A COMPENDIUM OF PMO CASE STUDIES:
Reflecting
PROJECT BUSINESS
MANAGEMENT CONCEPTS

PBMconcepts™

To view all *PBMconcepts* titles, go to: www.PBMconcepts.com.

Special discounts on bulk quantities of *PBMconcepts* books are available to professional associations, colleges, universities, corporations resellers, and other organizations.

For details, contact:

PBMconcepts
120 Beth Street,
Holland, MI 49424
E-mail: bookorders@PBMconcepts.com
Website: www.PBMconcepts.com

Praise for A Compendium of PMO Case Studies

"This book not only explains PMO principles but also illustrates PMO theory through case studies and specific examples of how PMOs are organizationally positioned and function within enterprises. This book provides the information needed to establish and operate a PMO, allowing you to benefit from the experiences of others."

Denise Callahan, PMP
PMO Manager
The Doe Run Corporation - Finalist, 2010 PMO of the Year

* * * * *

"In this book, Bolles and Hubbard have successfully continued to promote the concept of the business view of project management. Many books on project management take a theoretical approach with a mixture of examples that may not reflect reality. However, this compendium of project management offices (PMOs) case studies is based on the practical experiences of executives and managers regarding the undertaking of projects within their industry and enterprises. It is this practical basis, emphasizing enterprise-wide projects as a consequence of the current economic reality, which differentiates this book from conventional texts on project management.

The book through the presented research and case studies provides new insights into practices for undertaking projects that both executive management and project management practitioners will find interesting and useful for the advancement of their enterprises, particularly, the project business management aspect."

Dr Emanuel Camilleri
Visiting Senior Lecturer,
Faculty of Economics, Management & Accountancy, University of Malta,
Formerly: Director General (Strategy and Operations Support), Ministry of Finance,
Investments and the Economy, Government of Malta.
Author of *Project Success: Critical Factors and Behaviors*

✷ ✷ ✷ ✷ ✷

"*A Compendium of PMO Case Studies: Reflecting Project Business Management Concepts* will provide you with real life examples on how companies have found success in leveraging an enterprise-wide PMO as a differentiator in their industry. ... Valuable insights and examples are shared regarding the structure of various PMOs, key processes leveraged, and how they continuously improve and drive business value for their company. Read this book and take the first step in transforming your company."

Jennifer R. Bok, PMP
Assistant Vice President, Program Management
Nationwide Insurance

✷ ✷ ✷ ✷ ✷

"In their book, Bolles and Hubbard provide a window into a world of the next generation of PMOs. Experienced project offices and managers understand their organizations can no longer afford to approve, fund and implement projects in a bubble. Mistakes are more costly than ever before. A clear, concise and controlling strategy is a 'must have' for organizational success. It is imperative for leaders at all levels to understand how strong project management methodologies can positively impact the application of limited resources, business processes and cross-organization collaboration."

Michele Mills, PMP, FHIMSS
Director, ITS Program Management Office
University of Utah Health Care, Information Technology Services

✷ ✷ ✷ ✷ ✷

"The informed advancement in business discipline has been driven by project management authorities like Dennis Bolles and Darrel Hubbard. They have defined project business management and prescribed the character and structure of project management leadership and organizational structure. Now, these two experts with over 85-years of combined experience have advanced the formation of project business management to a survey-based business science. Their new book provides comprehensive definitions and observations of repeatable business project management experiments that form a foundation for sustaining project and process excellence."

William F. Bundy, Ph.D.
Professor, Leadership and Technology Research Development
Director, GRAVELY Naval Warfare Research Group

⋆ ⋆ ⋆ ⋆ ⋆

"This book is the next installment in defining the future of Project and Portfolio Management. Dennis and Darrel have succeeded in refining a future course for this critical management discipline. Anyone connected to project, program, portfolio management or change management of any kind will benefit from reading this book. The authors keep this discipline highly relevant at both the practitioner and executive levels through a continued focus on the realization of business value. This book is timely, insightful, and thought-provoking."

Greg Miller
Vice President, PMO
CareFirst BCBS

⋆ ⋆ ⋆ ⋆ ⋆

"This book is the most complete guide of real case studies about project offices described by organizations around the world. It contains real world reports from organization who are sharing how their PMO is implementing the Project Business Management practices that Dennis and Darrel have written about in their previous books. The PMO case studies include a wide variety where there are no two similar Project Offices and there are no two similar implementations. If you are a sponsor or a senior manager that needs to understand what kind of project office is the best approach for you, then please take a look at this book first in order to improve your decision."

Lic. Alberto G. Sirvent, MBA, PMP
Manager of Strategic Project Office
Banco Hipotecario S.A., Buenos Aires, Argentina

⋆ ⋆ ⋆ ⋆ ⋆

"This book expands the concept of Project Management from task to strategic capability. It draws upon a wealth of information from theory and practice to educate middle and senior management about the potential to improve business performance through a project management office. Dennis Bolles and Darrel Hubbard then provide practical guidance to help organizations gain additional value from Projects."

Nigel Williams
Senior Lecturer Project Management
Course Leader Engineering Business Management
The Business School, University of Bedfordshire, United Kingdom

＊ ＊ ＊ ＊ ＊

"This book draws insight from those actually in the trenches; it relates how things have advanced (and how they are advancing today) in the project management arena. This is a book that every PMO Department Library must have! Around the real-life scenarios and case studies, the supporting and descriptive text - just like it was done in the earlier go-to reference book *The Power of Enterprise-Wide Project Management*- it is very practically written and succinct, so as to not bog down experienced readers/ professionals with an overdose of theory. If you are responsible for advancing project management in your organizations, this is an opportunity to obtain something special."

Kenneth J. Fitzgerald
Vice President, Director - Program Management Office (PMO)
EMC Insurance Companies (Employers Mutual Casualty Company)

＊ ＊ ＊ ＊ ＊

"Dennis Bolles and Darrel Hubbard have responded to the elusive question about what makes a portfolio/program/project management office (PMO) successful. As we all know, there is no "PMO Cookbook" that we can go to for the recipe to make a successful PMO. But, their unique approach of soliciting case studies from a wide variety of high-performing PMOs provides the reader with practical insights that are readily applicable to their own organizations. It also confirms that there are numerous PMO approaches that are successful, and will inspire the reader with ideas for how to overcome challenges they may be experiencing. This book serves as an excellent reference for anyone who is establishing or running a PMO."

Ruth Anne Guerrero
Former PMI Standards Manager
Vice President, Enterprise Portfolio Management Office,
AmeriHealth Mercy Family of Companies

＊ ＊ ＊ ＊ ＊

"*A Compendium of PMO Case Studies: Reflecting Project Business Management Concepts* is a pragmatic reference for anyone interested in combining "Best-of-Breed" practices and real-world examples from field practitioners at the enterprise and executive level who are implementing project, program, and portfolio management offices. The "art" of applying the right approach with underlying operational support will vary for each organization depending on their business goals, strategic initiatives, and executive vision. This book provides a toolkit with hands-on references and contact information for those of us who are passionate about maximizing business value and realizing business benefits across an entire enterprise."

Barbara Bostian, PMP, MPM
Director, Project Management Office
Railinc - Wholly-owned subsidiary of Association of American Railroads

* * * * *

"There is a growing recognition of the synergies that exist between corporate strategic direction, project management, improved efficiencies and good, sound business management. Companies that effectively structure their organizations to properly integrate those functions will prove more successful in the future than their competition. This book provides a practical approach to that integration and supports that approach with extensive research and case studies."

John F. Bodensteiner, CFA
Assistant Vice President Strategic Planning & Analysis
Merchants Insurance Group

* * * * *

"Benefits Realisation and Value Creation have become the 'mantras' for achieving project management success. But how do you deliver these? Dennis Bolles and Darrel Hubbard show how this can be done in practice through a collection of industry case studies on Project Business Management Offices (PBMO) in their latest book titled *A Compendium of PMO Case Studies: Reflecting Project Business Management Concepts.* Their recent book is a must read for leaders where the authors have followed up the ideas that they espouse in their bestseller *The Power of Enterprise-Wide Project Management* with some implementable ideas."

Shankar Sankaran
Associate Professor - Course Director
PM School of the Business Environment
University of Technology Sydney

* * * * *

"Business efficiency, and more important effectiveness, is driving more mature approaches to the execution and achievement of business plans and targeted objectives. However, leaders in many organizations struggle to find appropriate guidance that is mature enough to apply to increasing levels of complexity and challenges that the current global economy provides. The concept of the Project Business Management Organisation discussed in this book could well be the 'model for success' that has eluded those striving for matrix management success. The structure of the book around context, discussion, research and case studies offers rigor to the ideas, concepts and models offered. The book should provide solid guidance and reference to those seeking to better align strategy to execution and goal achievement."

Iain Fraser, PMP
PMI Fellow, Past Chair, PMI Board of Directors
CEO, Project Plus Ltd

A COMPENDIUM OF
PMO CASE STUDIES:
Reflecting
PROJECT BUSINESS
MANAGEMENT CONCEPTS

A Validation of Project Business Management (PBM)
and the PBM Organization Model for
Achieving Business Benefits and Value

Dennis L. Bolles, PMP *and* Darrel G. Hubbard, PE

Published By

PBMconcepts™

This book is designed to provide accurate and authoritative information regarding the subject matter covered. It is sold with the understanding that the publisher is not engaged in rendering legal, accounting, or other professional service. If legal advice or other expert assistance is required, the services of a competent professional person should be sought.

This book contains information obtained from authentic and highly regarded sources. Reprinted material is quoted with permission, and sources are indicated. A wide variety of references are listed.

Disclaimer of Warranty / Limit of Liability: While the publisher and the authors have used their best efforts in preparing this book, they make no representations or warranties with respect to the accuracy or completeness of the contents of this book and specifically disclaim any implied warranties of merchantability or fitness for a particular purpose. The advice and strategies contained herein may not be suitable for your situation. You should consult with a professional where appropriate. Reasonable efforts have been made to publish reliable data and information, but the authors and the publisher do not assume any responsibility for the validity of all materials or for the consequences of their use.

Publisher's Cataloging-in-Publication data
Hubbard, Darrel G.
A compendium of PMO case studies : reflecting project business management concepts : a validation of project business management (PBM) and the PBM organization model for driving business benefits and value / Dennis L. Bolles, PMP, and Darrel G. Hubbard, P.E.
p. cm.
Includes bibliographical references and index.
ISBN-13: 978-0-9858484-0-8 (pbk.)
ISBN-10: 0985848405
1. Project management. 2. Project management --Case studies. 3. Management --Case studies. 4. Organization --Case studies. I. A compendium of project management office case studies : reflecting project business management concepts : a validation of project business management (PBM) and the PBM organization model for driving business benefits and value. II. Bolles, Dennis, L.

HD69.P75 .B655 2012
658.4/04 --dc23   2012948392

Trademark Notice: Product or corporate names may be trademarks or registered trademarks, and are used only for identification and explanation, without intent to infringe.

Please see pg. ii for additional information regarding logos, trademarks, and service marks.

Printed and bound in the United States of America. Printed on acid free paper.
Printing number
10 9 8 7 6 5 4 3 2

Dedication

To the executives and managers performing
the business management of enterprises,
and to the professionals
performing the management
of portfolios, programs, and projects,
who willingly and openly share
their knowledge and experiences
for the advancement of
project business management
and for their contribution to
the PMO knowledge base
of the project management profession.

Table of Contents

Forward

When the authors asked for contributions for their new book, which is the sequel to their book *The Power of Enterprise-Wide Project Management*, I was honored. After all, who wouldn't want to be recognized for exhibiting excellence and innovation in developing and maturing an organizational structure that supports effective project, program, and portfolio management?

Without hesitation, I began work to synthesize the journey VSP Vision Care has taken to improve the project management processes in our creation of a highly functioning, and continuously evolving PMO. Our situation was likely no different from that of any other organization. As the largest not-for-profit vision benefits and services provider in the United States, we are in constant need of efficient, innovative, and effective ways for managing the complex projects and programs that keep us at the top of our industry. We identified opportunities for growth, and to address these, we took some basic, but momentous steps. To find the key to our success and the success of others, you need to read the book!

Significant results took time, but improvement was enterprise-wide. Our demonstrated results culminated in requests for our project services that overwhelmed our capacity. The solution: a formal PMO to provide the structure and expertise needed to standardize processes and improve project success.

Bolles and Hubbard specialize in helping companies establish Project Management Centers of Excellence, and assist enterprises in maximizing operational effectiveness to deliver business benefits by implementing a Project Business Management Organization (PBMO). Together, they have over 85 years of experience in establishing effective processes to assist companies in developing, implementing, and measuring the success of their project processes.

A Compendium of PMO Case Studies: Reflecting Project Business Management Concepts is a remarkable book that provides valuable insights based on actual PMO experiences. Each case study illustrates the best practices, governance structures, and results of organizations that have successfully implemented formal PMOs.

The case studies provide the reader with actual information about PMOs that provide consistent benefits and value in achieving business results. Key topics include, PMO:

- Background; including scope, vision and mission, and position within the organizational structure
- Innovations and best practices

- Governance
- Standardization
- Capabilities
- Business Execution
- Sustainability
- Future Plans

After having led my organization through PMO structure development-- from grass roots coordination to virtual PMO to formal PMO, I can attest to the complexity, the sensitivity, the cooperation, and the persistence necessary. As a company, VSP recognizes the importance of knowledge sharing, and it is our hope that other enterprises will benefit from the learning contained within this case study compilation. The case studies in this book demonstrate specific actions that others have taken to establish an enterprise PMO model. You can be certain we will be leveraging the case studies in our efforts for the continuous education and growth of our staff.

"*A Compendium of PMO Case Studies: Reflecting Project Business Management Concepts* is a definite must read for any organization considering embarking on the road to excellence through standardizing project processes and formalizing a PMO governance structure.

Karen Casey
Vice President, Enterprise Project Solutions
VSP Vision Care
2011 and 2012 PMO of the Year Award Finalist

Preface

Global Business Performance Challenges

The business pressures during the recent period of global expansion and the following recession resulted in a growing number of organizations performing enterprise-wide projects. The additional requirements necessary to handle these projects exacerbated the issues already associated with what had been the normal ways many enterprises were conducting business. To put this into perspective, about twenty-five percent (25%) of all the goods and services produced in human history were produced in the last ten years. The global economy is influencing organizations to establish better means of managing portfolio, programs, and projects and to prioritize their projects and programs to effectively achieve business results and value more efficiently and proficiently. The challenges to the project management profession have only increased as enterprises, and their projects, programs, and portfolios, have grown in complexity.

During this time of change, another key challenge emerged for business. The time allotted for projects and programs to be vetted, and changes to be accommodated, is being condensed. This impacts the enterprise's ability to ensure projects and programs align with existing strategies that support the enterprise's mission and vision. Enterprises can no longer afford to continue to authorize, or fund, or execute projects without a clear controlling strategy.

The pressure continues to mount in the marketplace for management to apply more formal business management principles, practices, and processes to the projects in their portfolios and programs. Also, managers are beginning to recognize they need to apply those same portfolio / program / project management principles, practices, and processes to projects located within the operations side of the business.

As practitioners, we also understand the management of projects is as old as the heavy construction project management for the Egyptian pyramids and as current-day as the "Agile" project management methods being developed at the start of the 21st century for information technology projects. We see the practice and discipline of project management as constantly evolving as the physical and mental capabilities of humankind increase. These increased capabilities now allow an enterprise to attempt to plan and complete a greater number of projects and undertake even more complex projects, in shorter periods of time.

The project management profession has created sophisticated models, multiple methodologies, defined processes, a plethora of hardware and software tools, and technical disciplines. However, each project still competes for limited resources resulting in all too many projects and programs falling short in delivering their anticipated benefits and value to the enterprise.

Therefore, the misapplication of limited resources, sub-optimization of business processes, and lack of cross-organizational integration are being abandoned, for a more pragmatic and flexible structured project management office concept This business management approach leads to gaining business leverage over a multitude of corporate, divisional and departmental portfolios, programs, and projects, which cover research and development, capital expansion, new product lines, modified products, maintenance, and extensive process improvements.

However, establishing portfolio, program, and project management processes and integrating them within the enterprise's business management processes is a significant undertaking.

PMO Business Trends

Enterprises are now addressing the growing pressures from widespread competition and the global economy, which are creating global business challenges. These challenges have influenced organizations to establish enterprise-wide offices to manage their portfolio, programs, and projects. These offices prioritize their resources, projects, and programs to more efficiently achieve business results and value, and improve the alignment of project execution with corporate strategy. Another driving force influencing organizations to establish those enterprise-wide offices is the growing recognition that successful multi-project management within programs and portfolios is one of the major factors that establishes organizations as foremost leaders in their markets.

In addition, many programs and projects fail because of poor coordination, limited resources, faulty assumptions, not being the right project at the right time, or mid-management in-fighting. These issues are generally resolved at the executive level, where direction, priorities, and resources are determined and the final decisions are made. Therefore, if the executive level of the business establishes a more formal "project management office" type organization to manage the process of prioritizing, authorizing, and executing projects, those afore mentioned project failures can be minimized and maybe even eliminated.

These special organizations may be identified as project, or program, or portfolio management offices, but they all fit under the general business management heading of "PMO." Companies are implementing PMOs including those at the project level, originally called project support offices, to those at the C-suit level, commonly identified as enterprise PMOs.

As executive leadership's interest in, and recognition of, project management as a profession has grown, the trend to develop and establish enterprise level PMOs that are responsible for implementing portfolio/program/project management methodologies has also increased.

We believe the trend to develop enterprise-wide PMOs will continue to increase. Those organizations that are looking for the answer to meet the challenges of the global market will discover the answer is to implement a Project Business Management Organization. This will happen as more organizations begin to view the management of portfolio, programs, and projects as business functions and when they come to understand the need to create the executive level position, which owns the Project Business Management Organization.

Project Business Management (PBM) and the PBM Organization

The actions necessary to implement an integrated business approach to managing all the projects, programs and portfolios within the business is the concept we call Project Business Management. We coined and use the term *project business management* to eliminate any confusion and to suppress the reader's assumptions as to what the term *project management* means when used in a business context. Adopting and managing an approach that integrates portfolio, program, project management processes and best practices with the enterprise's business processes and best practices requires single ownership at an executive-level. This business unit, chartered to implement those integrated Project Business Management practices and processes, is the function we call the Project Business Management Organization.

The principles and concepts of project-related portfolio, program, and project management are complex, and the management processes involved are many, as are the organizational concepts established to provide the actual management. The blending of these project management principles and concepts with the principles, concepts, and varied processes of general business management motivated us to develop the concept of Project Business Management and the governance philosophy of the Project Business Management Organization.

We defined the Project Business Management (PBM) in our book *The Power of Enterprise-Wide Project Management* as, "The utilization of integrated general business management, and portfolio, program, and project management knowledge, skills, tools, and techniques in applying portfolio, program, and project processes. The purpose is to meet or exceed stakeholder needs, and to derive benefits from, and capture value through, any project-related actions and activities used to accomplish the enterprise's business objectives and related strategies."

We also defined, in that book, the Project Business Management Organization as, "A business unit positioned at the executive level of the enterprise, operating as an independent functional organization, and recognized by every level of the organization as having the autonomy, roles, responsibilities, and authority to implement and apply, on an enterprise-wide basis, those Project Business Management best practices developed specifically for the enterprise."

The premise that an executive level, enterprise-wide Project Business Management Office should be created to implement the Project Business Management methodology to direct diverse and resource intensive, portfolios, programs, and projects across the enterprise is deemed simple, yet brilliant by reviewers of our book, *The Power of Enterprise-Wide Project Management.*

Many executives and business unit leaders recognize that they depend on the proper application of specific business, portfolio, program, and project management processes. They realize the effective management of their projects has a measurable impact on their enterprise's bottom line. Consequently, those leaders have established, at a senior corporate management level of the enterprise, a related business management function. Doing so has helped ensure that executive management can direct the distribution of the enterprises funds and resources. It also assures the funds are effectively applied across the enterprise to only those projects that support business strategies and objectives, thereby giving them, from the very start, the best opportunity to succeed.

The Project Business Management Organization can support the evolution of project management as global businesses needs change and therefore as an enterprise's related needs evolve. This means the project management profession must support the PMO manager and the PMO in positioning themselves as value added managers and value added organizational problem solvers, who develop solutions which leverage the dynamics of project teams and increase the benefit results for projects and thus for the associated enterprise.

In an increasingly solution-focused business culture, each project, program, and portfolio must be positioned to provide solutions as well as being delivery focused. The Project Business Management Organization is the business function to address this opportunity and proactively lead project management into the 21st century.

Why This Book?

Our decision to research and write this case study compendium book is a result of the continued interest in our books *Building Project Management Centers of Excellence* and *The Power of Enterprise-Wide Project Management*, especially those portions related to Project Management Offices (PMOs) and corporate strategy. Our business experiences and reader feedback, since the publication of our second book, has shown a need for full-text case studies of Project Business Management Organizations that show how PMOs are organizationally positioned and currently function within an enterprise.

We wrote this book for executives and senior managers, as well as portfolio, program, and project managers, who recognize portfolio, program, and project management as business functions. It is for those who want to establish, within their enterprise (organization), a Project Business Management Organization at an executive organizational level. This book is a benchmark reference for management in forward-thinking companies who are establishing a Project Business Management Organization as an integrative business function. To that end, the book includes both the full-text and analyzed information from formal case studies.

The research makes the business case for the executive level PMO. This book validates the value proposition behind an enterprise-level Project Business Management Office. By doing so, it also provides assurance to both those who are testing the waters of establishing, and those who are currently implementing, a Project Business Management Organization and employing Project Business Management as a functioning business model.

With that in mind, we structured this book into four major sections as follows:

Section I establishes the context in which the PMO case studies were developed. We developed, using our combined 85 years of practical experience, a business oriented view and a business construct of the key functions of a PMO. We fully describe both the Project Business Management (PBM) concept and the Project Business Management Organization (PBMO) construct. We discuss the development of the PBMO model and lay out the evolution of the PBMO research model. The model we developed and employed is applicable to most PMO's most of the time.

Section II provides a discussion of our research methodology and the associated research instrument. To support the research discussion and analysis, we encapsulated the seven key business elements into a graphic, which we dubbed the Project Business Management House of Excellence, and it is shown on the cover of the book.

Section III delivers the research results and conclusions based upon the submitted case studies. We extracted and synthesized these results from those project business management organizations, generically known as PMO's that have manifested vision and business insightfulness in carrying out new ideas, methods, and processes. These PMOs have provided quantifiable improvements in the management of their projects, programs, and portfolios and demonstrated real business benefits and value for their enterprises.

Section IV includes the full-text of the formal PMO research case studies provided and written by those enterprises that have exhibited excellence and innovation in developing and maturing an organizational structure, which supports the effective management of projects, programs, and/or portfolios. These case studies provide the practical how-to information that profit, non-profit, and government enterprises are currently using to implement a Project Business Management Organization.

Darrel G. Hubbard, PE   Dennis L. Bolles, PMP
President   President
D.G.Hubbard Enterprises, LLC   DLB Associates, LLC

Acknowledgements

First and foremost, we want to acknowledge those enterprises who have given permission to print their case studies and those individuals who have graciously provided comments and endorsements for our book. Each has contributed to the research related to enterprises applying various aspects of the Project Business Management concepts.

We want to remember our mentors, peers, and those who have supported us in developing a business view of project management. We want to especially thank Sandra P. Schuster, MS for copy editing and contributions to the design, development, layout, and formatting of this book.

We acknowledge the member volunteers of the PMO Community of Practice and the OPM Community of Practice of the Project Management Institute (ww.pmi.org), who are advancing the knowledge bases related to Project Management Offices and Organizational Project Management. We also acknowledge PMSolutions, Inc., a project portfolio management consulting company (www.pmsolutions.com), for their ongoing contributions to and for promoting, since 2006 through its "PMO of the Year Award," the utilization of Project Management Offices.

Executives and managers of enterprises, who share relevant and real information regarding the portfolio / program / project management offices (PMOs) within their enterprises and industry, make this compendium of PMO case studies and similar research by others possible. They provide the project management professional with insights into how each of those PMOs function, is structured, and is organizationally positioned to provide value and benefits to the company and to its shareholders, stakeholders, and employees. This shared knowledge allows the profession of project management to understand the "what" and the "how" of creating and implementing a sustainable PMO, which itself is of business value to the enterprise.

The following enterprises and their PMO managers, who are contributors to this book, specifically deserve recognition for their efforts to advance the fields of project management and project business management, for the results they have helped achieve for their organizations, and for their value-centric implementation and operation of PMOs.

AmeriHealth Mercy Family of Companies
- Ruth Anne Guerrero, Vice President – Enterprise Portfolio Management Office
- Joanne McFall, Vice President and Chief of Staff for the Chief Operating Officer

Banco Hipotecario S.A.
- Alberto Gabriel Sirvent, Manager of Strategic Project Office
- Maximiliano Weber, Area Manager, Budget & Management Control
- Daniel Efkhanian, Area Manager, Controlling and Risk Management
- Fernando Rubin, General Manager

The Doe Run Company
- Denise Callahan, PMO Manager
- Sharon Gietl, Vice President of Information Technology and Chief Information Officer

EMC Insurance Companies
- Kenneth J. Fitzgerald, Vice President, Director – Program Management Office
- Ronald W. Jean, Executive Vice President – Corporate Development

ILLUMINAT (Trinidad and Tobago) Limited
- Owen Field, Regional Manager – Project Management Services – ILLUMINAT
- David Belgrave, Chief Executive Officer – ILLUMINAT
- Fenwick Reid, Chairman – Neal and Massy ITC Group

Merchants Insurance Group
- John F. Bodensteiner, Assistant Vice President Strategic Planning – PMO Director
- Kenneth J. Wilson, Chief Financial Officer

Nationwide Insurance
- Jennifer R. Bok, Assistant Vice President, IT Program Management
- J. Brian Smith, Vice President, Delivery Services
- Guru C. Vasudeva, Executive Vice President, Enterprise Chief Technology Officer

Railinc
- Barbara Cleary Bostian, Director, Project Management Office
- Treadwell Davison, Assistant Vice President, Business Operations
- Allen West, President

Southern California Edison
- Arlene Rocabado, Edison SmartConnect® PMO Project Analysts
- Campbell Hawkins, Senior Manager, Edison SmartConnect® Program Office
- Ken Devore, Director, Edison SmartConnect®

University of Utah Health Care
- Shannon Thayn, Senior Project Manager
- Michele Mills, Director – Program Management Office
- James Turnbull, Chief Information Officer

VSP Vision Care
- Karen Casey, Vice President – Enterprise Project Solutions Division
- Laura Costa, Chief Operations Officer

Section I

Project Business Management Constructs and Models

Since the early 1980's we, the authors, have been working within, consulting to, and studying project management organizations. We have been formally gathering data and information on project management processes since the mid-1970's and specifically on project management organizations since 1996. Our research of the literature on project related organizations began in 2000, which coincides with the beginning of major academic research on what has come to be called the project management office (PMO).

This academic research[3,4] is slowly providing insights into various aspects of PMOs and the forces that change PMOs. That research to date, which covers a range of PMO structures, in general has not provided significant business insights for practitioners to develop, implement, operate, or sustain a PMO.

During the past fifteen years we have, as part of our consulting practices, entrepreneurial endeavors, and applying our experiences with program and project offices, used heuristic methods to develop and refine our construct for the functioning of a PMO. Within this research methodology, a *construct* is something that has been systematically built or assembled from separate parts in an ordered way to create a theory as a result of systematic thought, especially a complex theory or subjective notion such as the functioning of a PMO.

A PMO construct developed in this way may be viewed as an *enterprise model*, which is a representation of the structure, activities, processes, information, resources, behavior, and constraints of an enterprise or portion thereof. From an operations' perspective, the enterprise model represents what is planned, what might happen, and what has happened. This PMO construct may also be viewed as a *business reference model*, which describes the business operations of an organization, where the operations are independent of the organizational structure that performs those functions.

Our PMO construct is a defined subset of the range of possible PMOs. The construct

1

is based upon, limited to, and restrained by, the authors' construct for Project Business Management (PBM), which is based upon an organizational management vantage point. Where PBM is defined[2] as the utilization of integrated general business management, portfolio, program, and project management knowledge, skills, tools, and techniques in applying portfolio, program, and project processes. The purpose being to meet or exceed stakeholder needs, to derive benefits from, and capture value through, any project-related actions and activities used to accomplish the enterprise's business objectives and related strategies.

Chapter 1

Project Business Management (PBM) Organization

1.1   Project Business Management Organization – The Construct

The authors defined the construct of the Project Business Management Organization in their second book[2] as a business unit positioned at the executive level of the enterprise, operating as an independent functional organization, and recognized by every level of the organization as having the autonomy, roles, responsibilities, and authority to implement and apply, on an enterprise-wide basis, those project business management best practices developed specifically for the enterprise.

To place this construct in a management context, the authors define a *Business Unit* as, "any sized functional organization within the enterprise that is charted to perform a relatively well defined business support operation, such as accounting, a service center, product production, sales, human resources, marketing or a project management office."

The Project Management Institute (PMI*) and the authors define an *Enterprise* as a company, business, firm, partnership, corporation, or governmental agency. This includes associations, societies, for-profit entities, and not-for-profit entities. They also define *Organization* as a group of persons organized for some purpose to perform some type of work within an enterprise. This includes business unit, functional group, department, division, or sub-agency.

The definition of the Project Business Management Organization established by the authors infers that it can include the three most common PMOs: Project Management Office, Program Management Office, and Portfolio Management Office.

The standards[5,6,7] promulgated by the Project Management Institute describes the function of the Project Management Office, as an organizational body or entity assigned various responsibilities related to the centralized and coordinated management of those projects under its domain. The responsibilities of the PMO can range from providing project management support functions to actually being responsible for the direct management of a project[5].

The PMI describes the function of the Program Management Office[6], as a critical portion of the program's infrastructure. The Program PMO is seen by PMI as supporting the program manager with the management of multiple, unrelated projects. While there are many varieties of program management offices within organizations, for the purposes of the program management standard, PMI views the PMO as providing support to the program manager by[6]: defining the program management processes that will be followed; managing schedule and budget at the program level; defining the quality standards for the program and for the program's components; providing document configuration management; and providing a centralized support for managing changes and tracking risk and issues.

In addition, for long, risky, or complex programs, PMI sees the program management office as providing additional support in the areas of managing personnel resources, managing contracts and procurements (especially international procurements), legal support, and other support as required[6]. Since some programs continue for years, PMI sees the PMO as assuming many aspects of normal operations that overlap with the larger organization's operational management[6].

PMI, within its standards, does not identify the Portfolio Management Office as an organizational entity[7]. PMI describes Portfolio Management specifically as a management activity and clearly defines the roles managers have with respect to projects, programs, and portfolios[7]. However, none of these roles' statements included the management of the related PMO.

The weaknesses in these PMI descriptions are that the PMOs are not seen to be organizations that manage, but rather are portrayed as administrative support functions to some manager and are therefore subject to the whims and vagaries of the operational aspects of the enterprise. These types of pseudo-PMOs were not part of our study. PMOs with those titles, but where the manager is responsible for management of the PMO, were part of our study.

Viewing the authors' higher level construct of the Project Business Management Organization from an executive perspective, it can be seen as the application of project business management practices and processes on an enterprise-wide basis using an enterprise-wide project business management office to support the management of the enterprise's non-operational and cross-functional projects, programs and portfolios.

The premise here is that an executive level, enterprise-wide Project Business Management Organization is created to implement the Project Business Management methodology to direct diverse and resource intensive, portfolios, programs, and projects across the enterprise. Many programs and projects fail because of poor coordination, limited resources, faulty assumptions, not being the right project at the right time, or mid-management infighting. These issues are generally resolved at the executive level, where strategies are set, business objectives are defined, and where direction, priorities, and resources are determined, and the final decisions are made.

1.2 Project Business Management Organization – The Model

The research of the general business literature and review of many works on organizational operations and project operations lead the authors to a perspective and understanding of the basic business elements that are commonly present in most functioning organizations, business units, and PMOs. These principles generally guide how an organization and its associated culture are perceived to behave or operate. This model has evolved and matured over the past decade.

2002 Project Management Center of Excellence Model

This initial model was created during the development of material for establishing and implementing project management centers of excellence and a set of associated documented project management methodologies with training programs. This material covered establishing formalized processes that help organize, plan, manage, and control the use of limited resources in project execution that is critical to continued growth and in some cases the very survival of an enterprise. There was a need to present this material to a diverse audience and to do that using a simple form to which everyone could relate and that would allow them to visualize those concepts. This need to help others visualize the concept of a project management center of excellence guided our decision to use a graphic to depict the concept of enterprise-wide project management. This visual representation of the institutionalization of project management within an organization in the form of a graphic (Figure 1-1 below), was presented in our first book[1].

FIGURE 1-1: PMCoE Model

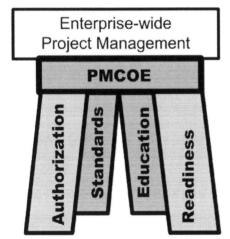

This initial graphical depiction took the form of a stylized four-legged stool. The integrity and stability of a four-legged stool depends on the strength of each leg as well as the connections (cross braces) between the legs. If one or more of the legs are weaker or shorter than the others, the integrity and stability (sustainability) of the stool is compromised and at risk of failure. The concept of the formation and sustaining of a project management center of excellence is seen as similar to a four-legged stool with similar characteristics, each having four supporting legs (elements).

The five elements within this model were selected and developed from a process development and methodology implementation perspective:

- *PMCoE*: The "Project Management Center of Excellence" represents the functions of the *Project Management Office* and the processes necessary to establish its *governance* and *sustain* its operation
- *Authorization*: Authorization is a foundation-building element that ensures alignment of projects with strategic goals and objectives. It, and the processes associated with it, involve the various components of *planning* and *execution*.

5

- *Standards*: Standards are the key to establishing a uniform and useful set of process *methodologies*.
- *Education*: Training and education are key components of developing, maturing, and *sustaining* human resource skills *capabilities*.
- *Readiness*: From a process viewpoint, readiness involves the availability of *capabilities* to be applied and approved plans to be *executed*.

2006 Enterprise-Wide Project Management House of Excellence Model

The next evolution of the model depicting the concept of enterprise-wide project management became the Enterprise Project Management Office (EPMO) House of Excellence. This graphic (Figure 1-2) was introduced in the Preface of our second book[2] The transition to the EPMO House of Excellence was the result of significantly expanding the concepts depicted by the four legged stool model to more fully incorporate all the components needed for the implementation of project management enterprise wide.

In addition to the process development and methodology implementation view of the project business management construct, this model incorporated the various aspects of program management and portfolio management with a business management view of the interrelationship and integration among the elements of the model. This required a new graphical representation that visually depicted the expanded model of enterprise-wide project management. The image of a house was chosen, because it is a familiar form recognizable by everyone. Building a house is a project and therefore it made sense to use that concept as the basis for creating a graphic that reflected the project management and business management concepts being presented.

FIGURE 1-2: Enterprise-Wide Project Management House of Excellence Model

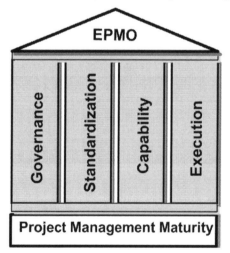

Input from a best practice benchmark study was used to help develop revised structure labels and initiate a supporting foundation. This house of excellence model represents a broader context for the concept of enterprise–wide project management with the four reframed major elements, or pillars, and the related foundation forming the framework of this expanded concept.

The designation of the 2002 *Authorization* element was replaced by the term *Execution* to more readily reflect its basic elements of *executing* and *planning*. The 2002 element title of *Standards* was broadened to *Standardization*. The 2002 *Education* and *Readiness* elements and the governing portion of the PMCoE model were combined, and then reformed, as the primary business elements they actually represent – *Capability* and *Governance*.

The added foundation symbolized that a maturing project management function and *sustained* organizational support, with related cultural and other changes, are needed to *sustain* an enterprise project management organization. This integrated framework with foundation was designed to allow the user to build a structurally sound enterprise-wide project management capability and is requisite to building and sustaining a successful EPMO, as represented by the roof of the house of excellence.

The various elements of the house of excellence model are as follows:

- *EPMO, the Roof* – Is a view of *project business management* from an executive's perspective. It represents the functions of the project management office and addresses enterprise-wide project management as a business concept, project management as a business function, and the EPMO as a business organization.
- *Governance* – Portrays the EPMO as a management method for setting policy, establishing charters, and providing an organizational model for the business management of projects, programs, and portfolios.
- *Standardization* – Provides identification and integration of processes and practices, development of standardized project business management processes, and documentation of enterprise-wide portfolio, program, and project management process methods and models, including their associated policies, practices, and procedures.
- *Capability* – Assesses the enterprise's abilities, develops a project management competency model, lays out an education and training program, establishes a career path progression plan, and outlines various key enterprise environmental factors and organizational process assets.
- *Execution* – Performs strategic business planning, tactical business planning, identifies business objectives and performs project prioritization, selection, and initiation, stage-gate reviews, and portfolio, program and project execution planning. Physically executes, monitors, and controls the planned work.
- *Project Management Maturity* – Matures project business management processes and practices, and evaluates the maturity of institutionalized project business management best practices required to *sustain* an enterprise-wide project management organization.

2012 Project Business Management Organization Model

The project management office interview follow-ups to the results of the authors' 1997 – 2006 PMO Survey research, combined with a more extensive review of the literature, lead us to a further refinement of the components within elements of the model. The majority of those components were reduced into, or summarized within, seven major business related constructs that would become the elements of the new model. This refined model incorporates aspects of organizational management, operations management, and organizational project management, in addition to addressing: 1) business management, 2) project, program, and portfolio management; and, 3) process and methodology views. The authors' visual representation of their PBM

Organization construct, called the "PBM House of Excellence," is shown below in Figure 1-3.

FIGURE 1-3: Project Business Management Organization Model

The *Execution* element within the 2006 model is split into its two main parts of *Execution* and *Planning,* to allow for better presentation of the two related functions within a business context. The 2006 element *Standardization* was renamed to the more encompassing term *Methodology* to allow for the incorporation of additional components. The foundation element in the 2006 model is modified to *Sustainability* to reflect the broader range of business practices that are required to sustain a project business management function and office.

The enterprise project management office designation for the roof element is updated to be the Project Business Management (PBM) Office, to reflect the greater range of project management offices that could be considered. The graphic form is now a historical architectural design symbolizing the long term stability exhibited by those houses from ages past

This final model is composed of these seven elements: Governance, Methodology, Capability, Planning, Execution, Sustainability, and the function of the Project Business Management Office. In general, these seven inter-related business based elements were found to be necessary to: 1) create, operate, and maintain a business organization such as a PMO, which the authors generically call the Project Business Management Organization, and 2) implement the PBM Organization as a business function.

Various interfaces and integrations were considered among the six supporting elements of the PBM House of Excellence, during the model development research, in refining the key components within each element. These research efforts and related changes to the model elements and their components lead to this enhanced model that was used for the PMO Case Study research.

This PBM Organization model provided the structure necessary to determine the type and style of questions that would provide the details on how each enterprise that submits a case study addressed specific aspects of creating and managing their PMO. This then provides the kind of information needed to do a comparative analysis of all the case study data collected from individual enterprises.

The basic concept and key components of each of the elements that comprise the PMO Organization model are given below in Chapter 2.

Chapter 2

Element Components of PBM Organization Model

The PBM Organizational Model is composed of seven elements, each with a number of components. These are common business components within operational management and project management for most enterprises. Each component has one or more operational business process and one or more project management business processes for applying and executing, that business oriented component.

2.1 Governance

The governance element of the model defines how the Project Business Management Organization will deliver the project business management methodology to the enterprise. Organizational governance used in performing project business management is a blend of several governance methods especially those of executive, operational, portfolio, program, and project management. It is employed at different decision-making levels of the enterprise to support implementation of specific business management objectives and their related business strategies. It creates the organizational model for the PBM Office and defines the relationship of the PBM Office and its management to the enterprise's operational management.

Governance establishes the roles, responsibilities and authority of each PBM Organization position, institutes the rules of conduct, and management protocols. It sets policy, establishes the charter, and provides the organizational structure for the business management of projects programs and portfolios. Governance involves adapting the Project Business Management (PBM) Organization concept, which also requires changing the enterprise's culture, and affects every level of the enterprise – from the boardroom to the office or plant floor.

The PBM Organization governance aligns resources to achieve the enterprise's Vision, Mission, Strategic Initiatives, and Business Objectives, which then enables translation of Vision, Mission, and Strategic initiatives into executable portfolios, programs, and projects. The governance structure is at the top level of the organization, in order to enable executive control and management - not just administration – of the enterprise portfolios, programs, and projects. The governance of the PBM Organization is positioned at the executive level, because organizational position is equated with:

- *Authority* that empowers decision making
- *Acceptance* that establishes a level of authority that ensures credibility
- *Adoption* that positions the PBMO as a business function
- *Autonomy* that secures self-direction

The PBM Organization is an independent top executive-level business unit for project / program / portfolio management that is organizationally an equal player in government politics and executive power. It has executive position and status, thereby ensuring the enterprise is doing the right things at the right time while maintaining enterprise-wide level focus on achieving all approved non-operational business objectives and related strategic initiatives.

2.2   Methodology

The methodology element of the model provides for the identification and integration of processes and practices, development of standardized project business management processes, and documentation of enterprise-wide portfolio program and project management processes methodology models, including their associated policies practices, and procedures. It establishes portfolio, program, and project management processes and integrates them within the enterprise's business management processes. Within the methodology construct, standardization means establishing a project business management methodology model composed of a set of defined and integrated project management and business management processes.

This element of the model is comprised of five integrated standard models each featuring their own sets of processes that follow the Initiating, Planning, Execution, Monitoring & Controlling, and Closing (IPECC) processes framework.

These standard models are:

- Enterprise Strategic Business Planning,
- Business Objectives Development,
- Portfolio Management,
- Program Management, and
- Project Management.

The five PBM Methodology standard models are closely aligned with development processes of the enterprise's products and services and are supported by associated written operational policies, plans, and procedures. There are four different types of standards documentation within the model:

- *Manuals* – Define what processes are required.
- *Handbooks of Procedures* – Define how to use those processes.
- *Standards & Work Instructions* – Provide guidelines for using the tools and templates to implement the processes.
- *Templates* – Provide common formats for implementing the processes.
- *Process Summaries* – Define the process flows, and indicate relationships and interactions. They provide the:
  - o   Process objectives,

o   Entry criteria exit criteria,
o   Inputs and outputs, and
o   Roles, responsibilities, and special activities.

Various standards, such as those from the Project Management Institute and the International Project Management Association as well as the enterprises own internal standards can be used in developing the methods and process used to conduct the enterprise's project business management activities.

2.3   Capability

Capability is the enterprise's state of having those specific attributes necessary for the performance and accomplishment of items from strategic initiatives down through project activities. The capability element in the model considers two major classes of capability attributes, which between them at the detail level include such things as the availability of qualified human resources, plant, facilities, technology, funds, and available education and training.

The first class of capabilities is *Enterprise Environmental Factors*, which are all the external environmental factors that either limit or enhance the enterprise's capabilities and all internal environmental factors that could influence the successful accomplishment of a project. These capability factors include organizational culture, organizational structures, infrastructures, existing resources (human and other), commercial databases, market conditions, tools, technology, and software.

The second class of capabilities is *Organizational Process Assets*, which are all process related assets that may be involved in planning and managing the project or can be used to influence the success of a project. These capability process assets include: formal and informal plans, policies, procedures, guidelines, education and training programs, methodologies, and knowledge bases such as lessons learned and historical information.

The capabilities within the enterprise environmental factors are applied to:
- Identification and selection of strategic initiatives, business objectives, portfolios, programs, and projects
- Establishing the structure and position of the PBM Organization
- Physical performance of the project work
- Management of the portfolios, programs, and projects

The capabilities within the organizational process assets are used for:
- Planning, documenting, selecting, prioritizing, and authorizing portfolios, programs, and projects
- Maturing the PBM Organization
- Talent management
- Process development and improvement

The enterprise's depth, quality, and strength within the above *factors* and *assets* have a profound impact on the enterprise's ability to complete successfully projects, programs, and portfolios.

2.4   Planning

The planning element in the model involves three different but related planning processes:

- *Strategic Planning* – Creates business-plan based strategic initiatives.
- *Tactical Planning* – Develops business objectives, identifies related portfolios, programs, and selects and prioritizes those business objectives, portfolios, programs, and projects, which support the strategic initiatives.
- *PBM Based Planning* – Authorizes projects from the selected and prioritized business objectives, portfolios, programs, and projects.

These three planning stages include developing Key Performance Indicators (KPIs).

Successfully planning requires high-level organizational support capable of overcoming internal organization and political obstacles. Executive and senior management are involved in the business initiating and supporting processes of strategic and tactical planning, that begin with identifying a single strategic initiative and progressing through to planning a project, since this is where up to eighty (80) percent of the value and benefits of the desired outcome can be created by senior management. It is also during these initiating and authorizing processes that executive and senior management's involvement and decision-making will have its maximum impact.

Strategic Planning

Performing strategic planning is the art and skill, of using stratagems in business endeavors. This form of planning is a common business exercise and is performed, to a greater or lesser extent, in all enterprises. PBM style strategic planning merges the business requirements of operations into portfolios, programs, and projects that support the future of the enterprise. It addresses market forces that can affect an enterprise's purpose or mission. The purpose is to define, refine, develop, and document the enterprise's strategic initiatives that must be accomplished by means of projects.

Initial business case submissions also need to adequately substantiate the request for any initial or incremental funding to further develop the initiative, by establishing the:

- Basis and need for incremental funding
- Resource allocation as it relates to incremental funding
- Benefits and value to be derived
- Enterprise's ability to execute the initiative
- Ability of the initiative, if implemented, to provide an adequate financial return

Strategic planning begins with the enterprise's updated vision and mission statements. It considers the impacts of internal and external Enterprise Environmental Factors, which influence the enterprise's ability to execute successfully its strategies. Those environmental factors include items such as culture, infrastructure, existing resources, and market conditions

Strategic planning is completed with the creation of a strategic business plan that includes only those strategic initiatives that have ranked strategic business cases for the next business cycle. The issued Business Plan:

- Articulates the intent and desired benefits and value of a business strategy in a feasibility study format
- Documents any associated business threat or opportunity related to the strategic initiative
- Provides information in a common format for use by business management, operations management, and the Project Business Management Organization
- Typically is divided into specific sections that reflect the type and style of business case being created
- Provides the basis for authorizing further planning and analysis activities
- Includes: Initiative Name, Description, Rational, Threats or Opportunities, Skills, Resources, Estimated Cost, Savings, and Duration
- Identifies Key Performance Indicators and Accomplishment Metrics to be used for measuring the level of strategy implementation.

Each strategic initiative with its business plan supporting documentation flows down from the strategic planning phase into the tactical planning process.

Tactical Planning

Tactical planning develops all of the specific Business Objectives and actions required to accomplish each of the enterprise's Strategic Initiatives. It considers the impacts of *Organizational Process Assets* that can affect the enterprise's ability to successfully accomplish each business objective. Those assets include such items as plans, policies, procedures, guidelines, and financial controls. It also considers the influence of *Enterprise Environmental Factors* of resource availability, and financial capability on the enterprise's ability to perform the objective.

Tactical planning begins with the ranked strategic business cases. It develops the supporting business objectives and related action items, which include portfolios, programs, and projects. It produces an Objective Profile and an Impact Study Package for each business objective. The Objective Profile is a document that lists criteria that are rated on a scale plus don't-know. The Impact Study Package document identifies program/project benefits, deliverables, cost benefit analysis, and risks

Prioritization and Selection processes are then used to rate and rank each Business Objective, Portfolio, Program, and Project. The processes begin by using the objective profile and associated potential impact study information to create the business objectives, portfolio, program, and projects objectives with a related action item tabulation. The impact of the enterprise environmental factors and the organizational process assets are reviewed to ensure they are clearly understood and can be effectively employed.

Tactical planning ends with the ranking and prioritization of every business objective, portfolio, program, and project. Key Performance Indicators and Accomplishment

Metrics are then formulated to support measuring the level of business objective, portfolio, program, and project accomplishment and completion.

Every ranked and prioritized business objective, portfolio, program, and project flows down from the tactical planning phase into the PBM based planning process.

PBM Based Planning

The PBM based planning process starts with each new business cycle or fiscal year. It begins with using the prioritized list of business objectives, portfolios, programs, and projects. It is driven by resource availability and the requirement to maintain alignment with the strategic initiatives and their supporting business objectives. These planning steps include portfolio planning, program, planning and project planning.

PBM based planning begins with selecting the prioritized business objectives, portfolios, programs, and projects based upon their priority and what resources the enterprise can make available during the time when the project is needed to be performed It ends with the authorizations to perform (execute) the selected portfolios, programs, and projects in the order of their prioritization.

This planning for the execution and turn-over of projects supporting programs and portfolios ensures those programs and projects support their specific related components of the enterprise's business plan, thereby reducing the possible impact that any misaligned project will result in the availability of funds being reduced and causing a counterproductive economic impact within the enterprise.

2.5   Execution

The execution element in the model involves directing and managing portfolios, programs, and projects to meet their respective Key Performance Indicators and Accomplish Metrics and produce the deliverables desired. It begins with the chartering of each portfolio, program, and project authorized during the PBM Base Planning phase. The execution processes initiate the work and establish the set of final Key Performance Indicators.

It applies the execution and monitoring and controlling process of the three PBM standardized model processes for portfolio, program, and project. During the course of executing programs and projects, changes in expected benefits, such as an anticipated risk-reducing benefit, may occur, when compared to the baseline at the time of selection. Execution assesses those and other changes as necessary to identify how well the project can remain on track. Project changes, risks, and opportunities that do occur are effectively managed to optimize these events to increase the project's likelihood of success in delivering the desired benefits and values for which it was selected.

The execution element maintains portfolio, program, and project alignment with the business objectives and related strategic initiatives. Execution is finalized when the portfolio, program or project is completed or terminated.

2.6   PMB Office

The PBM Office element of the model is composed of the executive and managerial personnel who will manage and supervise those enterprise business activities that are accomplished through projects and the related programs and portfolios of projects.

The PBM Office is established and functions as an independent business unit at the highest level of the enterprise to obtain the authority, acceptance, adoption, and autonomy necessitated to establish, monitor, and control the distribution of the resources demanded to successfully apply project business management best practices enterprise-wide. Using the executive level PBM Office to manage the processes of prioritizing, authorizing, and executing projects can eliminate or at least minimize the poor coordination, the application of inadequate resources, faulty assumptions, being the wrong project at the wrong time, and the inability to obtain cooperation due to mid-management in-fighting that is present in most enterprises. This result is achievable because these issues are generally resolved at the executive level, where direction, priorities, and resources are determined and the final decisions are made.

The PBMO has the authority and ability to improve efficiency, to support the adoption of new services and product offerings, and to enhance revenue-earning capability. Personnel from the executive level of the PBM Office function must be involved during strategic planning to ensure business strategic initiatives can be accomplished through the use of portfolios, programs, and projects. The PBM Office has the responsibility to assure the deliverables for authorized portfolios, programs, and projects remain aligned with their approved business objectives. It applies the PBM standardized model processes for portfolio, program, and project. The PBM Office applies metrics management to measure performance and accomplishments. The metrics addressed include:

- Key Performance Indicators addressed
- Completion of deliverables
- Degree that project requirements were met
- Level of desired benefits and value obtained

Execution requires carrying out the processes and methodologies involving: tracking time and budget; structuring of artifact repositories; applying the roles and responsibilities defined for performance of the work; establishing metric tracking methods; reporting metrics performance and accomplishments; and providing the analysis of variances; etc.

The PBM Office has ownership of, and the responsibility to institute and oversee, the effective application of the principles and practices of the Project Business Management methodology across the enterprise. The PBM Office ensures each authorized portfolio, program, and project gets off to the right start, with a readiness review. It provides a gate review check at the end of each phase to assure work is on the right track. It also assures at the end of each phase that the process captures lessons learned of what worked well, and what didn't work, so the enterprise can do it better the next time.

The PBM Office established at the executive level enhances the utilization of virtual project teams who are not exclusively located in the same building or even in the same city. The PBM Office also addresses the expanding managerial challenges of team members having a wider range of skills, knowledge, experience, perceptions, and diverse cultural backgrounds and who are typically spread out across multiple geographical locations.

2.7   Sustainability

The sustainability element of the model involves the PBM governance, methodology, capability, planning, and execution processes and their practice maturity as foundational requirements for a sustainable PBM Organization. Time and tenacity are employed to establish a mature sustainable PBM methodology and culture. Sustainability is focused on maintaining, over an extended time-period, a Project Business Management Organization as a functioning enterprise-wide business unit. Sustainability requires:

- Communicating the benefits and value of employing Project Business Management
- Institutionalizing PBM best practices enterprise-wide
- Assessing PBM processes and practices on a routine basis
- Identifying the gap between the assessed maturity state and the desired end state
- Implementing process improvement initiatives that address any identified maturity gaps
- Having a quality education and training program to mature development and implementation of PBM processes, practices, and personnel
- Establishing formally the roles and responsibilities of a PBM Organization and having them applied and commonly accepted
- Appointing a single executive who "owns" the Project Business Management Organization function

Education and training is a critical requirement for establishing a sustainable PBM Organization and having the talented human resources needed to manage it. This requires establishing a project management Career Path Program -- that includes quali-fication and certification steps -- from entry level through the advanced level.

To sustain a PMO, an effective training program is required for the following four audiences:

- General Population
- Project Teams
- Portfolio/Program/Project Managers
- Executives and Functional Managers

The institutionalization of project management occurs when the enterprise's cultural environment enables all of its employees to embrace the organization's project business management best practices as the normal way to do the project work that they do on a daily basis.

Chapter 3

Project Business Management – The Construct and Model

The authors' Project Business Management (PBM) initial concept was developed in 2002[1], it was expanded in 2006 into a construct, and then documented in their second book[2]. That construct was updated in 2008 to initiate additional research. It was refined and detailed in 2012 and the PMB Model finalized to support the PMO Case Study research process.

3.1   Project Business Management – The Construct

The discipline of Project Management has grown and matured during the past 60 years. It now encompasses the project aspects of program management and portfolio management. The "Y2K" debacle in the year 2000 in information systems and technology pushed project management into the arena of business. Project management's further involvement, during the following decade, in managing the projects producing the newest technology products and services, has cemented its place in business and has pulled it into the field of commerce. The lines between many portions of operations management and project management have been and will remain blurred and interlaced. Therefore, project management and business management must be integrated within the enterprise, if all projects are to be planned and managed to provide the desired benefits and value to the enterprise.

To address this need, Project Business Management provides for the utilization of integrated general business management, portfolio, program, and project management knowledge, skills, tools, and techniques in applying portfolio, program, and project processes. The underlying objective is to meet or exceed stakeholder needs, and to derive benefits from, and capture value through, any project-related actions and activities used to accomplish the enterprise's business objectives and related strategies.

Operations management, and project management, must coexist within the organizational structure and support the various business aspects of the enterprise. The PBM construct provides this holistic business view of the various aspects of project management, when coupled with the related business aspects of operations management.

3.2   Project Business Management – The Model

A visual representation of the PBM construct was created by the authors and called the Project Business Management Model. The PBM model is a simplified vision of the complex interfaces and interactions of operations business management and project business management. The model is useful to practitioners in analyzing interfaces and process interactions and designing a PBM organizational operation. This Project Business Management three-dimensional model, shown in Figure 3-1, graphically illustrates the integrative and interface aspects of the authors' Project Business Management construct.

FIGURE 3-1: Project Business Management Model

The top of the cube represents the Operations Business Management and the Project Business Management segments of the cube and indicates the two main business functions within an enterprise. This also illustrates the mutual need to distribute effectively the enterprises resources.

The left face of the cube shows both management functions being involved with distributing the enterprise's resources and employing the five common management constructs associated with the continuum from identifying a strategic initiative through determining what project may be required, to completing that project by meeting the stated business objectives of the enterprise.

The right face of the cube adds the third dimension, which is the previously defined PBM Organization Model that employs the five common business elements (governance, methodology, capability, planning, and execution). The location of the PBM Office on the graphic shows it managing the business aspects of the Project Business Management portion of the cube. The PBM Organization continues its operations when management employs the sixth common business element, shown in the PBM House of Excellence Model – sustainability.

An effective integration of the Operations Business Management and Project Business Management processes and best practices is necessary to consistently achieve strategic initiatives and meet business objectives that deliver the most desirable and effective business benefits and value. Those individuals involved within the Information Technology (IT) industry will see that this model can be a way of representing part of what is being called Business Process Management (BPM). For those involved with applying "Agile" project management, it can also be seen as applicable when specific interfaces are identified and a limited set of processes are selected to apply the model.

Section II

Research Methodology and Instrument

Chapter 4

Research Methodology

Interest in developing "Project Management Offices" of one type or another continues to expand. The number of articles related to project management offices (PMOs) continues to blossom as the growth of the project, program, and portfolio management practices also continues worldwide. However, useful information on how PMOs are now providing value and benefits to their enterprise, how those PMOs function, and how they are structured has been lacking.

This lack of current useful business information on PMOs, the continued interest in the project management office (PMO) portions of the authors' prior books[1,2], coupled with PMO community feedback lead to the decision to conduct this specific research. The combined feedback indicated a need for case studies of PMOs that show how various PMOs are organizationally positioned and function within an enterprise. The purpose for these case studies is to present to a wider audience those Project Business Management Organizations, generically known as PMOs (Project, Program, Portfolio or equivalent Offices), which have manifested vision and business insightfulness in carrying out new ideas, methods, or processes and that led to quantifiable improvements in project business management and demonstrated real business benefits and value for their organizations.

4.1 1997 through 2006 PMO Research Methodology

Availability of compiled data that identified the issues affecting the development, organization structure, and operation of project offices in organizations across multiple industries was generally non-existent in the mid-1990's. Establishing project management offices to facilitate the adoption of project management practices in various business units was an immerging concept at this time.

In 1997 a two-day PMI seminar entitled "Project Support Office: A Framework for Development" was developed and presented by Dennis Bolles at the PMI Symposium in Chicago, IL to 63 participants. Bolles then presented the seminar at five additional locations in the U.S. as part of the PMI seminars program in 1998 with over 200 participants attending these five sessions. The author began collecting case study data from the 1997/1998 seminar participants with data collection continuing today.

The methodology used was a PMO Survey tool, built from the key questions asked by the seminar participants, which contained 34 questions that are organized into the three phases of establishing a PMO:

- Phase One: Obtain Approval For The PMO (13 questions)
- Phase Two: Assess The Current Situation (19 questions)
- Phase Three: Document The PMO Design (2 questions)

The 1997-2006 survey tool was designed to require only short sentence fragment answers or the check-the-box for specific data items. The specific questions utilized in this PMO Survey tool are detailed in the Appendix. The detailed report of the 1997-2006 PMO Survey results is available on the publisher's website www.PBMconcepts.com.

4.2   2012 Research Methodology

The authors studied and built upon the information gathered in their prior 1997-2006 research. Information from PMO related literature searches, complied for future books, was incorporated into a possible set of PMO items that are of interest to the project management profession at-large.

The verbal input from practitioners and executives showed there was both an interest in and need for full-text PMO Case Studies that they could read and interpret for themselves. To address these needs, the authors' utilized their Project Business Management Organization model and the related Project Business Management (PBM) model as the basis for creating a comprehensive and cohesive case study instrument. (See Chapter 5 below).

The methodology employed was to require each PMO Case Study submitter to provide a full-text response to the each case study questions, as well as furnish demographic data about their organization and PMO structure. PMO Case Study participation for inclusion in the book was specifically by invitation only. The full-text formal case studies were only requested from those enterprises that have exhibited excellence and innovation in developing and maturing an organizational structure to support the effective management of projects, programs, and/or portfolios.

The research is designed and the instrument constructed to have each case study participant supply comprehensive responses to the case study information requests. The full-text qualitative case studies are meant to show the PMOs situated within the context of the enterprise's organization. The research resulted in a set of PMO case studies prepared and submitted in calendar year 2012 by both for-profit and non-profit commercial enterprises in response to the formal 2012 Case Study tool.

Chapter 5

2012 Research Instrument

The 2012 research process utilized an extensive questionnaire as the case study research instrument. The survey of 73 items included 11 demographic data questions and 62 questions requiring a written descriptive response. The questionnaire covered the seven common business elements within the PBM House of Excellence model (Figure 1-3) and the six management processes and interfaces in the authors' updated Project Business Management model (Figure 3-1). In addition, the instrument required the supply of data related to the enterprise and supporting non-textual items.

This 2012 Case Study instrument obtained PMO information and data in nine major areas, plus supporting items, as summarized below:

5.1   Enterprise Information

The instrument solicited specific enterprise demographic data such as: business name; industry; country and state/province; number of full-time employee equivalents; and size in annual sales revenue in U.S. dollars.

5.2   PMO Demographics and Structure Information

The instrument solicited PMO organizational and structural information and data, with respect to the PMO organizational structure, such as: name of business unit; title of leader/manager; position within the enterprise structure; reports to - title of person; PMO size in number of full-time employee equivalents; how is PMO internally structured; and annual operating budget in U.S. dollars.

5.3   Background, Innovations, Best Practices, and Future Impact

The research solicited specific information on:
- The PMO's background such as: scope, vision, mission, organizational description, and position within the enterprise's organizational structure
- Challenges the enterprise encountered prior to implementing any new PMO practices and how the PMO overcame those challenges

- The PMO's plans for 2012 and beyond - and how those plans will potentially impact the enterprise and its organizational structure
- Specific practices implemented and their effect on project, program, and/or portfolio and organizational success
- Innovations and best practices and potential future impact

5.4   Governance Information

The instrument solicited general descriptions related to: how the PMO presents itself as an executive-level management business function; how it addresses setting policy and establishing charters; how it provides an organizational model for the business management of portfolios, programs, and projects; how it provides an organizational model for the establishment of portfolio, program, and project management offices; and what the relationship of the PMO management is to the enterprise's operational management.

Specific operational information was requested on:

- Length of time the PMO has been in place and when it was started
- Relationship of the PMO management to the enterprise's operational management
- Internal PMO structure (positions, roles, responsibilities, etc.)
- Funding of the PMO's operations
- Position description summary of the PMO leader
- Position requirements used as a basis for selecting the PMO leader
- Whether the PMO is considered a profit and loss cost center, or overhead
- Current challenges with which the PMO is dealing

5.5   Methodology Information

The instrument solicited descriptions related to what methodologies and standardization the PMO implemented across the enterprise, and covered such items as: identification and integration of processes and practices; development of standardized Project Business Management processes; and documentation of enterprise-wide portfolio, program, and project management process methodology models, including their associated policies, practices, and procedures.

Specific process and methods information was requested on:

- Standards utilized by the PMO to ensure the enterprise's project/program/portfolio management goals and objectives are achieved
- Project management process guidelines being employed by the PMO
- Systems, tools, and templates that make the PMO successful
- Direct involvement of management at what levels in the development of the PMO and it processes
- Implementation plan used for establishing project/program/portfolio management standards across the enterprise

- Use by the PMO of project, program, and portfolio management standards to optimize its practices
- Those internal standards used that are based upon Project Management Institute's or other industry guides and if they are updated as new editions of the guides are released

5.6   Capability Information

The instrument solicited descriptions related to capabilities, such as: development and assessment of the enterprise's abilities; project management competency models; education and training programs; career path progression plan; and key Enterprise Environmental Factors [2,5, & Glossary] and Organizational Process Assets [2,5, & Glossary].

Specific capabilities information was requested for:
- Components of the enterprise's training program
- Education and training goals and objectives
- Value placed by the enterprise on education and training
- Any project management career path program
- Components of any project management career path program
- Measurements, metrics, and Key Performance Indicators (KPI's) utilized by the PMO to determine the organization's knowledge, skills, and level of achievement
- Any project management competency model employed by the enterprise

5.7   Business Planning Information

The instrument solicited specific descriptions related to planning items, such as: strategic business planning; tactical business planning; business objective (project) development and prioritization; and project identification, selection, and authorization.

Specific information related to planning was requested on:
- Organizational structure and process used for corporate strategic business planning
- Role PMO plays and the PMO's responsibilities in the corporate strategic business planning process
- Implementing the strategic plan with any project forecast plan
- Integrating strategic planning, culture, and selection of projects

5.8   Business Execution Information

The instrument solicited descriptions related to execution items, such as what role the PMO has in: project selection, prioritization, and initiation; portfolio, program and project execution planning; stage-gate reviews; and performance metrics selection and application.

Specific execution processes information was requested on:
- Selecting and initiating portfolios, programs, and projects

- Organizing and managing projects as a program and/or portfolio
- Prioritizing projects within a program and/or portfolio
- Enterprise's definition of what is project and program success
- PMO role in the management of projects considered operational in nature and the types of projects supported

5.9   Sustainability Information

The instrument solicited specific descriptions on the overall impact of the PMO over a sustained period (e.g., customer satisfaction, productivity, reduced cycle time, growth, building or changing organizational culture, etc.), and quantitative data to illustrate the areas in which the PMO has had the greatest business impact.

Specific information requested on sustainability covered:

- Elements included in a comprehensive project monitoring and control system and how that is implemented
- Structure of project start-up and gate review processes
- Project knowledge base system and its development
- Measurement, metrics, and Key Performance Indicators (KPIs) utilized by the PMO to measure project and program success
- Organizational benefits and value the PMO provides to the enterprise
- Economic benefits and value the PMO provides to the enterprise

5.10   Other Information

The instrument solicited additional comments and required providing the related figures, tables and other graphics, which supported the descriptive text.

Section III

Results and Conclusions

Chapter 6

Research Results

The PMO survey research information the authors obtained during the past one and one-half decades, combined with the additional research information produced from other sources, provides pertinent insights to the structure, operation, and future of PMOs.

1997-2006 PMO Survey Research

The authors' earlier research, obtained between 1997 and 2006, gathered data from various organizations that had recently set up their PMO, or were in the process of so doing. The responses were compiled into a summary report that was organized into five categories with a number of topics in each category, which were each cross-referenced to the original survey's 34 questions. This summary report is available on the publisher's website www.PBMconcepts.com.

The information gathered during this initial research phase was then used to expand the author's current PMO Case Study Survey instrument (see Chapter 5), which was used to gather the additional information contained in the PMO Case Study examples provided in Section IV.

2012 PMO Case Study Research Results

The expanded research resulted in a set of PMO case studies prepared and submitted in calendar year 2012 by various enterprises in response to the formal survey instrument. The full-text formal case studies were requested from those enterprises that have exhibited excellence and innovation in developing and maturing an organizational structure to support the effective management of projects, programs, and/or portfolios.

Each enterprise shared the "what" and the "how" details of the business actions they used to develop and manage their PMO. Those business case studies also gave descriptions that corroborated how each enterprise is successfully employing the Project Business Management model. The research results given below are based upon the prior research and the set of full-text case studies in Section IV that provide practical how-to information that profit, non-profit, and governmental enterprises can use to implement a Project Business Management organization.

6.1   Demographic Data Analysis

The following subcategories summarize the key demographic information included within each of the case studies.

6.1.1   Industries Represented

The enterprises included in the prior PMO Survey and the current Case Study research represent twenty-six diverse industries. The 2012 case study participants represent nine of those industries.

Table 6-1: Industries

- Banking
- Benefits Consulting & Administration
- Web Based Solutions & Enterprise Products
- Consulting Services
- Custom Applications, Network Installations, Support Services
- EPM Service & Training
- Eyecare and Eyewear
- Finance (Banking)
- Healthcare
- Information Technology and Communication
- Information Services
- Property Insurance
- Finance

- International Wholesale Banking
- Mining and Metals
- Office Automation / Dictation for Healthcare
- Casualty Insurance
- Semiconductor Development & Manufacturing
- Space & Aviation Components & Systems
- Telecommunications
- Transportation Logistics
- Transportation, IT and Software
- US Federal Government Banking Supervisor
- Utility
- Voice, Data, Video, Network Services
- Card Acquirer

6.1.2   Products and Services Represented

The 2012 PMO Case Studies and 1997-2006 PMO Survey Report include representation from organizations providing the following products and services:

Table 6-2: Enterprise Products and Services

- Telecommunications
- Consulting Services
- Office Automation/Voice Dictation
- Voice, Data, Video, Network Services
- Space and Aviation Components and Systems
- Information Services
- Project Management

- Retail Clothing
- Wholesale Banking
- Semiconductors
- Semiconductor Manufacturing
- Fully Integrated Rail Services (rail operations, engineering, training, technology, asset management)
- Financial

- Benefits Consulting
- Benefits Administration
- Software Services

- Software Development
- Biotechnology

6.1.3 PMO Function Titles

An outcome from the research confirmed the idiom…

"A PMO by any other name – is still a PMO,"

and produced an interesting list of PMO organization names. Examples of which are given in the table below:

Table 6-3: PMO Organization Names

- Corporate Project Management Office
- Project Support Office (PSO)
- Project Management Center of Excellence
- Delivery Services
- Enterprise Program Management Office
- Executive Project Management Office
- Enterprise Project Solutions
- Enterprise Portfolio Management Office

- Information Technology PMO
- IS PSO
- ITS Program Management Office
- Information Systems PMO
- New Product Development PMO
- Program Management Office
- Project Management Office
- Project Management Service Unit
- Strategic Project Office

Each enterprise has established a unique name for its PMO. The enterprise's culture and structure, and how it desires the PMO to be viewed within the enterprise, is reflected in the PMO title.

6.1.4 PMO Function within Enterprise Structure

The following table gives a cross-section of examples of the PMO title, the PMO leader's title, title of the position to which the PMO reports and the associated application span of the PMO within the enterprise:

Table 6-4: PMO Related Management Titles

PMO Title	Leader's Title	Direct Report Title	PMO Coverage
Corporate PMO	Assistant Vice President CPMO	Vice President Strategic Management	Enterprise-wide
PSO	PSO Leader	Department Manager	Enterprise-wide
Enterprise PMO	PMO Manager	Vice President -IT & CIO	Enterprise-wide
Executive PMO	Audit & Administrative Manager	Managing Director	Enterprise-wide
Program PMO	PMO Manager	Vice President Program Management	Enterprise-wide

Program Management Office	Director	CFO to CEO	Enterprise-wide
Enterprise Portfolio Management Office	VP Enterprise Portfolio Management Office	Chief of Staff for the Chief Operating Officer	Enterprise-wide
ITS Program Management Office	Director	CIO	Localized
IS PMO	PMO Supervisor	IS Director	Localized
PMO	PMO Leader	New Development Director/ GM	Localized
PMO	Director	Assistant VP, Products and Services	Localized

6.1.5   PMO Positioning and Its Affects

The research indicates that the title of the PMO leader, and the management level to which the PMO directly reports, drives both the perceived level of authority of the PMO and how the PMO is utilized within that enterprise. This positioning dictates whether the PMO services are provided enterprise-wide or are localized to a specific functional business unit or regional/divisional part of the organization.

The research also shows that the positioning of the PMO at the highest level of the organization has a direct influence on the PMO's acceptance across the enterprise, its level of authority, and the level of autonomy that the PMO has within the enterprise's structure. This positioning also influences directly the long-term sustainability of the PMO, and its ability to fulfill its role as a business function within the operational and business management structures of the organization.

The 1997-2006 PMO Survey organizations where not yet established at the enterprise-wide level, because in most cases they were just beginning to be developed.

Of the 2012 PMO Case Studies, 60% are functioning at the enterprise-wide level and report to a senior executive, and 85% of the enterprises' headquarters reside within the United States. Of these Case Study participants, 55% have firmly established their positions within their organizations as providing benefits and value, while the remaining 45% have executive support, have a clear vision, and have created a plan identifying what needs to be done to rise to the next level.

6.1.6   PMO Size

The following table identifies the breadth between the smallest and largest organization size of the 2012 Case Study participants as it related to annual sales volume, enterprise full time employees, PMO full time employees (FTEs), and PMO budgets. The 1997-2006 PMO Survey did not gather the data for PMO full time employees (FTEs), and PMO budgets, therefore it is not included in the table below.

Table 6-5: 2012 Case Study Size Related Data

Organization	Sales Volume	Total FTEs	PMO FTEs	PMO Budgets
Smallest size	$50 Million	225	1	$250,000
Average Size [Sales volume below $1 Billion]	$300 Million	6,200	60	$480,000
Largest size	$1 Billion +	33,000	450	$63,000,000

The PMO FTE's and Budgets of all the 2012 Case Study organizations vary depending on the industry they serve, the PMO positioning within the organization (enterprise-wide versus localized), and whether the industry is serving a global market or limited to a specific area or country-wide location.

6.1.7 Other Assessment Items

The following results from the 1997-2006 PMO Survey and 2012 Case Studies indicate a commonality between all study participants:

Table 6-6: Other Process Related Items

Self-assessed PM maturity levels: 39% = 0 (information not provided) 14% = 1.0 18% = 2.0 48% = 3.0	Corporate PM Policies: 73% Yes 27% No	PM Process Audit: 48% Yes 52% No
PMO coverage: 57% are enterprise-wide 43% support a business unit (primarily IT)	PM Job Descriptions: 70% Yes 30% No	Information Technology Infrastructure 85% Adequate 2% Inadequate 3% Needs Development
Resistance came primarily from: 48% No Resistance 21% Middle Management 12% Project Managers 12% Others	Commitment to PM Training: 70% High 12% Medium 18% Low	PM Technology Infrastructure 67% Adequate 3% Inadequate 21% Needs Development
PM Selection Criteria: 85% Technical Experience 21% Education Level 85% Previous PM Experience 54% PMP Certification	Management Level of Commitment to PM Processes and Procedures: 6% Non-supportive 55% Very Supportive 1% Neutral 55% Champion 48% Supportive	

33

6.2   Contextual Response Analysis – Business Questions

The research resulted in the following partial set of key business related factors, which are drawn as an analytical overview of the responses to the 2012 Case Study questions.

6.2.1   PMO Vision, Mission, and Scope/Goals

The PMO has emerged to address a basic need of enterprises for objective information about the state of their strategic initiative projects and to ensure their successful execution. The PMO mission, as stated in various ways by most of the organizations, is to create an environment of project management professionalism where: project success is the norm; project teams are proud of their work; internal customers reap the benefit of a carefully planned investment, and the external customer wins through improved service or lower cost.

The following are paraphrased Case Study excerpts related to visions, missions, goals and scope:

- The vision and mission is to build a type of corporate, or strategic, project office. It has a direct management dependency, which affords it a position of absolute neutrality in the handling of the interests of the different players.
- The vision for the PMO is to carry out those projects that really deliver value to the organization and position it with a business or operational advantage. A vision for the PMO is "the right projects, done right."
- The vision for the PMO is its striving to accomplish its mission by overseeing the project management/coordination, standardization, and communication on the company's portfolio of projects, delivering actionable decision-support information (including recommendations for project prioritization), and ensuring training and coaching are provided for successful project completion.
- The vision for the PMO is to achieve goals being worked that included: maximizing the value of the project portfolio by selecting the right projects; better planning; setting realistic expectations; improving the quality of information on projects; front loading the planning process so key decisions in direction are made early in the project when changes can have a significant positive impact and those changes can be made at a low cost; and providing processes for managing change.

6.2.2   PMO Innovations and Best Practices

The organizations included in this research have managed to establish a culture that supports prioritization of projects, executive committee presentations, and the understanding that the whole project is an investment. One challenge facing most enterprises is measuring the before and after of a project and creating a culture where the PMO is not seen as a bureaucratic body or a project auditor.

The following are paraphrased Case Study examples related to innovations and best practices:

- The need to address cultural changes resulted in establishing integrated multidisciplinary work teams from the conception of the project's product through to its implementation and operation.
- Organizations had their employees' complete training on how to manage external providers to ensure projects are delivered as promised, have seen significant improvements in project delivery. Improvements included not only the typical measurements of on-scope, on-time and on-budget, but more importantly in meeting the business objectives specified at the beginning of the project.
- The PMO institutionalized an integrated monthly meeting as a result of lessons learned from prior gaps in communications in a multi-year program. These meetings provide leadership with status reports of the project's financials, schedules, earned value, risks, contracts, change requests, and compliance.
- PMO project managers serve as a single point of contact and as process integrators for all PMO policies and procedures. The PMOs integration efforts assist the program and project managers to:
  o Ensure the flow of communications to mitigate any technology, process or resource gaps;
  o Gain trust and confidence as dedicated liaisons to all critical stakeholders to execute key initiatives by building relationships with client managers and utilize their interpersonal skills to help remove roadblocks and expedite critical activities and processes.
  o Provide the ultimate flexibility as matrix and cross-functional team-leads to provide service in all phases of the project.
- PMO project managers are provided on select projects to maintain and promote a consistent and standardized project management methodology throughout the company. Doing so also maintains and enhances the company's portfolio of projects; and facilitates widespread communication.
- The enterprise states it now has company-wide awareness, consistency, and standardization by delivering actionable decision-support information to the PMO oversight committee and the enterprise planning team.
- The PMO was created as an innovative way to plan and implement a major program to release a new innovative product. The PMO successfully implemented and integrated core project management methodologies.
- Not only did the PMO demonstrate the value of key project management tools in managing the day-today-day operations, but also in anticipating future challenges and ensuring the successful completion of the program.

6.2.3 PMOs Impact on the Enterprise Organizations

All of the PMOs in the Case Studies are recognized and accepted as an integral part of each enterprise's organizational structure. While, in most instances, there is no formal relationship between the PMO and operational management, the groups work together closely. Effective PMO's strive to understand each operation's business and issues to better understand proposed projects.

The following are paraphrased Case Study examples related to the impact the PMO has on the enterprise's organizations:

- PMO personnel visit operational units on a regular basis with the message "the PMO is here to help" rather than taking an approach of a distant unit in the corporate office formed to "enforce policy."

- The PMO fosters better working relationships by having PMO personnel situated side-by-side with operations staff to help develop business cases for projects, to provide advice on estimation techniques, and assess lessons learned at the end of the project. Improving the PMO and operations working relationships has resulted in a significant improvement in working relationships.

- PMO's included business analysts who are responsible for helping business units justify projects, establishing the scope for those projects, and gathering and documenting business requirements.

- The PMO is an enabling support services unit that creates a home for project management and supports project excellence.

- The PMO defines the path to developing project management maturity and competency within the organization.

- The PMO assesses project performance and implements continuous improvement initiatives to design, develop and deploy a common project management methodology that will ensure project and proposal success utilizing an integrated approach across the business.

- The PMO supports and facilitates project delivery success that is far superior to any competitor in the industry.

- The diversity of the organization's product lines resulted in "silos," where work for each product line was prioritized and managed without consideration of the other product lines. This sometimes led to competing priorities across the enterprise and an inability to see the "big picture" of all requested work across the enterprise. The introduction of portfolio management at the enterprise level enabled improved project prioritization and enabled project selection to be performed across all of the product lines in a consistent manner based on real business data and metrics.

- A corporate portfolio stakeholder committee, with representatives from all product lines and key corporate functional areas, was formed to manage the enterprise portfolio throughout the year.

- The new cost benefit analysis and business case required all proposed projects to be evaluated based on financial projections (cost and benefits), strategic alignment, risk, and other industry-specific characteristics.

- For the first time, an enterprise-wide approach was used to ensure that enterprise leaders were in consensus that the company was working on the "right" projects. The corporate portfolio is now a true reflection of the enterprises' top priorities.

- The PMO is an integral partner with the enterprise's operational management. All products and services currently provided by the enterprise, as well as the products and services under development, are supported by the PMO. The PMO also manages major software and technical infrastructure implementations and upgrades.

6.2.4 PMO's Value Added to the Enterprise

All of the 2012 Case Study PMOs provided some level of benefits and value to the enterprise by providing leadership of the improvement and expansion of project management best practices throughout the enterprise. Fully functioning PMOs all have a positive impact on the enterprise's selection and timely completion of those "right" projects, which provide value to the business by delivering the desired and promised benefits. Enterprises reported the value their PMO adds today to their organizations includes:

- Project management maturity advancement
- Increased success in producing winning sales proposals
- Increased market (customers) confidence in their ability to deliver
- Organization transformation of processes and systems
- Improved efficiency
- Strategic and competitive advantage
- Structured and coordinated approach to all projects
- Improved business results
- Improved positioning to win larger projects
- Improved assurance and reputation for successful projects
- Enterprise and talent capability advancement

The following are paraphrased Case Study examples related to the value added by the PMOs to the enterprise:

- PMO adds value to the organization by providing leadership for the improvement and expansion of company-wide project management best practices.
- Through partnering with the internal enterprise training team and external training partners, the PMO continues to add value by staffing increasingly complex projects and programs with highly skilled project professionals.
- The PMO adds value by reducing cost, improving productivity, and making the PMO department more efficient and/or effective.
- Value is added when executives, managers, supervisors, project sponsors, project managers, team leaders, and team members understand their roles in making projects successful and project managers and team leaders effectively manage projects and deliver them on time and within scope.
- The PMO adds value when it provides project managers with effective and well-documented tools, and templates that can help them effectively manage and deliver projects on time and within scope.

- The organization has an improved awareness of large project work, and hopefully a solid understanding of how an effective use of the PMO's methodology will aid in improved project execution, and as a result, an improvement in benefit realization, reduced costs, and an overall positive effect in the enterprises' bottom line.

- As project managers, trainers, coaches, and communicators, the PMO staff leads by example, through its steady and continuously improving competency. In addition, it has increased its number of Project Management Professional (PMP) credential holders.

- Proposals and projects are registered with the PMO for tracking, reporting, and strategic resources prioritization.

- The enterprise realized the first year benefits of project management and doubled its investment to increase the reach of the PMO unit. As a result, the PMO has actively participated in strategic planning sessions across the region.

- The PMO set and achieved the target to have 100% of the project managers become members of PMI and the local PMI chapter as well as becoming certified PMPs within 1 year, a feat no other company in the region has yet matched.

- The PMO in collaboration with the legal department of the parent company developed a contracting workshop for employees. The collaborative effort ensures that corporate risks are mitigated via contracts and managed via project management in accordance with the commercial agreement.

6.2.5 PMO Future Impact

The following are paraphrased Case Study examples of how enterprises see the future impacts of a PMO within the enterprise:

- One organization's next step is to take a baseline of current performance on all projects and implement steps to improve those project results. Because the PMO is decentralized and the PMO staff is small, success in this area will depend on educating project sponsors on best practices and making those project sponsors comfortable with holding project managers accountable.

- An area of focus for the PMO is resource management. The enterprise currently assesses potential resource bottlenecks using primitive tools that only reveal the most significant bottlenecks. To improve resource management, the enterprise's management will need to use improved tools and processes that require significant organizational change.

- The program management office has planned ongoing actions to ensure desired impacts by:
  o Monitoring and assessing PMO internal processes for both efficiency and effectiveness, and where applicable for expense reduction and/or for gains in efficiency or effectiveness;
  o Managing each assigned project according to the approved scope and estimated finish date;

- o Managing the PMO's overall training strategy regarding project management; and
- o Determining both the curriculum and most effective means of delivery.

- The enterprise uses project management and its maturing portfolio management methodologies, including the supporting tools, templates, and documentation, to improve any known weaknesses and requires appropriate individual application.
- The PMO is enhancing awareness of the value of the company's project management and maturing portfolio management methodologies.
- The PMO is effectively and confidently coaching project managers and team leaders through difficulties in dealing with various project management processes, tools, and templates, and various people management issues.
- To accommodate growth, the enterprise employed external team resources to support division-specific development and enhancement projects. This approach to project work resulted in minimal cross-divisional knowledge sharing and little coordination of project and business processes. Driven by the need to collaborate and share knowledge, a small, grassroots team of cross-divisional employees organized to address the ensuing lack of coordination among the lines of business.
    - o The team, known as the "project professionals," was comprised of project managers, business analysts, functional managers, and project sponsors.
    - o The project professionals met monthly on personal time to share experiences, network, and establish a standardized project management methodology and training program.
    - o The project professionals remained active project methodology advocates for nearly eight years before becoming members of structured and strategically located project management and business analysis teams.
- The program management methodology will evolve through streamlined processes that eliminate redundancy and the perception of bureaucracy. Each program will have a unified program plan endorsed by the program champions, program managers, and the governance team. The new program management disciplines will increase the speed to execution.
- The PMO is partnering with information technologies (IT) and operational business areas to develop standardized release management processes. The purpose is to find development, testing, and deployment efficiencies across multiple platforms for high exposure projects. The IT and PMO partnership will develop repeatable and measurable processes within the release management system, including the release plan and calendar.
    - o The outcomes will be improved productivity, decreased project resource competition, project technical architecture alignment, and preserved integrity and availability of production systems.

- o The PMO will also continue to emphasize the evolution and maturation of the portfolio analysis and support functions to facilitate organizational decision making and readiness.
- The PMO has formed partnerships with human resources to proactively provide portfolio data and input to strategically prepare for change and people management beyond the efforts at the project or program level. Likewise, partnerships are being formed with stakeholders representing external publics and customers to position change and value based on a longer term, aggregated view.
- The PMO is currently evaluating opportunities to streamline, enhance, and automate portfolio data capture and reporting to shift more attention toward higher value analysis and expanded influence. As the PMO matures, so must the skill sets of the project managers and business analysts.
- The PMO is a revenue generator due to its growth in project management maturity, industry leadership, and gaining recognition with its own external clients. The enterprise evolved the PMO unit and its resources during the transition from internally focused to balancing internal and external priorities and client demands.

6.3   Contextual Response Analysis – PBM Organization Elements

The author's research resulted in the following set of key project business management related points. Some of those points, which are drawn as an analytical overview of the responses to the 2012 Case Study questions related to the Project Business Management Organization model elements, are given below. Each enterprise's Case Study more fully shows the application of the Project Business Management Organization model elements. The Case Studies indicate how they have applied them to their organization's structure in the way they do business. Project Business Management concepts and the use of a Project Business Management Office construct are seen in the Case Studies as viable business approaches to managing the project-related business of an enterprise.

6.3.1   Governance

The enterprise PMOs in our research operate as an executive-level management business function in 61% of the organizations. They indicate that:
- Policies are set;
- Internal organizational models for the business management of portfolios, programs, and projects are established;
- An organizational model for the PMO is developed; and
- The relationships of the PMO management to the enterprise's operational management are established.

The likelihood of delivering the desired benefits, as work progresses leading to completion of the projects and portfolios, are greatly improved when senior and executive management leads the organization to adopt the necessary changes required for successfully delivering the strategic benefits and value to the enterprise.

Governance provides the business management view of projects, programs, and portfolios wherein the PMO staff works regularly with the heads of all the internal functions. The following are paraphrased Case Study examples with respect to PMO related governance within the enterprise:

- The PMO oversight committee is comprised of the company's president/CEO, and both executive vice presidents, including its chief operating officer. A vice president/branch manager representing one of enterprises' 16 independent branch offices/profit centers is included in the PMO oversight committee with the vice president/PMO director. The PMO director is also the facilitator of the PMO oversight committee, since roughly 80% or more of the enterprise's large projects involve information technologies.

- The PMO is integrated with each area of the organization, from commercial retail and wholesale to operations and systems and technology. Senior management at all levels is involved in the development of the PMO and its processes.

- The PMO reports to the CEO and the chairman of the holding company. The PMO has a flat hierarchy to foster a collaborative team focused on achieving common organizational objectives.

- The PMO utilizes the governance structure to obtain approval of the charter and to establish the initial baseline for the project.

6.3.2 Methodology

The 2012 Case Studies provide evidence from these best-in-class organizations that affirmatively answers the question, "Has the PBM Methodology best practices been implemented successfully by any enterprises?"

The number and depth of standardized practices and methodologies employed varied with both the organizational position of the PMO within the enterprise and the maturity of the PMO. Standardization involved documented policies, processes and procedures enterprise-wide. These included: prioritization process, business requirements, cost benefit analysis, charters, communication plans, action item reports, issues management, lessons learned, risk management, change management, performance evaluation, post-project evaluations, and life cycle management.

A function of the PMO is seen from the Case Studies as leading the design, development, and deployment of a common project management methodology that will ensure project and business objective success and utilizes an integrated approach across the business. The following are paraphrased Case Study examples related to the development and implementation of methodologies and standard processes for portfolio, project and program management:

- The PMO continues to refine and mature its portfolio, program and project management methodologies and tools and will be able to hold itself accountable to increasing levels of performance.

- Existing program and project management methodologies are reviewed regularly, and are republished throughout the year.
- The methodology enforces the use of standard project phase and deliverable names, enabling portfolio level tracking and reporting while ensuring a level of consistency across projects.
- One enterprise did not have the capability to develop a proprietary methodology. Therefore, it purchased a project management methodology designed for their industry's vertical market and customized the methodology to meet their enterprise's specific needs. That methodology provides them with a set of flexible processes, tools, and templates that are designed to manage their types of projects through their lifecycle.
- Portfolio tracking and reporting illustrates activities more commonly associated with the system development lifecycle (SDLC). This was a key attribute requested by the information systems department during the joint development effort of the methodology. As lessons learned surveys or sessions are conducted, improvements are made to these methodologies.
- Within the PMO, project management processes are the standard by which internal practices and controls are measured and they are optimized by establishing written policies governing the management of scope, time, budget, project governance, risk and procurement.
- The policies and processes are reviewed and updated periodically to reflect the latest program learnings by:
    o Focusing reporting to leadership in a manner consistent with project management practices;
    o Encouraging all levels of PMO staff to engage in continuing project management education; and
    o Ensuring that employee evaluations are aligned with program goals and targeted at improving project management acumen.
- The PMO has adapted Project Management Institute standards to the unique requirements of the enterprises regulatory environment. The PMO uses an integrated process control model that supports the project objectives while ensuring oversight through essential controls such as earned value and change management.
- The director of methodology and tools is responsible to assure, through planned stage gate assessments, that the project management team is adhering to the appropriate project methodology.

6.3.3 Capability

Gaining a competitive advantage requires the organization to focus on uninterrupted alignment of its resources to the right project at the right time. Focusing on maturing the balancing of resources and continuous resource alignment are seen as keys to having effective capabilities.

Capabilities described in the Case Studies covered:

- Project management competency models
- Education and training programs
- Career path progression plans
- Heavy investment in resources and in maturing them
- Making employee development a necessity
- Effective alignment of resources
- Investments in best in class tools
- A range of key *Enterprise Environmental Factors* and various *Organizational Process Assets*

The following are a few paraphrased Case Study examples with respect to the capabilities of the enterprises:

- Once processes were established, the PMO provided training to project managers and others involved in the project, including team members and project sponsors. Training is provided on the project management knowledge areas, soft skills such as leadership, and on tools.
- The PMO achieves organizational capability through project management training focused on the ten best practices from the methodology that will have the most positive impact on project delivery.
- Project managers use best practices and the supporting processes and templates to improve project results.
- The PMO facilitates risk management workshops for all major projects.
- The business diagnostic team analyzes operational performance capabilities and issues, industry and market trends, competitive threats and market forces, and financial data. The team then reports the findings to the executives, which they use as input in determining whether the current strategy and capability can be successful in the current market and industry and then revise the strategy as appropriate.

6.3.4 Planning

The Case Studies clearly show the roles the PMOs played in Strategic Business Planning, Tactical Business Planning, and Business Objective Development. The Case Studies show that strategic business planning (long term) sets the direction for developing the executable operating plans (annual, short term).

The exact role of each PMO related to project identification, selection, prioritization, and authorization is driven by its specific defined role within that enterprise. All PMOs supported the strategic selection and chartering of projects, and facilitated the project prioritization and authorization processes. The following are paraphrased Case Study examples with respect to range, methods, and types of planning that PMOs are performing:

- Planning team committees take part in the corporate planning process that helps establish the priority level for large projects. The enterprise's planning team is comprised of all executive officers, including all department heads.

- Departmental forecasted projects and programs are identified, prioritized, and listed as part of the departmental planning process, while others are listed as needed.

- New projects are integrated into the planning process by submitting a new project proposal form that is reviewed and authorized by a company vice president, which is then submitted to the PMO to initiate. This type of process allows projects to start if, and when, they are needed, as long as they are authorized by a company vice president, so the time required to start work on new projects is minimized.

- The business plan defines new business, sustainability, operations, systems and technology. The strategic plan is a map of projects ordered by project priority and then by timeline or deadline.

- There is a need to have an investment budget that can be used to track the planned work and the forecasted cost of the strategic plan.

- In the operating plan, corporate objectives and corporate action steps are identified, and then those are supported with departmental objectives and departmental action steps. Many forecasted projects are listed as a part of the annual departmental planning process; while others are initiated as they are needed.

- The organization selects and initiates programs, and projects through the development of business objectives that are identified during the annual strategic planning process.

- Prioritized projects and programs are selected according to a prior business case and prior budget approval process. Then, if the decision is made to move to the next stage, a detailed pre-project plan is prepared for that project initiative. The next step is to put this project into the portfolio to determine how it can be combined with the rest of the projects, resources, and capacities of the organization.

- Projects are usually prioritized by strategic target first and then by using variables such as cost and risks (including complexity and capacities). Not only business projects are included, but operational projects are also considered, when they are technological and sustainability projects.

- The PMO understands each of the business and support units' objectives and identified projects and develops a demand forecast for the project management office. The PMO also looks at its present strategic plans and its operational requirements and collates all the plans to create a budget and work. This is then allocated to the next level within the PMO in the form of work assignments, performance objectives, PMO development initiatives, annual operations events, and projects.

- Prioritization, selection and authorization of initiatives considers various factors such as, economic value, complexity, risk, strategic significance, strategic demand, liability, etc.
- Each year the annual plans are developed by various business and support units and presented collaboratively across the senior management level. This provides stakeholder input to the plans and considers the impacts of those plans to their plans.
- The integration of the strategic planning culture and selection of projects is evident as managers and senior managers understand the various levels of approval and so they only elevate the best developed business cases to the various stages of selection, thereby eliminating efforts on weak or poorly developed business opportunities.
- When the PMO has a clear understanding of which projects are to be worked on the following year, the projects are reviewed and grouped into existing or new programs and portfolios.
- Occasionally portfolios are renamed or rebalanced according to the anticipated workload.
- The PMO introduced a new portfolio management process to allocate funding by project, based on priority. As a result, limited funds are now distributed where they can have the greatest positive impact on the company as a whole.
- The PMO meets with each department and division at least six months prior to the beginning of the budget planning process to determine project requests for the upcoming fiscal year.
- Projects are divided into categories of non-discretionary spending (safety, regulatory, sustaining maintenance) and discretionary spending (profit improvement, strategic, cost reduction). Projects may also be grouped into programs of projects, depending on the need to coordinate resources or program outcomes.
- The PMO worked with the corporate portfolio stakeholder committee to identify the essential project data elements required for each project, and developed a cost benefit analysis and business case that used the data to prioritize the proposed projects.

6.3.5 Execution

Within execution, executive management is seen as directing the distribution of the enterprises funds and resources, and assuring the funds are effectively applied across the enterprise to only those projects that support business strategies and objectives thereby giving those projects, from the very start, the best opportunity to succeed. The following are paraphrased Case Study examples with respect to execution actions that PMOs are performing:

- Executive management is given actionable, decision-support information on topics involving project management best practices and the PMO' role and responsibilities.

- The PMO is responsible for project selection, prioritization and initiation within the project management services unit. However, in the other business and support units of the organization, the PMO provides input to the resource estimating, scheduling, risk assessment, etc. for the project selection, prioritization, and initiation by the units' management and the organization's executives.

- The enterprise-wide PMO works with executive sponsors, the information systems staff and other key business stakeholders to execute programs and projects. This collaborative effort considers many factors including finances, resource availability, technical releases, and the like. The execution is an ongoing effort, and collects feedback from planned changes, finance updates, resource information, and recommends adjustments.

- Once a concept is approved to issue a project charter, a project manager, business analyst, and systems analyst are assigned to begin charter development. Program roadmaps are developed for the larger, strategic efforts. Program managers and their champions work closely to define projects that will clearly support the program's vision and goals. The project selection committee approves and prioritizes enterprise projects that align with the enterprise strategies and yield the greatest business value and return on investment.

- Multiple categories of risk are assessed, including technical, project delivery, and operational risk. Each identified risk is prioritized and control strategies are developed for the higher level risks.

- To ensure projects get off to a good start, the PMO facilitates annual project briefing meetings. These meetings bring together project managers, project sponsors, and project owners to get agreement on how projects are going to be managed.

- For each project, it is determined what groups need to be involved and the key roles and responsibilities needed on each project team.

- The PMO participates in stage gate reviews, project performance report presentations to provide support and assurance to the executives that performance is on track and risks are mitigated.

- The PMO directly and indirectly develops or provides inputs to the project execution for the organization.

- Once a project is approved, the cost benefit analysis and business case is managed via the change control process, so any changes to it must be approved by the corporate portfolio stakeholder committee.

- The PMO has extended the definition of success from the traditional triple constraint project parameters of within budget, on schedule or earlier and within specification (scope and quality), to the greater business outcome parameters such as:
  o Client satisfaction and acceptance– testimonials
  o Repeat business – customer loyalty
  o Meet technical objectives
  o Commitment to quality

- o Meet business objectives (time to market) – improved client outcome
- o Set precedents/precedence
- o Functional reciprocity – valued teamwork
- o Delivered safely – no accidents, loss time due to health, safety, security or environmental issues
- The PMO Manager sets direction for portfolio, program and project management.
- Success is determined using the results of a post-implementation review.

6.3.6 PBM Office

The 2012 Case Studies provide clear evidence from a number of best-in-class organizations that affirmatively answers the question "Has a PBM Office been implemented successfully by any enterprises?" This research shows that enterprises have identified opportunities to improve the alignment of project execution with corporate strategies and objectives that support the enterprise's mission and vision, through the use of executive-level PMOs. Each company has established its "PMO" as a unique business function within its organization, rather than it being an add-on to an existing function or department.

PMOs are seen as taking on a variety of forms and functions. The PMOs that have the greatest impact on their companies, also have an influential structural position within the organization, and present themselves as an executive-level management business function.

The following are paraphrased Case Study examples related to the organizational structure and functioning of an enterprise PBM Office:

- The organizational structure has a direct reporting relationship of the project management team to the director of project managers. The project managers are responsible to the program director to complete the projects as planned, but are also held accountable to conform to the project methodology.
- The PMO is responsible for managing the enterprise portfolio of projects and it is led by the chief financial officer and chief operating office.
- The PMO was established as an enterprise-wide PMO with project oversight responsibility company-wide reporting to the chief information officer.
- The PMO is an independent, enterprise-wide department, which is vice president directed reporting directly to one of two executive vice presidents.
- The senior executive or PMO director is a member and facilitator of the PMO oversight committee and helps to set and communicate policy in the area of project management for the organization.
- The PMO conducts the following three key support functions: downward – providing support to project managers; horizontal – reporting about program health and status to internal and external organizations; and vertical – facilitating the governance structure.
- The PMO allows the four functional areas of the enterprise: 1) information

technology, 2) business design, 3) deployment, and 4) program office -- to focus their attention on their areas of responsibility.

- The reason for the PMO's dramatic growth is simple: the PMO has proven its ability to deliver a wide variety of projects, and its scope of responsibilities has continued to increase through the years.

- The PMO uses a unique approach to lessons learned, which is similar to a military after actions review. The questions asked are: What was supposed to happen? What actually happened? Why did it happen? What should be repeated? and What should be repaired?

- The most dramatic measure of PMO success is the enormous increase in the number of projects under PMO management, and their associated budgets. Over the past five years, there has been a fivefold increase in each of these. And, additional project requests continue to be approved and assigned to the PMO.

- Under PMO leadership, reporting moved from a focus on pictures of construction sites and vague descriptions of progress to objective reporting of schedule and cost versus baselines.

- The PMO led an effort to provide an integrated way to track project costs in the company financial system rather than on independent spreadsheets, leading to more accurate project reporting. This transparency has allowed management to see project trends monthly and make sure corrective action takes place sooner rather than later.

- Prior to the PMO, management lacked visibility into the strategic investment portfolio. Every year, millions of dollars would be invested without a consistent method to track return on investment. The PMO now conducts post-implementation audits on all major projects to evaluate whether or not business objectives were achieved. Results are communicated to the executive team to provide insight into the results of prior strategic decisions and the information is used to improve the decision-making process on future projects.

- The following is a list of typical PMO responsibilities and duties ascribed to by a number of PMOs in the research:
  o Advancing organizational project management maturity
  o Contribution in the sales process to winning proposals
  o Increasing confidence in the market of enterprises' ability to deliver
  o Improving collaborative effort and integration within the enterprise
  o Leading organizational transformation of processes and systems
  o Advancing organizational efficiency and the enterprise's capability
  o Improving strategic and competitive advantage
  o Proving a structured and coordinated approach to all projects
  o Establishing project documentation standardization and methodologies
  o Increasing business results
  o Establishing a PBM integrated approach across the enterprise
  o Positioning the enterprise to win larger projects
  o Increasing the enterprises reputation for successful project delivery

6.3.7   Sustainability

1997 – 2006 PMO Survey – Sustainability

The following are points drawn from the PMO Survey results analysis and interviews with some Survey participants.

- There are few significant differences in the responses submitted by participants between 1997 and 2006, which indicates most organizations believe they have a Stage 2 or lower PM maturity and are still struggling with implementing enterprise-wide project management.
- Project business management processes that are owned, controlled, and applied under the direction of the enterprise and not a supplier, can be improved and matured over time resulting in increased benefits and return on investment. This is particularly true where the enterprise has multiple projects being performed in whole or in part by third party suppliers over extended periods of time.

The significant results derived from analyzing the earlier 1997 – 2006 PMO research are the following:

- Approximately 45% of the PMO's ceased to exist during the survey period, based on follow-up research because:
  o The PMO did not deliver identifiable business benefits and value to the enterprise.
  o The PMO's could not define clearly either their purpose or role in supporting project management. This resulted in the PMO being viewed as ineffective and unable to produce business results to validate cost to exist.
  o The PMO lacked sufficient executive support to sustain its operating as a PMO.
- The issues that impacted effective PMO start-up and on-going operations were the same for those enterprises who joined the survey near the end, as they were for those enterprises that joined at the start.
- Implementing a Project Business Management Methodology that incorporates strategic and tactical planning fails for a number of reasons; such as:
  o Lack of executive support
  o Lack of clearly defined purpose
  o Lack of defined goals and critical success factors

2012 PMO Case Study Research – Sustainability

A common question previously asked of the authors is, "What actions need to occur to create a sustainable PMO?" The following is a partial list of actions, each of the submitters have communicated in some form or fashion as being required to create and maintain a sustainable PMO or that add to the sustainability of the PMO:

- PMO is instrumental in establishing best practices enterprise-wide.
- Benefits and value of operating a PMO and employing Project Business Management are communicated.

- PMO is routinely involved in assessing PBM processes and practices.
- PBM best practices are institutionalized enterprise-wide.
- PMO at the executive level is in a position to identify the gap between the PBM processes and practices assessed maturity state, and the desired end state.
- Senior members of the PMO coach the project managers of major projects.
- PMO has a quality education and training program to mature development and implementation of PBM processes, practices, and personnel.
- PMO is responsible for implementing PBM process improvement initiatives that address identified process or practice maturity gaps.
- PMO is assigned formally established and commonly accepted roles and responsibilities of a PBM Organization and they are applied.
- A single executive who "owns" the Project Business Management Organization function is appointed.

All of the PMOs in the case studies provide benefits and value to the company and are recognized and accepted as an integral part of their enterprise's organizational structure. Some have taken additional steps to have their executives and mid-management actively support their PMOs by providing leadership that drives the improvement and expansion of project management best practices throughout the company.

This is accomplished partially by establishing teams and committees led by executives and mid-management that add value to the organization by overseeing project management coordination, standardization, and communication on a portfolio of projects, delivering actionable decision-support information to an oversight committee, and ensuring training and coaching is provided for successful project completion. They lead by example rather than by edict.

The Case Study enterprises have exhibited excellence and innovation in developing and maturing an organizational structure to support the effective business management of projects. Their PMOs have manifested vision and business insightfulness in carrying out new ideas, methods, or processes that led to quantifiable improvements in project business management that demonstrate real business benefits and value for their organizations.

They have done so by developing teams and committees that are unique to their organization's culture with specific responsibilities that provide the opportunity for executive management to actively participate in the administrative functions that support their PMOs.

Chapter 7

Conclusions

The results of the authors' research led to many conclusions relating to the future of PMOs that are of interest to enterprise executive level managers and PMO managers who are either implementing or operating a PMO. These conclusions include those pertaining to the future of PMOs, such as: challenges being experienced in implementation and maturation; types of benefits and values being delivered; roles, responsibilities, and authorities; and positioning within the enterprise.

Three basic conclusions to be drawn from the literature research, prior to the 1997-2006 PMO Survey and the current 2012 Case Studies are that:

1) Establishing PMO's was a business practice starting in the post-World War II era with the Defense and Construction industries,

2) The practice of creating PMO's in other industries was just beginning to emerge in the 1990s, with the interest in developing "Project Management Offices" of one type or another growing since the mid-1990s, and

3) The level of acceptance, executive positioning, authority, and autonomy of the PMO within an organization's structure has only been achieved, to any great extent, in the past six years.

The research shows the sense of where PMOs are going is no longer in question. PMOs positioned at the executive level of an enterprise now play a key role in the strategic and tactical business planning, prioritization, authorization, and management of portfolios, programs and projects.

The PMO is now viewed as a beneficial change agent and unifying force within the enterprise. It has the ability to influence outcomes, lead projects that are enterprise-wide, and encourage and drive collaborative cooperation among various and disparate business units.

PMOs will oversee management of cross-enterprise projects and will ensure the projects within the operational business units are also managed to meet the enterprise's business needs and deliver the desired benefits and value.

Part of the purpose of the 2012 Case Studies was to obtain some partial answers to the following set of questions being asked by many project, program, and portfolio management practitioners:

1) What challenges are being experienced in PMO implementation and

    maturation?

2) What types of benefits and values are seen as being delivered by the PMO to the enterprise?

3) What are the function, position, and authority of a PMO, and why is important to understand how it perceived within the enterprise?

4) What will be the roles and responsibilities of the future PMOs?

5) What will be the authorities of the future PMOs?

6) Where will the PMO be positioned in the future within the enterprise?

7) How does a PMO at the executive level blend the management of portfolios, programs, and projects?

8) What level of autonomy will the PMO have within the enterprise's organizational structure?

The partial answers to the above questions as looked at through the results of the Case Studies are as follows, and many others can be drawn by reading the Case Studies.

7.1   PMO Implementation and Maturation Challenges

Establishing and implementing a sustainable PMO requires explicit executive action and continuing support. Some of the challenges faced include: raising the organization's project management maturity level enterprise-wide; improving operational transformation of project execution within the functional organization; and maturing the area of portfolio management especially within strategic planning and prioritization.

7.2   Benefits and Value Delivered by PMOs

The operation of these PMOs has led to quantifiable improvements in the management of the enterprise's projects, programs, and/or portfolios and demonstrated real business benefits and value for their organizations. Examples include: improved collaborative effort and integration of the organization; faster execution of specific political needs; more efficiency fostering lower cost; project management maturity advancement; organizational transformation of processes and systems; and improved business results.

7.3   PMO Function and Authority

The PMO organization must be positioned as a functional business unit with executive level authority to be accepted at all levels of the enterprise as having the authority to advance the efficient utilization of the enterprise's resource capabilities. With its position at the corporate level, the PMO has the authority to improve efficiency and revenue earning capability by including new services offerings and revenue streams.

Enterprises are addressing the misapplication of limited resources, sub-optimization of business processes, and lack of cross-organizational integration, by employing a more pragmatic and flexible structured PMO approach. This allows companies to gain business leverage over a multitude of corporate, divisional and departmental portfolios, programs, and projects. These projects cover the range from research and development, capital expansion, new product lines, modified products, and maintenance, to extensive process improvements.

Communicating the benefits of establishing a Project Business Management Office as a functioning enterprise-wide business unit is a critical step in making portfolio, program, and project management integral capabilities within all the enterprise's operations. The PMO organization must be positioned as a functional business unit with executive level authority to be accepted at all levels of the enterprise as having the authority to advance the efficient utilization of the enterprise's resource capabilities. With its position at the corporate level, the PMO has the authority to improve efficiency and revenue earning capability by including new services offerings and revenue streams.

7.4   PMO Roles and Responsibilities in the Future

In those organizations who have recently implemented a PMO, the role will be to establish it as an enabling functional unit providing services that create a home for project management and that supports excellence in project execution. The PMO will define the path to developing project management maturity and competency within the organization. It will assess project performance and implement continuous improvements. The purpose of the PMO will be to design, develop, and deploy a common project management methodology that will ensure project and proposal success utilizing an integrated approach across the business.

7.5   PMO's Authority In the Future

The future PMO will be established as an executive level business function, which can create a culture that evolves the organization to become superior to any competitor in project management performance. It will facilitate the enterprises' ability to consistently deliver business value and realize benefits that will result from the improvements in standardization, compliance, and enterprise alignment.

The PMO has become the change agent and unifying force within the enterprise, because of its ability to influence outcomes, lead projects that are enterprise-wide, and encourage and drive collaborative cooperation among the various, business units.

The research shows the executive PMO as a change agent and unifying force within the enterprise having the ability to influence outcomes, lead projects that are enterprise-wide, and encourage and drive collaborative cooperation among the various, and sometimes disparate, business units.

The trend to develop enterprise-wide PMOs will continue to increase. This will happen as more organizations begin to view the management of portfolio, programs, and projects as business functions and come to understand the need to create the executive level position who owns the Project Business Management Office organization.

7.6   Future Positioning of the PMO

The PMO will be positioned as a functional business unit owned by a senior executive with the PMO leader having the authority and responsibility to lead enterprise-wide the organizational changes necessary to achieve continuous improvements in all areas related to the management of projects. The research demonstrates that PMOs who oversee the management of cross-enterprise projects do ensure that projects within operational business units are managed to meet the enterprise's business needs.

7.7   Executive Blending of Portfolio, Program, and Project Management

PMOs utilize a portfolio governance discipline enabling the prioritization of company resources on critical projects and programs that sustains the organization's competitive advantage, continuous growth, operational excellence, and establishes a high-performing culture.

7.8   What Level of Organizational Autonomy Will PMOs Have?

Establishing a Project Business Management Organization at the corporate level provides the requisite authority, acceptance, adoption, and autonomy necessary to establish ownership of and responsibility to institutionalize and oversee the effective application of the principles and practices of the Project Business Management methodology across the enterprise. Those PMOs that are positioned as an integral partner with the operational management of an organization will have the ownership and responsibility for the direct development, implementation, and maintenance and consistent use of the portfolio, program, and project management methodologies by providing the tools and knowledge management in support of formulating best practices across the enterprise.

7.9   Summary

In the executive summary of their book, *The Project Management Office, A Quest for Understanding*, Hobbs and Aubry[4], state that a portion of their excellent academic research survey was to develop the answers to two questions: "What functions do they (PMOs) fill" and "How are PMOs structured." Hobbs and Aubry intimate that these may be the two underlining questions needing to be answered that could lead to a guideline or standard on PMOs[4]. However, Hobbs and Aubry also reflect that "If PMOs are temporary arrangements, it is impossible to answer these questions as they are presently being conceptualized[4].

The following, but paraphrased, findings[4], by Hobbs and Aubry are corroborated by the authors' 1997-2006 PMO Survey and 2012 Case Study research:

- Existing PMOs change every few years
- PMOs are varied

- PMOS in different industries, different regions, similar sized enterprises, or in private or public enterprises do not vary systematically in the manner in which they are structured or the functional roles they fulfill
- PMO organizational structure and the functional roles employed by a PMOs are driven by the enterprises political and organizational context
- PMOs are best established within a context specific setting

ESI™ in Section 4 of its study, *The 2012 Global State of the PMO*[8], noted the following finding:

"The lack of executive support was named as the number one reason for the disbandment of the PMO, according to survey respondents. These findings show that executive buy-in is crucial for the health of the PMO[8]."

The authors have a related finding that has been solidified through their many years of practical experience and those of other professional practitioners. It also has been corroborated by many off-the-record in-depth discussions with senior personnel who were involved in successful PMOs that were dismantled or disbanded. It will not appear as a specific point in any formal published case study or most academic research.

- The apparent temporary nature of many PMOs is a direct result of organizational politics and the selfish self-interest of personnel managing the competing permanent functions within the enterprises in which those PMOs were created.

A potential solution to this issue is suggested in the "Sand Boxes and Rice Bowls" subchapter of the Epilogue.

The authors agree with the Hobbs and Aubry research summary point that "When designing a PMO, an organization has a large number of choices as to how the PMO is organized and what role it plays[4]."

PMO Structures and Roles

The use of a Project Business Management Organization is shown by the research as a viable business organizational approach to managing the project-related business of an enterprise. The organizational structure of any specific PMO is dependent upon how the enterprise establishes and utilizes business units within its culture and business operations. For example, a PMO business unit might be a direct report to an executive and by its direct line position within the organization have the authority associated with any business unit at that level. Alternately, the PMO business unit could be located as a staff function to an executive, such as quality assurance usually is, and draw its authority directly from the executive to which it reports. Lastly, the PMO business unit could be established at the executive level as a permanent part of the enterprise's structure.

The research results confirm the experience of practitioners, which is the possible organizational structures for a PMO, will be as varied as the combination of industries and enterprises and the associated organizational and political contexts. That is why the PBM Office portion of the PBM Organization construct reflects the structure of the PBM office within the specific organizational structure of the enterprise where it is located. Therefore, because no two enterprises are alike, customization of the PBMO for business size and type is a given, as can be seen from the wide variety of PMOs in the earlier 1997-2006 PMO Survey and these 2012 Case Studies.

PMO Guideline Concepts

Based upon all the available research to date, the authors do not believe that PMOs can be, or should be, classified into some artificial types or groups by the project management profession in an attempt to create a guideline or a standard. Some of the significant reasons are:

- Organizational and political contexts are enterprise specific
- Political contexts vary by industry, geographical region, and country
- Enterprise Environmental Assets are enterprise specific
- Organizational Process Assets are enterprise specific
- Product and service focus is both enterprise and industry specific
- Enterprises intentionally establish a PMO as either temporary or permanent
- Project Support Offices and Project Administrative Offices do not manage and are not PMOs

However, since the Project Business Management and the use of a Project Business Management Organization are shown as an ubiquitous business approach to managing the project-related business of an enterprise, and are potentially usable by most enterprises most of the time, some basic PMO guidelines for establishing and operating a PMO can be suggested. Those simple guidelines and their relationship to the PBM Organization Model are:

- Establish whether the PMO is to be temporary or permanent (*governance*)
- Issue the PMO vision and mission statements (*governance*)
- Assign the PMO manager or executive (*PMO Office - governing*)
- Define the PMO reporting relationships and organizational structure (*governance*)
- Develop, document, and issue the methodologies to be used (*methodology*)
- Identify, acquire, and enhance the capabilities required to perform the mission (*capability*)
- Put in place the needed planning based upon the approved methodologies (*planning*)
- Manage and supervise the performance, monitoring, control, and completion of the projects in accordance with the issued plans and procedures (*execution*)
- For a permanent PMO or a multi-year mission PMO, institute and execute personnel training and process improvements (*sustainability*)

Section IV

PMO Case Studies

The research case studies contained within this Section present various Project Business Management Organizations (PBMOs), generically known as PMOs (Project, Program, Portfolio or equivalent Offices), from a variety of industries. These PMOs have manifested vision and business insightfulness and achieved business results for their organization. These full-text formal PMO case studies were written, with minor editing for format and consistency, by those enterprises that have exhibited excellence and innovation in employing their PMO and in developing and maturing an organizational structure, which supports the effective management of projects, programs, and/or portfolios. Each enterprise shares their actual business actions taken in the development, operation, and management of their successful PMOs.

These business oriented case studies provide the practical how-to information that profit, non-profit, and government enterprises are using to implement a Project Business Management Organization. Numerous graphics within the case studies help explain operational interfaces, process interactions, roles, responsibilities, and business linkages.

Each enterprise is notable as having developed a successful PMO operation, which displays quantifiable improvements in the management of projects, programs, and/or portfolios and demonstrates consistent business benefits and value for the enterprise.

The individuals and the enterprises who submitted these case studies are recognized by the Authors in the Acknowledgements Section at the front of this book. Each enterprise provides their enterprise information within their case study. These enterprises and their industries are:

Chapter 8: AmeriHealth Mercy Family of Companies
Health Care Industry

Chapter 9: Banco Hipotecaris S.A.
Finance and Banking Industry

Chapter 10: The Doe Run Company
Mining and Metals Industry

Chapter 11: EMC Insurance Companies
Insurance Industry

Chapter 12: ILLUMINAT
Information and Communications Technology Industry

Chapter 13: Merchants Insurance Group
Property and Casualty Insurance Industry

Chapter 14: Nationwide
Insurance and Finance

Chapter 15: Railinc
Transportation, Information & Software Technology Industry

Chapter 16: Southern California Edison
Utility Industry

Chapter 17: University of Utah Health Care
Healthcare

Chapter 18: VSP Vision Care
Eyecare and Eyeware Industry

Chapter 8

AmeriHealth Mercy Family of Companies PMO Case Study

The AmeriHealth Mercy Family of Companies (AMFC) is the nation's leader in health care solutions for the underserved. The company delivers excellence in publicly funded managed care services and products. The AmeriHealth Mercy Family of Companies is among the largest organizations of Medicaid managed care plans and related businesses in the United States, touching the lives of more than 4.5 million individuals covered by United States Medicaid, Medicare, CHIP and other insurance.

Headquartered in Philadelphia, the AmeriHealth Mercy Family of Companies is a mission-driven company with more than 25 years of experience serving low-income, chronically ill populations. AmeriHealth Mercy Family of Companies' core products include full-risk Health Management Organizations, management contracts, administrative services, pharmacy benefit management, care management services, and behavioral health care management services.

The AmeriHealth Mercy Family of Companies service is built on these values: • Advocacy • Care of the Poor • Compassion • Competence • Dignity • Diversity • Hospitality • Stewardship

8.1 AmeriHealth Mercy Family of Companies – Enterprise and PMO Office Survey Information

Enterprise Name: AmeriHealth Mercy Family of Companies

Country: United States of America

Industry: Healthcare

Enterprise – Annual Sales Revenue: Not Available

Enterprise – Full-time Employee Equivalents: 2,500

World Wide Web Site: www.amerihealthmercy.com

PMO Name:	Enterprise Portfolio Management Office (EPMO)
Title of PMO Leader:	Vice President, Enterprise Portfolio Management Office
PMO Position in Organizational Structure:	Enterprise-wide
PMO reports to in Organizational Structure:	Chief of Staff for the Chief Operating Officer.
PMO Annual Operating Budget:	Not Available
PMO – Full-time Employee Equivalents:	Approximately 80, but varies according to workload

The following are the PMO Case Study Survey question sets and associated responses as submitted by the AmeriHealth Mercy Family of Companies' Enterprise Portfolio Management Office, with minor editing for format and consistency.

8.2   AmeriHealth Mercy Family of Companies PMO Background, Innovations, and Impact

In the following three parts of this case study, the AmeriHealth Mercy Family of Companies' Enterprise Portfolio Management Office provides an overview of the background and structure of its PMO, various innovations and best practices by the PMO, and the potential future business impact of the PMO.

> **8.2.1 SURVEY – PMO Background:** Describe your PMO, including background information on its scope, vision, mission, and position within the enterprise's organizational structure.

Scope

The Enterprise Portfolio Management Office (EPMO) at the AmeriHealth Mercy Family of Companies is responsible for managing the Corporate Portfolio. As the number of projects in the Corporate Portfolio increased dramatically, it became apparent that the organization needed to develop sub-portfolios and in 2010, the Corporate Portfolio was subdivided into five smaller portfolios. Each of the five sub-portfolios are led by an Executive Sponsor who is accountable for the sub-portfolio they lead that support the goals of AmeriHealth Mercy Family of Companies current strategic plan and/or the annual operating plan goals.

The Corporate Portfolio is led by the Chief Financial Officer and Chief Operating Officer. In addition to the Corporate Portfolio work, the EPMO provides portfolio, program and project management support to all growth (new business activations) and major technical and infrastructure projects. This support extends across AmeriHealth Mercy Family of Companies diverse product lines, which include full-risk health plans, management and administrative services for health plans, intensive care management, pharmacy benefit management, and behavioral health care services.

Mission

The mission of the EPMO is to provide a centralized approach to assist the AmeriHealth Mercy Family of Companies (AMFC) in achieving its strategic and operational goals which focus on the organization's membership and provider networks. This approach brings discipline and standardization to the practice of project management across the organization through the use of project management best practices.

These best practices encompass tools and techniques, portfolio management, project and program methodologies, leadership, training, and guidance necessary to maximize the use of time and resources.

Vision

The EPMO vision utilizes a portfolio governance discipline that enables the prioritization of company resources on critical projects to sustain the organization's competitive advantage, continuous growth, operational excellence, and high-performing culture. The EPMO provides the tools, techniques, and education to ensure repeatable processes are followed, program and project performance is enhanced, resource utilization is maximized, and quality end-results are produced. Additionally, the EPMO manages and communicates the status of Corporate Portfolio, as well as ensures the quality of project deliverables.

8.2.2 SURVEY – PMO Innovations and Best Practices: Address the challenges your enterprise encountered prior to implementing the new PMO practices and how you overcame those challenges. Describe clearly and concisely the practices implemented and their effect on project, program, and/or portfolio and organizational success.

The diversity of AmeriHealth Mercy Family of Companies' product lines had resulted in "silos," where work for each product line was prioritized and managed without consideration of the other product lines. This sometimes led to competing priorities across the organization and an inability to see the "big picture" of all requested work across the enterprise. The EPMO's internal customers were dissatisfied when they experienced changes to project delivery dates and/or project budgets caused by resource contention.

The introduction of portfolio management at the enterprise level enabled improved project prioritization and enabled project selection to be performed across all of the product lines in a consistent manner based on real business data and metrics. A Corporate Portfolio Stakeholder Committee, with representatives from all product lines and key corporate functional areas, was formed to manage the Corporate Portfolio throughout the year.

The EPMO worked with the Corporate Portfolio Stakeholder Committee to identify the essential project data elements required for each project, and developed a cost benefit analysis/business case that used the data to prioritize the proposed projects. The new cost benefit analysis/business case required all proposed projects to be evaluated based on financial projections (cost and benefits), strategic alignment, risk, and other industry-specific characteristics. For the first time, an enterprise-wide approach was used to ensure that AmeriHealth Mercy Family of Companies leaders were in consensus that the company was working on the "right" projects.

AmeriHealth Mercy Family of Companies uses an annual budget process. The Corporate Portfolio Stakeholder Committee evaluates all programs and projects that are already in progress, as well those that are already "in queue" as a result of having been previously approved. These are evaluated against new requests for programs and projects that are received as part of the annual budget process. Analysis of all of the cost benefit analysis/business cases may result in adjustments being made to work in progress or planned.

This evaluation of work in progress, in queue, and newly requested work continues throughout the year, as our businesses are dynamic, and new needs are continually identified. As some projects are completed and new project requests are received, the EPMO oversees the "demand" and "delivery" aspects tied to the plan. The Corporate Portfolio is now a true reflection of AmeriHealth Mercy Family of Companies' top priorities.

8.2.3 SURVEY – PMO Future Impact: Briefly describe your PMO's plans for 2012 and beyond - please describe how those plans will potentially impact your enterprise and its organizational structure.

The EPMO will continue to refine and mature its portfolio, program and project management methodologies and tools so that it will be able to hold itself to increasing levels of performance. Its Portfolio Management methodology is under continual improvement to ensure the consistent, comprehensive management approach to the management of the portfolios that comprise the Corporate Portfolio. The existing program and project management methodologies are also under regular review, and are republished throughout the year. Several different paths through the project management methodology are planned, as the variety of projects has increased significantly.

There are also activities underway to enhance our demand and resource management capabilities. All of the PMO and Information Systems (IS) resources in AmeriHealth Mercy Family of Companies are now using a single tool to capture estimated and actual work effort. This data will be used to improve the organization's ability to estimate, forecast future resource shortages, and will also provide historical data which will be valuable as reference materials.

A separate but related improvement effort is the development of a staffing model that uses information about the project, such as its size, complexity, phase, etc. in conjunction with the assigned resource to determine the relative workload of each PMO resource. The target workload varies by seniority, but has proven to be an excellent tool to ensure equitable distribution of the workload, as well as a tool to justify the staff at any point in time. The intent is to be able to develop more accurate cost benefit analysis/business cases, and provide better financial forecasting and improved resource management.

The EPMO introduced a more robust portfolio Benefits Plan activity in 2012 to closely monitor benefits throughout the project's lifecycle. All changes to expected benefits are managed via the formal change control process, and require approval by the AmeriHealth Mercy Family of Companies Corporate Portfolio Stakeholders. This is being done to assure that forecasted benefits of the projects become realized benefits; or that deviations from the forecast are documented, understood and reviewed during the portfolio management throughout the year.

8.3   AmeriHealth Mercy Family of Companies PMO Model Components

In the following six parts of this case study, the AmeriHealth Mercy Family of Companies' Enterprise Portfolio Management Office provides its descriptions of how they implement the six key components of the Project Business Management Organization model: Governance; Methodology; Capability; Planning; Execution; and Sustainability.

> **8.3.1 SURVEY – PMO Governance:** Describe how your PMO presents itself as an executive-level management business function, how it addresses setting policy and establishing charters, and how it provides an organizational model for the business management of portfolios, programs, and projects and the establishment of portfolio, program, and project management offices.

The EPMO reports directly to the Chief of Staff for the Chief Operating Officer of the company. This serves to position the EPMO as an executive-level management business function. In addition, the VP of the EPMO is included in executive level meetings, with her peers across the AmeriHealth Mercy Family of Companies.

All proposed projects are required to create a cost benefit analysis/business case that captures the overall "value" of the project, which is a composite score of its strategic value (determined by which strategic goal(s) are supported), financial value (estimate of the value of the benefits expected to be delivered by the project), and the magnitude of the project risk (takes various factors into consideration such as whether the project regulatory/contractual, uses new technology, organizational impact, etc.). The cost benefit analysis/business cases also capture estimated costs for hardware, software, and project personnel. This process enables all proposed projects to be evaluated in a consistent manner by the Corporate Portfolio Stakeholder Committee.

Once a project is approved, any changes to the cost benefit analysis/business case are managed via the Change Control Process, and require the approval of the Corporate Portfolio Stakeholder Committee.

However, the role of the Corporate Portfolio Stakeholder Committee is much broader than the mere review and prioritization of proposed projects. It also plays an on-gong oversight role that reviews all in-process and proposed projects on a monthly basis, and approves or denies requests for funding, schedule and other proposed project changes.

The Corporate Portfolio is comprised of five sub-portfolios: Growth, Medical Management, Operations, Corporate, and Technology. Each of these portfolios has an executive sponsor who is also part of the Corporate Portfolio Stakeholder Committee. When changes are needed, it is the executive sponsor who makes the case to the Corporate Portfolio Stakeholder Committee. The EPMO is the facilitator of this process, not the decision maker. This means that the EPMO provides information to the Corporate Portfolio Stakeholder Committee that enables them to make well-informed decisions.

Today, the AmeriHealth Mercy Family of Companies has a single enterprise-wide EPMO that supports all of its diverse products and services, as well as the underlying technology that supports the entire enterprise. Since the Corporate Portfolio was first broken down into sub-portfolios, the EPMO groups some of the proposed projects into programs, and builds sub-portfolios from the proposed projects and programs as part of the annual planning process. Each sub-portfolio has an Executive Sponsor and an EPMO Director who manage the portfolios together as a team. They are accountable to the Corporate Portfolio Stakeholder Committee for timely and within budget delivery of the projects and programs, as well as the expected benefits.

8.3.1.1 – How long has the PMO been in place? When was it started?

In 2004, the AmeriHealth Mercy Family of Companies formed its first iteration of a Program Management Office (PMO), which was the result of organizational recognition of the importance of creating a resource pool of project managers who were well skilled at delivering projects.

The PMO began creating a set of standard templates and reports that the organization uses to this day to execute and monitor the performance of its projects.

8.3.1.2 – What is the relationship of PMO management to the enterprise's operational management?

Today's EMPO is an integral partner with the operational management of the AmeriHealth Mercy Family of Companies.

All of the products and services currently provided by the enterprise, as well as the products and services under development are supported by the EPMO. The EPMO also manages major software and technical infrastructure implementations and upgrades.

8.3.1.3 – How is the PMO internally structured (positions, roles etc.)?

The EPMO consists of various levels of project managers and business analysts, which are depicted in Figure 8-1 (see at end of case study): AMFC Enterprise Portfolio Management Office (EPMO). Each of these resource types is managed as a "pool" and overseen by managers.

There are also Directors that support the five sub-portfolios and directors of Methodology and Tools, Resource and Demand Management, and Finance support roles that complete the organization.

The organizational structure illustrates the direct reporting relationship of the project management team to the director of project managers; however, the project managers are matrixed to one or more projects that may be in multiple portfolios. They are responsible to the program director to complete the projects as planned, but are also held accountable to conform to the project methodology. The director of methodology and tools is responsible to assure, through planned phase assessments, that the project management team is adhering to the appropriate project methodology.

8.3.1.4 – How are the PMO's operations funded?

The EPMO is a department that has an annual operating budget, as well as responsibility for the budget associated with the annual Corporate Portfolio.

8.3.1.5 – What is the summary position description of the PMO leader?

The Vice President of the EPMO is responsible for developing and leading the enterprise-wide, strategically-oriented Enterprise Portfolio Management Office.
The Vice President will interact with the highest levels of the organization leading the evolution of the company's culture and practices towards a future state of world-class program management.

8.3.1.6 – What position requirements are used as a basis for selecting the PMO leader?

- A bachelor's degree or equivalent work experience is required, with a Master's degree preferred.
- Previous leadership or management experience in process improvement or change management required.
- Minimum of seven years of experience as a project manager required.
- Project Management certification required.
- Must possess good, solid leadership skills.
- Demonstrated ability to influence and facilitate cultural change.
- Must be able to instill confidence at all levels of the organization including the Executive level.
- Must possess a strong technical background in project management methodologies and process improvement.
- Demonstrated ability to manage multiple priorities and be a self-starter.
- Strategic orientation, strong organizational and budgetary skills.
- Excellent verbal and written communication skills.

8.3.1.7 – Is the PMO a Profit & Loss cost center or considered overhead?

Historically, the PMO has been viewed as overhead.

However, with the recent introduction of cost benefit analysis/business cases, and the focus on benefits realization, it is slowly changing to be viewed as a Profit and Loss center.

8.3.1.8 – What current challenge is the PMO dealing with?

The AmeriHealth Mercy Family of Companies has grown very rapidly in a short time period. As a result, its maturity levels vary across the organization. The EPMO is working to raise the organization's project management maturity, as well as acting as a partner to mature other corporate functions as well.

One of the challenges facing the EPMO is that there is not a single "work intake and prioritization" process for work beyond the management control of the EPMO. While all work that the EPMO is responsible to manage is required to create a cost benefit analysis/business case, which is used to prioritize and schedule projects, there is additional risk to the organization due to additional requests for work that occur outside of these processes. This sometimes leads to resource contention and confusion.

The EPMO is working with other corporate areas to develop an improved work intake process, which will include more global and standardized ways to evaluate all requests against common, objective criteria.

Another historical challenge has occurred when a project completes. In the past, the EPMO has not reviewed the benefits that were delivered and compared them to the anticipated benefits.

The EPMO added this step to our project management methodology and is partnering with our finance area to ensure that a benefits review is conducted on all completed projects, and any variances are researched and communicated. It is expected that this process will enable the organization to do a more precise job of predicting project benefits.

Many of the projects that the EPMO manages introduce significant organizational changes. These changes were not consistently anticipated nor planned for until recently. The EPMO is partnering with our human resources area to incorporate "organizational change management" into our project management methodology and implementing a process that require analysis and preparation for organizational changes that will result from project implementations.

8.3.2 SURVEY – PMO Methodology / Standardization: Describe what standardization your PMO has implemented across the enterprise that examines: identification and integration of processes and practices; development of standardized Project Business Management processes; and documentation of enterprise-wide portfolio, program, and project management process methodology models, including their associated policies, practices, and procedures.

The EPMO has recently implemented process improvements for:
- Project methodology and supporting tool set
- Work intake
- Cost benefit analysis/business case
- Business analysis methodology and supporting tool set

8.3.2.1 – Describe the standards utilized by the PMO to ensure the enterprise's project / program / portfolio management goals and objectives are achieved.

The EPMO project management methodology is divided into multiple phases as shown in Figure 8-2 (see at end of case study): AMFC Enterprise Project Management Methodology. The methodology enforces the use of standard project phase and deliverable names, enabling portfolio level tracking and reporting while ensuring a level of consistency across projects.

A unique feature to the methodology is that it also illustrates activities more commonly associated with the System Development Lifecycle (SDLC). This was a key attribute requested by the IS department during the joint development effort of the methodology since its inception several years ago.

The most recent improvement is the introduction of a Director of Methodology and Tools position in the organization and the addition of process measures that identify the key customers of the process, critical characteristics of the process, measurement criteria and identify upstream processes within the methodology. Process measures allow the organization to measure the level of success and compliance within the methodology. The new methodology also requires phase gate reviews in which an assessment of the project's approved deliverables is completed against the requirements of the methodology for that project phase.

8.3.2.2 – Describe the project management process guidelines being employed by the PMO.

Referring again to Figure 8-2 (see at end of case study), there is a Pre-Initiation phase, during which project requests are received, an impact analysis is performed, and a cost benefit analysis/business case is prepared to document the qualitative and quantitative benefits of the project. This documentation includes what will be measured, when it will be measured, and who will measure and report it.

The cost benefit analysis/business case is then presented to the AMFC Corporate Portfolio Stakeholder Committee to approve the proposed budget and timing, as well as any other changes that may be needed for "work in progress" or planned projects to accommodate this new request.

During the annual budgeting process, many project requests are received, and an annual planning process is performed. As the year progresses, the Pre-Initiation process allows new requests to be considered against all of the other previously approved work.

The next phases are broken into Elaboration and Construction activities.

During the Elaboration Activity, the phases are Initiation, Planning, and High-Level Design. Each of these phases requires several project artifacts to be created. The EPMO project management methodology provides templates for each of these artifacts. These artifacts may be customized to meet unique project needs as necessary. A phase assessment sign-off is also required to ensure that all required project artifacts were created and approved. Our Internal Audit Department works with the EPMO to conduct audits to ensure compliance with our methodology.

During the Construction Activity, the phases are Design, Development and Testing. As in the Elaboration Activity, these phases require the creation of project deliverables. The EPMO project management methodology also includes project deliverables that are created by our Information Systems staff as part of the AMFC System Development Life Cycle (SDLC). This serves to provide the "big picture" of all of the project work that needs to be accomplished, ensure that all members of the project "speak the same language" relative to phases and deliverables, and results in a uniform approach to projects.

The next project phase is Execution or Deployment, and consists of all reviews that are required to ensure that the technical components are ready to be deployed to a production environment. The impacted business areas are also walked through the proposed changes and impacts to verify that all needed training, policies, procedures, staffing changes, etc. are in place.

The final phase is called Stabilization and Benefit Realization. In this phase, the benefits that were documented in the cost benefit analysis/business case are used to see if the project delivered its intended benefits. The content of this document guides the benefits verification process, as it documented previously agreed to information as to what would be measured, when it would be measured, and who would measure and report it.

This project phase also includes gathering lessons learned. Depending on the size and impact of the project, the lessons may be collected either by survey or a facilitated session. The findings must be "actionable," and are then used to enhance the AMFC Project Management Methodology or to make other organizational recommendations and changes. Throughout the life of the project, monitoring and controlling and change management processes are performed.

8.3.2.3 – What systems, tools, and templates make your PMO successful?

The AMFC Project Management Methodology is a tool that is used to ensure consistency and completeness in the execution of projects. Updates to the methodology are deployed several times a year, and the project managers have a great deal of input into the improvement process. All changes are reviewed with information systems to be sure that the synchronization between the project management methodology and the SDLC remains intact.

The EPMO also uses a hosted Portfolio Project Management (PPM) tool, to automate some of the routine status reporting that is performed. High-level milestones and artifacts are tracked in the PPM tool, as are the resources assigned to those tasks. Issues and risks are tracked in the PPM so that standardized reporting can be communicated to key stakeholders in a consistent manner. Detailed project plans are maintained in Microsoft Project.

More importantly however, are the processes that we have put in place to ensure project success. Every portfolio has an executive sponsor and an EPMO director who work together to deliver the planned projects and their benefits. This teamwork enables the prompt resolution of issues that threaten to impede project progress.

The EPMO consists of both project managers and business analysts. The EPMO is working to improve the skills, methodology and tools used by our project managers, while also maintaining a focus on the development of business analysts. The EPMO Business Analysis team has developed a business analysis methodology, which is shown in Figure 8-3 (see at end of case study): AMFC Business Methodology Phases with PMO Program Methodology. This methodology is integrated with the project management methodology and provides structure and guidance to the business analysts while ensuring consistency across projects. Business analysis training took place over the past few years to instill proficiency and standardization in elicitation techniques, use cases and other essential skills.

The most recent productivity improvement in the business analysis area has been the introduction of a tool to develop requirements in a more systematic method, which allows for improved collaboration between the EPMO Business Analyst , IS Systems Analyst and development teams, and the key business subject matter experts. This tool is used to capture business and functional requirements, including use cases. The product interfaces with our testing tool, providing us with more confidence that each business requirement is captured by one or more functional requirements and test scripts. The expectation is that over time we will be able to build a library of reusable requirements components, which should improve the productivity and quality of our analysis work.

8.3.2.4 – Describe how management at all levels is directly involved in the development of the PMO and it processes.

Corporate executives are briefed monthly regarding the status of the work that the EPMO is managing. This is an audio and video teleconference that allows executives from across the company to participate. Each portfolio of projects is reviewed, and updated financial information and projections are also shared.

There is also a group of executives one-level down that are members of the AMFC Corporate Portfolio Stakeholders Committee. This is the group that meets monthly or as needed to review the status of the AMFC Corporate Portfolio including financial, schedule, and resource issues. As project plans and/or budgets change, and new project requests come into the EPMO, the AMFC Corporate Portfolio Stakeholders can react by recommending changes to in process or planned work. They can also recommend budget increases when needed.

To be sure that projects are on track and issues are resolved quickly, the EPMO chairs a weekly AMFC Corporate Portfolio Review meeting. Focus at this meeting is on off target and on alert projects, but this is an open forum where any project concerns regarding resources, schedules, vendors, etc. can be discussed with a cross section of AMFC staff from the business, information systems, and the EPMO. This has proven to be a successful way to communicate and resolve issues and concerns, as well as to share information about upcoming releases and other pertinent data.

The Vice President of the EPMO holds a weekly Direct Reports meeting that includes all of the EPMO management. This is a place where information can be shared regarding recent corporate developments and upcoming corporate plans. The meeting also provides an opportunity for the EPMO management to discuss any issues that are internal to the EPMO. The Vice President of the EPMO also meets weekly with each direct report in a one-on-one meeting so that detailed issues can be discussed and either resolved or escalated.

The rapid expansion of the EPMO and its staff has made regular communication, both internal and external to the EPMO, essential to its success.

8.3.2.5 – Describe the implementation plan you used for establishing project / program / portfolio management standards across your enterprise.

Over the past 5 years, the EPMO has been on a journey to maturity. In 2007, the project management methodology was updated and enforced. An external OPM3 Assessor/Consultant performed an OPM3 assessment in 2008. The findings were used to develop an improvement plan that consumed the next 18 months. A second OPM3 assessment was performed in 2010, which also generated an improvement plan that spanned another 18 months.

Highlights of improvements made include a revised AMFC project management methodology. We have also created an AMFC program management methodology, which is currently being rolled out.

The cost benefit analysis/business case was a major organizational change that required communication across the entire enterprise. Currently, we are planning to formalize Phase Gate reviews. We plan to develop an AMFC Corporate Portfolio Management standard within the next 12 months.

8.3.2.6 – How does the PMO use project, program, and portfolio management standards to optimize its practices?

Are they based on PMI˚ or other

Our home-grown business analysis, program, and project management methodologies are under continuous review and improvement

As Lessons Learned surveys or sessions are conducted, improvements are made to the methodologies. Our business analysts and project managers also can submit recommendations for changes and frequently form small teams to develop needed improvements.

industry guides and are they updated as new editions of the guides are released?	Our methodology aligns with the content of the *PMBOK® Guide*, and we have been using Organizational Project Management Maturity Model (OPM3®) over the past 4 years to perform two maturity assessments, followed by the development and implementation of improvement plans.

> **8.3.3 SURVEY – PMO Capabilities:** Describe development and assessment of the enterprise's abilities, describe any project management competency model, summarize any education and training program, describe any established career path progression plan, and outline key Enterprise Environmental Factors.

The EPMO engaged an independent OPM3 assessor/consultant to conduct OPM assessments in 2008 and 2010. These provided an objective view of which best practices the organization met, and which were lacking. Armed with this information, in 2008 an improvement plan was developed that guided many improvements over the following 18 months. In 2010, a second OPM assessment was conducted and we are nearly complete with that improvement plan. A third OPM assessment is targeted for late 2012.

The value of the OPM assessment is that it not only looks at project management capabilities, but also evaluates the overall organizational factors that are critical to project management success. This broad focus has enabled the EPMO to not only focus on project management and business analysis skills, but also to look across AMFC to be sure that the key stakeholders of the AMFC Corporate Portfolio, its programs and projects are adequately engaged and informed.

In 2011 we conducted a rigorous series of classes for business analysts and PPM tool training for project managers. There is no formal training program in place today, although many project management classes have been brought in house in recent years.

There is a formal career path for both project managers and business analysts. The job family for project managers consists of project coordinators, project managers, senior project managers, program managers and program directors. Similarly, for business analysts, the jobs are business analyst, senior business analyst, and lead business analyst.

All of the roles in the EPMO are depicted in Figure 8-1 (see at end of case study): AMFC Enterprise Portfolio Management Office.

8.3.3.1 – Describe the components of your enterprise's training program.	All of our project managers at a senior project manager level and above are required to hold a PMP credential. We provide educational assistance to them to prepare for the exam. We have also brought classes in-house on a variety of topics to help our project managers to improve their skills.

As the number of projects assigned to the EPMO has expanded rapidly, we also developed an EPMO on-boarding process for both employees and contractors. It consists of overviews of our business analysis project management methodologies and tools, and other useful topics.

The introduction of the on-boarding process has greatly shortened the length of time it takes for new EPMO project resources to become productive. It also provides reference materials for new EPMO members to use as they are getting acclimated to AmeriHealth Mercy Family of Companies.

8.3.3.2 – Describe the value your enterprise places on education and training and its goals and objectives.

The AmeriHealth Mercy Family of Companies provides educational assistance for all associates to pursue job related degree programs. The EPMO periodically offers PMP preparation classes for project managers needing a PMP, as well as classes that focus on specific skills that need improvement.

8.3.3.3 – Does the enterprise have a project management career path program? If so, what are the components?

There are several jobs in the project management career path at the AmeriHealth Mercy Family of Companies. These are depicted in Figure 8-1 (see at end of case study).

The entry level position is called project coordinator. We also have project managers, senior project managers, program manager and program director jobs. Each of these positions has a more comprehensive scope of responsibilities and increasing experience requirements.

8.3.3.4 – Describe the measurements, metrics, and Key Performance Indicators (KPI's) utilized by the PMO to determine the organization's knowledge, skills, and level of achievement.

All of our project managers report to a single manager, who is aware of their skills and background, as well as current and past performance. The project managers are managed as a pool, and are matrixed to projects where they will be given every opportunity to grow and succeed. There is a wide diversity of project work available to them, and some have more interest in technology, while others want to become more expert in operations or regulatory matters.

The EPMO has a Director of Methodology and Tools who is responsible to ensure that the methodology is being followed, and the tools are being used as required. Our Internal Audit department partners with the EPMO to verify EPMO compliance with our project management methodology.

In 2012, a panel of EPMO and business management conducted a one-time project review of each project in the AMFC Corporate Portfolio. This activity enabled the EPMO to see on a project by project basis, if there were challenges with the project managers' use of the methodology or tools. As a result of this exercise, several improvements to the project management methodology were made and additional in-house training for the project managers was performed. Starting in the third quarter of 2012, regular Phase Gate reviews will replace this one time exercise.

The Manager of Project Managers and Program Directors works with the Director of Methodology and Tools to assess the performance of the project managers, and make recommendations to improve their performance.

8.3.3.5 – Does the enterprise employ a project management competency model? If yes, please describe it. If no, why not?

There is no formal project management competency model in place other that the position descriptions, which serve as the basis for annual performance reviews. The long-term vision of the EPMO is to develop such a model, but other priorities must be completed first.

> **8.3.4 SURVEY – PMO Business Planning:** Discuss strategic business planning, tactical business planning, business objective (project) development and prioritization, and project identification, selection, and authorization.

AmeriHealth Mercy Family of Companies develops multi-year strategic plans to guide its corporate focus, and is currently following its 2010-2012 strategic plan. The current strategic goals were developed to drive AmeriHealth Mercy Family of Companies "to pursue for and accomplish excellence and innovation … Our vision and commitment provide the foundation for our … strategic goals and will drive the prioritization of key ... initiatives during this timeframe."

A cross-functional group of executives worked together to develop the current strategic plan, and the EPMO was an active participant in that process. Each year, the AmeriHealth Mercy Family of Companies strategic plan serves as a framework for the development of annual operating plan goals. These are, in turn, cascaded throughout the AmeriHealth Mercy Family of Companies organization, and are further supported by the development of departmental and eventually, individual employee goals. The goals also result in project proposals. This link between the strategic plan, annual operating plan, and proposed projects is depicted in Figure 8-4 (see at end of case study): AMFC Project Methodology.

Two of the Guiding Principles contained in the current AmeriHealth Mercy Family of Companies strategic plan are:

- We will target and prioritize our investments and decisions based on the value they deliver to the Enterprise
- We will leverage lessons from past performance across (AmeriHealth Mercy Family of Companies), using a cost benefit analysis/business case to evaluate every initiative.

In order to ensure that this would be performed, the EPMO worked with Corporate Finance to develop a draft "strategic scorecard" based on the value drivers associated with AmeriHealth Mercy Family of Companies strategic and annual operating plan goals. Changes were made to the project management methodology to require all proposed projects to complete a cost benefit analysis/business case template that captures consistent project information, and uses the information provided to develop scores for strategic alignment, financials, and risk. This process is also shown in Figure 8-4 (see at end of case study), which depicts the link between the strategic plan and portfolio governance.

Once the AmeriHealth Mercy Family of Companies annual business planning process is complete, the EPMO works with the project sponsors to prepare cost benefit analysis/business cases for the newly proposed projects so that it can demonstrate how the proposed projects align with the strategic plan and support the strategic and annual operating plan goals. The information captured in the cost benefit analysis/business case is used by the Corporate Portfolio Stakeholders Committee to develop a composite score for each project, and is used to prioritize the body of project work requested for the coming budget year.

Each year, the AMFC Corporate Portfolio Stakeholders Committee is responsible for developing a recommended Corporate Portfolio. They evaluate projects already in progress, projects previously approved and scheduled to begin at a future point in time, and newly proposed projects. They begin with the default prioritization scoring that results from the cost benefit analysis/business cases, but they are empowered to revise the priority of a project, provided there is consensus. Regulatory and contractual projects are typically given a high priority based on their impact to the organization. This process is shown in Figure 8-5 (see at end of case study): AMFC Business Case Process the cost benefit analysis/business case process. Finally, there is always a need to tailor the Corporate Portfolio to fit within the approved budgets.

As the year progresses, proposed changes to cost benefit analysis/business cases (time, cost, etc.) follow the EPMO Change Management process, and must be resubmitted to the AMFC Corporate Portfolio Stakeholders Committee for evaluation. Proposed changes may be approved or denied by the AMFC Corporate Portfolio Stakeholders Committee. This continuous process ensures that AMFC is working on the projects that are expected to deliver the most benefits to the overall company.

As previously noted, the AmeriHealth Mercy Family of Companies Corporate Portfolio is subdivided into 5 smaller portfolios, each led by an Executive Sponsor, responsible for a particular set of programs and projects that support the goals of

AmeriHealth Mercy Family of Companies current strategic plan and/or the annual operating plan goals. Each of these smaller portfolios has an EPMO Portfolio Director and Executive Sponsor, who work as a team to ensure that the programs deliver their intended benefits. This has proven to be an effective model for AmeriHealth Mercy Family of Companies. Not only are the Portfolio Director and Executive Sponsor responsible to deliver the projects within scope, budget and on-time, but they are also accountable to deliver the expected benefits. AmeriHealth Mercy Family of Companies views its project budgets as investments, and as such, expects a "return" on those investments.

The project management methodology was modified to add a new project phase called "Benefit Realization" so there would be a formal review of the delivered benefits, with explanations of any variances. This is shown in the Stabilization and Benefit Realization phase in Figure 8-2 (see at end of case study): AMFC Enterprise Project Management Methodology.

In addition to the Corporate Portfolio work, the EPMO provides program and project management support to many major technical and infrastructure projects. A project comes under EPMO management when it will have a wide impact across AmeriHealth Mercy Family of Companies, or is on the critical path of other strategic projects that cannot be delayed. Other areas of responsibility include all new business activations, and new product development and delivery. As AmeriHealth Mercy Family of Companies continues to grow, EPMO responsibilities were added to also grow to support facilities expansions across the country. This increase in EMPO responsibilities is a result of the need to provide a more disciplined approach to this diverse body of work, and to minimize risk to other planned projects.

8.3.4.1 – Describe the organizational structure and process used for corporate strategic business planning.

Does the PMO play a role in the process? If so, describe the PMOs role and responsibilities.

AmeriHealth Mercy Family of Companies is currently developing a strategic plan to guide it through 2013 – 2016. A cross-functional team, which includes the EPMO, is working together to develop this new strategic plan.

The EPMO will not only participate in laying out the new strategic vision, it will also participate in the identification of projects that will need to be executed in order to turn the vision into reality. Areas of focus in the strategic plan will become programs and projects in the new multi-year Corporate Portfolio. The EPMO will work with the Executive Sponsors to develop cost benefit analysis/business cases for all proposed projects, and will work with the AMFC Corporate Portfolio Stakeholders to prioritize and schedule the work.

This is a significant effort, as all new ideas must be evaluated against in-process projects and scheduled projects. In addition, a multi-year perspective must be developed to ensure that all of the planned goals will be realized.

8.3.4.2 – How is the strategic plan implemented with a project forecast plan?

A multi-year portfolio will be developed that will consist of work on the Corporate Portfolio, new business activations, new product development and implementation, key technology projects, as well as facilities expansions.

This all-encompassing, multi-year schedule is needed to ensure that all goals are adequately supported by a "realistic" portfolio of programs and projects. "Realistic" is defined as having adequate funding, availability of resources, and achievable, quantified benefits. Regular evaluation of status will be reported, and will include schedule and budget analysis for in-process projects, and benefits realization analysis for completed projects.

8.3.4.3 – How is strategic planning, culture, and selection of projects integrated?

The creation and communication of AmeriHealth Mercy Family of Companies strategic plan serves to focus the entire company on the key goals for the coming years. Linking annual operating plan goals to the strategic plan, and cascading the goals to departments and employees further serves to make everyone feel a connection to and responsibility for the strategic plan.

Since each project's cost benefit analysis/business case shows how it is linked to strategic goals, the members of the project teams also can realize how the project work that they are performing serves to further the organization's strategic goals. Everyone is following the same roadmap, and working together to ensure that the strategic goals will be met, and the expected benefits delivered.

8.3.5 SURVEY – PMO Business Execution: Describe what role the PMO has in project selection, prioritization, and initiation; in portfolio, program and project execution planning; in stage-gate reviews; and in performance metrics selection and application.

The EPMO works closely with the AMFC Corporate Portfolio Stakeholders to review cost benefit analysis/business case documents associated with projects on the Corporate Portfolio. The information is presented in an objective manner, and contains sufficient detail so that the Corporate Portfolio Stakeholders can make informed decisions regarding which projects to select, prioritize, and initiate. Additionally, all changes to the portfolio must be approved by this committee, which ensures that the company remains focused on the projects with the highest priorities. In this role, the EPMO is a moderator of this committee, not a decision maker. All of the Executive Sponsors of the sub-portfolios are members of this committee as well, and can respond to any concerns or questions immediately.

The EPMO works with Executive Sponsors, the Information Systems staff and other key business stakeholders to plan the execution of programs and projects. This collaborative effort takes many factors into consideration including finances, resource availability, technical releases, and the like. This planning is an ongoing effort, and collects feedback from weekly status changes, finance updates, resource information, etc., and recommends adjustments as needed.

The EPMO Director of Methodology and Tools will chair Phase Gate reviews, targeted to begin later in 2012, but key project stakeholders from Information Systems, Operations and other corporate functions will participate. The goal is to ensure that all required project artifacts were created and received the required approvals.

The EPMO is an enterprise-wide PMO. For data within its control (project financial and schedule performance, number and type of change requests, etc.), it has the freedom to select the performance metrics to drive higher levels of project success. However, developing a more comprehensive set of metrics that include data the EPMO does not control, will require collaboration with other organizational areas, and in some instances, developing new processes and tools to capture the needed data.

8.3.5.1 – How are portfolios, programs, and projects selected and initiated?

In 2010, the EPMO divided its work into five sub-portfolios that are led by an Executive Sponsor who is accountable for the successful delivery of projects that support the goals of AmeriHealth Mercy Family of Companies current strategic plan and/or the annual operating plan. The five sub-portfolios: are Growth, Medical Management, Operations, Corporate, and Technology.

AmeriHealth Mercy Family of Companies conducts an annual budgeting process where new project proposals are submitted for consideration as part of this process. Each proposed project goes through the Pre-Initiation process that was previously described, which results in a set of cost benefit analysis/business case documents. These newly proposed projects are evaluated against the value of projects in progress and projects previously approved and planned for future execution.

Changes to current or planned work may be made by the AMFC Corporate Portfolio Stakeholders committee.

When the EPMO has a clear understanding of which projects will be worked on the following year, the projects are reviewed and grouped into existing or new programs and portfolios. Occasionally the portfolios are renamed or rebalanced according to the anticipated workload.

During the course of the year, new project proposals are accepted. They complete the Pre-Initiation phase, and can be evaluated against in progress or future planned projects. The AMFC Corporate Portfolio Stakeholders committee can make recommendations for changes to the AMFC Corporate Portfolio as business needs and priorities change throughout the year. This process has proven to be effective.

8.3.5.2 – How are projects organized and managed as a program and/or portfolio?

Projects are grouped into programs if there is synergy between them. This synergy can be sharing a common technology, customer or sponsor, or corporate goal.

The 5 portfolios that make up the AMFC Corporate Portfolio consist of projects and programs. The executive sponsor and EPMO manager are jointly responsible for the body of work (projects and programs) that make up their portfolio.

8.3.5.3 – How are projects prioritized within a program and/or portfolio?

The AMFC Corporate Portfolio Stakeholders Committee prioritizes the projects based on the cost benefit analysis/business case documents. Since the executive sponsor is ultimately accountable to the AmeriHealth Mercy Family of Companies for the delivery of anticipated project benefits, they work with the EPMO Program Director to make sure that they are managing according to the priorities.

8.3.5.4 – How does the enterprise define what project and program success is?

The AmeriHealth Mercy Family of Companies views project budgets as investments, and expects benefits to be delivered as documented in the cost benefit analysis/business case.

The project management methodology recently added Benefit Realization, and several projects have gone through the Benefit Measurement activity.

Results have been reported, and we are working to identify and remediate the root cause of any deviation from what was expected.

8.3.5.5 – Does the PMO support the management of projects that would be considered operational in nature? If so, describe the types of projects.

The EPMO manages a wide variety of projects including projects that directly impact operations.

Recently completed projects that had a large organizational impact were the replacement of our workflow system, which required retraining of over 1,000 associates.

We also manage large financial system changes that have an impact across the entire company. Some projects focus more on analysis and remediation of business trends, and may not require any systems changes to complete.

However, many of these projects enable the attainment of AmeriHealth Mercy Family of Companies' strategic and annual operating plan goals, so they are critical to AMFC's overall success. For this reason, the EPMO sometimes manages these projects as well.

8.3.6 SURVEY – PMO Sustainability: Describe the overall impact of the PMO over a sustained period (e.g., customer satisfaction, productivity, reduced cycle time, growth, building or changing organizational culture, etc.). If available, please provide quantitative data to illustrate the areas in which the PMO has had the greatest business impact.

The EPMO has endured since 2004 because it has established credibility across the AmeriHealth Mercy Family of Companies. When the current Vice President joined the organization in 2007, there was a staff of seven already in place. A total of 19 projects were completed that year.

Five years later, the full time staff fluctuates with contractors to meet demand, but has averaged about 80. The number of projects completed in the first six months of 2012 was 47 out of a total of 131 projects. The reason for this dramatic growth is simple: the EPMO has proven its ability to deliver a wide variety of projects, and its scope of responsibilities has continued to increase through the years.

In 2007, many project sponsors were reluctant to have their projects added to the AMFC Corporate Portfolio to be managed by the EPMO. Today, the demand for EPMO support continues to increase. Most recently the EPMO has been asked to manage facility work across the USA, and also to manage projects for customers for which we provide "third party administration" or TPA services. The EPMO has built its credibility project-by-project, and similarly its portfolio of projects.

8.3.6.1 – What is included in a comprehensive project monitoring and control system and how is it implemented?

The AMFC projects are all tracked in a centralized tool that records expected dates by phase for project deliverables.

Changes to these dates are controlled by the change management process, which also controls changes to scope and the cost benefit analysis/business case. Issues and risks are also captured in this tool, and are reported on a weekly basis.

On a weekly basis, a project review meeting takes place with all of the EPMO Directors. Special attention is placed on reviewing off target and on alert projects, but any project can be discussed. This forum provides a first level escalation for project teams to resolve issues.

8.3.6.2 – How are project start-up and gate review processes structured?

All proposed projects are required to create a cost benefit analysis/business case, which captures the overall "value" of the project, a composite score of its strategic value (determined by which strategic goal(s) are supported), financial value (estimate of the value of the benefits expected to be delivered by the project), and the magnitude of the project risk (takes various factors into consideration such as whether the project regulatory/contractual, uses new technology, organizational impact, etc.).

The cost benefit analysis/business cases also capture estimated costs for hardware, software, and project personnel. This process enables all proposed projects to be evaluated in a consistent manner by the Corporate Portfolio Stakeholder Committee.

Once a project is approved, the cost benefit analysis/business case is managed via the Change Control Process, so any changes to it must be approved by the Corporate Portfolio Stakeholder Committee.

In the third quarter of 2012, the EPMO will partner with our internal audit department to introduce Phase Gate reviews. The purpose of the Phase Gate review is to verify that all required project artifacts were delivered and approved. Any deficiencies will be noted, and a service level agreement will require remediation to occur within 5 business days.

8.3.6.3 – Describe the project knowledge base system and how is it developed?

The EPMO uses a unique approach to "lessons learned," which is similar to a military "after actions review."

The questions asked are:
- What was supposed to happen?
- What actually happened?
- Why did it happen?
- What should be repeated?
- What should be repaired?

For large projects, a facilitator from the human resources department may run the session(s), but the goal is to develop recommendations for improvements. The EPMO and participants view this as an opportunity to improve future projects. The recommendations are documented and used to improve the project management or business analysis methodologies.

8.3.6.4 – Describe the measurement, metrics, and Key Performance Indicators (KPIs) utilized by the PMO to measure project and program success.

The most dramatic measure of EPMO success is the enormous increase in the number of projects under EPMO management, and their associated budgets. Over the past five years, there has been a fivefold increase in each of these. And, additional project requests continue to be approved and assigned to the EPMO.

The EPMO strives to be a transparent organization. A comprehensive set of reports is issued each week across the enterprise, and are posted to the EPMO intranet site as well. Anyone in the company can access current or historical reports. The ability to analyze this information over time also provides insight into the EPMO's span of control and levels of performance.

Additionally, key indicators include weekly evaluation of the project schedule, project risk management and issue resolution. The organization utilizes health indicators (On Target, On Alert and Off Target) to measure the projects performance in the areas of Scope, Schedule, Resources, Budget, Quality, and Vendor Engagement. Beyond the weekly reviews, the portfolio is measured monthly on financial health at the project, program and portfolio levels. These metrics are communicated to governance teams on a monthly basis and reported to the Chief Financial Officer quarterly.

8.3.6.5 – Describe the organizational benefits and value the PMO provides to the enterprise.

The EPMO brings a consistent approach to all AMFC Corporate Portfolio projects, along with accurate and transparent reporting. The EPMO has been able to support the AmeriHealth Mercy Family of Companies growth strategy, and recently expanded its responsibilities to include nationwide facility acquisition and expansion projects. Through the consistent use of project management and business analysis methodologies, it is delivering more predictable outcomes, and working as a catalyst for AmeriHealth Mercy Family of Companies organizational change and maturation.

When the EPMO organized the AMFC Corporate Portfolio into sub-portfolios, it aligned each sub-portfolio with the organizational structure. Each executive sponsor oversees the work that is essential to their role, so they are well informed and able to make critical decisions. This model has been highly effective, in part because of the close working relationship between the Portfolio Directors and executive sponsors.

Many large projects have project sponsors, who are selected based on the role they have in the AmeriHealth Mercy Family of Companies organization. This ensures that critical project decisions can be made and issues resolved in a timely manner.

8.3.6.6 – Describe the economic benefits and value the PMO provides to the enterprise.

The use of cost benefit analysis/business cases has enabled AmeriHealth Mercy Family of Companies to think of project budgets as investments. As such, projects are now expected to deliver benefits or a return on their investment. This has been a significant, but needed organizational change. All companies have more good ideas than they can afford to implement, and being able to evaluate all project ideas consistently positions AmeriHealth Mercy Family of Companies to make the best choices.

The EPMO also recognized the need for closer collaboration with the procurement, financial and legal departments. Cross-functional improvement efforts have been completed with regard to the RFP and contracting processes, and have resulted in more consistent contract terms.

The EPMO recently added dedicated finance staff to manage project, program and portfolio level cost management. In addition to the finance team's role in cost budget management, they facilitate management of a large number of contracts and associated invoicing and accounting processes. They play an integral role in the monthly and quarterly reforecasting activities, as well as in the development and tracking of the cost benefit analysis/business case documents. The expertise and objectivity they provide to the project management staff has been greatly appreciated by the EPMO, but has also increased the credibility of the processes utilized.

8.3.7 SURVEY – Additional Comments: Please provide any additional comments

The AmeriHealth Mercy's Enterprise Portfolio Management Office did not provide any additional comments.

FIGURE 8-1: AMFC Enterprise Portfolio Management Office (EPMO)

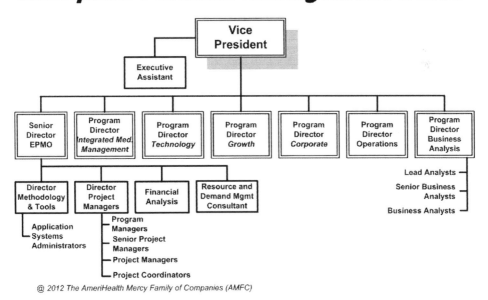

FIGURE 8-2: AMFC Enterprise Project Management Methodology

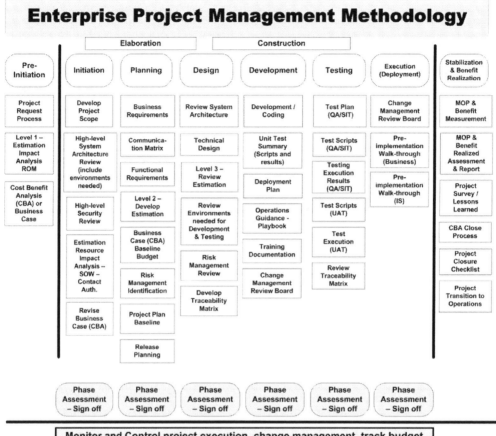

Enterprise Project Management Methodology

	Elaboration		Construction			

| Pre-Initiation | Initiation | Planning | Design | Development | Testing | Execution (Deployment) | Stabilization & Benefit Realization |

| Project Request Process | Develop Project Scope | Business Requirements | Review System Architecture | Development / Coding | Test Plan (QA/SIT) | Change Management Review Board | MOP & Benefit Measurement |

| Level 1 – Estimation Impact Analysis ROM | High-level System Architecture Review (include environments needed) | Communication Matrix | Technical Design | Unit Test Summary (Scripts and results) | Test Scripts (QA/SIT) | Pre-implementation Walk-through (Business) | MOP & Benefit Realized Assessment & Report |

| | | Functional Requirements | Level 3 – Review Estimation | Deployment Plan | Testing Execution Results (QA/SIT) | Pre-implementation Walk-through (IS) | |

| Cost Benefit Analysis (CBA) or Business Case | High-level Security Review | Level 2 – Develop Estimation | Review Environments needed for Development & Testing | Operations Guidance - Playbook | Test Scripts (UAT) | | Project Survey / Lessons Learned |

| | Estimation Resource Impact Analysis – SOW – Contact Auth. | Business Case (CBA) Baseline Budget | Risk Management Review | Training Documentation | Test Execution (UAT) | | CBA Close Process |

| | | Risk Management Identification | Develop Traceability Matrix | Change Management Review Board | Review Traceability Matrix | | Project Closure Checklist |

| | Revise Business Case (CBA) | Project Plan Baseline | | | | | Project Transition to Operations |

| | | Release Planning | | | | | |

| | Phase Assessment – Sign off | Phase Assessment – Sign off | Phase Assessment – Sign off | Phase Assessment – Sign off | Phase Assessment – Sign off | Phase Assessment – Sign off | |

Monitor and Control project execution, change management, track budget via budget book and risk mitigation

Project Change Management process includes overall project re-evaluation and approval (CBA Required)

Organizational Change Management (OCM) Assessment (PM Decision)

@ 2012 The AmeriHealth Mercy Family of Companies (AMFC)

FIGURE 8-3: AMFC Business Methodology Phases with PMO Program Methodology

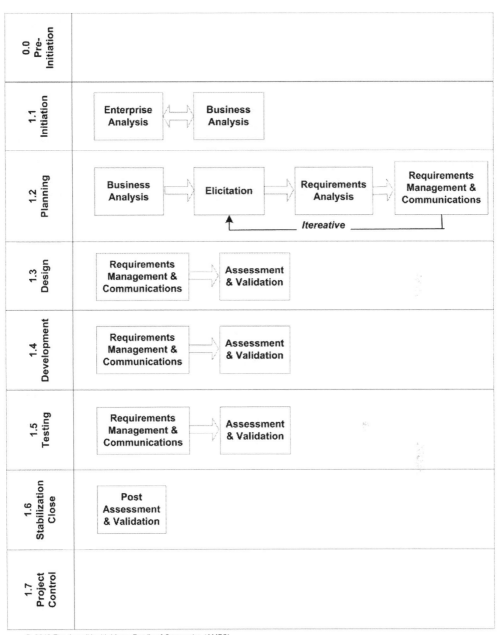

@ 2012 The AmeriHealth Mercy Family of Companies (AMFC)

FIGURE 8-4: AMFC Project Methodology

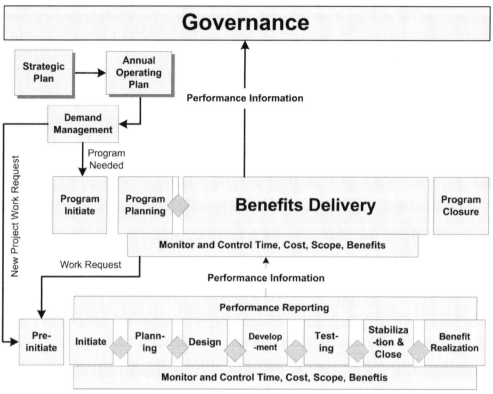

@ 2012 The AmeriHealth Mercy Family of Companies (AMFC)

FIGURE 8-5: AMFC Business Case Process

AmeriHealth Mercy Family of Companies Business Case Process

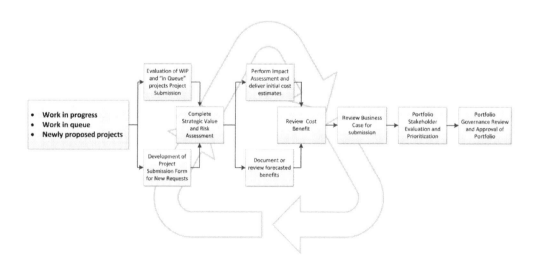

Chapter 9

Banco Hipotecario PMO Case Study

Banco Hipotecario S.A. provides banking services primarily in Argentina. The group focuses mainly on the real estate lending market. It offers loans for the purchase, construction, or improvement of residential properties, repayment of mortgages originally designed for home purchases, and home equity. The group also underwrites insurance related to its mortgage lending activities, and services its own and third-party mortgage loan portfolios. In addition, it provides real estate brokerage services and property management services. As of July 31, 2012, it operated 52 branches.

9.1 Banco Hipotecario S.A. – Enterprise and PMO Office Survey Information

Enterprise Name:	Banco Hipotecario S.A.
Country:	Argentina
Industry:	Finance (Banking)
Enterprise – Annual Sales Revenue:	Small; less than $100 Million US Dollars
Enterprise – Full-time Employee Equivalents:	1,800
World Wide Web Site:	www.hipotecario.com.ar
PMO Name:	Strategic Project Office
Title of PMO Leader:	Manager
PMO Position in Organizational Structure:	Enterprise-wide
PMO reports to in Organizational Structure:	Area Manager (Budget & Management Control)
PMO Annual Operating Budget:	$270,000 US Dollars
PMO – Full-time Employee Equivalents:	5 (including the manager)

The following are the PMO Case Study Survey question sets and the associated responses as submitted by the Banco Hipotecario S.A. Strategic Project Office, with editing for format, English as a second language, and consistency.

9.2   Banco Hipotecario S.A. PMO Background, Innovations, and Impact

In the following three parts of this case study, the Banco Hipotecario S.A. Strategic Project Office provides an overview of the background and structure of its PMO, various innovations and best practices by the PMO, and the potential future business impact of the PMO.

> **9.2.1 SURVEY – PMO Background:** Describe your PMO, including background information on its scope, vision, mission, and position within the enterprise's organizational structure.

Our project management office emerged to address a basic need of the banks' organization for objective information about the state of their main projects.

During many prior years, there was a project office in systems and operations, that had created many standards for the management of IT projects. Those standards were implemented correctly, but the project office was seen as an Office Bureaucracy, utilizing additional time for IT staff and having only an informational role.

Banco Hipotecario determined that a properly managed and implemented strategic plan could provide a definite business advantage, as shown below in Figure 9-1.

The bank management then decided to build a type of corporate, or strategic, project office named the Strategic Project Office.

The Strategic Project Office has a direct management dependency on the Area Budget and Management Control (depending also on the Risk and Controller Area Manager), which gives us a position of absolute neutrality in the handling of the interests of the different players. On the other hand, we have the strongest support that a Project Management Office can have, which is the corporate level sponsorship of the General Management of the Bank and the Management of the Controller Area, as well as the rest of the top Management of the Bank.

After being formally established, we began to do something that would *not be* seen as "bureaucratic," that would be "simple," but which in turn could ensure the control of all stages of a project (evaluation, design, preliminary, draft, and post-implementation). Our vision for the PMO is to carry out those projects that really give value to the Bank and position the Bank with a business or operational advantage.

FIGURE 9-1: Banco Hipotecario – Why Strategic Planning

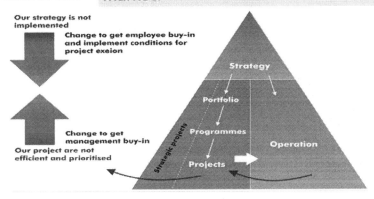

© 2012 Banco Hipotecario S.A.

9.2.2 SURVEY – PMO Innovations and Best Practices: Address the challenges your enterprise encountered prior to implementing the new PMO practices and how you overcame those challenges. Describe clearly and concisely the practices implemented and their effect on project, program, and/or portfolio and organizational success.

The main challenges facing the Strategic Project Office were to measure the before and after of a project and to establish the correct "stage gates" within each stage, by involving everyone (and not only systems and IT). We are creating a culture where the PMO is *not* a bureaucratic body, is *not* a project auditor, and is *not* an implementer of projects. We also integrated multidisciplinary work teams from the conception of the project's product through to its implementation and operation.

We have managed to establish a culture that supports prioritization of projects, presentations to Executive Committees on investments, and the understanding that the whole project is an investment. An overview of the Investments Budget and Strategic Plan interface is shown below in Figure 9-2.

The Strategic Project Office developed a strategic decision making process composed of five decision steps that address fifteen specific business points. This process selects and prioritizes Business Cases and their associated Projects.

Decision 1: Decide what strategic initiatives, benefits, and resource limitation *Criteria* (i.e. measures) to use for project filtering and portfolio ranking.
   1) What are our resource objectives?
   2) What are our critical resource limitations?

Decision 2: Either decide which *Criteria* are most important to achieve, or decide which Weightings will control critical trade-offs to be made during portfolio optimization.
   3) What do we think is most important?

Decision 3: Decide which project ideas or needs are worth developing into *Business Cases*.
   4) Which ideas and needs are worth development into business cases?
   5) What strategic initiatives does this project support?
   6) Does the value equation, fully consider all uncertainty and risk?
   7) What are the inter-project dependencies?
   8) Why are we doing this project?

Decision 4: Decide which *Business Cases* should be considered as part of the portfolio.
   9) Which business cases should be considered for inclusion in the portfolio?
   10) What are the key risk areas for each project?

Decision 5: Decide which specific *Projects* to include in the *Portfolio*, and decide why to include them.
   11) Which current projects and proposed new projects should be in the portfolio?
   12) Will a project cause excessive multitasking or delay other critical work?
   13) What are the risk areas for each portfolio?
   14) What areas of uncertainty endanger the benefits?
   15) Why are we doing this project?

The strategic decision making process incorporates the PMO "strategic lines of action" as shown below in Figure 9-3 and reflects the following three stages of Banco Hipotecario's Strategic Project Office prioritization methodology:
   1) Strategic Planning: Drives criteria development and importance weighting, thus developing the measures for the organization's success;
   2) Project Proposal: Project Sponsors develop business cases for ideas opportunities and needs; and
   3) Portfolio Building: Proposed projects chosen for funding and resource allocation.

The key business roles involved in the project prioritization process are:
- Affected governance board or committee
- Strategic PMO
- Project Sponsor

The results of the strategic planning and prioritization process are captured in a "Map of Projects," a sample of that documentation is shown below in Figure 9-4.

FIGURE 9-2: Banco Hipotecario Investments Budget Process

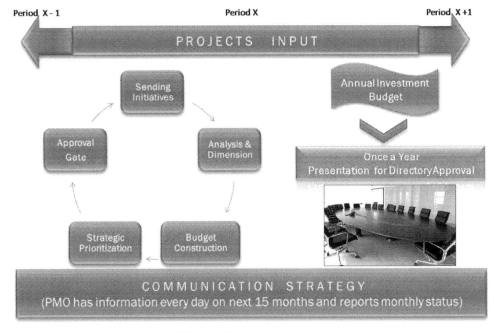

© 2012 Banco Hipotecario S.A.

FIGURE 9-3: Banco Hipotecario PMO Strategic Lines of Action

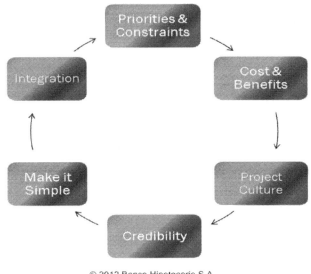

© 2012 Banco Hipotecario S.A.

FIGURE 9-4: Banco Hipotecario Prioritization Process Sample Results

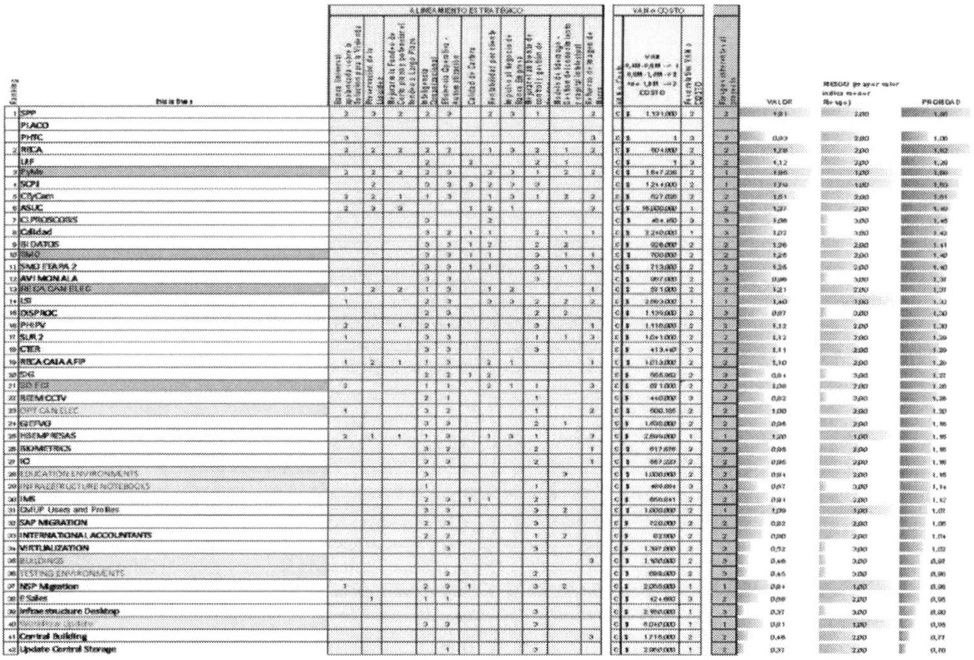

© 2012 Banco Hipotecario S.A.

> **9.2.3 SURVEY – PMO Future Impact:** Briefly describe your PMO's plans for 2012 and beyond - please describe how those plans will potentially impact your enterprise and its organizational structure.

We have several plans underway, including:

- Achieving development of products using "Agile" methods, while maintaining quality;
- Internally developing a tool for Portfolio and Demand Management and possibly acquiring a tool that is currently in market;
- Structuring different PMOs within companies linked to the economic group;
- Improving the system of risk matrixes;
- Further improving productivity in projects, by making improvements in metrics and diagnostics of maturity; and
- Enhancing the reviews made on an annual basis and conducted during the months of January to March each year.

9.3   Banco Hipotecario S.A. PMO Model Components

In the following six parts of this case study, the Banco Hipotecario S.A. Strategic Project Office provides its descriptions of how they will implement the six key components of the Project Business Management Organization model: Governance; Methodology; Capability; Planning; Execution; and Sustainability.

> **9.3.1 SURVEY – PMO Governance:** Describe how your PMO presents itself as an executive-level management business function, how it addresses setting policy and establishing charters, and how it provides an organizational model for the business management of portfolios, programs, and projects and the establishment of portfolio, program, and project management offices.

9.3.1.1 – How long has the PMO been in place? When was it started?	The Strategic Project Office has been in place for two years. The PMO was formed in April 2009.
9.3.1.2 – What is the relationship of PMO management to the enterprise's operational management?	The PMO is integrated with each area of the organization; from Commercial Retail and Wholesale to Operations and Systems and Technology.
9.3.1.3 – How is the PMO internally structured (positions, roles etc.)?	• 1 – Manager • 2 – Specialists (Senior Analyst) • 2 – Semi-Senior Analysts
9.3.1.4 – How are the PMO's operations funded?	PMO operations are covered by an internal Area Budget.
9.3.1.5 – What is the summary position description of the PMO leader?	Not Provided

9.3.1.6 – What position requirements are used as a basis for selecting the PMO leader?	• PMP Certificated • Bachelor Degree or Superior • IT and Systems Know How • Financial and Economic Know How (a related degree is desirable)
9.3.1.7 – Is the PMO a Profit & Loss cost center or considered overhead?	PMO is considered overhead.
9.3.1.8 – What current challenges is the PMO dealing with?	Project Leader needs to work with middle management personnel in the organization. Because we are not matrixed nor organized by projects, we would like to work with Intermediate Managers or Chiefs in order to be more effective in the operational transformation, which implies project execution in a functional organization.

> **9.3.2 SURVEY – PMO Methodology / Standardization:** Describe what standardization your PMO has implemented across the enterprise that examines: identification and integration of processes and practices; development of standardized Project Business Management processes; and documentation of enterprise-wide portfolio, program, and project management process methodology models, including their associated policies, practices, and procedures.

9.3.2.1 – Describe the standards utilized by the PMO to ensure the enterprise's project / program / portfolio management goals and objectives are achieved.	The PMO uses the following internally documented tools: • Preliminary Scope • Global Scope • Detailed Scope • Risk Analysis w/Matrix Situation (not quantitative only qualitative) • Project Prioritization Matrix • Resource Allocation Form • Business Case Presentation • Investment Committee Presentation • Project Template • Project Tracking Report • Test Tracking Report

- Close Document
- Lessons Learned Document
- Post Implementation Review input into the Investment Committee (see Figure 9-5 below)

9.3.2.2 – Describe the project management process guidelines being employed by the PMO.	The following internal guidelines are employed: - Pre-feasibility - Preliminary Draft - Initiation - Planning - Execution - Closing - Post Implementation Review (see Figure 9-5 below)
9.3.2.3 – What systems, tools, and templates make your PMO successful?	The preliminary scope document is the tool used to initially detect and then correct the need for, and strategy of, the project in question, and to establish the basis for the project's correct prioritization and the assembly of the preliminary business case. Another key tool is the presentation to the Investment Commission of the pre-feasibility and preliminary draft, which puts the project into the organization's scope of control. Microsoft Project is the tool used for detailed plans. We are still in the process of finding a tool to use for Portfolio & Demand Management, which will meet our needs and requirements. We also provide a Monthly Report Status through our home-made tool for reporting and storing the project's information. Other templates and tools used are the Lessons Learned and the Post Implementation Review Process (see Figure 9-5 below).
9.3.2.4 – Describe how management at all levels is directly involved in the development of the PMO and it processes.	Senior Management at all levels have been involved in the development of the PMO and its processes. This involvement is described in our internal document named "Politic or Procedures of the Strategic Project Office."

9.3.2.5 – Describe the implementation plan you used for establishing project / program / portfolio management standards across your enterprise.

- Establish Senior Management expectations
- Share the planned prioritization of the strategic targets with all the Senior Managers and the CEO, and show the different weightings according to the project position in the prioritization structure
- Prioritize the Project Portfolio using the established primary weightings, and then use additional weighting variables like risks, budget, VAN, complexity and teams interrelations necessary for implementing the project
- Define an explicit Policy and Standard for management of Strategic Projects within the organization that is signed by the Senior Management
- Have the Investments and Equipment Commission rank the projects (something similar to a Project Steering Committee)
- Utilize a simple process
- Employ simple templates that are easy to use
- Have only a few key documented processes (In our culture, many well documented processes are not always a good sign, because the PMO could be seen as a bureaucracy, so we defined specific documentation needs for processes and also for audit purposes)
- Specified and succinct Life Cycle (see Figure 9-6 below)
- Post Implementation Review used for continuous improvement (see Figure 9-5 below)

9.3.2.6 – How does the PMO use project, program, and portfolio management standards to optimize its practices?

We base our methodology and practices on PMI, and also specific items from PRINCE, because we perform a lot of work in the very first part of the project analysis. The PMI standards do not seem to cover this analysis part, nor the Post Implementation Reviews.

Are they based on PMI or other industry guides and are they updated as new editions of the guides are released?

Yes, they are based upon PMI® standards and PRINCE® standards.

98

FIGURE 9-5: Banco Hipotecario PMO Post Implementation Reviews

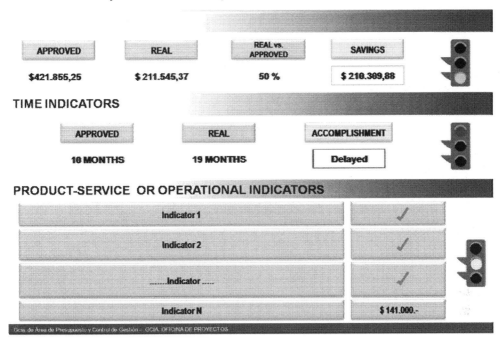

© 2012 Banco Hipotecario S.A.

FIGURE 9-6: Banco Hipotecario PMO Simple & Virtuous Project Life Cycle

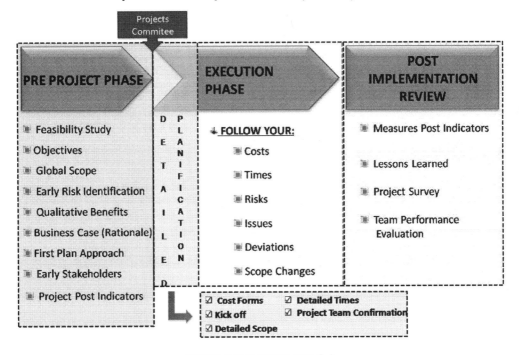

© 2012 Banco Hipotecario S.A.

99

> **9.3.3 SURVEY – PMO Capabilities:** Describe development and assessment of the enterprise's abilities, describe any project management competency model, summarize any education and training program, describe any established career path progression plan, and outline key Enterprise Environmental Factors.

We don't have a specific Project Management competency model. We are strongly integrated with the Organizational Development Area in order to identify the right Project Managers. The assignment of a Project Manager is decided based on experience, position, and principally by consensus among the different stakeholders, because the Project Manager needs to have time dedicated for the specific projects.

9.3.3.1 – Describe the components of your enterprise's training program.	Key components are: • Trainings in PMI Methodology (5 days a year) • Specific Coach and Mentoring for new Project Managers (8 to 40 Hours / Year) • General Management Training (Negotiation, Conflict Management, Business, Leadership)
9.3.3.2 – Describe the value your enterprise places on education and training and its goals and objectives.	Our enterprise places a high value on education and training through an Annual General Programme for different disciplines through the Organizational Development Area.
9.3.3.3 – Does the enterprise have a project management career path program? If so, what are the components?	No, establishing a project management career path program is a gap that we still want to address. Currently we decided in a sensible and political matter just to prepare Project Managers within the organization and to promote the culture of integrated teams. We measure the people that work for the projects and the Project Managers by objectives that are used in the annual evaluation process.
9.3.3.4 – Describe the measurements, metrics, and Key Performance Indicators (KPI's) utilized by the PMO to determine the organization's knowledge, skills, and level of achievement.	We use a standardized template to evaluate every project manager in each project. We actually have an annual exercise of Objectives Measure within the whole organization, which has objectives by area, sector and person, and that also has a specific set of capacities for the whole organization that needs to be achieved by every coworker.

9.3.3.5 – Does the enterprise employ a project management competency model? If yes, please describe it. If no, why not?

No, that is a gap that we still want to address, but it is politically sensitive inside the organization. However, we think that with the way that PMO is emerging within the organization as a structured, integrated, and enterprise-wide function, that we will insist, starting in 2013, to have this process established in a more structured way.

> **9.3.4 SURVEY – PMO Business Planning:** Discuss strategic business planning, tactical business planning, business objective (project) development and prioritization, and project identification, selection, and authorization.

9.3.4.1 – Describe the organizational structure and process used for corporate strategic business planning.

Does the PMO play a role in the process? If so, describe the PMOs role and responsibilities.

Yes, the PMO plays a role in the definition of the Investments for the current year. This is done during the Business Plan development and strategic planning for the next 3 (three) years.

This Business Plan defines new business, sustainability, branches, retail and wholesale business, operations, and Systems and Technology.

9.3.4.2 – How is the strategic plan implemented with a project forecast plan?

The strategic plan is a "Map of Projects" ordered by project priority and then by timeline or deadline (see Figure 9-4 above).

In addition, we have a Continuum Investment Budget where we can track the planned work and the forecasted cost of the strategic plan.

9.3.4.3 – How is strategic planning, culture, and selection of projects integrated?

We have a strong strategic planning culture. We initiate the strategic planning process every year during August in order to complete the whole business plan during November, and then have it approved by the Directory during the second week of December.

9.3.5 SURVEY – PMO Business Execution: Describe what role the PMO has in project selection, prioritization, and initiation; in portfolio, program and project execution planning; in stage-gate reviews; and in performance metrics selection and application.

9.3.5.1 – How are portfolios, programs, and projects selected and initiated?

They are selected and initiated through the Continuum Investment Budget process. The project idea is received and then it is prioritized according to a prior Business Case and a prior budget.

Then, if the Steering Committee decides to move to the next stage, we continue with the detailed pre-project phase for that project initiative. We next put this project into the portfolio to determine how it can be combined with the rest of the projects, resources, and capacities of the organization.

9.3.5.2 – How are projects organized and managed as a program and/or portfolio?

We have both Programs and Portfolios.

Within a program, we have one or more strategic projects.

9.3.5.3 – How are projects prioritized within a program and/or portfolio?

They are prioritized by strategic target first and then by using variables such as cost, VAN, risks (including complexity and capacities).

9.3.5.4 – How does the enterprise define what project and program success is?

Success is determined using the results of the Post-Implementation Review.

9.3.5.5 – Does the PMO support the management of projects that would be considered operational in nature? If so, describe the types of projects.

Yes, of course.

Not only business projects, even technological and sustainability projects.

Substantially all of the business cases are related to operations (Example: Improvements in Credit Cards Administration and those type of business cases imply automation of administrative and control functions).

9.3.6 SURVEY – PMO Sustainability: Describe the overall impact of the PMO over a sustained period (e.g., customer satisfaction, productivity, reduced cycle time, growth, building or changing organizational culture, etc.). If available, please provide quantitative data to illustrate the areas in which the PMO has had the greatest business impact.

Banco Hipotecario uses the following six Benefit Performance Indicators to show the value of the Strategic Project Office:

- Decrease in failed projects
- Projects delivered under budget
- Improvement in productivity
- Projects delivered ahead of schedule
- Cost savings per project
- Increase in resource capacity

9.3.6.1 – What is included in a comprehensive project monitoring and control system and how is it implemented?

- Milestones
- Planning Tracking
- Open Risks and New Risks
- Issues

These are implemented through a Specific Report prepared by the Project Management, with the assistance of the PMO.

9.3.6.2 – How are project start-up and gate review processes structured?

- Start Up: Steering Committee or Investment Committee
- Pre-Project to Project through Investment Committee
- Kickoff after detailed planning phase
- Monitoring during Execution
- Closing Phase with Lessons Learned
- After several months: Post Implementation Review

9.3.6.3 – Describe the project knowledge base system and how is it developed?

Simply, we have developed a shared directory, which contains the best documents and templates that we have put in place.

We have designed a web page for the Strategic PMO, and we are working to make it available on mobile devices.

9.3.6.4 – Describe the measurement, metrics, and Key

The following are the Key Performance Indicators:
1) Percent of investment decisions influenced by PMO participation and provided data

Performance Indicators (KPIs) utilized by the PMO to measure project and program success.	2) Percent of projects aligned with organizational goals 3) Percent of projects completed within budget versus cost overruns 4) Number of projects completed during this financial year vs. previous year (productivity) 5) Percent of projects completed on time - deliverables (On time versus late) 6) Percent of projects with deliverables (Accepted versus Rejected) 7) Percent of projects with post-project reviews 8) Percent of projects have supporting and validated business cases 9) Project Manager satisfaction score of value of PMO services (survey) 10) Organizational customer satisfaction perception of PMO value contribution to project management within the organization (survey) Total number of risks open (Size, Schedule, Quality, Staffing, and Cost) on a monthly basis
9.3.6.5 – Describe the organizational benefits and value the PMO provides to the enterprise.	• Integration between Interdisciplinary Teams • Methodology • Fast execution of specific and political needs • Alignment with Senior Management expectations • Leadership • Business measurement
9.3.6.6 – Describe the economic benefits and value the PMO provides to the enterprise.	We develop those projects that have a real impact on the bottom line and will have positive results.

9.3.7 SURVEY – Additional Comments: Please provide any additional comments

The Banco Hipotecario S.A. Strategic Project Office did not provide any additional comments.

Chapter 10

Doe Run Company PMO Case Study

The Doe Run Company, based in St. Louis, Missouri, is a privately held natural resource company focused on metals mining, smelting, recycling, and fabrication. Doe Run is the largest integrated lead producer in the Western Hemisphere and the third largest total lead producer in the world. Doe Run operates the world's largest, single-site lead recycling facility, located in Missouri.

The company retrieves and recycles more than 150,000 tons of lead annually from manufactured products such as batteries and telephone cables. Doe Run produces zinc and copper, along with valuable by-products.

Doe Run facilities feature advanced technology and produce a consistently pure product. Doe Run's mills offer state-of-the-art automation to maximize the recovery of metals from ore, and its recycling facility is the most technologically advanced, environmentally sound and safest of its kind in the world.

Doe Run is organized into four divisions in the United States and operates facilities in Missouri, Washington and Arizona.

10.1 Doe Run Company – Enterprise and PMO Office Survey Information

Enterprise Name:	The Doe Run Company
Country:	United States of America
Industry:	Mining and Metals
Enterprise – Annual Sales Revenue:	Medium, between $100 Million and $1 Billion US Dollars
Enterprise – Full-time Employee Equivalents:	1,500
World Wide Web Site:	www.doerun.com
PMO Name:	Enterprise PMO
Title of PMO Leader:	PMO Manager

PMO Position in Organizational Structure:	Enterprise-wide
PMO reports to in Organizational Structure:	Vice-president of Information Technology and Chief Information Officer
PMO Annual Operating Budget:	$350,000 US Dollars
PMO – Full-time Employee Equivalents:	3

The following are the PMO Case Study Survey question sets and the associated responses as submitted by The Doe Run Company's Enterprise PMO, with minor editing for format and consistency.

10.2   Doe Run Company PMO Background, Innovations, and Impact

In the following three parts of this case study, The Doe Run Company's Enterprise PMO provides an overview of the background and structure of its PMO, various innovations and best practices by the PMO, and the potential future business impact of the PMO.

> **10.2.1   SURVEY – PMO Background:** Describe your PMO, including background information on its scope, vision, mission, and position within the enterprise's organizational structure.

The Doe Run Company's PMO was established as an enterprise-wide PMO in 2006. The PMO reports to the Chief Information Officer and is staffed by three people: PMO Manager, PMO Specialist and Business Analyst. The PMO was established with a decentralized structure where engineers in each division serve as Project Managers but do not report directly to the PMO. The PMO is responsible for providing coaching and oversight on projects company-wide, including construction and engineering projects as well as corporate and information technology (IT) projects. The PMO provides oversight to approximately 40 projects at any point in time, with projects ranging in size from $10,000 to $150 million.

Vision

The vision of the PMO is "the right projects, done right."

Mission

The PMO mission is to create an environment of Project Management professionalism where:

- Project success is the norm

- Project teams are proud of their work
- Internal customers reap the benefit of a carefully planned investment
- The external customer wins through improved service or lower cost

Strategic Goals

Strategic goals for the PMO include:

- Maximize the value of the Doe Run project portfolio through selection of the right projects
- Reduce surprises in projects through better planning, setting realistic expectations and improving the quality of information on projects
- Front load the planning process so key decisions in direction are made early in the project, when changes can have a significant positive impact and changes can be made at a low cost
- Provide processes for managing change

In pursuit of these goals, the PMO established the following objectives:

1) Direct development, implementation, and maintenance of consistent project management practices:
    - Develop an effective and efficient project management methodology for use by Doe Run to improve project quality and on-time/on-budget/on-scope delivery of projects;
    - Sell the concept of the project management office (PMO) across the company and gain commitment from all divisions and departments to use PMO practices and resources; and
    - Lead efforts to continuously improve Doe Run's ability to execute projects.
2) Direct development, implementation, and maintenance of consistent portfolio management practices:
    - Develop a standard definition of a project and what projects are to be considered as part of a managed project portfolio;
    - Develop process for initiating, selecting, and approving a project;
    - Develop process for prioritizing projects in the project portfolio and determining resource needs; and
    - Participate in the development of Doe Run strategic plans.
3) Build Project Management Professionalism among Doe Run Staff:
    - Train Doe Run employees in effective project management practices, tools, and techniques;
    - Coach Project Managers;
    - Work with Human Resources on developing career paths for Project Managers;
    - Identify gaps in project management expertise and execution and develop and implement plans to remediate; and
    - Provide training to all levels so each Project Sponsor, functional manager, team member, and executive understands their role in making projects successful.

4) Provide tools and knowledge management in support of project and portfolio management practices:

- Select Project and Portfolio Management tools for organization-wide use;
- Maintain documentation of Doe Run project and portfolio management policies and procedures;
- Develop systems that integrate with financial systems for project reporting; and
- Maintain and publish a "Lessons Learned" repository.

5) Manage and Support projects as requested in pursuit of Doe Run strategic objectives. The PMO primarily serves in one of three roles:

- Management of the project. Because of limited resources, PMO employees serve as Project Manager on a limited number of projects.
- Coaching of the Project Manager. It is more common for the PMO to provide assistance by coaching Project Managers on key projects. The PMO is actively involved in these projects, coaching Project Managers from inception through project closure.
- Scoping and requirements definition. In a "scoping" role, the PMO Business Analyst assists each department or division to help define project scope and required functionality.

6) Measure project performance and keep Doe Run's management team and project management community informed:

- Maintain information on the project portfolio;
- Develop systems and metrics to track and report on projects regarding cost, scope, quality, schedule and business results; and
- Report to Doe Run Executive Team on: the status of strategic projects in the Doe Run portfolio, metrics that measure PMO effectiveness and the progression of the organization in regards to project management maturity.

10.2.2 SURVEY – PMO Innovations and Best Practices: Address the challenges your enterprise encountered prior to implementing the new PMO practices and how you overcame those challenges. Describe clearly and concisely the practices implemented and their effect on project, program, and/or portfolio and organizational success.

Prior to 2006, The Doe Run Company had no formal portfolio or project management in place. Projects were funded based on historic financial allocation by area, regardless of the current business situation. Project funding approvals were based on a one paragraph scope description. While project performance was not routinely tracked, there are examples of projects completing 100% to 200% over schedule and budget.

There was no formal training in project management processes for Doe Run personnel. Most projects were managed by external Project Managers with little Doe Run oversight. After years of projects being delivered significantly over schedule and over budget (and not delivering agreed-upon business objectives), ownership lost confidence in Doe Run's project management capabilities. As a result, every project estimated to cost over $10,000 required pre-approval from the Board of Directors.

In response to these issues, an enterprise-wide PMO was established in 2006. Over a period of several years, the PMO implemented standard processes for portfolio, project, and program management as described below. Once processes were established, the PMO provided training to Project Managers and others involved in the project, including team members and Project Sponsors.

Training is provided on the project management knowledge areas, soft skills such as leadership and on tools such as Microsoft Project. While Doe Run still relies on external Project Managers in many cases, now a Doe Run employee is appointed as Project Manager to represent Doe Run interests. Those employees complete training on how to manage external providers to ensure projects are delivered as promised.

As a result, Doe Run has seen significant improvements in project delivery, including not only the typical measurements of on-scope, on-time, and on-budget, but more importantly in meeting the business objectives specified at the beginning of the project. For more detail, see metrics listed below.

> **10.2.3 SURVEY – PMO Future Impact:** Briefly describe your PMO's plans for 2012 and beyond - please describe how those plans will potentially impact your enterprise and its organizational structure.

The future focus for the Doe Run PMO will be in use of project management best practices for all projects in the organization. In the past, much of the Doe Run PMO focus has been on the largest, most strategic projects (typically those projects anticipated to cost over $500,000). As a result, project delivery has significantly improved on those projects.

The next step is to take a baseline of current performance on all projects at Doe Run and implement steps to improve those project results. Because the PMO is decentralized and the PMO staff is small, success in this area will depend on educating Project Sponsors on best practices and making those Project Sponsors comfortable with holding Project Managers accountable.

In support of this effort, a simplified version of the Doe Run project management methodology has been created for use on smaller projects. Additionally, Project Managers will be trained using an updated development curriculum and coached through on-the-job practice.

A second area of focus for the Doe Run PMO is resource management. Doe Run currently assesses potential resource bottlenecks using primitive tools that only reveal the most significant bottlenecks. To improve resource management, Doe Run will need to convince the organization to use improved tools and processes that require significant organizational change.

10.3   Doe Run Company PMO Model Components

In the following six parts of this case study, The Doe Run Company's Enterprise PMO provides its descriptions of how they implement the six key components of the Project Business Management Organization model: Governance; Methodology; Capability; Planning; Execution; and Sustainability.

> **10.3.1 SURVEY – PMO Governance:** Describe how your PMO presents itself as an executive-level management business function, how it addresses setting policy and establishing charters, and how it provides an organizational model for the business management of portfolios, programs, and projects and the establishment of portfolio, program, and project management offices.

10.3.1.1 – How long has the PMO been in place?
When was it started?

In 2006, Doe Run executives and the Board of Directors were frustrated with poor project delivery as described above. Key executives wanted to improve project results, but were resistant to take any steps that appeared to "add bureaucracy."

However, the "tipping point" came when the company struggled with a large enterprise resource planning implementation which was led by a functional manager with no project management experience. That project finished one million dollars over budget and a year late. In response, the Project Management Office was created in 2006 with one person, a PMO Manager, who was brought in as a consultant with a right-to-hire clause and given one year to show progress toward "delivering projects as promised."

10.3.1.2 – What is the relationship of PMO management to the enterprise's operational management?

While there is no formal relationship between the PMO and operational management, the groups work together closely. The PMO strives to understand each operation's business and issues to better understand proposed projects.

PMO personnel visit divisional operations on a regular basis with the message "the PMO is here to help" rather than taking an approach of a distant unit in the corporate office formed to "enforce policy." PMO personnel are situated side-by-side with operations staff to help develop business cases for projects, to provide advice on estimation techniques and assess lessons learned at the end of the project.
Within two years of the PMO implementation, management

recognized the positive impact of the new processes. One division general manager commented: "We used to do planning on the back of a napkin. Now we research alternatives and provide fully thought-out plans with detailed cost analyses."

10.3.1.3 – How is the PMO internally structured (positions, roles etc.)?

The Doe Run PMO is led by a PMO Manager who supervises the work of a Business Analyst and a PMO Specialist. The PMO Manager sets direction for portfolio, program, and project management at Doe Run.

The Business Analyst is responsible for helping business units justify projects, establishing the scope for those projects, and gathering and documenting business requirements.

The PMO Specialist provides administrative and operational support for the PMO, including project tracking and reporting and supports Project Manager development through training classes.

All three members of the PMO coach Project Managers of major project efforts.

10.3.1.4 – How are the PMO's operations funded?

PMO operations are funded out of the annual IT budget.

10.3.1.5 – What is the summary position description of the PMO leader?

The primary purposes of the PMO Manager position is to:
- Assist in establishing strategic plans and objectives for Doe Run;
- Optimize the project portfolio to ensure compliance with Doe Run strategy and objectives; and
- Provide the methodologies, tools and training to improve project delivery in terms of quality, schedule, cost, and scope.

10.3.1.6 – What position requirements are used as a basis for selecting the PMO leader?

Position requirements used in selecting the leader of the PMO are:
- Minimum 7 to 10 years of experience in initiating and leading a Project Management Office;
- Master's degree in Project Management, Information Technology or Engineering;
- Project Management Professional certification from the Project Management Institute; and
- Demonstrated competency in building organizational talent, change leadership, communicating with impact, developing strategic relationships, execution, and operational decision-making.

10.3.1.7 – Is the PMO a Profit & Loss cost center or considered overhead?

The Doe Run PMO is considered overhead.

10.3.1.8 – What current challenge is the PMO dealing with?

Because the Doe Run PMO is decentralized, the PMO depends heavily on operations managers to hold Project Managers accountable for providing business value and in delivering projects on-scope, on-time and on-budget. The PMO is not staffed to be an enforcement organization nor are there plans to serve in that role.

The Doe Run organizational culture is relationship based as operations are located in small towns where employees are friends and family members. The PMO is constantly challenged to show the value in project management best practices and how accountability for following best practices is good for the Project Manager, Project Sponsor and the organization.

Behavior change is slow, but encouraged through publicizing positive business outcomes for projects managed using best practices. The PMO also works with operations management to build project related goals into annual employee performance reviews for both Project Managers and Project Sponsors.

10.3.2 SURVEY – PMO Methodology / Standardization: Describe what standardization your PMO has implemented across the enterprise that examines: identification and integration of processes and practices; development of standardized Project Business Management processes; and documentation of enterprise-wide portfolio, program, and project management process methodology models, including their associated policies, practices, and procedures.

10.3.2.1 – Describe the standards utilized by the PMO to ensure the enterprise's project / program / portfolio management goals and objectives are achieved.

The PMO works closely with the Financial Analysis and Planning group at Doe Run in creating and maintaining a standard economic model for calculating potential project financial return. The PMO assists business units with creating the business case for projects, including completing the financial model. Project funding requests must include a description of the current problem or opportunity, alternatives that were evaluated, and a detailed description of the proposed solution. PMO approval is required for all project funding requests.

The PMO coordinates the annual project proposal cycle, including grouping related projects into programs and maintaining the project portfolio.

10.3.2.2 – Describe the project management process guidelines being employed by the PMO.

Doe Run purchased a Project Management methodology designed for the mining vertical market and customized the methodology to meet specific Doe Run needs. The methodology is named the "Project Delivery System" and provides a set of flexible processes, tools and templates that were designed to manage a project through its lifecycle.

Doe Run Project Management training focuses on the ten best practices from the methodology that will have the most positive impact on project delivery. Those ten best practices are:
1) Documenting project scope in detail
2) Communicating team roles and responsibilities
3) Analyzing project stakeholders and creating a Communication Plan
4) Holding a project kickoff meeting
5) Regularly updating the project schedule
6) Managing scope change through a formal process
7) Regularly updating project cost forecasts and assessing cost status
8) Regularly assessing and mitigating risk
9) Providing written project status updates
10) Documenting project lessons learned and using them to improve project performance next time

Project Managers use these "best practices" and the supporting processes and templates to improve project results. For example, the methodology provides guidelines on how to assess and manage project risks. The PMO facilitates risk management workshops for all major projects. The PMO helps ensure input is solicited from all key stakeholders and provides risk breakdown structures and prior project lessons learned to trigger ideas on potential risks. Multiple categories of risk are assessed, including technical, project delivery and operational risk. Each identified risk is prioritized and control strategies are developed for the higher level risks. This process helps Doe Run look at all possible things that could go wrong with a project. Because many in Doe

Run management started as engineers, there was a tendency in the early days of the PMO to only focus on technical risk.

In order to ensure projects get off to a good start, the PMO facilitates annual "project briefing meetings" on all projects scheduled to start during the next fiscal year. These meetings bring together Project Managers, Project Sponsors and Project Owners to get agreement on how projects are going to be managed. For example, the Project Managers and Project Sponsors agree on the frequency of status reporting and the criteria for escalating scope changes or issues to the Project Sponsor. The Project Sponsor also ranks priorities for the project in terms of scope/quality, time and cost. For each project, it is determined what groups need to be involved and the key roles and responsibilities needed on each project team. These project briefing meetings ensure expectations of all parties are in alignment as projects are initiated.

10.3.2.3 – What systems, tools, and templates make your PMO successful?

In addition to the processes and templates provided in the Project Delivery System methodology, Doe Run uses tools such as standard cost estimate practices from the Association for the Advancement of Cost Engineering International (AACEI). AACEI provides guidelines on the type and detail level of planning documentation required to arrive at desired cost accuracy for each major phase of the project. For example, at the stage gate after a pre-feasibility study, if the required planning has been completed, the estimate should be accurate to -10% to +30%.

Contingency funding is modeled with Monte Carlo analysis using tools such as Crystal Ball. Use of these tools in conjunction with training on cost estimation practices and review of historical information on project costs has greatly increased the accuracy of estimates.

Microsoft Project is the standard tool used for developing and managing project schedules. Training is available to Project Managers on how to develop the initial schedule, how to manage to that schedule and how to use the Microsoft Project tool.

Microsoft SharePoint is used as a collaboration tool for project teams. SharePoint provides a centralized repository for all project-related documentation.

Other tools are based on Microsoft Excel. For example, the PMO forecasts resource usage for projects using input from the Project Managers and a standard Excel template. This information is used to prevent bottlenecks when scheduling projects.

10.3.2.4 – Describe how management at all levels is directly involved in the development of the PMO and it processes.

When the PMO was initially established, Doe Run executives recommended a Portfolio and Project Management governance team be appointed to assist the PMO Manager. Team members were selected based on their ability to influence others, whether through formal authority (for example, a division general manager) or informal authority (for example, a well-respected engineer). Representatives were selected from each major operational division. The team also included a mix of employees with many years seniority and newer employees with experience at companies other than Doe Run.

Just as the Portfolio and Project Management team provided insight into the direction for the initial implementation of PMO processes, a governance body continues to provide guidance on new and revised processes. The governance body is made up of the general managers of each major division within Doe Run. These managers often serve as Project Sponsors and understand the pain points around project management and whether or not a process will add value. Having the backing of the governance body helps ensure adherence to PMO best practices, particularly since the Doe Run PMO serves in a supportive role rather than as the "PMO Police."

10.3.2.5 – Describe the implementation plan you used for establishing project / program / portfolio management standards across your enterprise.

Doe Run treated the implementation of project, program and portfolio management standards as a project. The Portfolio and Project Management team created a project charter that outlined the mission and vision, identified objectives and critical success factors, determined resource needs and analyzed stakeholders.

The first action of the team was to identify pain points with the current situation. There was agreement that the primary pain point was the slow turnaround time for project funding approvals, which was delaying critical projects. The goal of the team was to restore management confidence through improved project performance, eventually leading to reduced turnaround time for project funding approvals.

Next, the team identified the current state and desired future state for Doe Run project management. Then the team looked at three areas needed to move toward the future state: process, people and tools. Doe Run decided to first focus on standard project management processes. Having standard processes in place first would help us determine necessary tools and training. Doe Run obtained a project management methodology and considered the best approach for implementing the best practices.

Before implementing the new methodology, the team assessed the current organizational culture. At the time, Doe Run had very few standardized processes around project management or other areas of the business including procurement, job performance assessment or mine planning. Doe Run had used the same operational processes for 140 years and was extremely slow to adopt changes. In the past, Project Managers had not been held accountable for performance and were rewarded for completing a project regardless of whether schedule or budget was met or business objectives were realized.

The team also evaluated techniques used in the past to introduce changes to the organization and what techniques worked and did not work. They found a higher success rate when changes were introduced slowly from the bottom-up rather than top down from the executives.

The team then adopted a framework for assessing organizational change that looks at the internal and external context for change to determine what needs to be changed, who will lead and who will follow. For example, executives never mandated that projects follow a gated approval process. Instead the PMO worked closely with Project Managers and Project Sponsors to "sell" the benefit of getting an official "stamp of approval" for proceeding on a project in order to prevent wasting engineering costs when projects were cancelled late in the process or did not deliver promised benefits.

A critical new product development project was chosen as a pilot for the new methodology. Despite a lack of project management experience, the assigned Project Manager was willing to adhere to the new standard practices. The methodology proved a major help to the team as they considered alternatives for the project in regards to technology, location and production capacity. This initial success was communicated throughout the organization and the Project Manager served as cheerleader for the new process. The Project Manager, Vice President of Research and Development, shared:

"Without the Doe Run project management processes, it would not have been possible to organize the details of a very complex project in order to move the project forward through approval gates. The Doe Run processes helped insure that we had the right people involved throughout the project, forced us to analyze and address risks to the project and provided a framework for cost estimates. I've taken the concepts I've learned from the project management methodology and applied them to other projects that I've been involved with to improve business processes throughout the company."

Organizational indicators that the new practices have been accepted and welcomed as part of the culture of Doe Run include:

- Project Managers preparing formal business cases for projects even when not required.
- Team members reminding each other that project and portfolio management processes are "just the way we do things" and holding each other accountable.
- Projects that would have received immediate approval in the past are now deferred due to inadequate justification.

10.3.2.6 – How does the PMO use project, program, and portfolio management standards to optimize its practices?

Are they based on PMI or other industry guides and are they updated as new editions of the guides are released?

The Doe Run Project Delivery System methodology is similar to the Project Management Body of Knowledge (PMBOK) from PMI. However, the methodology was customized to incorporate best practices for the mining and metals industry. For example, the methodology includes checklists for typical contents of a Detailed Feasibility Study report, which are standard within the mining industry. Having this alignment with standard practices within the industry simplifies the process for obtaining financing for large capital projects.

The approach to program and portfolio management at Doe Run is loosely based on PMI standards but the specific processes and templates were developed by Doe Run. PMO staff review new editions of the *PMBOK® Guide* and the *PMI Standard for Program Management* and *PMI Standard for Portfolio Management* as updates are released. PMO staff is also involved in local and national organizations that support project management and use information from those groups to continuously improve internal processes.

10.3.3   SURVEY – PMO Capabilities: Describe development and assessment of the enterprise's abilities, describe any project management competency model, summarize any education and training program, describe any established career path progression plan, and outline key Enterprise Environmental Factors.

10.3.3.1 – Describe the components of your enterprise's training program.

The Doe Run Project Management development program identifies recommended training classes for six target audiences:

- Project team members;
- Part-time Project Managers;
- Project Managers;
- Project Directors;
- Department Managers/Project Sponsors; and
- Executive Management.

Part-time Project Managers are those employees who do not have a Project Manager title but perform as Project Managers at times in addition to regular job duties.

Internal courses are provided by Doe Run PMO staff and are conducted through classroom training or formal coaching. The PMO also provides recommendations on project management training courses offered by external sources. External courses are also offered via web-based training and instructor led interactive training using the web.

Internal courses focus on the Doe Run project management methodology, best practices and terminology. Courses include:

- Project Management Overview
- Scheduling using Microsoft Project
- Cost Estimation
- Risk Management
- Building a Business Case
- Tracking Project Costs
- Leading Organizational Change
- Managing External Service Providers

Because of the importance that all project stakeholders speak a common language, a brief overview of the project management methodology and practices is included in the orientation program for all new Doe Run managers. Project Sponsors throughout the organization attend a three-hour overview on the

Project Sponsor role in project success. Guidelines are provided on what a Project Sponsor should expect from a Project Manager and tools such as standard status report formats and "Key Questions to Ask About the Project" are provided to Project Sponsors. This training helps Project Sponsors become comfortable with their role in holding Project Managers responsible for project delivery.

10.3.3.2 – Describe the value your enterprise places on education and training and its goals and objectives.

In order to reduce reliance on external expertise for project management, Doe Run is striving to build internal competence in project management. Project management courses are coordinated through the organization's learning management system, the company pays for external courses, and training plans are included in employee performance goals.

10.3.3.3 – Does the enterprise have a project management career path program? If so, what are the components?

Doe Run has an informal project management career path. There are three levels of Project Managers: part-time Project Managers; full-time Project Managers; and Project Directors who manage the most complex and costly projects. Doe Run categorizes projects into one of four categories based on size and complexity and Project Managers are assigned to projects based on proven expertise and skill.

10.3.3.4 – Describe the measurements, metrics, and Key Performance Indicators (KPI's) utilized by the PMO to determine the organization's knowledge, skills, and level of achievement.

Doe Run uses two methods to determine the organization's knowledge and skills in project management.

First, Doe Run annually reviews its level on a project management maturity model. Using the maturity model developed by Dennis Bolles and Darrel Hubbard in their book *The Power of Enterprise-Wide Project Management*, from 2006 to 2010, project management maturity at Doe Run moved from Stage 1 (Evolving) to Stage 2 (Defined/Emerging). Since 2010, some functions are now starting to move into Stage 3 (Managed/Controlling) with processes fully documented and implemented and personnel trained. Since the return on the investment in project management increases as processes mature, the current goal is to drive maturity into Stage 4 (Optimized/ Improving).

Second, Doe Run analyzes the percentage of projects meeting the following metrics:

- Within 10% of baseline schedule
- Within 5% of approved project amount
- Actual Net Present Value (NPV) at least 90% of projected NPV
- At least 90% of stated business objectives achieved

For 2011, the goal was to have 53% of projects meeting schedule targets, 71% of projects meeting budget targets, 89% of projects meeting NPV targets and 85% of projects meeting business objective targets.

10.3.3.5 – Does the enterprise employ a project management competency model? If yes, please describe it. If no, why not?

Doe Run does not employ a project management competency model. In 2012, Project Managers will be assigned to projects based on demonstrated results on prior projects. Doe Run is interested in possible use of a competency model, but will first assess the impact of making assignments based on project complexity and Project Manager expertise.

> **10.3.4 SURVEY – PMO Business Planning:** Discuss strategic business planning, tactical business planning, business objective (project) development and prioritization, and project identification, selection, and authorization.

10.3.4.1 – Describe the organizational structure and process used for corporate strategic business planning.

Does the PMO play a role in the process? If so, describe the PMOs role and responsibilities.

Every year, executives re-evaluate the long-term strategic business plan for Doe Run. Input to the strategic planning process is provided by a Business Diagnostic team, led by the PMO Manager. The Business Diagnostic team analyzes:
- Operational performance capabilities and issues
- Industry and market trends, competitive threats and market forces
- Financial data

The team then reports findings to the executives which they use as input in determining whether the current strategy and capability can be successful in the current market and industry and revise the strategy as appropriate.

The PMO also facilitates the use of tools such as Strength-Weakness-Opportunity-Threat (SWOT) Analyses and Risk Assessment with company executives to assist in determining overall company strategic direction.

10.3.4.2 – How is the strategic plan implemented with a project forecast plan?

The project planning cycle is coordinated with the strategic planning cycle, so projects can be based on the goals and initiatives established by the Executive Team in annual meetings. See the Doe Run PMO Activity Timeline in Figure 10-1, shown at the end of this case study.

10.3.4.3 – How is strategic planning, culture, and selection of projects integrated?

The Doe Run business strategy and strategic goals are cascaded annually from the executive level to senior leadership. Senior leaders in each department and division then use the strategy and goals to develop tactical objectives for their business unit. The PMO is involved via the annual project planning process in helping determine the initiatives and projects necessary to meet those tactical objectives. Each department and division explains the link to business strategy as a part of every project proposal.

One of the key selection criteria for projects is the impact on company culture and required organizational change. Each project proposal must include comments on the number of people impacted by the change and the type of impact. Once projects are selected for funding, the PMO coordinates a second look at the projects to determine the overall impact on organizational change based on proposed timing for the project. If the executives, in conjunction with the PMO, determine that there is too much organizational change during a time-period for the company to manage effectively, projects will be rescheduled.

10.3.5 SURVEY – PMO Business Execution: Describe what role the PMO has in project selection, prioritization, and initiation; in portfolio, program and project execution planning; in stage-gate reviews; and in performance metrics selection and application.

10.3.5.1 – How are portfolios, programs, and projects selected and initiated?

Prior to the PMO, project funding was allocated to each division based on historical funding levels. The PMO introduced a new portfolio management process to allocate funding by project, based on priority. As a result, limited funds are now distributed where they can have the greatest positive impact on the company as a whole.

The PMO meets with each department and division at least six months prior to the beginning of the budget planning process to determine project requests for the upcoming fiscal year. Planning for these projects may have begun months or years prior to this date, depending on the amount of engineering required to make a reasonable estimate of costs.

Projects are divided into categories of non-discretionary spending (safety, regulatory, sustaining maintenance) and discretionary spending (profit improvement, strategic, cost reduction). Projects may also be grouped into programs of projects, depending on the need to coordinate resources or program outcomes.

Each business case contains a complexity assessment that assigns a number in regards to the risk of the project. For example, projects that affect large numbers of users over a large geographic area would have a higher score than a project that impacts only a few users in one location. These numerical ratings are used to compare the risk of one project to another.

All proposed projects for the budget cycle are placed on a risk/reward bubble chart so they can be compared as part of the project selection and ranking process. In the sample Excel chart in Figure 10-2 (shown at the end of this case study), complexity is shown on the x-axis and Internal Rate of Return is shown on the y-axis. The size of the bubble indicates the total cost of the project. The most desirable projects are high and to the left on the chart – high potential reward with low complexity. The least desirable projects are low on the chart and to the right – low potential reward with high complexity. Just as with a financial portfolio, the objective is to provide a desired level of reward and risk.

Each division and department then presents the business case for each program or project at an annual three-day meeting aligned with the budget planning cycle. Information for each project is provided on:
- Financial, environmental and social impact
- Risks
- Resource availability
- Organizational change impact

After review of this information, company executives and senior leaders categorize projects as "must have," "should have" or "nice to have." Projects are ranked in order and projects are included in the budget based on anticipated funding availability. See a diagram of the portfolio selection process in Figure 10-3, shown at the end of this case study.

10.3.5.2 – How are projects organized and managed as a program and/or portfolio?

The Doe Run project portfolio is managed by the PMO. Planned projects for the next five years are maintained in a Microsoft Project schedule, which the PMO uses to help determine optimal timing of projects based on project interdependencies, funding availability and resource availability.

Any set of projects managed as a consolidated "program of projects" are managed by a program manager who will coordinate the work of the individual Project Managers.

10.3.5.3 – How are projects prioritized within a program and/or portfolio?

Projects are prioritized at budget time based on the criteria listed above. Priorities are reviewed on a monthly basis and projects are re-prioritized if changing business conditions dictate.

Typically, all projects in the "regulatory" category are due on fixed dates provided by government agencies, so all other project work must be scheduled around regulatory commitments.

10.3.5.4 – How does the enterprise define what project and program success is?

The PMO considers a project to be a success when the following are true:
- Pre-defined Business Objectives and Project Goals are achieved or exceeded (i.e., the project satisfied the need that created it)
- A high-quality product is fully implemented and utilized
- Project delivery met or beat schedule and budget targets
- There are multiple winners: Project participants have pride of ownership and feel good about their work, the customer is happy, and management has met its goals
- Project results increase credibility in project management capability

10.3.5.5 – Does the PMO support the management of projects that would be considered operational in nature? If so, describe the types of projects.

Operational projects with anticipated spending of at least $500,000 are managed and monitored to the same standard as capital projects.

A typical operational project for a mining and metals company such as Doe Run would be the annual rebuild of a furnace. While the rebuild is a routine effort, major cost expenditure and significant risk of potential production downtime dictate that the effort run as smoothly as possible.

10.3.6 SURVEY – PMO Sustainability: Describe the overall impact of the PMO over a sustained period (e.g., customer satisfaction, productivity, reduced cycle time, growth, building or changing organizational culture, etc.). If available, please provide quantitative data to illustrate the areas in which the PMO has had the greatest business impact.

10.3.6.1 – What is included in a comprehensive project monitoring and control system and how is it implemented?

Under PMO leadership, reporting moved from a focus on pictures of construction sites and vague descriptions of progress to objective reporting of schedule and cost versus baselines. The PMO led an effort to provide an integrated way to track project costs in the company financial system rather than on independent spreadsheets, leading to more accurate project reporting.

Projects in progress are reported on monthly via dashboards that provide an appropriate level of detail for the audience and support "drill down" to details if desired. Key projects are discussed in monthly business reviews and reprioritized as necessary. This transparency has allowed management to see project trends monthly and make sure corrective action takes place sooner rather than later.

10.3.6.2 – How are project start-up and gate review processes structured?

A key component of the Doe Run project management methodology is a gated process for approving projects. The methodology is flexible and the number of approval gates varies with the size and complexity of the project. In the past, significant expenditures would have been made on engineering before a request for funding was made for the entire project cost. Once such major expenditures were made, management was reluctant to cancel these projects in progress due to the "sunk cost." The goal of the gated approval process is to provide just enough information at each phase of the project to make a good business decision whether or not to fund the next phase of the project. As a result, several major projects have been cancelled in early stages of development, when it was determined capital expenditure requirements were too high for the potential benefit or that the project no longer fit with company strategy.

10.3.6.3 – Describe the project knowledge base system and how is it developed?

Part of the Doe Run project management knowledge base system is a central repository for capturing lessons learned on each project. The PMO strives for continuous improvement, and using lessons learned to improve PMO processes and training programs is a key part of that process. Also, as part of the kickoff meeting for any new project, there is a review of pertinent lessons learned from prior projects and a discussion on how to apply the lessons learned to improve results on the current project.

Information is also captured on the performance of external service providers used on the project. For each external service provider, we collect data on:

- Scope of work
- Type of contract
- What the provider did well
- What the provider could have done better
- Recommendations on future engagements (for example, we ask "Would you use this provider again and, if so, in what capacity?)

This information is made available to other project teams who may be looking for similar resource providers.

All lessons learned data is posted to a common portal along with PMO templates, reference material, project portfolios, project status reports, and the training calendar.

10.3.6.4 – Describe the measurement, metrics, and Key Performance Indicators (KPIs) utilized by the PMO to measure project and program success.

Prior to the PMO, management lacked visibility into the strategic investment portfolio. Every year, millions of dollars would be invested without a consistent method to track return on investment. The PMO now conducts post-implementation audits on all major projects to evaluate schedule, scope and budget performance, stakeholder satisfaction, and whether or not business objectives were achieved.

Actual Net Present Value is tracked against target Net Present Value, isolating variables within the project's control (for example, excluding the impact of commodity price changes on project return). Results are communicated to the executive team to provide insight into the results of prior strategic decisions and the information is used to improve the decision-making process on future projects.

Specific goals for each project are:
- Within 10% of baseline schedule
- Within 5% of approved project amount
- Actual Net Present Value (NPV) at least 90% of projected NPV
- At least 90% of stated business objectives achieved

Management holds Project Managers and team members accountable for project performance based on metric results revealed in post-project audits. These metrics are incorporated into both the Doe Run Global Performance Management system (used for evaluating employee performance) and variable pay (bonus) calculations.

10.3.6.5 – Describe the organizational benefits and value the PMO provides to the enterprise.

Projects are now planned in advance, instead of the day before budget submissions are due. Collecting resource management information as part of the process had led to better resource allocation and less project bottlenecks. Interdependencies between projects and production work are identified to ensure projects are scheduled appropriately and don't face unnecessary delays. Reviewing the project portfolio has ensured better alignment with company strategy, encouraged involvement of key stakeholders, eliminated company silos, increased employee 'buy-in' for new initiatives and improved communication.

10.3.6.6 – Describe the economic benefits and value the PMO provides to the enterprise.

It is difficult to assign a dollar figure to the impact of the PMO on the enterprise, but much anecdotal evidence shows a positive impact on the company For example:
- Projects are ranked in priority order and priorities are re-evaluated monthly. Having this process in place allowed Doe Run to move quickly to address a changing economic situation in late 2008. Having reliable information available on cash flow and business benefits made it much easier to determine which projects to suspend until the economy improved.
- The Stage Gate process supports evaluating the feasibility of projects early-on, before significant expenditures are made.

For example, Doe Run cancelled a planned plant expansion after the pre-feasibility stage, when it was shown that the project would not yield the desired financial return.

- The Doe Run portfolio management process has encouraged managers to break down silos and to support what is best for the company as a whole. For example, now during project proposal meetings, a general manager of one division may be seen arguing for funding for another division.

- Many more projects are being completed on-time and on-budget. Improved planning is eliminating the re-work that resulted in many projects being over budget and over schedule. A baseline measuring the impact of the PMO on project results was taken at the end of 2007 after new processes had been in place for one year. By the end of 2011, the percent of projects meeting schedule objectives increased from the baseline of 14% to 67% and the percent of projects meeting cost objectives increased from 57% to 89% (see Figure 10-4 shown at the end of this case study).

- A focus on having specific business objectives stated upfront and measuring those results throughout the project has increased the number of projects delivering promised business benefits. For example, between 2007 and 2011, the percent of projects achieving stated business objectives dramatically increased from 57% to 100%.

When the PMO was organized in 2006, the major pain point identified with projects was the delay in obtaining project funding. Through the work of the PMO, confidence in the ability of Doe Run personnel to successfully deliver projects has increased to a level that the Board of Directors raised the dollar limit for requiring Board approvals from $10,000 to $500,000. The average time for project funding approval has dropped from 98 days to an average of 22 days, so now critical projects can be completed as needed to meet operational needs.

By mid-2010, project performance had improved so dramatically, the Doe Run PMO was awarded first runner-up in the PMO of the Year award, second only to IBM.

The PMO of the Year award is an international competition, sponsored by the PMO Community of Practice of the Project Management Institute (ww.pmi.org) and the PMSolutions Group (ww.pmsolutions.com).

> **10.3.7 SURVEY – Additional Comments:** Please provide any additional comments

The Doe Run Company's Enterprise PMO did not provide any additional comments.

FIGURE 10-1: Doe Run PMO Activity Timeline

Doe Run PMO Activity Timeline

Quarter 1			Quarter 2			Quarter 3			Quarter 4		
NOV	DEC	JAN	FEB	MAR	APR	MAY	JUN	JUL	AUG	SEP	OCT
Start of fiscal year			Review corporate strategy	Executive planning conference (1 year horizon)			Non-discretionary project proposals	Discretionary project proposals; project prioritization and initial selection	Project resource allocation; review overall project timing	Final budget; Final project portfolio for next fiscal year	Executive strategic planning conference (5 year horizon);
Project kickoffs for current fiscal year			Detailed planning for projects for next fiscal year								

Ongoing Activities

Daily	Monthly	Periodic
Individual on-the-job mentoring Business case development Business requirement gathering	Project portfolio review Strategic project assessment Project spend and forecast monitoring	Project management training classes Opportunity framing workshops Audits of project performance Project approval gate reviews

FIGURE 10-2: Doe Run Proposed Projects Risk versus Reward Bubble Chart Example

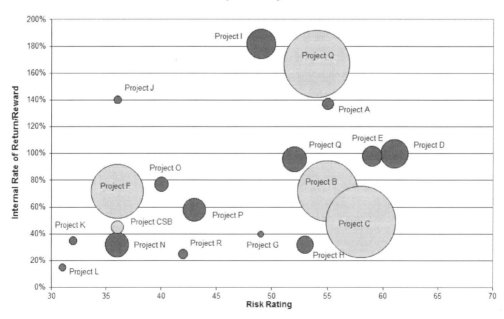

FIGURE 10-3: Doe Run Portfolio Selection Process

Doe Run Portfolio Selection Process

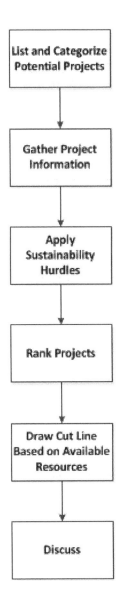

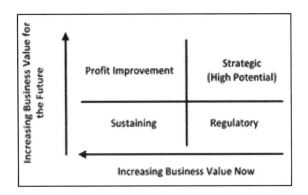

Ranking	Description	Spending
1	Project A	$10,500,000
2	Project B	$2,750,000
3	Project C	$540,000
4	Project D	$1,000,000
5	Project E	$2,400,000
6	Project F	$750,000

FIGURE 10-4: Doe Run PMO Performance Metrics

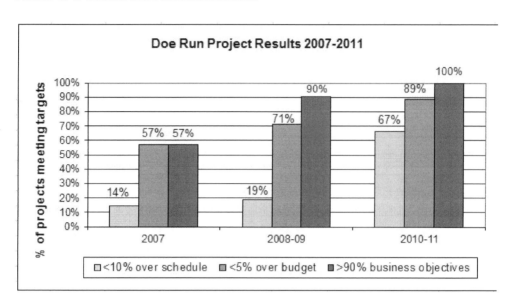

Chapter 11

EMC Insurance Companies PMO Case Study

EMC Insurance Companies ranks among the top 60 insurance organizations in the United States and is one of the largest property and casualty companies in Iowa, based on net written premium. EMC Insurance Companies (EMC) is the trade name used by Employers Mutual Casualty Company (EMCC), several subsidiaries and affiliated insurance companies and the EMC Insurance Group Inc.

EMC Insurance Group Inc. (EMCI) is one of 39 small-capitalization companies included on the "100 Most Trustworthy Companies" list published by Forbes on April 5, 2010. The Forbes list identifies companies that are "the most transparent and trustworthy businesses that trade on American exchanges."

Founded in 1911, EMC Insurance Companies is financially solid, built on 100 years of serving policyholders and independent insurance agents. Today, EMC employs more than 2,500 employees in 16 locations across the country.

EMC sells its products solely through independent insurance agencies in more than 40 states. EMC believes their partnership with independent agents brings a superior level of personalized service to the insurance process.

11.1 EMC Insurance Companies – Enterprise and PMO Office Survey Information

Enterprise Name:	EMC Insurance Companies (Employers Mutual Casualty Company)
Country:	United States of America
Industry:	Insurance
Enterprise – Annual Sales Revenue:	Large, greater than $1B US Dollars
Enterprise – Full-time Employee Equivalents:	2,200

World Wide Web Site:	www.emcins.com
PMO Name:	Program Management Office (PMO)
Title of PMO Leader:	Vice President, Director - Program Management Office (PMO)
PMO Position in Organizational Structure:	Executive level, Enterprise-wide Department
PMO reports to in Organizational Structure:	Executive Vice President, Corporate Development
PMO Annual Operating Budget:	$375K-$654K US Dollars
PMO – Full-time Employee Equivalents:	4

The following are the PMO Case Study Survey question sets and the associated responses as submitted by EMC Insurance Companies' Program Management Office, with minor editing for format and consistency.

11.2 EMC Insurance Companies PMO Background, Innovations, and Impact

In the following three parts of this case study, the EMC Insurance Companies' Program Management Office provides an overview of the background and structure of its PMO, various innovations and best practices by the PMO, and the potential future business impact of the PMO.

> **11.2.1 SURVEY – PMO Background:** Describe your PMO, including background information on its scope, vision, mission, and position within the enterprise's organizational structure.

Position within Organization

The PMO is an independent, enterprise-wide department, which is Vice President directed and reports directly to one of two Executive Vice Presidents.

Mission

Add value to the organization by providing leadership for the improvement and expansion of project management throughout the company. The PMO will strive to accomplish this mission by:

- Overseeing the project management/coordination, standardization, and communication on the company's portfolio of large projects (PMO Oversight Projects),

- Delivering actionable decision-support information (including recommendations for project prioritization) to the PMO Oversight Committee (POC) and EMC Planning Team (as needed), and
- Ensuring training and coaching are provided for successful project completion.

> **11.2.2 SURVEY – PMO Innovations and Best Practices:** Address the challenges your enterprise encountered prior to implementing the new PMO practices and how you overcame those challenges. Describe clearly and concisely the practices implemented and their effect on project, program, and/or portfolio and organizational success.

__Challenge__: Inconsistent and un-standardized project management, coordination, standardization, and communication of project work.

__PMO Practice__: Provide PMO project managers on select projects (as capacity allows); maintain and promote a consistent and standardized PM methodology throughout the company; maintain and enhance the company's database/portfolio of those large projects; and facilitate wide-spread communication on project work.

__Effect__: EMC now has company-wide awareness, consistency, and standardization on these topics.

__Challenge__: Inconsistent and un-standardized project recognition and decision making by executive management.

__PMO Practice__: Deliver actionable decision-support information (including, but not limited to, recommendations for project prioritization) to the PMO Oversight Committee (POC) and EMC Planning Team (as needed). The POC is comprised of the company's:

- President/CEO;
- Both Executive Vice Presidents (including its Chief Operating Officer);
- The Senior Vice President of IT (since roughly 80% or more of EMC's large projects involve IT);
- A Vice President/Branch Manager (representing one of EMC's 16 independent branch offices/profit centers); and
- The Vice President/PMO Director (who is also the facilitator of the POC).

The EMC Planning Team is comprised of all executive officers (including all Department Heads) of EMC.

__Effect__: Executive management now has every-other-month, actionable, decision-support information on topics involving PM and the PMO.

Since PMO inception in November 2006, the POC has met - with 100% attendance - on 29 consecutive occasions. Likewise, the PMO has always had a seat at the EMC Planning Team table over those 5 years (and 29 consecutive meetings) and has presented to that executive committee on at least a dozen different occasions.

Challenge: Inconsistent and un-standardized company-wide communication and awareness of large project work.

PMO Practice: Require and receive timely status reports from all project managers and timely stage gate reports from all project sponsors, consolidate that information, and provide the company's executives with a summary of critical project information (including recommendations on prioritization), as well as with requests for necessary input and/or support.

Effect: Company's executives are regularly briefed and consulted, using all different sorts of media (internal website, email, posters, meetings, presentations, one-on-ones, fliers, handbooks, video sessions, etc.).

Challenge: Inconsistent and un-standardized Project Management (PM) training.

PMO Practice: Ensure training, as well as coaching (for all large projects), are provided for successful project completion. Ensure on-going training, as well as one-on-one coaching for all large projects, is provided to all levels of EMC staff so that executives, managers/supervisors, project sponsors, project managers, and project team members understand their roles in making projects successful.

This also includes ensuring PMO project managers (and select employees outside the PMO where project coordination is a significant job requirement/responsibility for their positions; e.g., those frequently asked to be project Team Leaders (TLs) obtain professional continuing education.

As coaches, PMO employees are responsible for guiding/instructing TLs (as needed and in a scalable manner) through their PM responsibilities with both the processes and the people involved; and to a lesser extent (if needed), for helping project sponsor(s) and team members work through their unique roles.

This coaching effort provides a connection between the TLs and the PMO, which in turn promotes involvement and ongoing knowledge and skill development that benefits not only the TL, but also the PMO and the company in general.

The training and coaching are two-fold – process responsibilities and people responsibilities:

Process Responsibilities:
- Guiding/instructing the TL in defining the project; completing the Cost Benefit Analysis (CBA), participating in the Project Initiation meeting(s), building the project management plan; building and managing the schedule; managing communications, issues, risks, scope, quality, metrics, and the stage gating process; and working with the project sponsor(s), team members, and other stakeholders
- Reinforcing, within the context of a "real" project, previous educational elements, with the TL
- Identifying educational resources to help broaden TL knowledge

People Responsibilities:
- Guiding/instructing the TL with both project leadership and direction-setting;

       for example, with communicating; delegating; holding accountability; team building; and addressing morale, behavioral, and/or performance issues involving employees on project team (plus other employees supporting the project team)

- Building/maintaining a supportive relationship with the TL and providing a confidential, neutral sounding board throughout the project

Effect: Executives, managers/supervisors, project sponsors, project managers, team leaders, and team members all now understand their roles in making projects successful. In addition, all large projects have PMO coaching provided.

11.2.3 SURVEY – PMO Future Impact: Briefly describe your PMO's plans for 2012 and beyond - please describe how those plans will potentially impact your enterprise and its organizational structure.

    The following are the Program Management Offices planned ongoing actions and desired impacts.

1) Monitor and assess PMO internal processes for both efficiency and effectiveness, and where applicable for expense reduction and/or for gains in efficiency or effectiveness, implement necessary changes.

    Impact: Reduce cost, improve productivity, and hopefully make the PMO department. more efficient and/or effective.

2) Manage each assigned project according to the approved scope and estimated finish date agreed upon among the project manager(s) - representing the project team - and the project sponsor(s).

    Impact: Projects will be effectively managed and be delivered on time and within scope.

3) Manage the PMO's overall training strategy regarding project management - focusing on project managers/team leaders, sponsors, team members, resource managers, and other key stakeholders (as appropriate); taking into consideration both basic-type training as well as more-advanced training for select employees; and determining both the curriculum and most-effective means of delivery (inside or outside courses, e-classes, etc.).

    Impact: Executives, managers/supervisors, project sponsors, project managers, team leaders, and team members will understand their roles in making projects successful; and project managers/team leaders will effectively manage projects and deliver them on time and within scope.

4) Regarding the company's project management and maturing portfolio management methodologies - including the supporting tools, templates, and documentation - improve any known weaknesses and continuously monitor and require appropriate individual usage/application.

Impact: For PM, with effective and well-documented tools, templates, and techniques, projects will be effectively managed and delivered on time and within scope; for Project Portfolio Management (PPM), the company will continue to mature in the areas of strategic planning, prioritization, portfolio management, and resource allocation with an attempt to deliver the most beneficial projects in a more rapid time frame.

5) Effectively and confidently coach project managers/team leaders through difficulties in dealing with various project management processes, tools, and templates, as well as with various people management issues.

Impact: Team leaders outside of the PMO will effectively manage projects and deliver them on time and within scope.

6) Enhance awareness of the value of the company's project management and maturing portfolio management methodologies.

Impact: The organization will have an improved awareness of large project work, and hopefully a solid understanding of how an effective use of the PMO's methodology (PM and PPM) will aid in improved project execution, and as a result, an improvement in benefit realization, reduced costs, and an overall positive effect in EMC's bottom line.

7) Evaluate and improve the overall project management competency level of PMO Department staff.

Impact: As project managers, trainers, coaches, and communicators, our PMO staff will lead by example (because of its steady and continuously-improving competency). In addition, its number of PMP credential holders will increase.

11.3   EMC Insurance Companies PMO Model Components

In the following six parts of this case study, the EMC Insurance Companies' Program Management Office provides its descriptions of how they implement the six key components of the Project Business Management Organization model: Governance; Methodology; Capability; Planning; Execution; and Sustainability.

> **11.3.1 SURVEY – PMO Governance:** Describe how your PMO presents itself as an executive-level management business function, how it addresses setting policy and establishing charters, and how it provides an organizational model for the business management of portfolios, programs, and projects and the establishment of portfolio, program, and project management offices.

The Program Management Office is an executive level management business function. The Vice President/PMO Director is an active participant on the PMO Oversight Committee (POC) and EMC Planning Team committees, takes part in the corporate planning process, and helps establish the priority level for all large projects (as a member, and facilitator, of the POC).

As a member and facilitator of the POC, the Vice President/PMO Director helps set and communicate policy in the area of Project Management (PM) for EMC. Project sponsors, on the other hand, approve charters - but they are sanctioned and subject to review and question by the POC.

Provides an organizational model for business management of projects, programs, and portfolios (P, P, & P) - the PMO staff works, regularly, with the heads of all departments on the PM methodology, templates, and software tool – "cordin8" - in discussions about both PM and PPM in regard to small, non-PMO projects. A few departments (of our 16) have their own portfolio of small projects and apply a subset of our PM methodology.

Establishment of P, P, & P offices - our PMO is an enterprise-wide PM department; in the areas of P, P, & P, we do not want any other offices established here at EMC.

11.3.1.1 – How long has the PMO been in place? *When was it started?*	The PMO has been in place for 5 plus years. The PMO was started November 2006.
11.3.1.2 – What is the relationship of PMO management to the enterprise's operational management?	The Vice President/PMO Director is a member of the EMC Planning Team, which can be considered to be EMC's operational management team, with all Department Heads, all executives, and the company's top leadership.
11.3.1.3 – How is the PMO internally structured (positions, roles etc.)?	One Vice President/PMO Director and three Project Managers. The responsibilities for the PMO Department are all listed above; while the project managers are required to manage their own large projects, that is only about half of their overall responsibilities, the other half is a requirement to support the PMO Department's responsibilities.
11.3.1.4 – How are the PMO's operations funded?	The PMO has its own annual budget; an allocation out of the Executive Area. The PMO does not charge back effort to other functional areas.

11.3.1.5 – What is the summary position description of the PMO leader?

Under the general direction of the POC, the PMO Director assumes responsibility for day-to-day operational management of all activities and functions of the PMO Department.

- Develops, implements, and evaluates program policies, procedures, and standards.
- Determines program service levels and enhancements.
- Develops and monitors program budget issues.
- Provides technical advice and/or supervision to project managers and to other department project team leaders and project team sponsors.
- Manages/coordinates projects and ensures successful completion.
- Promotes consistent, company-wide usage of approved project management tools, terminology, and processes and techniques.

11.3.1.6 – What position requirements are used as a basis for selecting the PMO leader?

Education and Experience:

- Bachelor's degree along with a minimum of 10 years of experience in project-related coordination required.
- Experience may be substituted for college education at the rate of two years of experience for each year of college.
- PMP development is required.
- Any insurance-related professional development is helpful.
- Prior supervisory experience required.

Knowledge, Skills, and Abilities:

- Knowledge of all aspects of PM is required.
- Must have a sound understanding of EMC's specific PM methodology, its corporate culture, and its organizational structure (to ensure effective communication).
- Excellent leadership and interpersonal skills with the ability to manage, direct, lead and counsel employees are required.
- Must possess solid organizational and analytical abilities.
- Exceptional communication skills, including the ability to speak effectively before groups, are required.
- Must maintain high standards of professional competence and conduct.
- A valid driver's license with an acceptable motor vehicle report per company standards is required.
- Regular attendance is required on the job, with the ability to work the hours established for the specific location.

11.3.1.7 – Is the PMO a Profit & Loss cost center or considered overhead?	The PMO is considered overhead.

11.3.1.8 – What current challenge is the PMO dealing with?	**Challenges include:** • Resource allocation; • Upfront estimating; • Training new project managers; • Maturing in the area of Project Portfolio Management (PPM) (especially with respect to strategic planning, prioritizing, and accelerating high-benefit projects); and • Using consistent scheduling tools/techniques throughout the organization.

> **11.3.2 SURVEY – PMO Methodology / Standardization:** Describe what standardization your PMO has implemented across the enterprise that examines: identification and integration of processes and practices; development of standardized Project Business Management processes; and documentation of enterprise-wide portfolio, program, and project management process methodology models, including their associated policies, practices, and procedures.

We have enterprise-wide, standardized, documented policies, practices, and procedures for the following:

Action Items, Business Requirements, Charters, Communication Plans, Issues Management, Lessons Learned, Project Health, Schedules, Risk Management, Roles and Responsibilities, Scope Change Management, Sponsor Post-Project Evaluations, Stage Gating, Status Reporting, Time Tracking, Glossary and Acronyms, Cost Benefit Analysis (CBA), Archiving, Performance Evaluation, New Project Proposals (NPP), Portfolio Oversight, Project Escalation, Project Initiation, PM Requirements, Prioritization Process, Best Practices, Lifecycle Management, PM Phases, PM Process, Sponsorship, Team Member Handbooks, and substantial "help" for the cordin8 PM software.

The "cordin8" product is a scalable out-of-the-box enterprise portfolio / program management office solution technology offered by cordin8, LLC, which supports the Ten Step, Inc. methodology.

11.3.2.1 – Describe the standards utilized by the PMO to ensure the enterprise's project / program / portfolio management goals and objectives are achieved.

The PMO coaches every large project; and we project manage about 25% of them ourselves.

We monitor the Status Reports; we monitor the Stage Gate reports; and we ask for a formal project update for all managers and supervisors twice a year.

About every three years, we conduct a PM Process Review (sort of an Audit) to see how the project managers are following our required methodology.

In addition, 4-to-12 months after project completion, we ask the project sponsor to provide the POC (and in some instances the EMC Planning Team) with a post-project evaluation of benefits being received.

11.3.2.2 – Describe the project management process guidelines being employed by the PMO.

We have the following set of required processes for all large projects:
- Action Items,
- Business Requirements,
- Charter,
- Change Log,
- Communication Plan,
- Cost Benefit Analysis (CBA),
- Issue Log,
- Lessons Learned,
- Meeting Agendas and Minutes,
- New Project Proposal (NPP),
- Roles,
- Risk Log,
- Schedule,
- Stage Gate Report,
- Status Report, and
- Time Tracking.
- We also ask for the following (as needed project by project):
  - Implementation Plan,
  - Procurement Plan,
  - System Design Specifications,
  - Test Plan,
  - Training Plan, and
  - Transition Plan.

There is published documentation for all of the above.

11.3.2.3 – What systems, tools, and templates make your PMO successful?	We use cordin8 project management software (cordin8, LLC). That product originates with the TenStep methodology and templates (TenStep, Inc.), which is then customized by our PMO staff to fit EMC.

11.3.2.4 – Describe how management at all levels is directly involved in the development of the PMO and it processes.	The POC governs the PMO. Included within the POC is EMC's Executive Management Team (its President/CEO and his two Executive VPs)…these three gentlemen have governance over all of the company's executives - the entire organization reports up to one of these three.

All PMO plans for company change and/or advancement are first proposed to the POC for approval; once approved, the POC provides its direction to the entire organization.

In addition, all of EMC's top management is a part of the EMC Planning Team, including all members of the POC (including the PMO Director). At the direction of the POC, this larger committee is routinely briefed about POC-approved company changes and advancements in the area of PM and PMO activities. As a result of Executive Management Team support, the trickle-down affect starts to take place with all of those reporting Department Heads.

11.3.2.5 – Describe the implementation plan you used for establishing project / program / portfolio management standards across your enterprise.	We started with a scaled-down approach for all large projects (just asking for a Charter, Schedule and Time Tracking for each project) when the PMO first started.

Later, we divided the portfolio of large projects into two piles: complex and larger in size, and more straightforward and smaller in size. Then we applied a mature set of PM requirements to the complex/large-project set and a smaller set of PM requirements to the straightforward/small-project set.

A little over a year ago, we determined the mature set of PM requirements identified above, should just apply only to all large projects.

Requested POC approvals, detailed company-wide communication plans, and adjustments to both cordin8 and our documentation helped introduce the changes.

11.3.2.6 – How does the PMO use project, program, and portfolio management standards to optimize its practices? Are they based on PMI® or other industry guides and are they updated as new editions of the guides are released?	The standards are based on the TenStep methodology. Elements of PMI's structure offer influence, and much of the final product has EMC customization added to it. Both TenStep and PMI do have updates, which the PMO reviews, and after analysis, we determine *if* our standards will be changed (and if so, then how/when/etc.).

> **11.3.3 SURVEY – PMO Capabilities:** Describe development and assessment of the enterprise's abilities, describe any project management competency model, summarize any education and training program, describe any established career path progression plan, and outline key Enterprise Environmental Factors.

Enterprise's Abilities

Before the PMO, the company was already running large projects fairly well. The PMO established prioritization, standardization, consistent execution, role definition (including responsibilities and accountabilities), and significantly more transparency about these important projects.

Competency Model

We do not yet have a formal competency model. However, outside of our PMO project managers, we look for talented employees in the business units, including IT, to manage large projects. We consider their company knowledge, PM training to-date, prior project work, and people skills before turning the reins over to them. Then the PMO provides coaching for every large project. Inside the PMO, we expect our PMs to continue with their ongoing education, pursue the PMP designation, and work through regular leadership initiatives.

Training Program

Our PMO provided Basic Training to nearly a hundred interested and potential project managers. We also provided Sponsorship training to our entire forty-executive sponsor base. Ongoing, we have created hundreds of pages of our documentation; we host the TenStep library and its wealth of PM materials; we maintain a fantastic PMO website (a one-stop shop for all things dealing with PM); we maintain our own Training Library, and we are creating e-classes for critical deliverables such as Charters, Risk Logs, etc.

Career Path

Our company's project managers reside in the PMO. While we rely on employees in the business units, and IT as well, to manage large projects also (in addition to their own jobs), it is the career path within the PMO that is fully dedicated to project management. Soon, the PMO will add a Senior Project Manager title to its existing two levels: Project Manager and Associate Project Manager. This is all in addition to the position of the PMO Director.

Enterprise Environmental Factors

Our company has cultural elements of slower-pace change, minimal cutting-edge change, and conservative thinking. This is why the culture-change initiative of implementing a PMO Department took a good two years to take root, another year to cultivate, and the past two years to thrive, take hold, and become the new cultural way of doing things around EMC.

We are heavily regulated, so our documentation requirements on large projects, especially those involving financial matters, are significant. Specifically on the PM side, we do have and use an excellent PM tool - cordin8 - for collecting, collaborating on, and distributing information.

Lastly, at EMC, we are fortunate to have a great number of hard working and caring employees. This lends itself to a host of talented project managers to draw upon (when needed), a great group of sponsors, and a ton of team members who care a lot about what they are doing personally, and also about the company for which they work.

11.3.3.1 – Describe the components of your enterprise's training program.	Initial Basic PM Training (roughly a 2-day workshop) - based on the TenStep methodology and incorporating the cordin8 PM software. This is customized to fit what we do here at EMC. If we cannot form a full workshop, our PMO uses the materials to individually train.
	Sponsor Training (roughly a half-day workshop) - similarly based on the TenStep methodology, incorporating the cordin8 PM software, and customized to fit what we do here at EMC. Today, the PMO uses the materials to individually train (when needed).
	Training Library (this is continuously maintained). E-class Training on various PM components (this is ongoing). Team Member Handbooks (very detailed; provided to ALL project team members).
	PMO coaching services are provided for every large project.

11.3.3.2 – Describe the value your enterprise places on education and training and its goals and objectives.

When we first offered Basic PM Training, over one-hundred employees (who are dedicated to IT programming, underwriting, adjusting claims, litigating, providing actuarial services, etc.) asked to be included - and all were accommodated.

When we first offered Sponsor Training, every executive (forty in total, including our CEO, two Executive Vice Presidents, and all Senior Vice Presidents) was in attendance.

Today, the PMO continues to provide these same training opportunities to all of those who either missed these sessions or are new to EMC.

It is all well-funded, kept current, and highly regarded.

11.3.3.3 – Does the enterprise have a project management career path program? If so, what are the components?

As mentioned in the introduction, our company's project managers reside in the PMO. While we rely on employees in the business units, and IT as well, to manage large projects in addition to their own jobs, it is the career path within the PMO that is fully dedicated to PM.

Soon, the PMO will add a Senior Project Manager title to its existing two levels: Project Manager and Associate Project Manager. This is all in addition to the position of the PMO Director.

11.3.3.4 – Describe the measurements, metrics, and Key Performance Indicators (KPI's) utilized by the PMO to determine the organization's knowledge, skills, and level of achievement.

We currently measure performance based on the completion of a project according to its *scope* (as agreed to by the project team and approved by the sponsor) and *time frame* (also as agreed to by the project team and approved by the sponsor, as well as by the PMO Director).

So we use evaluation forms to gather information, continuously review the portfolio for date changes, monitor all stage gate activity (referencing health and including commentary by both the project manager and sponsor), and frequently review status reporting.

Since the PMO coaches every large project, we have a good first-hand observation of the knowledge and skills being utilized; and overall, on the collective achievement of all large projects in the portfolio.

11.3.3.5 – Does the enterprise employ a project management competency model? If yes, please describe it. If no, why not?

Inside the PMO, yes; outside the PMO (so enterprise-wide), no.

Our inside model consists of using the performance management process to factor in these PM competencies/job factors (initially presented and defined, reviewed at an interim period, and then formally evaluated at a final period:

- Interpersonal skills (5%),
- Problem solving/decision making (5%),
- Teamwork (5%),
- Planning/organizing (5%), and
- Leadership (5%).

This comprises a total of 25% of their annual performance review; and in the process, it is used to review and determine competencies in these areas and to make the proper adjustments as needed along the way.

11.3.4 SURVEY – PMO Business Planning: Discuss strategic business planning, tactical business planning, business objective (project) development and prioritization, and project identification, selection, and authorization.

11.3.4.1 – Describe the organizational structure and process used for corporate strategic business planning.

All company Department Heads, plus the CEO and its two Executive Vice Presidents, comprise the EMC Planning Team. Through every-other-month meetings, this committee establishes the strategic business plan, ensures tactical business planning, and oversees business objective development.

Does the PMO play a role in the process? If so, describe the PMOs role and responsibilities.

The PMO Director is a member of this committee. He routinely presents on matters of project support to this process; and he regularly works directly with the head of the Planning Team - the Executive Vice President for Corporate Development (his boss), on preparation work and pre-planning for the larger-scale Planning Team involvement.

11.3.4.2 – How is the strategic plan implemented with a project forecast plan?

Our strategic plan (long-term) sets the direction for our operating plan (annual, short-term). In our operating plan, we identify corporate objectives and corporate action steps, and then we support those with departmental objectives and departmental action steps.

In those departmental action steps, we ask for forecast plans on whether that work will take place in the form of a large PMO-level project, a smaller project, or other work. Through the Planning Team, we then report out on progress regarding these annual plans.

11.3.4.3 – How is strategic planning, culture, and selection of projects integrated?

Many forecasted projects (if known upfront) are listed as a part of the annual departmental planning process; while others are initiated as they are needed. To get a project integrated, a New Project Proposal form is completed by a functional area, authorized by a company Vice President (VP), and submitted to the PMO to be initiated. For the most part, unless resource managers can all agree to a different approach, the culture here is to start all projects if/when they are needed as long as they are authorized by a company VP, so we tend to get work started quickly on all new projects.

The PMO, and its governing POC committee, are setting the stage for future project reviews upfront to then determine/sanction that start, consider postponement (of that project or of another resource-competing project), and/or factor in other alternatives.

11.3.5 SURVEY – PMO Business Execution: Describe what role the PMO has in project selection, prioritization, and initiation; in portfolio, program and project execution planning; in stage-gate reviews; and in performance metrics selection and application.

Project Selection, Prioritization, and Initiation

Here at EMC, the functional areas (not the PMO) select which projects are needed; they then send to the PMO a New Project Proposal (NPP) that outlines the project and identifies the Vide President (VP) who is authorizing the project's start. Based on the project's alignment to, and support of, the company's priority issues and aligned objectives - as well as its cost-benefit analysis - the PMO then compares that project to the others in the portfolio and provides a priority recommendation to the POC.

We use two tiers: Tier I (high priority) and Tier II (all other). The POC then determines the actual priority level, and the PMO communicates that to the company - asking that our limited resources be allocated accordingly. Once a project is submitted to the PMO (via the NPP), while the priority analysis, recommendation, and approval processes are taking place, the PMO also facilitates a Project Initiation process with all of the resource managers involved.

This helps determine resource allocation, other priorities, etc. and it sets the stage for the proper development of the cost-benefit analysis process. The project continues once there is "consensus" among the Project Initiation participants/managers and continues on with a PMO/POC priority level either at that time or shortly thereafter (depending on POC meeting time frame).

Portfolio, Program and Project Execution Planning

At this time, the PMO is not involved with portfolio planning (just not quite ready for that yet - still maturing) and we do not use programs. On the project side, we require planning and documenting the project (by the project manager), using our templates to do so (Risk, Communications, etc.); we facilitate the Project Initiation meetings (which is a planning session for the resource managers); and we monitor the execution of those plans through our coaching efforts and stage gate reviews.

Stage-Gate Reviews

Stage gate passages are required here as follows: at the end of initiating (obtaining the sponsor's direction to continue starting the project), every 4 months throughout the project (obtaining the sponsor's direction to continue), and then at the end of implementing (obtaining the sponsor's direction to close down the project).

Prior to each POC meeting, the PMO collects all sponsor direction/comments presented since the last meeting and facilitates a review session of those at the meeting. In addition, the entire PMO portfolio of projects is presented to the POC so it can see all gate passage time frames, GO/NO GO statuses, health conditions at the gate, current health, names and other dates. This puts all of the stage gate activity into a portfolio perspective. Throughout all of this, the PMO also serves as a coach to the sponsors (if needed).

Performance Metrics Selection and Application

The PMO selects and applies metrics to both individual projects as well as to the collection of projects in the portfolio. As needed, the PMO then analyzes those metrics and provides the POC and/or EMC Planning Team with thoughts/opinions, needs for correction, requests for feedback, etc.

The PMO also uses that information to determine coaching changes, training needs, and communication pieces. Findings may also lead to topics addressed in Knowledge Sharing sessions, White Papers, or Performance Management matters.

11.3.5.1 – How are portfolios, programs, and projects selected and initiated?

Portfolios - currently, our portfolio set-up is as follows:
1) Corporate Operating Plan (for all departments),
2) Large (PMO-level) projects (that span all departments), and
3) Select department portfolios for small projects (we have 6 of 16 departments with these).

Any additional corporate-level portfolios would be initiated in conjunction with the PMO, POC, and EMC Planning Team.
Any additional departments wanting to manage its small projects in this manner would initiate those through the PMO.
In all cases, we use the cordin8 PM software.

Programs - we do not use programs at this time.
Projects - as addressed above.

11.3.5.2 – How are projects organized and managed as a program and/or portfolio?

We do not organize projects as a program nor do we organize projects as a portfolio.

If large enough, they are a component of our company's portfolio of large (PMO-level) projects and land in that listing and under the oversight of the PMO.

If smaller, and if a department is using a portfolio concept to manage small projects, then they are a component of that department's portfolio of small projects and land in that listing and under the oversight of that Department Head.

11.3.5.3 – How are projects prioritized within a program and/or portfolio?

We do not prioritize projects within a program.

For PMO-level projects (in the PMO portfolio), that priority process is spelled out above.

For smaller projects (in applicable departmental portfolios), that priority process is similar to the one in the PMO - some use Tiers, others use a level of priority (1 to 5), etc. This is unique for the 6 areas. For all of the ways, however, the Department Head has the final say on the priority level. The PMO and POC have little to do with these portfolios, projects within, or priority levels assigned - other than to maintain an awareness and keep an eye open for resource conflicts with the larger projects at the PMO level.

11.3.5.4 – How does the enterprise define what project and program success is?

Two-fold defining of success:
First, throughout the project and at its end, it was managed according to scope, in the time frame needed, as agreed to by the project team and approved by the sponsor.

Second, in a time frame no less than 4 months and no greater than 12 months after project close, we (PMO and POC) ask for a standardized Sponsor Post-Project Evaluation. These focus on the benefits realized, as well as the success of the project that helped obtain those. In all instances, these are written synopses for the POC; in most instances, unless the project was very small, these are also verbal presentations to the POC with Q&A. In a few instances (large, company-wide benefits), these are also verbal presentations to the EMC Planning Team with Q&A.

11.3.5.5 – Does the PMO support the management of projects that would be considered operational in nature? If so, describe the types of projects.

The PMO oversees <u>all</u> projects that require five hundred or more hours of employee time.

These projects could be operational in nature.

All projects are overseen in the same manner and require the same level of PM rigor and requirements.

11.3.6 SURVEY – PMO Sustainability: Describe the overall impact of the PMO over a sustained period (e.g., customer satisfaction, productivity, reduced cycle time, growth, building or changing organizational culture, etc.). If available, please provide quantitative data to illustrate the areas in which the PMO has had the greatest business impact.

The EMC Program Management Office has had the following impacts:

Customer Satisfaction

Projects are now initiated better and with management support. There is a corporate priority level established to reduce or eliminate departmental differences of opinion, they are consistently managed according to a well-known scope and time frame and with standardized and well-documented tools and processes. There is company-wide transparency as a result of these, and customer satisfaction has been increased. Customer surveys over the years have validated this.

Productivity

Teams are now formed in a quicker fashion, the processes used today are well known, the PM tool (cordin8) has been used repeatedly, and employees now understand their roles better. As such, productivity has increased to some degree. Again, customer surveys have validated this over the years.

Reduced Cycle Time

Projects now have a quicker start up, have more visibility throughout, and as such, the start to end time has been somewhat reduced. The planning and closing phases are better understood now, and we've seen an acceleration of those activities too. The great unknown, project to project, is in the phase of executing and the PMO has little influence over this actual in-the-trenches work so it is too variable to indicate any reduction.

Growth

If a project focuses on corporate growth, it is likely going to receive a Tier I (high priority) priority level; as such, it will likely get the resources it needs and be executed in the time frame desired.

Building or Changing Organizational Culture

The PMO has been gradually changing culture at EMC since its inception in November 2006. We now have a culture of "doing projects right." The projects are consistently managed, standardized, prioritized, and transparent. With that foundation in place, we are trying to change culture once again, this time towards "doing the right projects." We are one year into this culture change initiative toward project portfolio management and things are going well.

11.3.6.1 – What is included in a comprehensive project monitoring and control system and how is it implemented?

1) PMO staff coach all large projects (i.e., those that they do not manage themselves).

2) All large projects roll up into the one portfolio, so the PMO can oversee all.

3) The PMO facilitates the Project Initiation process for all new projects...and throughout the project, it monitors the monthly status reports and the time sensitive stage gate activity (along with the POC).

4) Two times a year, the PMO asks for a status summary which it then compiles into one portfolio booklet and distributes that to all managers/supervisors in the organization, which is nearly one-hundred-twenty-five employees.

5) Every two years, the PMO works through an extensive review process by which it looks at the completeness and quality of the PM deliverables, processes, logs, etc.

11.3.6.2 – How are project start-up and gate review processes structured?

The first step in project startup begins once there is "consensus" among the Project Initiation participants/managers.

Stage gate passages are required at the end of initiating, every 4 months throughout the project, and then at the end of implementing.

11.3.6.3 – Describe the project knowledge base system and how is it developed?	In addition to information we have already covered, we also hold Knowledge Sharing sessions about once every quarter by which all active project managers and any project manager who was active in the prior year, congregate and share experiences, ask questions, and build camaraderie.
	The PMO keeps track of the project manager base and has a good set of records as far as knowledge, skills, abilities, and training received to date.
11.3.6.4 – Describe the measurement, metrics, and Key Performance Indicators (KPIs) utilized by the PMO to measure project and program success.	Metrics are selected and applied to both individual projects as well as to the collection of projects in the portfolio.
	The PMO analyzes those metrics and provides the POC and/or EMC Planning Team with information that can be used to make decisions.
11.3.6.5 – Describe the organizational benefits and value the PMO provides to the enterprise.	Economic times are still tight, the insurance industry continues to be in a soft market, and our company just experienced one of its most catastrophic loss years in its 100-year existence. Resources are extremely limited, so it is crucial that we achieve our goals and objectives as efficiently and effectively as possible.
	From the Planning Team level down to the individual project team member, the PMO helps make the connections and establishes the transparency so the entire organization sees how the planning process fits together and is accomplished all the way down to the individual departmental action steps and project work. Everyone can now see "where the rubber actually meets the road."
	Plus, the processes must be consistent, understood, and utilized and when this is the case, projects start up much quicker and are managed more efficiently. And we also have a better "solution fit" the first time around. The PMO coaching and its training certainly helps in this regard along with all of the available documentation and examples.
	We manage risk better and we're better at predictability. And last, we maintain a solid set of Best Practices which are shared. We add to that bank of practices regularly through a standardized

approach to gathering and reporting out on Lessons Learned.

11.3.6.6 – Describe the economic benefits and value the PMO provides to the enterprise.

In most instances, faster or more efficient fosters lower expenses. With consistent, understood, and utilized processes, projects start up much quicker and are managed more efficiently today.

Plus, after a project closes (within a 4-to-12 month window), the PMO and POC obtain a benefits realization evaluation from the sponsor.

11.3.7 SURVEY – Additional Comments: Please provide any additional comments

---

In the 5 plus years of the EMC Insurance Companies' Program Management Office existence, since November 2006, here are the following highlights:

The PMO's Involvement with Projects

- Have worked on 93 different PMO-level projects to-date
- At inception, we started with an initial set of 25 projects
- Completed 69 projects over those 5 years
- On average, we typically have 23 active projects any given time
- We start just over 15 new projects each year; and we close just under 15 each year
- As far as those projects with a high priority status of Tier I level, the ratio is 25% to 75% at about any given time
- Average duration of PMO-level projects is just under 24 months
- Average effort per project is now just over 5,000 labor hours
- Average cost at END for each of these projects, which is mostly internal labor so salaries are already allocated, is approximately $300,000
- Average Net Present Value projected benefits over projected costs is approximately $1.5 million

The Involvement of EMC People

- To-date, 54 different project managers, from 5 different departments (out of 16); 80% of those PM's have received extensive training
- We've had 40 different sponsors and executive sponsors from 8 different departments
- We have used 334 different team members out of an employee base of about 2,200, including about 1,000 employees in the home office headquarters, where most project work takes place, and
- For increased competency, we've added 5 PMPs in these 5 years, 2 in the PMO and 3 elsewhere

Chapter 12

ILLUMINAT PMO Case Study

ILLUMINAT is a member of one of the largest conglomerates, the Neal and Massy Group of Companies (N&M), founded in 1932, which has been a leading force in business in the Caribbean for almost a century. ILLUMINAT was formed in 2001 from its founding companies that, for almost five decades, have pioneered the field of information technology and communications in the Caribbean. ILLUMINAT's parent company is the Neal and Massy ITC Group.

ILLUMINAT is in the information technology and communications business – providing products, services, and solutions that help effectively manage, develop, and troubleshoot businesses. It has strategic alliances and partnerships with global leaders in information and communications technology products, services and solutions integration. ILLUMINAT designs, implements, and maintains systems that allow their customers to exploit technology to achieve quantifiable improvement in business efficiency. It has a regional team of approximately 450 employees and main offices in Jamaica, Antigua, Barbados, Trinidad, and Tobago and partnerships in Belize, Cayman Islands, St. Lucia, St. Vincent, Grenada, Guyana, and Suriname.

12.1   ILLUMINAT – Enterprise and PMO Office Information

Enterprise Name:	ILLUMINAT
Country:	Trinidad and Tobago, West Indies
Industry:	Information and Communications Technologies (ICT)
Enterprise – Annual Sales Revenue:	Small, less than $100 Million US Dollars
Enterprise – Full-time Employee Equivalents:	Approximately 450
World Wide Web Site:	www.illuminatnm.com
PMO Name:	ILLUMINAT Project Management Services Unit

Title of PMO Leader:	Regional Manager – Project Management Services
PMO Position in Organizational Structure:	Enterprise-wide
PMO reports to in Organizational Structure:	CEO of ILLUMINAT and Chairman of the Neal & Massy ITC Group
PMO Annual Operating Budget:	$900,000 US Dollars
PMO – Full-time Employee Equivalents:	Approximately 12, distributed across 3 countries (Trinidad, Barbados, Jamaica)

The following are the PMO Case Study Survey question sets and the associated responses as submitted by the ILLUMINAT Project Management Services Unit, with minor editing for format and consistency.

12.2   ILLUMINAT PMO Background, Innovations, and Impact

In the following three parts of this case study, the ILLUMINAT Project Management Services Unit provides an overview of the background and structure of its PMO, various innovations and best practices by the PMO, and the potential future business impact of the PMO.

> **12.2.1 SURVEY – PMO Background:** Describe your PMO, including background information on its scope, vision, mission, and position within the enterprise's organizational structure.

ILLUMINAT Project Management (PM) Services are available throughout the Caribbean region and can draw upon full-time or contract resources to support any project or customer. As an example of our reach (footprint), we have completed IT projects from the Bahamas in the North through to Suriname (Dutch Guiana) in South America.

The Project Management Office at ILLUMINAT is staffed with a complement of Managers, Project Managers and Project Office Administrators. Our team has expertise locally, regionally and internationally in Project, Program and Change Management delivering Information and Communications Technology (ICT) Solutions projects across multiple industries such as Telecommunications and IT, Financial Services, Government, Energy, Retail, Education, Utilities, Manufacturing, etc.

Our Project Management resources are a select group of business professionals with the ability to manage project challenges. They are the liaisons between business, technical, contractor, vendor, and customer teams on a project and serve as the single point of communication and coordination, attending to details while keeping a greater focus on the macro elements of the project. Using our methodology and tools to formally manage projects, our team provides stakeholders the assurance of productivity, governance, and benefits management to ensure project progress and success.

Our employees are members of the Project Management Institute (PMI) and the local PMI Chapters in the Caribbean and avidly ensure continuous professional development. ILLUMINAT's project management practitioners are PMI Project Management Professional (PMP) certified and comply with the PMI Code of Ethics and Professional Conduct.

The Regional Management of the PMO was established in January 2006 with the recruitment of the Regional Manager, Project Management Services. The office has a base in Trinidad with a mandate to establish a standard project management methodology throughout the region.

The Regional Manager is responsible for the planning, direction, and coordination of project management activities of the Organization regionally, to maximize the strategic use of project management and manage project governance, processes, methodology, and standards compliance. The Regional Manager's responsibilities includes improving effectiveness and efficiency (performance) of the projects, while integrating with the business units and identifying and implementing areas for improvement to help satisfy our clients expectations and returns on investment, as well as, to develop the Project Management IQ, maturity and competencies within the organization.

The PMO reports directly to the CEO in each territory and is considered a Support Unit to the organization. It is independent of any Business Unit in order to provide services across the Enterprise and across the Region. Collectively the three Enterprise PM Offices form the Regional PM Services structure given below in Figure 12-1.

FIGURE 12-1: ILLUMINAT Regional Project Management Services Structure

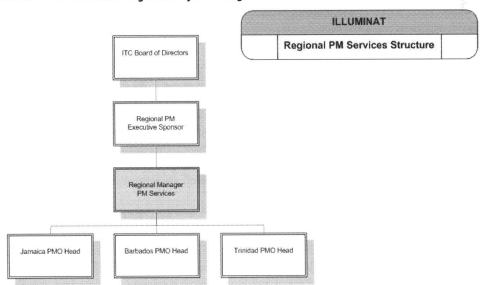

ILLUMINAT Project Management Office (PMO) Mandate
- The PMO is an enabling support services unit that creates a home for project management and supports project excellence at ILLUMINAT.
- The PMO defines the path to developing PM maturity and competency within the organization.
- The PMO assesses project performance and implements continuous improvement initiatives.

PMO Purpose Statement
- To design, develop, and deploy a common Project Management Methodology that will ensure project and proposal success utilizing an integrated approach across the business.
- To provide enterprise-wide project management services, delivering within budget and on time, maximizing efficiencies and ensuring customer satisfaction while enhancing the skills of the human resources involved.
- To support and facilitate project delivery success that is far superior to any competitor in the region.

PMO Objectives
- Develop a Common Project Management Methodology
- Ensure Adherence of Business Practices - Ensure "Good Business"
- Ensure Success of Projects
- Ensure Success of Proposals
- Enable an Integrated approach for Business
- Provide Project Management Tools, Best Practices, and Support across the Business

PMO Services
- Project Information Management
- Professional Development
- Project Management
- Project Consulting

PMO Services Taglines
- *External*: ILLUMINAT Project Management Services – Executing Projects, Managing Business Transformation, Delivering Results
- *Internal*: The Project Management Office "Empowering for Success"

12.2.2 SURVEY – PMO Innovations and Best Practices: Address the challenges your enterprise encountered prior to implementing the new PMO practices and how you overcame those challenges. Describe clearly and concisely the practices implemented and their effect on project, program, and/or portfolio and organizational success.

ILLUMINAT was established in 2001 as a result of the merger of three Neal & Massy (N&M) companies operating in the Information and Communications Technology (ICT) sector. As such, there were various organizational cultures and processes brought together into one company. The effects of these variations prompted the need for organizational integration, as ILLUMINAT became a products, services, and solutions provider to the largest clients in the Caribbean including several governments throughout the Caribbean.

The company attempted to accomplish this integration through the application of 1 or 2 project managers assigned to major projects. However, challenges remained such as uncoordinated implementations, excessive rework, overburdened resources, inadequate project documentation, scope creep, poor communications, poor scheduling, and estimating (time and cost), high project costs, schedule overruns between 6 to 24 months and millions of dollars not billed as project change control was often absent. This caused about 75% of the projects to be considered challenged or failed projects and prompted ILLUMINAT executives to formulate a strategy to implement a Project Management Services Unit and to invest in Project Management.

The CEO and Chairman recruited a Regional Manager for the Project Management Services Unit who defined the role and the department's mandate or "Charter" by soliciting the business needs from the Senior Management across the enterprise. A five-year-plan was then developed to elevate the Project Management Maturity Level and to integrate Project Management into the culture of the organization.

In 2006, the PMO in its current form was officially established with 2 resources, both working on the largest or most strategic projects for the organization while building the Project Management (PM) framework and supporting methodology, tools, and templates as well as providing various training programs for the Managers, Team Leaders, and Technical resources.

The greatest challenge besides developing the methodology expeditiously was to have it distributed and adopted across the organization. Emphasis was placed on Organizational Change Management to influence communications, resistance to change, process adoption, and culture change.

We employed several strategies such as creating a corporate email address for the PMO and a presence on the corporate intranet with simple PM training materials. The PMO Newsletter was developed and distributed bi-monthly. We also distributed several communiqués via email to all employees. We established a community of practice and met monthly commencing with a handful of employees that grew to 10% of the organization's employees at a time.

By the end of 2006, customers were beginning to notice a change in ILLUMINAT's approach to project delivery. ILLUMINAT's proposal win ratio began to improve as the quality of proposals improved, thereby winning larger projects up to 7 times the average project size.

The PM resources were in high demand and a Project Office Administrator was recruited to the unit to support the Project Managers and the operations of the PMO. Proposals and Projects were registered with the PMO for tracking, reporting, and strategic resources prioritization. Due to the high demand, further efforts were made to develop the Senior Engineers and Senior Technical resources to manage the smaller projects while the Project Managers managed the larger more strategic projects.

Guidelines were developed to assist the employees to determine when to engage the PMO based on project value, estimated project duration, and project complexity, including the number of departments involved in a cross-functional solutions project, risks and liabilities, PM Maturity of the client organization and strategic importance of the client or the solution to the organization.

The Organization realized the first year benefits of project management and doubled its investment to increase the reach of the unit. The PMO actively participated in the strategic planning sessions across the region since that year. The PMO set and achieved the target to have 100% of the Project Managers become members of PMI and the local PMI chapter as well as certified Project Management Professionals (PMPs) within 1 year.

The PMO in collaboration with the Legal Department of the parent company developed a contracting workshop for employees. The collaborative effort ensures that corporate risks are mitigated via contracts and managed via Project Management in accordance with the commercial agreement.

ILLUMINAT has built an integrated framework, combining procedures and tools from international standards and various project management methodologies. This combination creates a rich and robust set of methods, tools and standards to optimize the Project Management practice at ILLUMINAT which has been recognized by the ICT industry for excellence and awarded "Project of the Year" and "Project Manager of the Year."

By the end of the second year, the ICT Society of Trinidad & Tobago hosted an awards ceremony for Project Excellence where ILLUMINAT was evaluated by an international panel of judges and awarded the following honors.

- *Winner* – Project Manager of the Year Award
- *Winner* – Mobile Technology Project of the Year
- *Finalist* – Business to Business Project of the Year

The ICT industry's peers now recognized ILLUMINAT for its selection of projects and its ability to deliver these projects.

The PMO's contribution to the organization was an overall improvement in the following:
- Image of ILLUMINAT

- Employee Morale
- Employee Productivity
- Customer Service & Quality
- Good Business Practices
- Expense Management
- Receivables and Inventory Management
- Operational Efficiency

Seeking to embed Project Management across the organization while integrating the organization, the PMO developed the "*Orientation to the PMO*" for all new employees to the organization, which is hosted monthly.

The *Annual PMO Awards and Recognition Ceremony* was established to encourage the practice of the PM Methodology with continuous improvement towards raising the organization's PM maturity level and to reward and recognize employees for their contribution. Each year there are 2 team awards, the "*Excellence Team Award*" and the "*Commendation Team Award*". Also, there is an individual award, the "*Special Recognition Award.*" Nominations are submitted by employees and evaluated by the PMO team.

ILLUMINAT's Regional Manager was appointed to the local PMI Chapter's Board of Directors further demonstrating ILLUMINAT's position in the industry and its rise in just a few years with such a small team.

The organization also rewarded all the Project Managers as they attended the PMI North America Congress in Denver, in 2008, as part of their professional development plan, and to celebrate their PMP certification achievement.

The Enterprise again realizing the benefits and value of Project Management increased its investment for a third time, allowing the unit to recruit more Project Managers where the top 1% of applicants were selected. The response to the recruitment was the largest ever seen demonstrating the reputation in the industry and making the ILLUMINAT PM Services a highly sought after and competitive organization with which to work.

ILLUMINAT PMO employees were appointed to 3 more Board positions on the local PMI Chapters in the Caribbean and several Committee positions as well. ILLUMINAT was the leading Sponsor in the PMI Southern Caribbean Chapter Conference, which is the largest Project Management Conference in the Caribbean. The PMO thus became a brand ambassador for the organization.

The PMO also developed a partnership approach/model to professional development when it provided training in Business Analysis for all PMs as well as other employees from 5 departments across the organization.

For the commemoration of the 2009 Annual International Project Management Day, the PMO hosted an event featuring 6 presentations on key aspects of the PM methodology and a podcast by Dr. H. Kerzner, which was attended to full capacity by employees including the Senior Executives across the enterprise.

The PMO implemented "Spotlight," a bi-monthly focus on a successfully delivered project that highlights benefits realization to the client, the company, the development of the Caribbean, etc. It highlights these projects and the challenges and innovations applied on the project that enabled success.

The PMO won new clients and is providing its PM professional services to clients directly, while still supporting the implementation projects coming through the sales organization.

The Project Managers also develop Project Cash Flow reports that feed into the Organization's financial reporting. This assists the Senior Management to determine when to expect sources of revenue as well as where and when sources of funding are required to manage and balance the organization's portfolio.

Performance Objectives for the Project Managers include quantitative metrics such as Customer Satisfaction, Utilization, Erosion, Productivity and other measures of project success.

In order for Project Managers to develop broad experience across Telecommunications and Information Systems in both the private and public sectors, they are assigned to diverse projects within their nation and culture as well as those in other nations and cultures. Some projects are large or long and some are smaller or quicker.

This gives our Project Managers a diversity that makes them versatile and adaptable to any situation they encounter.

ILLUMINAT and its PM Services Unit were featured in Dr. Harold Kerzner's 2010 book, *Project Management Best Practices – Achieving Global Excellence* Second Edition. Harold Kerzner, Ph.D. is Senior Executive Director with International Institute for Learning, Inc. He is a globally recognized expert on project, program, and portfolio management, total quality management, and strategic planning and the author of several best-selling books about project management.

The PMO hosted an event to commemorate the International Project Management Day 2011 with a Corporate Group-wide seminar, which included attendance from 4 countries, 15 companies and presentations from CEOs discussing the role of Project Management in Corporate Strategy.

The team continues to meet bi-weekly where the agenda items focus on what is happening in the industry, in the organization, and within the department. The projects' updates are given and challenges or issues are discussed with different approaches or solutions offered to assist peers. This encourages the team to share learning and offer insights based on diverse experiences and develops a supportive environment for Project Management capability enhancement.

Lastly, the PMO achievements in the last year included:

- Increased level of certifications in ITIL and PMI (PMP and CAPM)
- Increased affiliations and leadership positions in industry such as PMI, the ICT Society of Trinidad & Tobago, the World Information Technology and Services Alliance (WITSA)
- Increased training offered to external organizations
- Increased external business closing on target
- Hosted 4th Annual PM Recognition and Awards

- Hosted level 2 employee training where registration was filled within 24 hours with 240 hours of training time provided, and 80 certifications awarded.
- PMO process alignment with the ITIL Service Management Framework
- Hosted International Project Management Day with Executive presentations via webinar
- Provided project support to other Neal & Massy ITC Group companies
- Issued Regional PM Newsletter and Project Spotlights

At ILLUMINAT, we have built project management capability to seize and execute attractive opportunities and have utilized our skills regionally servicing our customers' projects. We have continued to evolve and develop PM maturity, capability and competency across the organization and improved project performance and organizational performance. We have deployed a common PM Methodology that has contributed to project and proposal success utilizing an integrated approach across the organization. The PMO has facilitated project delivery success that is demonstrating a far superior approach to any competitor in the region and this is evidenced by the major deals that we attract. The PMO is a repository for project information and best practices vital to improving the knowledge assets of the organization that creates a competitive advantage for the company and enables competition with the traditional consulting firms in terms of the provision of project management services. The PMO continues its efforts to integrate the organization and to elevate even further the Organizational PM Maturity level.

Greatest Impact to the Organization

The ILLUMINAT PMO now has a structured coordinated approach to all projects. Project documentation is now standard on all projects whereas before it was isolated and adhoc. Change is both managed and billed, thereby reducing the revenue erosion, and vast improvements were made to the scheduling and estimating (time and cost), thereby improving business results. Now the company is integrated and positioned to win larger projects than it did before. The overall result is the assurance and reputation of the company for being able to deliver projects successfully for our clients, hence added value and business growth.

> **12.2.3 SURVEY – PMO Future Impact:** Briefly describe your PMO's plans for 2012 and beyond - please describe how those plans will potentially impact your enterprise and its organizational structure.

PMO's Plans for 2012

1) Further enhance governance process and Enterprise Project Management and Document Management capability

2) Focus on enterprise wide project reviews and audits

3) Further develop Project Management training curriculum and performance measurement, analysis and reporting tools.

4) Continue with the standard services offered and increase new services capability

5) Grow Project Management Services External Business

Impact to the Organization

- Superior Performance and Industry Leadership
- Enterprise and resource capability advancement
- Improved efficiency and revenue earning capability including new services offerings and revenue streams
- Demonstrated value and benefits realization
- Improved standardization, compliance and enterprise alignment

Some Measures of Success

- *Erosion* – Improvements in estimating and the application of project change control enabled a 100% reduction in PMO revenue erosion in 4 years - exceeding targets for the first 3 years
- *Employee PMO Satisfaction* – Improved by 9% over last year. The PMO continues to be ranked as a leading department in the organization
- *Client Project Management Satisfaction* – Improved by 9% over last year.
- *Resource Productivity* – 20% above target
- *Resource Utilization* – Improved by 7% over last year
- *PMO Employee Performance* – 12% above target
- *Revenue* – PMO moved from a cost centre to a revenue generator

12.3   ILLUMINAT PMO Model Components

In the following six parts of this case study, ILLUMINAT Project Management Services Unit provides its descriptions of how they implement the six key components of the Project Business Management Organization model: Governance; Methodology; Capability; Planning; Execution; and Sustainability.

12.3.1 SURVEY – PMO Governance: Describe how your PMO presents itself as an executive-level management business function, how it addresses setting policy and establishing charters, and how it provides an organizational model for the business management of portfolios, programs, and projects and the establishment of portfolio, program, and project management offices.

The PMO operates as an Executive Level management business function by attending all Senior Management meetings and by providing support to the Executive Strategy Implementation (5-year corporate strategy) progress meetings. The PMO provides the N&M ITC Group Chairman with benchmarking reports and comparative analysis reporting in Project Management. PM Maturity Audits are done across the enterprise, Project Cash-flow reporting feeds into the financial reporting. Continuous Improvement initiatives are planned and executed annually.

Whitepapers and reports are authored and submitted to the Chairman for business evolution. Corporate Risk and Quality Management functions reside with the PMO which manages organizational work plans, resourcing and execution. The PMO also issues policies, templates, methods and tools across the enterprise, delivers presentations at the employee and managerial levels, and supports the business' objectives while growing its own external business, thus truly demonstrating returns on investment.

12.3.1.1 – How long has the PMO been in place? *When was it started?*	The PMO has been in place for six years. The PMO in its present configuration was established January 2006 with the recruitment of a Regional Manager for Project Management Services.
12.3.1.2 – What is the relationship of PMO management to the enterprise's operational management?	The PMO reports to the CEO of ILLUMINAT and the Chairman of the Neal & Massy ITC Group. It provides support to the 4 business units and this year has officially become a business unit as well, moving from a cost centre to a revenue generator.
12.3.1.3 – How is the PMO internally structured (positions, roles etc.)?	The Managers, Project Managers and Project Officers and Administrators all report to the Regional Manager for Project Management Services. The PMO has a flat hierarchy to foster a collaborative team focused on achieving common organizational objectives.
12.3.1.4 – How are the PMO's operations funded?	The PMO in past years was fully funded by the business units, however, in this financial year, the PMO is only partially funded as the PMO is now a revenue generator due to its growth in PM maturity, industry leadership, and recognition with external clients of its own.

12.3.1.5 – What is the summary position description of the PMO leader?	The PMO Leader position is responsible for the planning, direction and coordination of project management activities for the organization regionally, to maximize the strategic application of project management and maintain functions such as project governance, processes, methodology, and standards compliance. This role also manages a team of project managers and other project management resources.

12.3.1.6 – What position requirements are used as a basis for selecting the PMO leader?

- Diverse Experience
- PMO experience
- Personal Maturity
- Project Management Maturity
- Leadership qualities and skills
- Demonstrated capability and thorough domain expertise.
- Cultural approach and disposition
- Behavioral and personality traits
- Attitude and aptitude for excellence
- Persistence, determination, dedication
- As well as, the traditional tertiary level education, industry experience, industry credentials, etc.

12.3.1.7 – Is the PMO a Profit & Loss cost center or considered overhead?	The PMO is now only partially funded by the business units, since the PMO has become a revenue generator and profit center.
12.3.1.8 – What current challenge is the PMO dealing with?	Evolving the unit and its resources during the transition from internally focused to balancing internal and external priorities and client demands. Managing competing demands and balancing internal and external portfolios is a new challenge that will fade when we complete our year of transition and operation under the new business model.

Success can be challenging and in professional services, the reward for good work is more work.

12.3.2 SURVEY – PMO Methodology / Standardization: Describe what standardization your PMO has implemented across the enterprise that examines: identification and integration of processes and practices; development of standardized Project Business Management processes; and documentation of enterprise-wide portfolio, program, and project management process methodology models, including their associated policies, practices, and procedures.

ILLUMINAT has built an integrated framework (the core of which is based on the PMI PMBOK Guide) combining procedures and tools from international standards and project management methodologies such as ISO, PMBOK and PRINCE2.

To complement the ILLUMINAT Methodology, the framework also adopts certain tools and procedures from other professional disciplines. This combination creates a rich and robust set of methods, tools and standards to optimize the Project Management practice and profession at ILLUMINAT.

Training, Tools, Templates, Processes and practices have been developed and are annually reviewed and improved to evolve the organization in the quest for excellence. Project Managers working across the enterprise aid in the utilization and distribution of common practices as well as annual training programs available to all employees and delivered by the PMP credentialed Project Managers.

The PMO function is also improving its knowledge assets and processes by aligning operations with the IT Infrastructure Library (ITIL) Standard for Service Management Framework. Of course, the PMO is customizing its alignment with ITIL to suit a PMO environment versus an IT Operations environment.

Lastly, various systems embedded in the operations processes and practices ensure compliance and standardization across the enterprise. Such systems include Financial Systems, Time Reporting Systems, Project Performance Reporting, Performance Appraisal System, Client Satisfaction Surveying and Reporting, and other custom built PMO and project tools.

12.3.2.1 – Describe the standards utilized by the PMO to ensure the enterprise's project / program / portfolio management goals and objectives are achieved.

ILLUMINAT has built an integrated framework combining procedures and tools from international standards and project management methodologies such as the *PMBOK Guide* 4th edition and PRINCE2.

To complement the ILLUMINAT Methodology, the framework also adopts certain tools and procedures from other disciplines such as IT Infrastructure Library (ITIL) Service Management Framework, Occupational Safety and Health (OHSAS 18001 and the regulatory OSH Act), Contract Management, Supply Chain and Logistics Management, Organizational Change Management (PROSCII and Change Wheel Model), Document and Configuration Management, Contracting and Procurement Management, Internal Auditing, Quality Management (ISO 9000:2000, ISO 9001:2000, ISO 9004:2000) as well as other best practice implementation methodologies from our technology partners and other professional networks such as ORACLE (AIM), PeopleSoft, CISCO, EMC, AVAYA, (COMPASS), (CVP), etc.

12.3.2.2 – Describe the project management process guidelines being employed by the PMO.

The project management process guidelines follow a typical cascade/waterfall model spanning the entire project/program lifecycle starting with Pre-Sales, Sales, Contracting, Initiating, Planning, Executing and Controlling, and Closing.

Further, the project management process is integrated with the Systems Development Life Cycle (SLDC) or Systems Implementation Life Cycle (SILC), which includes Definition, Design, Development, Testing, Knowledge Transfer, Deployment, etc. Flow Charts and Job Aids visually depict and guide practitioners and employees on the integration of Project Management Deliverables with IT and Telecommunications Product Deliverables.

12.3.2.3 – What systems, tools, and templates make your PMO successful?

It is difficult to identify specific items to answer this question. The Framework is an integrated system of People, Processes, and Tools. Success is derived by the continuous evolution of the practice at ILLUMINAT in the quest for excellence. The components for success include:

- Professional Development;
- Performance Appraisals;
- PMO assignments for continuous improvement of tools and templates;
- Application of standards and best practices to define the processes and deliverables for successful project outcomes; and
- Utilization of project management tools and business systems to provide the quantitative metrics and key performance indicators necessary to manage the PMO and its resources to meet the objectives of the organization.

Such Key Performance Indicators include :
1) Customer Satisfaction
2) Employee Satisfaction
3) Productivity
4) Efficiency
5) Utilization
6) Erosion
7) Performance
8) Revenue/Profitability
9) Brand reputation
10) Organization integration
11) Regional integration

12.3.2.4 – Describe how management at all levels is directly involved in the development of the PMO and it processes.

Feedback is elicited via the quarterly internal client satisfaction surveys. Feedback is assessed, analyzed and actioned for continuous improvement. Feedback is received both via formal and informal means. The Chairman and the CEO set the objectives and targets for the PMO annually and conduct the performance appraisal on the PMO Leader at the half year and end of year. Client demands and needs also serve as inputs for PMO development and evolution.

The PMO is a service organization in the business of providing services required for the business to achieve it objectives. Given the above feedback mechanisms to the PMO, the management has a direct contribution to the development of the PMO.

12.3.2.5 – Describe the implementation plan you used for establishing project / program / portfolio management standards across your enterprise.

When ILLUMINAT recruited the Regional Manager for Project Management Services, he immediately met with all Executives and Senior Management to understand the challenges of the past and to identify the needs and expectations of the organization. This formed the job description for the Regional Manager. The Project Management Office then created a PMO Mandate Document to guide the purpose and strategy of the PMO. This was initially set for 3 years and included the following objectives and goals;

Objectives

Develop a Common PM Methodology
- Develop Standards compliant with (PMI)
- Tools
- Process
- Templates
- Archives

Ensure adherence of Business Practices
- Implement a Governance Structure
- Project Selection
- Prioritization
- Definition
- Resource Allocation
- Budget Approvals
- Exit Gates – Approval to Continue
- Compliance to Methodology
- Work Authorization Sanctioning and Payment – Contractors

Ensure Success of Projects
- Customer Relationships
- Building Capability with Clients
- Guidance
- Planning
- Resource Scheduling
- Estimating/Costing (Analysis)
- Skill set and Caliber of resources

Ensure Success of Proposals
- Evaluate Business Opportunity
- Facilitate development of Complex Proposals
- Screen Proposals and Sanitize
- Ensure Professional Presentation/Appeal

Enable an Integrated approach for Business
- Collaborative Approach across the Business relating to the Integrated ILLUMINAT Solutions Approach
- New Business Acquisition Process (Sales)
- Corporate policy compliance (Receivables, Payables, HR)
- Integrated Team Approach
- Commitment/Negotiator for resource Allocation and Resource Retrieval

Provide Project Management Tools, Best Practices and Support across the Business
- Acquire Tools (Visio, MS Project Licenses)
- Certify/Maintain Certification Requirements/Forums/Conferences/ etc.
- Staged approach to Training – Beginner/Intermediate/Advance
- Scheduled Communication
- Informative Sessions
- Apprenticeship/Mentorship
- Special Interest Sessions
- Industry Specific Knowledge

Goals
1) Framework is widely communicated/distributed accessible
2) Improved Project Metrics in efficiencies & effectiveness
3) Evident improvement of PM IQ of the organization

4) Transition from a Tactical / Delivery approach to a Strategic /Consultative approach
5) Integrated Program Management
6) Integrated Portfolio Management

It was well known that as a matter of priority, a Project Management Framework and Methodology was needed and then the adherence to that methodology would be required.

The Methodology selected was based on International Standards and Best practices in alignment with PMI's PMBOK. Over a 3-month period, simple tools and templates were developed as well as training presentations. A Community of Practice was initiated and training was rolled out across the organization. Several Communiques and Newsletters were also developed and distributed.

In the first year, frequent communications from the Regional Manager and the CEO were required to reinforce the importance of the PMO to the organization and the adoption of the PM procedures to the way we do business at ILLUMINAT.

Additional investment was made in recruitment to double the strength of the PMO and ensure sufficient coverage across the Enterprise. Senior Management received specific training with customized integrated Legal, Business and Project Management training. Similarly, training was customized for Sales and Technical Implementation teams with guides being developed and distributed as well.

Year after year, the PMO continues to host a minimum of 2 to 3 training cycles. It creates, at least annually, a strategic plan for continuous improvement, with 10 to 12 development initiatives executed and deployed for PMO evolution and Organizational Project Management Maturity improvement.

12.3.2.6 – How does the PMO use project, program, and portfolio management standards to optimize its practices?

As detailed in the answers to Survey Questions 12.3.2.1 and 12.3.2.2 above, the PMO at ILLUMINAT has built an integrated framework combining procedures and tools from many international standards, project management methodologies, and other professional disciplines.

Are they based on PMI' or other industry guides and are they updated as new editions of the guides are released?

As new editions of the various standards and guide are released, the ILLUMINAT framework and methodology is updated, where it is deemed appropriate.

12.3.3   SURVEY – PMO Capabilities: Describe development and assessment of the enterprise's abilities, describe any project management competency model, summarize any education and training program, describe any established career path progression plan, and outline key Enterprise Environmental Factors.

The PMO conducted several qualitative assessments utilizing PM Solutions Maturity Assessment, Kerzner's Maturity Assessment and PMI's OPM3 Assessment. However, in 2010, a benchmark study was performed on all 3 territory Enterprise PMOs using a Maturity Assessment Template. The Maturity Assessment Tool examines a number of factors and provides results in categories aligned to the 9 Knowledge areas of the PMBOK. The result of that study led to the development of an action log to move the organization and the PMO from a level 2 to a level 3. That plan contained eighty-three (83) areas to be developed and implemented before the Enterprise conducted another quantitative assessment. The plan is now 93% complete and the next benchmark study is expected in 2012 where a quantitative result of Level 3 is the target.

The PMO also assesses Project Managers and other Project Management resources twice a year. Further, career path and competency development consider both training and experiential exposure.

Attendance at conferences, subscriptions and memberships, assignments on committees, various projects, certification, etc. are all factored at the beginning of each year and reviewed during the year and achievements evaluated at the end of the year.

Annually the PMO team plans the training required for the organization by reviewing areas of non-conformance, incident and issue recurrences, areas for advancement to the next level of competency, areas based on market demand or regulatory requirements, areas based on client feedback, etc. This way the training in any particular year is of immediate need and benefit to the enterprise.

12.3.3.1 – Describe the components of your enterprise's training program.

Annually the PMO team plans the training required for the organization by reviewing areas of non-conformance, incident and issue recurrences, areas for advancement to the next level of competency, areas based on market demand or regulatory requirements, areas based on client feedback, etc. This way the training in any particular year is of immediate need and benefit to the enterprise.

The training for the Organization's employees have included the following:

- Proposal Preparation
- Project Charter
- Project Change Control
- Requirements Gathering
- Value of Project Management
- Roles and Responsibilities on Projects
- Work Breakdown Structures
- Schedule and Cost Estimating
- Scope Management
- Communications
- Risk Management
- Project Reporting
- Understanding Contracts – A business approach
- Linking Project Management to Leadership & Strategy
- Project Management Capability & Capacity in executing Strategy
- Case Study review of a High Risk Major Project from Structuring, Governance & Strategy
- Project Management for Sales Teams
- Project Management for Implementation Teams
- Project Management for Supporting Teams
- Project Management Methodology Fundamentals
- Project Planning
- Project Closure
- Stakeholder Analysis
- Leadership in Project Management

The training for PMO's employees have included the following:

- Business Analysis
- Understanding personalities for teamwork
- Consulting and Relationships
- Organizational Change Management
- Power, Politics, Leadership, Influence
- Negotiation
- Strategy Formulation
- PMI Chapter monthly meetings
- PMI Chapter Conferences
- PMI North America Congress
- ITIL Foundations
- Business Continuity Planning

12.3.3.2 – Describe the value your enterprise places on education and training and its goals and objectives.

Our organization is in the business of technology. Therefore as a service provider, we are critically dependent on the expertise of our human resources.

As such, ILLUMINAT places great value and investment in competency development and certifications. Likewise, the PMO invests annually in its resources' competencies advancement.

The PMO has invested in all employees becoming PMP or CAPM certified as well as ITIL certified, Business Continuity Planning (BCP) certified, etc. Training is both formal and informal, local and international, in-house and outsourced.

A library has been developed, employees attending training return and present on their learning experience with their peers. Meetings are scheduled twice a month for peer to peer reviews and learning. A lessons learned and best practice library has been developed with inputs from all members of the team.

Value is derived from improved capabilities in technocratic, strategic, and relational domains and the PMO invests continuously in advancing the team in the quest for excellence. Both time and budget are allocated throughout each year.

The PMO also invests in subscriptions and memberships for its resources and assists with industry leading appointments on committees. All members of the PMO attend PMI Chapter technical sessions, seminars and conferences.

12.3.3.3 – Does the enterprise have a project management career path program? If so, what are the components?

Yes, ILLUMINT has developed a Career Path Program that is presently going through its second iteration in 2012.

The components of this include everything from the job posting, to the recruitment of a new hire, to the orientation of the new hire, to the experience levels, salary levels, performance review cycles, succession plans, components of compensation, training requirements, certification requirements, job profile hierarchy, affiliations and leadership assignments, etc.

Further, Career Path and Competency Development consider both training and experiential exposure.

12.3.3.4 – Describe the measurements, metrics, and Key Performance Indicators (KPI's) utilized by the PMO to determine the organization's knowledge, skills, and level of achievement.

As described under the general Survey Question 1.3.3 above, the PMO has conducted several qualitative assessments utilizing various maturity assessment models. These assessments are performed on all 3 territory Enterprise PMOs

Other Key Performance Indicators include:
1) Customer Satisfaction Index
2) Employee Satisfaction Index
3) Awards and Recognition
4) Affiliations and Industry Leadership roles
5) Industry Presentations, Publications and Invitations for participation
6) Portfolio Expansion

12.3.3.5 – Does the enterprise employ a project management competency model? If yes, please describe it. If no, why not?

Yes. The PMO assesses Project Managers and other Project Management resources twice a year, which incorporates the PMI Project Management Competency Development Framework areas of Knowledge, Performance, and Personal Attributes assessments.

Attendance at conferences, subscriptions and memberships, assignments on committees, various projects, certification, etc. are all factored at the beginning of each year and reviewed during the year and achievements evaluated at the end of the year. The Performance Appraisal also includes Performance Objectives, Compliance Objectives, Behavioral Objectives, Employee's self-assessment, Manager's assessment, and Professional Development Plans.

12.3.4 SURVEY – PMO Business Planning: Discuss strategic business planning, tactical business planning, business objective (project) development and prioritization, and project identification, selection, and authorization.

The PMO participates at the Organization's Strategic Level and participates in the Strategic Planning annually. The PMO understands each of the Business and Support Units objectives and identified projects for the coming year and develops a Demand Forecast for the Project Management Office.

The PMO also looks at its present Strategic Plans and its Operational Requirements and collates all the Plans to create a budget and work plan for the year. This is then allocated to the next level within the PMO in the form of work assignments, performance objectives, PMO development initiatives, annual operations events and projects. This spans 4 main portfolios. Operations, Communications, Systems and New Business. The Regional Manager works with the PMO Team members for the execution of these Programs/Portfolios for the fiscal year.

Prioritization, Selection and Authorization of initiatives considers various factors such as, economic value, complexity, risk, strategic significance, strategic demand, liability, etc. Besides the Annual Planning, reviews of the plan and modifications are made at the half year and quarterly if required.

12.3.4.1 – Describe the organizational structure and process used for corporate strategic business planning.	The Organization has 5 business units (profit centers) and 6 support units (cost centers). Corporate Strategic Planning is done for 5-year plans, 3-year plans, and annual plans.
Does the PMO play a role in the process? If so, describe the PMOs role and responsibilities.	Each year the annual plans are developed by various business and support units and presented collaboratively across the Senior Management Level. This provides all stakeholders input to the plans and to consider impacts of the plans to their plans. The PMO is present in all Strategic Plans as the PMO is a key stakeholder for execution of the plan. The PMO reviews the plan and provides input to resourcing, budgeting, scheduling, risk mitigation and contingency planning, executing, organizational change management, quality and reporting.
12.3.4.2 – How is the strategic plan implemented with a project forecast plan?	The 5-year strategic plan is divided into different Goal Horizons i.e. 1-year, 3-year and 5-year plans. This is then further developed into annual strategic plans with annual budgets allocated during the annual budget and forecast planning period, usually in Q3 of each fiscal year. The annual plan is then assessed for the demand forecast on human resources, cost, time and materials. The annual plan priorities are then determined and the budget allocated for the next fiscal year. When the prioritized projects are ready to be initiated, a request for resources is submitted, resources are identified and allocated to the project for planning and execution. A project manager is assigned to manage and oversee the implementation of the project for the sponsoring organization.

The project objectives, milestones, schedule, targets, etc. are defined in the initiating and planning stages. After the planning stage is completed, the project team executes the project to achieve the required business outcomes.

12.3.4.3 – How is strategic planning, culture, and selection of projects integrated?

The ILLUMINAT organization is a subsidiary company of a major conglomerate consisting of over seventy (70) companies. The Strategic Planning Culture has been established over eighty (80) plus years of operations across the group of companies.

There are several layers of project selection decision-making. The first level is at the Business Unit management layer followed by the Senior management. This is then presented at the Executive level and Board level. Based on the size of the investment required, the Holdings Company for the Group of companies requires presentation and approval of the business case from the investment committee for the group.

Overall, the process is a mature one rooted in finance and set on making wise investments to ensure good business decisions and to maximize returns. A formal business case is required including Market Analysis, Evaluation of Alternatives, Risk Assessments, etc.

The integration of the Strategic Planning Culture and Selection of Projects is evident as managers and senior managers understand the various levels of approval and so they only elevate the best developed business cases to the various stages of selection, thereby eliminating efforts on weak or poorly developed business opportunities.

> **12.3.5 SURVEY – PMO Business Execution:** Describe what role the PMO has in project selection, prioritization, and initiation; in portfolio, program and project execution planning; in stage-gate reviews; and in performance metrics selection and application.

The Regional Manager of the PMO is responsible for the project selection, prioritization, and initiation within the PM Services Unit. However, in the other business and support units of the organization, the PMO provides input to the resourcing, estimating, scheduling, risk assessment, etc. for the project selection, prioritization and initiation by the units' management and the organization's Executives as required.

The PMO also participates in stage gate reviews, project performance report presentations, etc. to provide support and assurance to the Executives that performance is on track and risks are mitigated. The PMO directly and indirectly develops or provides inputs to the project planning and execution for the organization.

12.3.5.1 – How are portfolios, programs, and projects selected and initiated?	Various business and support units in the organization identify, select, and prioritize projects for their areas of business. Once approval is granted by the Executives, the business unit engages the PMO to initiate, plan and execute the projects.
12.3.5.2 – How are projects organized and managed as a program and/or portfolio?	Projects are categorized or organized in programs and portfolios aligned to the business reporting of the company and the organizational structure of the company. This spans 4 main portfolios: Operations, Communications, Systems, and New Business.
12.3.5.3 – How are projects prioritized within a program and/or portfolio?	The Business Unit sponsoring the project within their program/portfolio prioritizes projects using various factors such as, economic value, complexity, risk, strategic significance, strategic demand, liability, etc.

12.3.5.4 – How does the enterprise define what project and program success is?

The PMO at ILLUMINAT has extended the definition of success from the traditional triple constraint project parameters of within budget, on schedule or earlier and within specification (scope and quality), to the greater business outcome parameters such as:

- Client Satisfaction - Testimonials
- Repeat Business – Customer loyalty
- Met Technical Objectives (Finished /Scope completed), Commitment to Quality
- Met Project Objectives (On schedule/On Budget/Meeting Specification - Scope completed) – Client Acceptance
- Business Objectives (Time to market), Improved outcome for client
- Set Precedents/Precedence
- Reciprocity – Valued Teamwork
- Delivered Safely – no accidents, loss time due to Health, Safety, Security or Environmental issues
- Managed Changes – no Erosion of business

12.3.5.5 – Does the PMO support the management of projects that would be considered operational in nature? If so, describe the types of projects.	Yes, the PMO is engaged by the organization's IT Unit to assist with the effective implementation of some routine operations such as a Telephony (PBX) upgrade or an IT application software upgrade.

The IT unit engages the PMO to assist with the project management considerations such as risk management, communications management, methodology compliance, organizational change management etc. This allows the Technical resources to remain focused on the technical considerations such as implementation, configuration, testing, release management, etc.

The collaborative approach between the PMO and the IT Unit leads to successful technology deployments with no significant disruption to the rest of the organization's business operations.

12.3.6 SURVEY – PMO Sustainability: Describe the overall impact of the PMO over a sustained period (e.g., customer satisfaction, productivity, reduced cycle time, growth, building or changing organizational culture, etc.). If available, please provide quantitative data to illustrate the areas in which the PMO has had the greatest business impact.

Overall Impact of the PMO Over a Sustained Period

1) *Customer Satisfaction* – Delivering to standards and expectations with professionalism
2) *Employee Satisfaction* – Eliminating inter-unit conflict for resources via an Enterprise PMO clearing the path for employees to deliver
3) *Productivity* – Significantly improved due to professional development and culture to achieve superior results
4) *Efficiency* – Developed capability through methodology and tools to do more with less
5) *Utilization* – Improved the standardization of professional services billable time tracking and management
6) *Erosion* – Significantly reduced revenue leakage due to poor estimating and effort not invoiced due to poor change management
7) *Revenue* – Develop new revenue channel and revenue recovery capability
8) *Brand Reputation* – Excellence in project delivery, formal and informal industry recognition. Clients and Partners actively seek to do business with ILLUMINAT.
9) *Organization Integration* – Uniform processes and standards, organizational capability improvement
10) *Regional Integration* – Benchmarking and standards. The Regional PMO

Integration process is providing synergies across the Caribbean where PM expertise from one territory can be applied in another, as well as the cross cultural innovations and learning are shared and applied across territories.

Impact to the Organization

- Superior Performance and Industry Leadership
- Enterprise and resource capability advancement
- Improved efficiency and revenue earning capability including new services offerings and revenue streams
- Demonstrated value and benefits realization
- Improved standardization, compliance and enterprise alignment

Some Specific Measures of Actual Success

- *Erosion* – Improvements in Estimating and the application of Project Change Control enabled a 100% reduction in PMO Revenue Erosion in 4 years - exceeding targets for the first 3 years
- *Employee PMO Satisfaction* – Improved by 9% over last year. The PMO continues to be ranked as a leading department in the organization
- *Client Project Management Satisfaction* – Improved by 9% over last year
- *Resource Productivity* – 20% above target
- *Resource Utilization* – Improved by 7% over last year
- *PMO Employee Performance* – 12% above target
- *Revenue* – PMO moved from a Cost Centre to a Revenue Generator

12.3.6.1 – What is included in a comprehensive project monitoring and control system and how is it implemented?

Some of the methods for Project Monitoring and Controlling at ILLUMINAT include:

- Project Performance Reporting
- Variance Analysis (Planned versus Actual)
- Risk Reviews
- Health Checks and Compliance Audits
- Peer Reviews
- Lessons Learned and Improvement plans based on learning
- Dashboard reporting and quantitative KPI reporting

These methods are implemented by the project managers on each project and by the PMO in its reporting to the Executives.

The Project Managers have in their performance appraisal objectives some of the above as requirements on their projects such as the performance reports, health checks and compliance audits, contribution of lessons learned, etc.

The Regional Manager reviews these items and provides further guidance where deemed appropriate.

12.3.6.2 – How are project start-up and gate review processes structured?

When a project has been selected and budgeted by a business unit, a request is sent to the PMO for a Project Manager to be assigned. The Project Manager then requests the Sponsor to register the project, create the Charter for the project, provide all supporting business case deliverables, preliminary scope state-ment etc. Once the Project Manager receives these documents, other resources are identified and assigned to the project to commence the project planning followed by execution.

The gate review processes are determined based on the mile-stones of the project. When a project reaches a major milestone, the project deliverables and documentation must be presented for review and an Executive review similar to a steering meeting presentation is performed by the Project Manager and Sponsor. The following are some factors required for presentation:

- Project Performance Reporting
- Variance Analysis (Planned versus Actual)
- Risk Reviews
- RAG Status
- Health Checks
- Lessons Learned
- Critical Issues
- Outlook
- Achievements

12.3.6.3 – Describe the project knowledge base system and how is it developed?

The project knowledge base includes the capture of lessons learned from all projects in the PMO over several years. Projects are categorized and deliverables are maintained for potential review in the event of similar or near similar deployments in the future. The PMO presently uses a shared network drive and is migrating this to a SharePoint system for the project deliverable and documentation repository.

Besides capturing project Lessons Learned, reviews are done to capture the Turning Points in a project or the critical lessons learned which are those activities that had they not occurred, the project would have been challenged or those activities that because they occurred, the project challenges were overcome.

This repository is constantly updated and reviewed and has become the ILLUMINAT Best Practice Library. It is a subset of all the lessons learned but holds a greater strategic value to the organization.

12.3.6.4 – Describe the measurement, metrics, and Key Performance Indicators (KPIs) utilized by the PMO to measure project and program success.

The PMO utilizes the following KPIs to measure success and the progress of various initiatives for continuous improvement in the projects and programs we undertake:

- Customer Satisfaction
- Employee Satisfaction
- Productivity
- Efficiency
- Utilization
- Erosion
- Brand Reputation
- Organization Integration
- Regional PMO Integration
- Training Hours in Project Management and Certifications awarded
- Enterprise and resource capability advancement
- Compliance to methodology
- PMO Employee Performance
- Repeat Business – Customer loyalty
- Health and Safety Training and reporting
- Maturity Level rating
- Program and Portfolio Value and number of projects
- Portfolio Health Index and Corporate risk
- Business Pipeline and Proposals Win Ratio

12.3.6.5 – Describe the organizational benefits and value the PMO provides to the enterprise.

Organizational benefits and value the PMO provides includes:

- Project Management Maturity advancement
- PM's contribution in the sales process for winning proposals
- Additional Professional Services revenue
- Increased confidence in the market of ILLUMINAT's ability to deliver
- Improved collaborative effort and integration of organization
- Organizational action and achievement orientation
- Organizational transformation of processes and systems
- Improved Efficiency
- Strategic and Competitive advantage

- Structured and coordinated approach to all projects
- Project documentation standardization
- Change management and reduced revenue erosion
- Improved scheduling and estimating (time and cost)
- Improved business results
- Integrated approach across the enterprise
- Positioned to win larger projects
- Improved assurance and reputation for successful project delivery
- Enterprise and resource capability advancement

At ILLUMINAT, we have built project management capability to seize and execute attractive opportunities and have utilized our skills regionally servicing our customers' projects. We have continued to evolve and develop PM maturity, capability and competency across the organization and improved project performance and organizational performance.

We have deployed a common PM Methodology that has contributed to project and proposal success utilizing an integrated approach across the organization. The PMO has facilitated project delivery success that is demonstrating a far superior approach to any competitor in the region and is evidenced by the major deals that we attract.

The PMO is a repository for project information and best practices vital to improving the knowledge assets of the organization that creates a competitive advantage for the company and enables competition with the traditional consulting firms in terms of the provision of project management services.

The PMO continues its efforts to integrate the organization and to elevate even further the Organizational PM Maturity level.

12.3.6.6 – Describe the economic benefits and value the PMO provides to the enterprise.

Economic Benefits of the PMO include the following;
- *Additional Professional Services revenue* - Alternate Revenue Channel PMO Direct Sales – over $400K
- *Alternate Revenue Channel PMO Project Change Control* – over $2.5M
- *Expense savings* – over $400K
- *Efficiency* – $120K
- *Utilization* – $250K
- *Productivity* – $60K

- *Performance* – $150K
- *Training and Capability Development* - $20K
- *Business Pipeline support* - $20K

Other Value the PMO provides:
- Project Management Maturity advancement
- PM's contribution in the sales process for winning proposals
- Increased confidence in the market of ILLUMINAT's ability to deliver
- Improved collaborative effort and integration of organization
- Organizational action and achievement orientation
- Organizational transformation of processes and systems
- Improved Efficiency
- Strategic and Competitive advantage
- Structured and coordinated approach to all projects
- Project documentation standardization
- Improved scheduling and estimating (time & cost)
- Improved business results
- Integrated approach across the enterprise
- Positioned to win larger projects
- Improved assurance and reputation for successful project delivery
- Enterprise and resource capability advancement

12.3.7 SURVEY – Additional Comments: Please provide any additional comments

The ILLUMINAT Project Management Services Unit did not provide any additional comments.

Chapter 13

Merchants Insurance Group PMO Case Study

Merchants Insurance Group, with its headquarters in Buffalo, New York, is comprised of the Merchants Mutual Insurance Company, Merchants National Insurance Company and the Merchants Preferred Insurance Company. These companies provide a variety of property and casualty insurance products for commercial and personal lines. Merchants provides high-quality and affordable insurance for home owners, automobile owners, and many businesses, such as contractors and business owners. Merchants' core states of operation are Massachusetts, Michigan, New Hampshire, New Jersey, New York, Ohio, Pennsylvania, Rhode Island and Vermont.

13.1 Merchants Insurance Group – Enterprise and PMO Office Survey Information

Enterprise Name:	Merchants Insurance Group
Country:	United States of America
Industry:	Property and Casualty Insurance
Enterprise – Annual Sales Revenue:	Medium; $100 Million to $1 Billion US Dollars
Enterprise – Full-time Employee Equivalents:	330
World Wide Web Site:	www.merchantsgroup.com
PMO Name:	Project Management Office
Title of PMO Leader:	Director
PMO Position in Organizational Structure:	Independent Department
PMO reports to in Organizational Structure:	Chief Financial Officer; dotted line to Chief Executive Officer

PMO Annual Operating Budget: $220,000 US Dollars

PMO – Full-time Employee Equivalents: 3

The following are the PMO Case Study Survey question sets and associated responses as submitted by the Merchants Insurance Group's Project Management Office, with minor editing for format and consistency.

13.2   Merchants Insurance Group PMO Background, Innovations, and Impact

In the following three parts of this case study, the Merchants Insurance Group's Project Management Office provides an overview of the background and structure of its PMO, various innovations and best practices by the PMO, and the potential future business impact of the PMO.

13.2.1   SURVEY – PMO Background: Describe your PMO, including background information on its scope, vision, mission, and position within the enterprise's organizational structure.

Background

Merchants Insurance Group determined that a more disciplined approach to project management ("PM") was necessary to achieve the maximum benefit from business investments. Introducing a standard, repeatable PM methodology and mentoring Project Leads to use the methodology effectively was the first step. Implementing a Project Management Office (PMO) and staffing it with professional project managers would advance the initial successes realized.

Mission

To turn Merchants' ability to complete projects, which add value to customers, into a competitive advantage.

Vision

To better satisfy the needs of Merchants' customers by being:

- The Center of Excellence for project management, equipping project teams with the knowledge, tools, and skills to initiate, plan, execute, and close projects using a set of consistent and repeatable PM Best Practices.

- The support organization that dramatically increases the likelihood of projects being delivered on schedule, within budget, and meeting quality expectations.

13.2.2 SURVEY – PMO Innovations and Best Practices: Address the challenges your enterprise encountered prior to implementing the new PMO practices and how you overcame those challenges. Describe clearly and concisely the practices implemented and their effect on project, program, and/or portfolio and organizational success.

Merchants Insurance Group faced a number of challenges in the project management area before the creation of the PMO, including:

- Resource capacity/need across the entire project portfolio was not well defined.
- Project management skills among the business managers were lacking.
- The IT department was the de facto controller of the project arena.
- There was no clear alignment between the project queue and corporate strategy.

The reality of a property-casualty insurance company is that it primarily does two things – processes transactions and works on projects.

As Merchants strove to improve the speed and accuracy of its transaction processing through automation, the required projects increasingly involved the Information Technology (IT) area of the company. Accordingly, the IT area defaulted into the company's center of knowledge for project scheduling and portfolio management.

One of the first tasks that the PM consultants achieved, when they were engaged in 2008, was to redirect the responsibility for projects back to the business users, and to set up a system of PM governance that recognized the IT area as a significant and talented resource to project completion, but not the center of project management.

This was a huge culture change for the company and a challenging transition for our IT colleagues – one that still poses the occasional challenge to the PMO.

The PMO has been instrumental in smoothing that transition by successfully partnering with the IT area to clarify, establish and enforce new guidelines in such areas as:

- Project change requests: placing responsibility for all PCR's with the business lead, and establishing a formal process for PCR review and approval;
- Project sign-offs: designing a new "turnover form" and sign-off process for each phase of the project;
- Requirement specifications: introducing (and making ongoing modifications to) a requirements specifications form, and ensuring that all projects have these in as detailed and comprehensive manner as necessary; and
- Post-deployment items: establishing responsibility for ensuring that all requirements are met before deployment of a project, identifying when IT is still "on the hook" for unmet requirements, and determining the guidelines for setting up a new project that is tied to the original project that deployed with items that were missed by the requestor in the original requirements.

> **13.2.3 SURVEY – PMO Future Impact:** Briefly describe your PMO's plans for 2012 and beyond - please describe how those plans will potentially impact your enterprise and its organizational structure.

For 2012, there are a number of goals yet to accomplish as a PMO:

- Expand our expertise more to the Process Improvement area, as increasingly more initiatives in the company are concerned with doing things more efficiently and with better quality.
- Begin the process of upgrading our project repository to improve the views, workflow, reporting ability, and other functionality that will simplify and improve the project process for our business users, and provide the PMO and other departments with more and better information.
- Develop a process to fast-track approval and completion of smaller "micro" projects that seem now to get burdened by oversight.
- Raise the awareness of "value-added" for each project, requiring formal business cases on larger projects.
- Look at the idea of "project scoring" to better gauge the value of individual projects.
- Training continues to be an important service area for us. In addition to ongoing classes on PM basics, we look forward to expanding into some soft skills training as well as a supplemental tutorial on navigating the new project repository.

13.3   Merchants Insurance Group PMO Model Components

In the following six parts of this case study, the Merchants Insurance Group's Project Management Office provides its descriptions of how they implement the six key components of the Project Business Management Organization model: Governance; Methodology; Capability; Planning; Execution; and Sustainability.

> **13.3.1 SURVEY – PMO Governance:** Describe how your PMO presents itself as an executive-level management business function, how it addresses setting policy and establishing charters, and how it provides an organizational model for the business management of portfolios, programs, and projects and the establishment of portfolio, program, and project management offices.

The PMO Director is also the Assistant Vice President of Strategic Planning and the Chief Risk Officer, with over 30 years of experience in the company. Throughout the year, he leads the staff of senior executives in planning sessions, enterprise risk management committee meetings, as well as numerous meetings regarding projects.

He facilitates the Executive Review Group (all of senior staff) in monthly meetings to review all new project requests and project change requests. He also facilitates the Project Management Council ("PMC", a subset of senior staff) in monthly meetings to review all strategic projects in the company and provide assistance and guidance.

The PMC also sets overall project governance and policy guidelines and Project Charters are required on every project.

As important subject matter experts on the capacity planning team for projects, the PMO members identify which groups of projects comprise a program, and coordinate the project prioritization process of the project queue.

13.3.1.1 – How long has the PMO been in place? *When was it started?*	The PMO has been in place for three years. The Merchants Insurance Group PMO, officially chartered in November 2008, was fully staffed with two certified PMP's by December 2008.
13.3.1.2 – What is the relationship of PMO management to the enterprise's operational management?	The PMO is not part of the operations to the extent that it is not responsible directly for the profit and loss of any unit of the company. Instead, it works over and with all other departments in the company to facilitate better project management and process efficiency.

13.3.1.3 – How is the PMO internally structured (positions, roles etc.)?

Aside from the PMO Director, there are two certified PMPs on staff. Their responsibilities include (but are not limited to):

- Provide expert PM assistance and transfer PM knowledge to all departments by mentoring, coaching, training and assisting project leads and team members in developing and executing their projects and project strategies;
- Manage select projects on behalf of the project sponsor and/or business lead, coordinating project activities, and team members;
- Establish new and maintain existing project schedules (MS Project), as well as other project portfolio and resource monitoring tools;
- Develop, document and maintain a repository of a standard PM methodology, including a set of tools, templates, and consistent, repeatable processes used for projects; and
- Act as PM thought leader and senior advisor to the PMO Director; communicate PM-related information to appropriate parties.

13.3.1.4 – How are the PMO's operations funded?	The PMO has a separate budget center.
13.3.1.5 – What is the summary position description of the PMO leader?	• Provides guidance and leadership to the business planning process, and ensures communication of results versus plan. • Oversees the Project Management Office and PM policies, and manages the PMO staff. • Oversees the Enterprise Risk Management process, and reports to all stakeholders. • Provides the analysis related to AROE bonus compensation, A.M. Best and other rating agencies, reinsurance programs, and the evaluation of business initiatives.
13.3.1.6 – What position requirements are used as a basis for selecting the PMO leader?	Rank and relationship with senior executives; exceptional skills in the areas of leadership, organization and communication; involvement with strategy setting of the company; experience with project management.
13.3.1.7 – Is the PMO a Profit & Loss cost center or considered overhead?	The PMO is considered overhead.
13.3.1.8 – What current challenge is the PMO dealing with?	Career development profiles are difficult with such a small staff. There is still some resistance from the IT function in dictating how projects (and which projects) should be managed. The PMO needs to keep evolving – continue to illustrate its value-added to the organization.

13.3.2 SURVEY – PMO Methodology / Standardization: Describe what standardization your PMO has implemented across the enterprise that examines: identification and integration of processes and practices; development of standardized Project Business Management processes; and documentation of enterprise-wide portfolio, program, and project management process methodology models, including their associated policies, practices, and procedures.

The PMO has standardized project request prioritization, project request submission, change control, project approval workflow, resource capacity planning, deployment planning, project initiation and planning, project execution and monitoring, and project closeout.

13.3.2.1 – Describe the standards utilized by the PMO to ensure the enterprise's project / program / portfolio management goals and objectives are achieved.

The Project Managers develop a business case for each project, and after deployment, measure actual results to the plan.

They develop schedules and track progress against baseline dates. Where information is lacking, they estimate activities using a best practice rule of thumb.

They track resource usage across related projects, ensuring the proper allocation of resources.

Project Managers monitor the progress of each project.

13.3.2.2 – Describe the project management process guidelines being employed by the PMO.

The PMO has created guidelines for categorizing projects in terms of size, complexity, and strategic alignment.

The PMO has developed a rule of thumb to estimate the size of future projects.

The PMO has developed a resource-planning model to estimate the capacity of the organization to address future projects.

13.3.2.3 – What systems, tools, and templates make your PMO successful?

The PMO uses:
- Microsoft Project for schedules,
- WBS Chart Pro for work breakdown structures.
- A Lotus Notes application serves as a repository of all project documentation, as well as a workflow tool for request review and approval, involving phase gates and change control procedures.

13.3.2.4 – Describe how management at all levels is directly involved in the development of the PMO and it processes.

The PMO Director is a corporate officer.

Our Executive Review Group (consisting of all senior officers) reviews requests and approves projects and changes.

Our Project Management Council (comprised of the President, CFO, COO, VP of Claims and PMO Director) meets monthly to review strategic projects.

Functional resource managers are responsible for finding and applying their resources to the projects.

13.3.2.5 – Describe the implementation plan you used for establishing project / program / portfolio management standards across your enterprise.

The PMO grew iteratively.

- First, the organization developed project reporting capabilities.
- Next, employees were trained to understand project schedules.
- Then, employees were trained on the use of the Lotus Notes document repository.
- Finally, employees were trained to become familiar with the automated workflow capabilities of the repository.

13.3.2.6 – How does the PMO use project, program, and portfolio management standards to optimize its practices?

Every service of the PMO is based on PMI standards and guidelines.

Are they based on PMI® or other industry guides and are they updated as new editions of the guides are released?

Both project managers are active in the local PMI Chapter and often attend professional development activities, returning with suggestions to enhance the offerings of the PMO.

13.3.3 SURVEY – PMO Capabilities: Describe development and assessment of the enterprise's abilities, describe any project management competency model, summarize any education and training program, describe any established career path progression plan, and outline key Enterprise Environmental Factors.

The PMO uses the PMO maturity model developed by PM Solutions to guide its growth opportunities. This provides suggestions for future enhancements to the PMO. The PMO conducts training for all employees who, by nature of their position, serve on project teams. This includes training on project management concepts, an introduction to the tools, an overview for executives, and soft skill training on topics like leadership and communication. Because both project managers are certified and fairly senior, no career progression path has yet been identified.

13.3.3.1 – Describe the components of your enterprise's training program.	Project managers are certified by PMI and maintain their proficiency with periodic training.

Employees are periodically trained on:
- Project management topics,
- Soft skills, or
- Methodology-specific training.

The PMO tracks the percent of the workforce who has been through its training.

13.3.3.2 – Describe the value your enterprise places on education and training and its goals and objectives.

Employees are allowed time to attend training.

An established metric for the PMO is the percent of the workforce that has been trained, which is evidence that the organization desires a trained workforce.

13.3.3.3 – Does the enterprise have a project management career path program? If so, what are the components?

Project managers are given increasingly more responsibility as they become familiar with the organization.

These responsibilities have grown to include business case development, resource planning, involvement with the strategic planning process, program management, and portfolio management.

13.3.3.4 – Describe the measurements, metrics, and Key Performance Indicators (KPI's) utilized by the PMO to determine the organization's knowledge, skills, and level of achievement.

The PMO evaluates itself and the organization's achievements by tracking whether projects are completed on time, the length of projects, the utilization of project resources, and customer satisfaction.

13.3.3.5 – Does the enterprise employ a project management competency model? If yes, please describe it. If no, why not?

Project Management Professionals (PMP's) were hired, to ensure a minimum level of competency.

Each project manager is expected to actively manage their own training, and to contribute to the enhancement of the PMO.

> **13.3.4 SURVEY – PMO Business Planning:** Discuss strategic business planning, tactical business planning, business objective (project) development and prioritization, and project identification, selection, and authorization.

13.3.4.1 – Describe the organizational structure and process used for corporate strategic business planning.

Does the PMO play a role in the process? If so, describe the PMOs role and responsibilities.

The Assistant Vice President for Strategic Planning is also the PMO Director.

The annual process for preparing and presenting the business plan is run like a project, with executive support from the CEO and CFO, and input from every area of the company. The overall process would be too complicated to detail here, but at the very foundation it is:

- An assessment of industry data and company trends;
- An understanding of our strategic priorities and how they help us to achieve our Mission and Vision;
- An assessment of the competition and marketplace in general;
- A corporate Strengths-Weaknesses-Opportunities-Threats analysis; and
- A review of the projects that will help us to achieve our strategic priorities.

13.3.4.2 – How is the strategic plan implemented with a project forecast plan?

Early on in the planning process, a separate group of officers (Resource Planning Committee) meets over the course of two months to review all potential projects for the coming year(s). They classify them as strategic or operational, prioritize them using decision criteria tied to the current key objectives and strategic priorities of the company, and graph the timing and capacity available for completing these highest priority projects.

Throughout this process, the PMO is involved in facilitation, expert consultation and coordination of the activities, and the end result.

13.3.4.3 – How is strategic planning, culture, and selection of projects integrated?

For a company of our size, and a PMO of our maturity level, the resource planning and capacity planning for all projects are detailed and documented extensively.

All projects are tied to the key objectives of the strategic plan, and prioritized using criteria that includes measures of profitability, customer service and value added to the company.

13.3.5 SURVEY – PMO Business Execution: Describe what role the PMO has in project selection, prioritization, and initiation; in portfolio, program and project execution planning; in stage-gate reviews; and in performance metrics selection and application.

13.3.5.1 – How are portfolios, programs, and projects selected and initiated?

As an insurance company with recurring rate reviews, product enhancements and compliance with occasional regulatory changes, there are many of these projects that are "fast-tracked" through the approval process with an executive sponsor overseeing each one.

For all other projects (whether strategic or operational), any person in the company has the ability to initiate a project through our Lotus Notes-based Project Repository.

The PMO reviews each project before forwarding it to the executive sponsor for initial approval or declination.

After appropriate documentation is prepared, the Executive Review Group comprised of all senior officers, and facilitated by the PMO Director reviews all new project requests (excluding the rate review and legal/mandatory projects) monthly.

13.3.5.2 – How are projects organized and managed as a program and/or portfolio?

The PMO maintains all reports regarding the current project queue, all closed projects, and all projects that are in the early stages of initiation.

Strategic programs/projects are managed using a PMP from the PMO, and led by a business lead. Those projects/programs are also reviewed each month by a smaller subset of senior officers (facilitated again by the PMO Director) called the Project Management Council.

13.3.5.3 – How are projects prioritized within a program and/or portfolio?

Every project is required to have some estimate of its value to the company.

Larger projects have formal business cases attached. Business benefit is one of the most highly regarded criteria for prioritization, along with the fulfillment of customers' needs and alignment with strategic priorities.

Aside from the annual prioritization that takes place during the planning season, the project queue is re-prioritized by the Resource Planning Committee on a quarterly basis (or as needed).

13.3.5.4 – How does the enterprise define what project and program success is?

Project success is predicated upon a mixture of product quality, project delivery (time and cost) and resource management. Product deliverables should trace back to business requirements. The quality of business requirements is gauged through the number of project change requests and scope changes that occurred.

Project schedules are closely monitored by phase. Team morale and training are important aspects of our project management reviews.

The formal PM Metrics that are reported quarterly to the Project Management Council include measures of project efficiency, project duration, project productivity, on-time deployment, PCR monitoring, PM training of employees, and a customer satisfaction survey.

13.3.5.5 – Does the PMO support the management of projects that would be considered operational in nature? If so, describe the types of projects.

Yes, the PMO supports the management of projects considered operational.

To a certain extent, the PMPs are involved in all projects except for the very small legal and mandatory ones.

The PMP level of involvement and the level of project management oversight applied to a project depends upon the size and impact of the project.

13.3.6 SURVEY – PMO Sustainability: Describe the overall impact of the PMO over a sustained period (e.g., customer satisfaction, productivity, reduced cycle time, growth, building or changing organizational culture, etc.). If available, please provide quantitative data to illustrate the areas in which the PMO has had the greatest business impact.

13.3.6.1 – What is included in a comprehensive project monitoring and

Strategic projects have the most extensive monitoring. For each of those projects, the business lead provides the Project Management Council ("PMC") with a monthly Status Report that

control system and how is it implemented?	includes an update on recent milestones, any new issues encountered, accomplishments, next steps and a review of the overall schedule.
	The PMC must approve all scope and budget changes.
13.3.6.2 – How are project start-up and gate review processes structured?	The start-up process was previously discussed. Business cases are updated throughout the project life cycle as one component of a gate review process – if the benefit of a project falls below desired expectations, the project is cancelled.
13.3.6.3 – Describe the project knowledge base system and how is it developed?	Project Management training is the responsibility of the PMO. The target is to have 100% of all project team members trained in the basics of PM. A requirement of project managers in the PMO is that they are PMP certified.
13.3.6.4 – Describe the measurement, metrics, and Key Performance Indicators (KPIs) utilized by the PMO to measure project and program success.	The formal PM Metrics that are reported quarterly to the Project Management Council include measures of project efficiency, project duration, project productivity, on-time deployment, PCR monitoring, PM training of employees, and a customer satisfaction survey.
13.3.6.5 – Describe the organizational benefits and value the PMO provides to the enterprise.	Largely because of the process and governance that the PMO has established around projects the past few years, the outstanding project queue has been reduced from over 200 projects to an average of around 50 projects. We now focus more on the projects that matter, and resources are more optimally managed.
	There is better communication, teamwork, and meeting management throughout the company, in large part because of the processes and practices that the PMO has established.
13.3.6.6 – Describe the economic benefits and value the PMO provides to the enterprise.	Because the PMPs of the PMO can more efficiently manage projects (compared to the business leads, which used to manage them), we are seeing real efficiency gains in terms of hours spent on some of the administrative and managing functions of projects.

Improvements in communication and meeting management are less quantifiable, but real all the same.

13.3.7 SURVEY – Additional Comments: Please provide any additional comments

---

The Merchants Project Management Office has benefited from day one by having the support of our highest-ranking officers in the company. We chose wisely in selecting the right people to champion the PM cause and to staff the PMO positions. Constant attention to innovation and improvement in the area of project management will guide the PMO's continuing success.

Chapter 14

Nationwide PMO Case Study

Nationwide is one of the largest insurance and financial services companies in the world. Over the last 80 years, Nationwide has grown from a small mutual auto insurer owned by policyholders to one of the largest insurance and financial services companies in the world, with more than $135 billion US dollars in statutory assets.

Nationwide is a long-standing Fortune 500 company focusing on domestic property and casualty insurance, life insurance and retirement savings, asset management and strategic investments.

Their property and casualty businesses serve customers through five operating brands: Nationwide Insurance, Allied Insurance, Scottsdale Insurance, Titan Insurance, and Nationwide Agribusiness. Financial services are offered through three operating brands: Nationwide Financial, Nationwide Retirement Solutions, and Nationwide Bank.

Nationwide is a company where every voice is heard and valued. Nationwide understands the importance of associates with different backgrounds, experiences and perspectives coming together to serve their customers. Nationwide believes true diversity is all-inclusive and seeks out a winning combination of academic backgrounds, ages, cultures, life circumstances, thinking styles and interests.

14.1 Nationwide – Enterprise and PMO Office Survey Information

Enterprise Name:	Nationwide
Country:	United States of America
Industry:	Insurance and Finance
Enterprise – Annual Sales Revenue:	Large, greater than $1 Billion US Dollars
Enterprise – Full-time Employee Equivalents:	33,000
World Wide Web Site:	www.nationwide.com
PMO Name:	Delivery Services
Title of PMO Leader:	Vice President, Delivery Services

PMO Position in Organizational Structure:	Enterprise-Wide
PMO reports to in Organizational Structure:	Senior Vice President, Enterprise Chief Technical Officer
PMO Annual Operating Budget:	$63 Million US Dollars (does not include project spending)
PMO – Full-time Employee Equivalents:	Approximately 450 (300 associates, 150 contractors)

The following are the PMO Case Study Survey question sets and the associated responses as submitted by Nationwide' Delivery Services, the PMO, with minor editing for format and consistency.

14.2   Nationwide PMO Background, Innovations, and Impact

In the following three parts of this case study, Nationwide's Delivery Services provides an overview of the background and structure of its PMO, various innovations and best practices by the PMO, and the potential future business impact of the PMO.

14.2.1 SURVEY – PMO Background: Describe your PMO, including background information on its scope, vision, mission, and position within the enterprise's organizational structure.

Before the transformation to the current centralized Program Management Office, Nationwide operated 10 plus Program Management Offices, each with their own priorities and governance processes. In May of 2009, approximately 300 Project / Program Managers, who were managing over 500 programs and projects were centralized into an enterprise-wide PMO organization named Delivery Services (DS).

The mission of Delivery Services is to provide effective, efficient and predictable project delivery services that create business value for Nationwide customers while improving the company's project management capabilities.

With this transformation of the PMO, Nationwide has achieved the foundation for "Delivery Done Right" through:

- Stronger partnerships that enable business and Information Technology (IT) success;
- Associates that are empowered and leaders that are accountable; and
- Implementing consistent project delivery methodology and performance standards.

Delivery Services, Nationwide's PMO organization, basically provides two types of services: program/project delivery services and on demand services.

Program/Project Delivery Services

Program/Project delivery services cover:

- Placing the right project manager on the right project – highly capable PMs managing an appropriate level of work;
- Providing coaching to the project manager to drive efficient, effective, and successful delivery; and
- Ensuring appropriate delivery methods are leveraged – fit to purpose.

FIGURE 14-1: Nationwide Information Technologies Delivery Model – View by Component

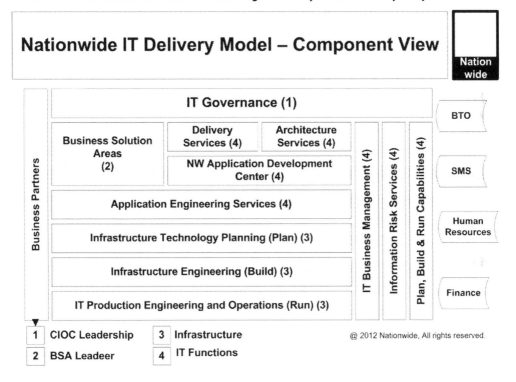

On Demand Services

On Demand Services are requested by the Business Solution Area (BSA) or recommended by the Program/Project Manager (PM) Coach. The services consist of:

- Program / Project efficiency reviews;
- Enterprise Solution Delivery (Nationwide Project Management Methodology) adoption workshops;
- Solution delivery reviews done by external industry experts; and
- Plan to Build transition activities - Program/ Project framing and sizing, pre-initiate consulting, and high-level estimating.

Delivery Services Journey to Effectiveness

The Delivery Services leader was accountable for centralizing the PM profession, capabilities, and all project managers into a single organization that is focused on continuous growth and improvement in project delivery capabilities. The Information Technology Delivery Model shown above in Figure 14-1 provides more details.

The PMO journey over the past three years has been planned and focused around operational alignment, efficiency, and effectiveness as shown below in Figure 14-2.

FIGURE 14-2: Nationwide Deliver Services Organization (PMO) Journey

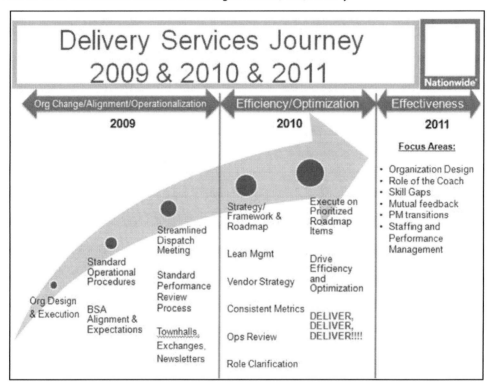

Delivery Services Challenges Becoming a Centralized PMO

In June 2009 when we centralized, we were faced with:

- Inconsistent demand process;
- Inconsistent vendor management;
- Project evaluations conducted inconsistently;
- Inconsistent resource alignment and project funding; and
- Inconsistent role expectations and performance management.

Organizational Change – Alignment - Operationalization

In the second half of 2009, we did the following:

- Created a centralized model aligning our PM Coaches and PM Service Owners (15:1 associate to coach ratio) that face off to Chief Information Officer areas;

- Created a standard operational plan and procedures (had varying operating models coming into centralized model that had to be revised and agreed upon and then rolled out);
- Focused on organizational change and communication of the new centralized model both internally within Delivery Services and to our partners;
- Created a process for demand/resource management and a method to manage it via a dispatch meeting;
- Created common expectations, objectives and calibration for all roles in Delivery Services; and
- Revised and rolled out new Post Implementation Commitment Review (PICR) to enable consistent review and improve process governance.

Efficiency and Optimization

In 2010, we accomplished the following:

- Developed service level agreements (SLAs) and project health metrics and began consistent operations reviews; began to focus on the high number of PM transitions;
- Created a consistent feedback process with our partners and project team members, since no mutual feedback process existed;
- Ensured there was a consistent performance management process, including promotion and demotion activities;
- Realigned headcount achieving a 70:30 ratio of PMO associate to contractor;
- Developed and executed a vendor strategy across all locations, PMs and Requirements Analyst (RA) focused on streamlining 19 vendors to nine vendors in nine months and managed to reduce contractor rates down within the PM and Requirements Analyst (RA) space;
- Created common roles and expectations for all PMs and Requirements Analyst (RA);
- Utilized Lean Management practices and tools to streamline our demand management and resource allocation processes; and
- Developed roadmap for Delivery Services which focused on People, Capability and Business Solution Areas, which drives our 2011 focus on "effectiveness."

Effectiveness Focus

In 2011, we accomplished the following:

- Achieved a significant increase in our overall Gallup Engagement Score (0.20 considered meaningful growth);
- Rebalanced our PMs aligning them to the coaches corresponding to appropriate Chief Information Officers and Business Solution Areas;
- Reduced the frequency and number of transitions of PMs throughout the

organization. Socialized and reported transition triggers and impacts across the organization. Renewed focus on delivery success by conducting project Health Assessments and in-flight project leading indicator reviews;

- Matured PM best practices in working with the standing team model. Particular focus was on the Iteration and Project Manager interactions. The standing team model is relativity new for our organization; however we now have 25% of our project teams successfully delivering using this model; and
- Assumed leadership role in creating a work force strategy for all IT positions throughout the organization.

14.2.2 SURVEY – PMO Innovations and Best Practices: Address the challenges your enterprise encountered prior to implementing the new PMO practices and how you overcame those challenges. Describe clearly and concisely the practices implemented and their effect on project, program, and/or portfolio and organizational success.

When the staff implemented the new Delivery Services (PMO) strategy, it transformed how the PMO could leverage our Program and Project Management talent. This included the centralization of our entire PM staff. Prior to implementing this change, PMs were aligned across company business areas (de-centralized) to PM Competency Coaches within their IT organization.

This included a matrix relationship to a centralized skills capability uplift and methodology deployment group.

With the de-centralized model:

- Program/Project Managers were limited to assignments within their business area;
- Program/Project manager expectations varied across business areas;
- Program/Project manager support varied across business areas;
- Little opportunity existed for reassignment outside of business area to leverage talent and build skills;
- Limited career path (limited by business area); and
- Limited best practice sharing and reuse (was not done between business areas).

Figure 14-3 below provides an example of the situation before PMO centralization of a de-centralized model that was operational in just one line of business. Each line of business had inefficient models where there were PM Coach-to-PM ratio inefficiencies along with level stratification inefficiencies.

While Figure 14-4 below illustrates the new Delivery Services organizational model, which streamlines the PM Coach-to-PM ratios and minimizes the number of executives.

FIGURE 14-3: Nationwide Example Business Area PMO Organization Chart [Prior to Centralization]

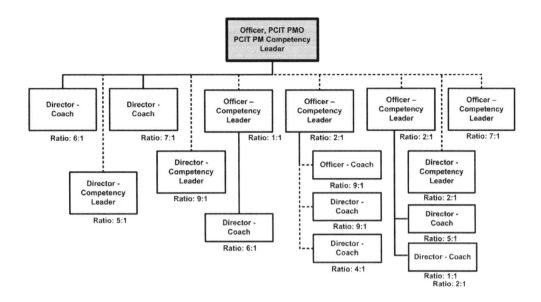

FIGURE 14-4: Nationwide Delivery Services (PMO Organization) Model [After Centralization]

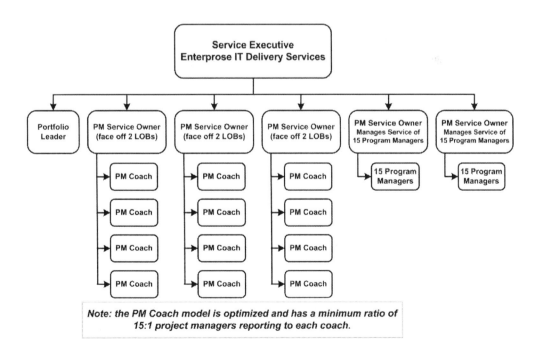

FIGURE 14-5: Nationwide Associate Point of View – Centralized versus De-centralized PMO Function

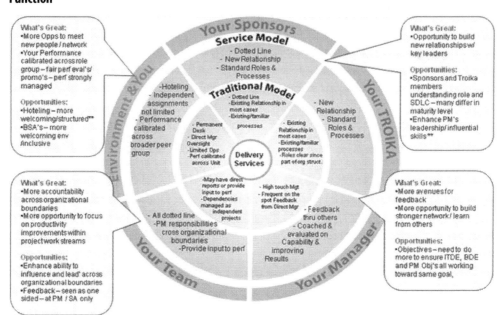

These two figures (one above and one below) depict the benefits of operating as a Service Model (Centralized) [Figure 14-5] versus the Federated/Traditional Model (De-centralized) [Figure 14-6], both from a PMO Associate's and Customer's point of view.

FIGURE 14-6: Nationwide Customer Point of View – Centralized versus De-centralized PMO Function

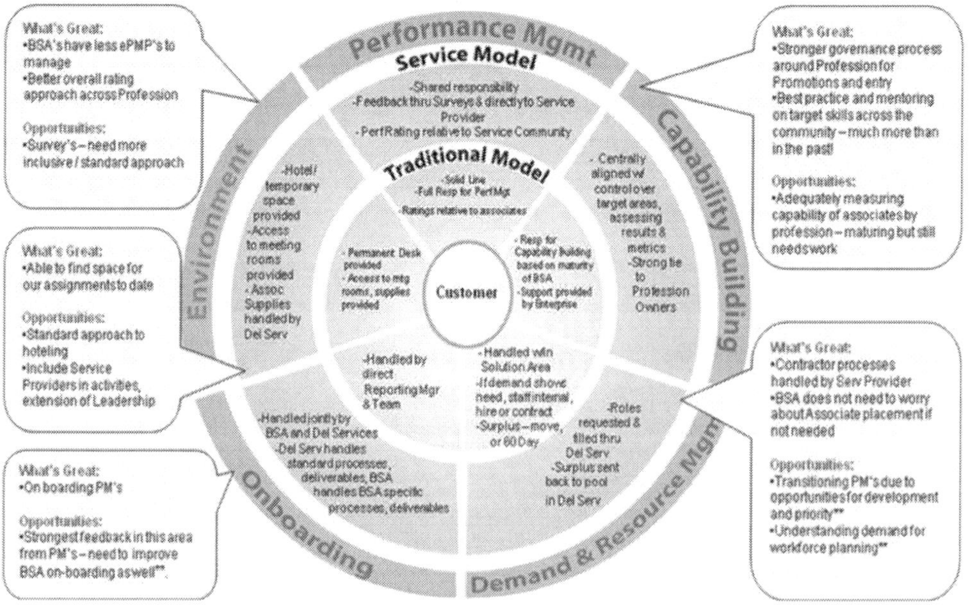

In the centralized model, PM assignments are based on the capability and skill of the resource, which are matched to the size and complexity of the project. PMs are endorsed to a maximum Project Tier Level category (see Figure 14-7) and projects are staffed accordingly.

Project Tier definitions are used to categorize projects (see Figure 14-8). Projects are assigned a Tier Level (see Figure 14-8) based on various factors including project size, complexity, team size, organization impact, interfaces, etc.

FIGURE 14-7: Nationwide Project Tier Definitions for Staff Endorsement and Assignment

	Tier 1	Tier 2			Tier 3		Tier 4	
Endorsement Tier	T1	T2H	T2M	T2L	T3H	T3L	T4H	T4L
Staffing Level	Executive PM Senior PM	Senior PM	Lead PM	Lead PM	Lead PM	PM	PM	PM

FIGURE 14-8: Nationwide Project Category Definitions by Project Tier

Tier	Summary
T1	Typically these are very large projects or programs, which are highly visible and are reflected as an OCEO level effort. While in most cases, the hours involved with these efforts are very large, these efforts may be identified as T1 due to their overall importance to the organization these projects or for Senior Level Project Managers or Program Managers.
T2	Typically these are large projects or programs costing approximately $1 million or more and with labor in excess of 15,000 hours. Given the cost and size of these efforts, there is increased visibility and focus on these efforts. These programs or projects are staffed with strong, experienced Senior Level Project Managers or Program Managers.
T3	Typically these are projects costing under $1 million, with less than 15,000 hours of labor. These projects are primarily managed by Project Manager Consultants or solid Project Management Specialists
T4H	Typically these are projects costing under $300,000 and with less than 4,000 hours labor. These projects are preliminary managed by entry-level Project Management Specialist or project manager candidates in the pipeline.
T4L	In general, Delivery Services provides very limited coverage for T4L efforts. Coverage is limited to infrastructure projects or bundled small project work. Application projects at this tier are typically run within the Business Solutions Areas. These projects are good hands-on opportunities for candidates in the project management pipeline.

It was important as the PMO staff implemented the Project Tier and Categorization model that they improved associates' understanding of their role, uplifted the capability of the PMs, and were viewed as an enabler to the Nationwide IT solution area partners, and not seen as a roadblock.

The PM profession is the foundation by which the PMO organization is structured (see Figure 14-4). The PMO has twenty "PM Coaches" who directly manage and develop project managers. They are responsible for assigning project managers with the right skills to the "right project" at the "right time." Each PM Coach is assigned to a specific business unit to develop project delivery support partnerships.

IT Associates Outside of Delivery Services - Our Pipeline

In addition to the encouraging feedback from our associates, we also have seen an increase over time of individuals outside the organization who want to become part of

Delivery Services. They understand that in order to become a great PM, Delivery Services has the support and opportunities available to make their desire a reality.

Customers – Solution Areas

When Nationwide first implemented the Delivery Services PMO model, there was much resistance from the IT solution areas (where these resources were coming from) due to a concern of control. There were many instances of customers trying to bypass Delivery Services and staff using their own contractors.

Over a period of time the PMO has built a very trusting relationship with our solution area partners. We no longer have any instances where our internal customers bypass us – they leverage us, because they know the Delivery Services PMO ensures alignment of the right PM, to the right work, at the right time.

Ability to Deliver

Delivery Services ability to deliver moderate to extremely complex initiatives within Nationwide continues to be a strength for IT and the business. Through the implementation of this Nationwide PMO model, we are now able to leverage our talent more effectively to ensure we limit delivery risk. In addition, we have realized efficiencies in starting up programs and projects by ensuring we do not staff a PM until there is a clear understanding of work, and the key resources are aligned to the project effort to efficiently kick it off.

Opportunities for Higher Levels of Success

PM Coaches were spending too much time and effort on transactional activities like assigning and interviewing resources. The areas on which coaching is focused is being realigned, as illustrated in Figure 14-9.

FIGURE 14-9: Nationwide Monthly Allocation of PM Coach Time – Curent and Future

Monthly Allocation of PM Coach Time							
		Class Room Training	Misc	Internal	Transactional	Interfacing with IT Partners	People Development
Average Allocation	Current	2%	4%	16%	18%	22%	38%
	Future	2%	4%	12%	7%	15%	60%

PMs were removed from projects at rates higher than expected (see Figure 14-10) due to the mismatch of the necessary experience and skills with their assigned projects, thereby impacting the project.

Too many external-staff augmentation vendors (see Figure 14-11 below) created high variability with contractor on-boarding time, which were both reduced after implementation of consolidation through Deliver Services.

FIGURE 14-10: Nationwide Change in PMs Being Transitioned Off from Projects

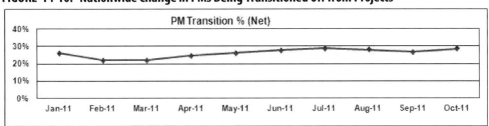

FIGURE 14-11: Nationwide Reduction in Vendor Count with Centralized PMO (Delivery Services)

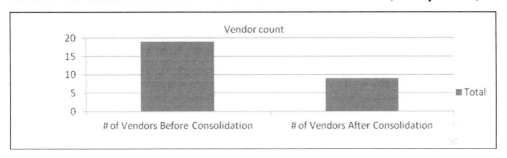

FIGURE 14-12: Nationwide Lean Management Principles

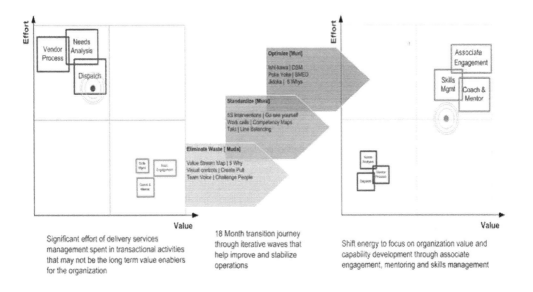

Continuous Improvement

Reduce amount of time on transaction activities: After searching across various industries for ideas to improve our resource management and capacity planning to become more efficient and effective, we discovered a large IT offshore company who had successfully applied Toyota's Lean Management principles and techniques to solve similar problems for its organization. Through a successful partnership with this organization, we were able to train our management team, including the PM Coaches, on those Lean Management principles and techniques.

Using the Lean Management principles (see Figure 14-12 above), we were able to shift wasted time spent on low value-add transactional activities like assigning resources, to value-added activities such as coaching, PMO associate engagement, and skills development.

Specific action steps taken by the Delivery Services PMO to shift or eliminate wasted time spent on low value-added transactional activities:

Step 1: Eliminated waste by creating a standard resource request form.

Step 2: Defined consistent metrics and Key Performance Indicators (KPIs) used to measure effectiveness and efficiency.

Step 3: Implemented a consistent skills and experience capability assessment framework.

Step 4: Created a matching solution where projects' attributes are matched to the ideal resource characteristics.

FIGURE 14-13: Nationwide PM Competency Framework

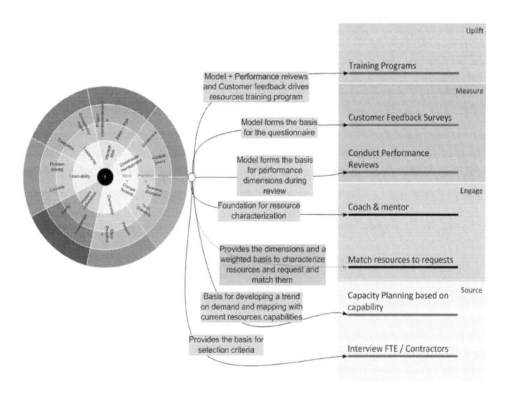

208

Ensure project manager skills and experience aligns with project needs: As a next step in our Lean Management initiative, we completed a skills and experience baseline of all our associates targeted to be assigned to programs and projects. Nationwide partnered with the Project Management Office Executive Council who captures and measures various project manager skills and experience across numerous industries.

We selected this organization because they surveyed hundreds of companies and discovered there were about 40 key competencies that successful project managers possess and successfully leverage. In addition, the Project Management Office Executive Council has completed thousands of assessments using this framework for various Fortune 500 organizations with similar complexity and levels as Nationwide.

A key factor in improving the successful placement of PMs to projects was to enhance our resource request form to include additional project characteristics. These new project characteristics allow us to match parameters aligning with the Project Management Office Executive Council skills and experience completed for each PM. Additionally, we are in the early stages of piloting a new matching tool which quickly assesses how closely each need aligns to various PMs. This tool calculates a "fit index" based upon the project attributes and the project manager's competencies and experience (see Figure 14-13 above).

Reducing the amount of vendors and improving the contractor on-boarding process: The number of external staffing vendors created high levels of variability with contractor performance and on-boarding time. There were approximately 20 vendors who supplied contractors, and all with varying processes and techniques.

To become more efficient, we approached nine vendors we believed could be our future strategic vendors with the idea of forming a competitive environment amongst each other. We guaranteed they would get a larger share of our staff augmentation requests at a fixed rate. This would reduce their effort of generating leads, negotiating hourly rates and provide more valued services, like training contractors and associates on our tools and processes.

One of our strategic partners played an instrumental role in developing our Agile and Project Management methodologies. This included implementing the tools, education and training aligned with those methodologies.

One key component of the partnership involved a unique arrangement of a single vendor leading a small "consortium" of other Nationwide preferred vendors in partnership with Nationwide's Sourcing Group. In addition, this vendor utilized their expertise in filtering, screening, and final selection of potential consultant candidates. The vendor also provided targeted training to newly engaged consultants providing increased reliability, performance, and "right fit" of the consultants. Nationwide realized administrative cost savings and decreased project delays associated with incorrect skill-sets or poor performance on a project and gained productivity, consistency, and "healthier" project teams.

14.2.3 SURVEY – PMO Future Impact: Briefly describe your PMO's plans for 2012 and beyond - please describe how those plans will potentially impact your enterprise and its organizational structure.

The Delivery Services 2012 priorities are listed in Figures 14-14 and 14-15.

FIGURE 14-14: Nationwide Delivery Services PMO 2012 Priorities

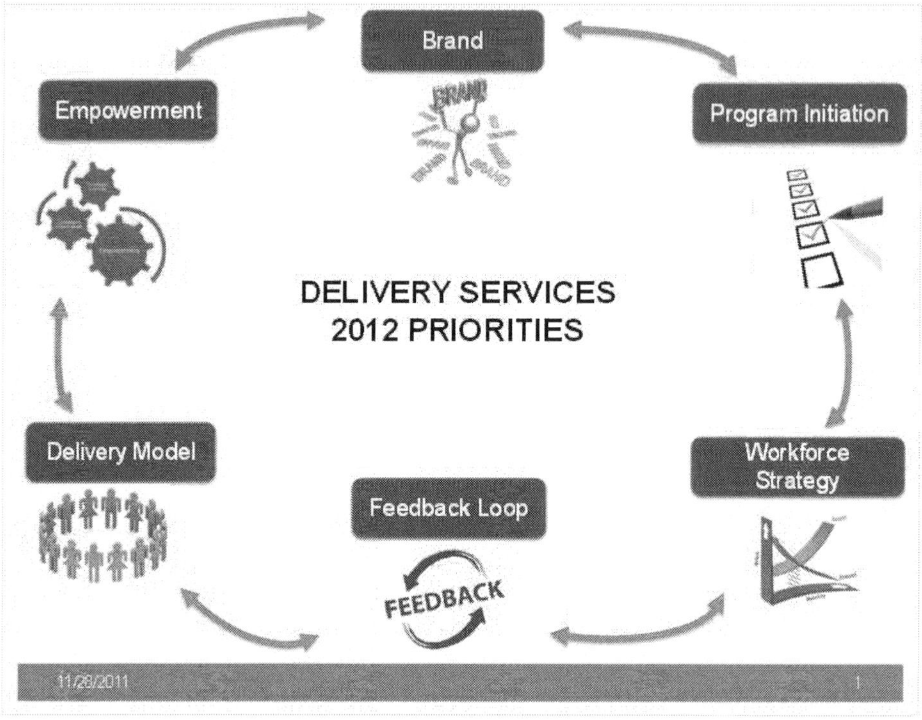

14.3   Nationwide PMO Model Components

In the following six parts of this case study, the Nationwide PMO, Delivery Services, provides its descriptions of how they implement the six key components of the Project Business Management Organization model: Governance; Methodology; Capability; Planning; Execution; and Sustainability.

14.3.1 SURVEY – PMO Governance: Describe how your PMO presents itself as an executive-level management business function, how it addresses setting policy and establishing charters, and how it provides an organizational model for the business management of portfolios, programs, and projects and the establishment of portfolio, program, and project management offices.

FIGURE 14-15: Nationwide Delivery Services Meaning of PMO 2012 Priorities

EMPOWERMENT
Empower associates to define Standard Work; Continuously improve processes; Establish a culture of a learning organization

DELIVERY MODEL
Transform to be responsible for the portfolio level "Delivery Quality"

PROGRAM INITIATION
Develop and offer capabilities to enable effective program/project initiation

WORKFORCE STRATEGY
Develop a multiyear workforce plan to support the build portfolio

BRAND
Provide visibility to our services and successes

FEEDBACK LOOP
Establish a two way feedback loop

11/28/2011   2

14.3.1.1 – How long has the PMO been in place?

When was it started?

The centralized PMO had been in place since 2009.

The enterprise PMO – called Delivery Services, was formed in April 2009 when Nationwide combined all Project Management professionals into one centralized team.

14.3.1.2 – What is the relationship of PMO management to the enterprise's operational management?

Within the IT organization, the PMO is closely aligned with operational management.

We consider projects to be covered under "Build" and operational to be covered under "Run."

Part of the project process is to consider the impact to our Run organization once a project is implemented.

Most projects maintain a warranty period of 30-90 days prior to handing over the future support and enhancements to the Run organization.

14.3.1.3 – How is the PMO internally structured (positions, roles etc.)?	The structure of the Delivery Services (PMO) organization is displayed above in Figure 14-4.
14.3.1.4 – How are the PMO's operations funded?	Delivery Services currently provides project management services to projects totaling over $450 million in project spending.

Delivery Services is funded, as an operating item necessary to perform project build functions, from Enterprise IT. It is funded out of the enterprise by charging back the cost of the Delivery Services function to each business unit based on their allocation of use.

Therefore, all Business Solution Areas that need IT project management services are funding the Delivery Services PMO organization.

14.3.1.5 – What is the summary position description of the PMO leader?

Vice President, Delivery Services:
The position is responsible for defining and running a service organization which provides PM and Analysis services to all IT Lines Of Businesses.

This PMO type organization is run and operated as an internal consulting company within "One IT" at Nationwide to drive the necessary competencies into the PM and Analysis areas to ensure the right people are staffed at the right time on the right work.

Key areas of focus are the following:
Program / Project Management– responsible for project and program management capability building, advisory services and a centralized delivery model for all project management staffing.

Solution Analysis – responsible for defining best practices within this discipline as well as engaging and delivering on large projects to ensure requirements are properly defined; this also is a centralized area for all solution analyst staffing.

SQA (Software Quality Assurance) - via a matrixed relationship, responsible for driving competency and best practices into the system, test analysis and overall IT quality areas of the organization which are represented in each of the Business Solution Areas (BSA).

Quantitative Scope: The following are the number of direct reports and the number of indirect reports; assets managed; reserve responsibilities; operating budget, etc., applicable to this position.

- There are 432 full time equivalents (FTE) in the Delivery Services organization with 10 direct reports (4 Assistant Vice Presidents, 5 Directors, and 1 Executive Administrative Assistant)
  - o 127 contractors are included in the FTE number above
- 37 FTE (22 Senior Quality Analysts and 15 BCL) are in a matrixed reporting relationship to Delivery Services across the software development domains
- Two IT Professions are represented in Delivery Services:
  - o The PM Profession Owner is responsible for managing a profession of ~300 associates
  - o The Analysis Profession Owner is responsible for managing a profession of ~800 associates
- Annual overall budget of $62.8 million

Position Purpose: The following is the position's primary purpose or primary contribution to the department, the business unit, and the Enterprise.

This office serves multiple purposes. First, we provide advisory services, capability building and execution across several of the key domains (project and program management, solutions and systems analysis, and testing). More specifically, we:

- Direct a central resource pool of highly skilled project/ program management and solution analyst resources that are deployed to drive the completion of key IT projects which includes:
  - o Attracting and retaining highly skilled professionals
  - o Developing consistent tools and processes for project/program management and requirements management
  - o Providing leadership of the PM and Analysis professions across One IT
- Formulate policies, implement processes, and review all IT initiatives to mitigate program and project management issues.
- Develop and administer the governance structure necessary to oversee the execution of all IT initiatives.

213

- Lead strategy and competency development for the systems analysis and testing domains across One IT from a Thought and Personal Leadership perspective through matrixed management of 22 Senior Quality Analysts to ensure better end-to-end quality of our IT Application and Project Portfolios
- Maintain key leadership positions on both the Build and ITWE Leadership Teams (See Figure 14-2)

14.3.1.6 – What position requirements are used as a basis for selecting the PMO leader?

Essential Responsibilities: List the position's essential or most critical functions and responsibilities. Then approximate the percentage of time spent on each core accountability (may not equal 100%).

% Time	Critical/Core Responsibilities
30 %	Provide leadership of the Project Management and Solutions Analysis organizations
20%	Development and management of direct reports
20%	Development and execution of overall Test and Quality Strategy
10%	Provide leadership of the SQA matrixed organization
10%	Develop project and program management policies, standards and methods; oversee project/program management and analysis trending; recommend remedial actions; present management information to Chief Information Officer Staff and Line of Business cabinets
10%	Prepare strategies and provide executive oversight for enterprise initiatives affecting the IT community, (Profession Leadership (ITWE), Build Leadership)

Employment Guidelines: The following are the education, experience and skills necessary to perform competently the position's most critical functions and core responsibilities.

Education: Undergraduate studies in management information systems, mathematics, business administration or related fields. Strategic planning in a management information systems environment. Expert level knowledge of program and project management.

Certification: PMI's PMP Certification desired.

Experience: Fifteen or more years related leadership experience in information systems, system delivery and defining, organizing, developing and managing large organizations.

14.3.1.7 – Is the PMO a Profit & Loss cost center or considered overhead?

The PMO is not a Profit & Loss cost center. The leadership within the PMO does not charge time to projects and therefore would be considered overhead.

All of the Project Managers, Program Managers and Requirement Analysts are allocated to projects and bill to those projects.

14.3.1.8 – What current challenge is the PMO dealing with?

In 2011, Delivery Services focused on becoming more effective in a few key areas: organizational design, role of the PM Coach, key skill gap areas, mutual feedback, undesirable number of PM transitions, and staffing and performance. We called this work: Delivery Services Effectiveness and it was one aspect of a larger objective to improve our IT Delivery Model effectiveness. See brief descriptions in the chart Figure 14-16.

In 2011, we addressed the design of the organization by reorganizing the PM Coaches so the PM resources working in their Business Solution Area report to them administratively. While we were addressing this design concern we also focused on the PM Coach having more time to focus on project delivery and less on staffing.

Skill gap improvements are now wrapped into continuous improvement for the organization in efforts to enhance our skills and capabilities. Mutual feedback will continue to be a focus in 2012.

At the end of 2011 we made huge improvements on providing formal feedback on all project roles to help with the overall performance of the project team and organization. In regards to PM transitions, this item has matured and will not be a large concern for 2012.

The last item, staffing and performance management, is being linked into our overall workforce strategy for 2012. We have made great strides at the end of 2011 to hire a bench of personnel and to staff directly without as many interviews to slow the process. In addition, we have worked out a managed service concept with local vendors to staff contracting resources without interviews.

FIGURE 14-16: Nationwide Delivery Services PMO Effectiveness

Delivery Services Effectiveness

Nationwide®

1. **Organization Design** – Assumed extreme fungibility of resources; Over 2 years this has resulted in coaches not having a critical mass of resources working in support of the BSA they faceoff with. This design also limited our ability to build depth of knowledge in line of business or operational areas

2. **Role of the Coach** – Currently focused on staffing, capability, resource management, and BSA coordination; Role expectation of coaches did not include responsibility for project delivery.

3. **Skill Gaps** – There are opportunities to improve certain core PM capabilities (e.g. schedule predictability); Leadership and managerial courage is another area of opportunity. Finally, we don't have sufficient visibility to long-term demand for certain types of work and the needed PM skills (a.k.a. Package)

4. **Lack of mutual feedback loop** – We get inconsistent feedback about the performance of PMs on projects. We don't have an opportunity to provide feedback about other roles in the project structure.

5. **Undesirable number of PM transitions** – Mainly due to undefined and/or change of scope and lack of lead time.

6. **Staffing and Performance Management** – While we are structured like a consulting organization, we don't have all the levers consulting organizations have such as a bench, ability to performance manage quickly or the ability to give a second chance. Another obstacle is the desire by the ITDEs/BSA Execs to interview each proposed resource before being staffed.

11/28/2011   4

14.3.2 SURVEY – PMO Methodology / Standardization: Describe what standardization your PMO has implemented across the enterprise that examines: identification and integration of processes and practices; development of standardized Project Business Management processes; and documentation of enterprise-wide portfolio, program, and project management process methodology models, including their associated policies, practices, and procedures.

Delivery Services reports to the Enterprise Chief Technology Officer (Enterprise Chief Technology Officer (ECTO)). This allows the organization to see impacts to the entire organization. Also reporting to the Enterprise Chief Technology Officer (ECTO) is the Enterprise Architecture, Enterprise Risk Management, IT Strategy, Application Development Center (ADC) and Build Capability. All of these functions are critical to project delivery success hence the departments work closely together. The ADC is a fairly new department which operates as a software development factory to support project teams in delivery success.

14.3.2.1 – Describe the standards utilized by the PMO to ensure the enterprise's project / program / portfolio management goals and objectives are achieved.

The PMO leverages a Post Implementation Commitment Review (PICR) to ensure that the projects goals and objectives are achieved. The Post Implementation Commitment Review (PICR) is a score that sets a baseline after design and then a grade is given after implementation on the project's baseline in the following areas: Scope, Schedule, Cost, Quality, Architecture and Value. The grades are:

- Exceeds: A
- High Achieves: B
- Achieves: B-
- Low Achieves: C
- Does Not Meet: F

Post Implementation Commitment Review (PICR) Report Commitment Criteria: The following contains commitments, commitment evaluation criteria and commitment delivery assessments.

- **Scope Commitment:** Provide a high level list of the Features and Deliverables (e.g., Feature List) that the program or project will deliver.
- **Scope Criteria:** Provide criteria for the corresponding assessment level or indicate "N/A" if there is no meaningful criterion for the corresponding level. The criteria that the template provides may be sufficient to describe assessment criteria for your program or project. The Business Delivery Executive, IT Delivery Executive, and PM should use their best judgment to define critical and noncritical variances.
- **Scope Commitment Delivery Assessment:** Select from the drop down list the assessment value that the Business Delivery Executive, IT Delivery Executive, and PM agree most accurately describes how the program or project delivered on the Scope Commitment based on the criteria specified. Enter this field during program or project delivery assessment.
- **Schedule Commitment:** Provide the planned implementation date.
- **Schedule Criteria:** Provide criteria for the corresponding assessment level or indicate "N/A" if there is no meaningful criterion for the corresponding level. The criteria that the

template provides may be sufficient to describe assessment criteria for your program or project.

- **Schedule Commitment Delivery Assessment:** Select from the drop down list the assessment value that the Business Delivery Executive, IT Delivery Executive, and PM agree most accurately describes how the program or project delivered on the Schedule Commitment based on the criteria specified. Enter this field during program or project delivery assessment.

- **Cost Commitment:** Provide the approved budget for the project or release.

- **Cost Criteria:** Provide criteria for the corresponding assessment level or indicate "N/A" if there is no meaningful criterion for the corresponding criteria level. The forecast is the dollar estimate to complete for the project. The criteria that the template provides may be sufficient to describe assessment criteria for your program or project.

- **Cost Commitment Delivery Assessment:** Select from the drop down list the assessment value that the Business Delivery Executive, IT Delivery Executive, and PM agree most accurately describes how the program or project delivered on the Cost Commitment based on the criteria specified. Enter this field during program or project delivery assessment.

- **Quality Commitment:** Provide the program or project commitment in the area of Quality.

- **Quality Criteria:** Provide criteria for the corresponding assessment level or indicate "N/A" if there is no meaningful criterion for the corresponding criteria level. The criteria that the template provides may be sufficient to describe assessment criteria for your program or project.

- **Quality Commitment Delivery Assessment:** Select from the drop down list the assessment value that the Business Delivery Executive, IT Delivery Executive, and PM agree most accurately describes how the program or project delivered on the Quality Commitment. Enter this field during program or project delivery assessment.

- **Architecture Commitment:** Provide the program or project commitment in the area of Architecture.

- **Architecture Criteria:** Provide criteria for the corresponding assessment level or indicate "N/A" if there is no meaningful criterion for the corresponding criteria level. The criteria that the template provides may be sufficient to describe assessment criteria for your program or project.

- **Architecture Commitment Delivery Assessment:** Select from the drop down list the assessment value that the Business Delivery Executive, IT Delivery Executive, and PM agree most accurately describes how the program or project delivered on the Architecture Commitment. If the Business Delivery Executive, IT Delivery Executive, and PM cannot determine, with certainty, whether the solution will support achievement of all Critical Success Factors and satisfies all Stakeholder Needs, they should concur on the most probable result. Enter this field during program or project delivery assessment.

- **Value Commitment:** Provide the program or project commitment in the area of Value.

- **Value Criteria:** Provide criteria for the corresponding assessment level or indicate "N/A" if there is no meaningful criterion for the corresponding criteria level. The criteria that the template provides may be sufficient to describe assessment criteria for your program or project.

- **Value Commitment Delivery Assessment:** Select from the drop down list the assessment value that the Business Delivery Executive, IT Delivery Executive, and PM agree most accurately describes how the program or project delivered on the Value Commitment. If the Business Delivery Executive, IT Delivery Executive, and PM cannot determine, with certainty, whether the solution will achieve the expected business value, they should concur on the most probable result. Enter this field during program or project delivery assessment.

Completion Guidelines

The Post Implementation Commitment Review Report is required for OCEO projects or programs and by projects or programs whose Post Implementation Commitment Reviews are being tracked by the line of business Delivery Services organization. The Post Implementation Commitment Review Report is created, maintained and completed as follows:

- **Post Implementation Commitment Review Report Creation:** The Business Delivery Executive, IT Delivery Executive and PM use the Post Implementation Commitment Review Report template and complete all sections and fields, with the exception of the Approval date and the Commitment Delivery Assessments, within 10 days of the end of the Design Phase.

- **Post Implementation Commitment Review Report Maintenance:** The Business Delivery Executive, IT Delivery Executive, and PM may change baseline commitments as a result of program or project Change Requests throughout the Develop Phase. However, not all Change Requests are eligible to drive changes to baseline commitments. The Change Requests that are eligible to drive updates to baseline commitments are the same as those that are eligible to drive work plan baseline changes. See Work Plan Change Request Management Guidelines for further direction.

- **Post Implementation Commitment Review Report Completion:** The Business Delivery Executive, IT Delivery Executive, and PM complete the Approval date and the Commitment Delivery Assessments within 30 days after implementation. The IT Delivery Executive or Business Delivery Executive may revise the assessment 90 days after implementation or at the end of the warranty period, whichever is later.

14.3.2.2 – Describe the project management process guidelines being employed by the PMO.

We leverage a home grown methodology called *Enterprise Solution Delivery Methodology.* It is broken into Classic and Agile methods and provides a process, deliverables, and work products to be leveraged based on the method used.

For example, Enterprise Solution Delivery methodology classic components include:

- Five project phases: Initiate, Solution Scoping, Design, Develop and Implement
- Four dimensions: People, Process, Technology and Program Management
- Eight disciplines: Organizational Change, User Experience, Requirements, Architecture, Application, Production Readiness and Project Management

Our Enterprise Solution Delivery methodology (ESDm) that is a Classic methodology is shown below in Figure 14-17 at the end of this survey area.

We also have Enterprise Solution Delivery Agile methodology, which we just recently developed for the enterprise.

14.3.2.3 – What systems, tools, and templates make your PMO successful?	The Project Management tool set is Clarity. Clarity Workbench is leveraged for work-plan management, resource management (charging hours to projects), financial management, portfolio management, demand management, billing, and reporting.
	We leverage deliverable templates and store example documents for all major deliverable documents. These are stored on-line and available for any team member to utilize.
	In addition to storing deliverable documents, we also leverage a website to collect improvement ideas to make the templates better.
14.3.2.4 – Describe how management at all levels is directly involved in the development of the PMO and it processes.	There is an executive team made up of IT Profession Owners and leaders that form the Build Leadership Team. This team is focused on improving the build process, tools, and capabilities for IT development. Subteams are formed to work on initiatives that improve these processes at all levels of the organization.
	The PMO includes PM and Requirements Analyst (RA) professionals and reports up to the Office of the Enterprise Chief Technology Officer (ECTO), which also includes the enterprise architects. Therefore, this team has a close working relationship and fills key roles on all projects.
14.3.2.5 – Describe the implementation plan you used for establishing project / program / portfolio management standards across your enterprise.	Delivery Services partners with our Build Leadership Team on process changes and improvements related to delivering projects.
	We leverage experts in organizational change management to rollout any changes to the resource and the organizations. Communication and training plans are managed closely to ensure all parties are informed and prepared.
	Prior to any major changes, we obtain the correct sponsorship and approval from our Chief Information Officers.
14.3.2.6 – How does the PMO use project, program, and portfolio management standards to optimize its practices?	The standards leveraged by the PMO are based on PMI practices and tailored to fit the organization. The PMO encourages investment in all employees, therefore, we often attend and support local PMI chapter development days. In addition, we have partnered with Stanford University to raise the bar on PM learning and have brought Stanford's Advanced Project Management Certification program on-site to Nationwide.

Are they based on PMI® or other industry guides and are they updated as new editions of the guides are released?

In regards to improvements, they are mostly based on developments and ideas surfacing from the Build Leadership Team and sponsored by our IT Strategy Council.

FIGURE 14-17: Nationwide Enterprise Solution Delivery methodology (ESDm)

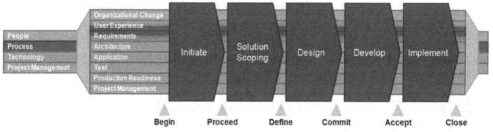

14.3.3 SURVEY – PMO Capabilities: Describe development and assessment of the enterprise's abilities, describe any project management competency model, summarize any education and training program, describe any established career path progression plan, and outline key Enterprise Environmental Factors.

14.3.3.1 – Describe the components of your enterprise's training program.

We have developed a Project Management Learning Roadmap. This roadmap is a 3 year plan to raise the bar on our PM education.

We have partnered with Stanford University to offer courses onsite. One class is called PM Fundamentals, which focuses on the basics of project management. For the more advanced PMs, we are sponsoring Stanford's Advanced Project Management Certification program.

In addition, we have a variety of other classes that are offered for unique needs, i.e. negotiation skills. In addition, we have specialized tool training, and on-boarding classes.

We also encourage associates to leverage seminars and other training opportunities that fit into their own self-development plan.

We work closely with our Enterprise Learning Solutions team (training department) to bring the appropriate classes to our company.

14.3.3.2 – Describe the value your enterprise places on education and training and its goals and objectives.

We have a department dedicated to education and training, called Learning Solutions. Our organization partners with Learning Solutions to enhance training and look for new courses.

In addition, the Delivery Services organization has formed a team of practitioners to work together to develop creative ways to further develop our organization and associates in the PM and Analyst profession.

Budget is set aside for each associate to use for training and development on a yearly basis. All training is linked to the associate's individual development plan.

14.3.3.3 – Does the enterprise have a project management career path program? If so, what are the components?

The program / project management career path is illustrated in Figure 14-18 below.

There are Profession Guides for each profession at Nationwide IT.

14.3.3.4 – Describe the measurements, metrics, and Key Performance Indicators (KPI's) utilized by the PMO to determine the organization's knowledge, skills, and level of achievement.

Delivery Services maintains metrics on staffing, customer satisfaction of resources and Post Implementation Commitment Review results.

We are also in the process of enhancing our associate database which will house key metrics on their background, skills, level, areas of expertise, etc.

In our monthly operation reviews we review several KPIs, including:
- Staffing Trends
- Resource Requisitions
- PM Transitions (See Figure 14-10)
- Lead Times from Business Solution Areas for resources
- Financials
- People metrics (turnover, hiring, etc.)

See some sample graphs that are produced and reviewed each month are shown below

In Figure 14-18, Figures 14-19, Figures 14-20, and Figures 14-21:

14.3.3.5 – Does the enterprise employ a project management competency model? If yes, please describe it. If no, why not?	Yes, Delivery Services uses a PM competency model. Our levels are included below in the career path information of Figure 14-22 and are also found and detailed in our Profession Guide.

FIGURE 14-18: Nationwide PM Staffing Requests and Fulfillment

PM Requests	Jan-11	Feb-11	Mar-11	Apr-11	May-11	Jun-11	Jul-11	Aug-11	Sep-11	Oct-11
Demand In (Gross)	60	60	50	40	20	28	27	63	48	32
Cancelled Demand	4	6	4	6	1	0	0	0	1	3
Demand In (Net)	56	54	46	34	19	28	27	63	47	29
Demand Filled	70	63	49	43	24	32	29	50	32	34
Transitions In (Gross)	25	12	14	19	15	18	18	21	10	24
Cancelled Transitions	5	1	1	1	3	1	2	0	1	0
Transitions In (Net)	20	11	13	18	12	17	16	21	9	24
Transitions Filled	20	16	16	15	12	14	21	22	10	21
Total Requests In (Net)	76	65	59	52	31	45	43	84	56	53
Total Requests Filled	90	79	65	58	36	46	50	72	42	55
Transition YTD % (Net)	26%	22%	22%	25%	26%	28%	29%	28%	27%	29%

FIGURE 14-19: Nationwide Delivery Services Resource Requisitions

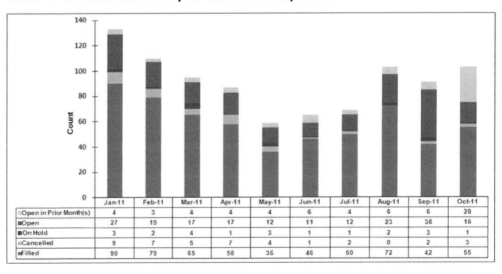

	Jan-11	Feb-11	Mar-11	Apr-11	May-11	Jun-11	Jul-11	Aug-11	Sep-11	Oct-11
Open in Prior Month(s)	4	3	4	4	4	6	4	6	6	28
Open	27	19	17	17	12	11	12	23	38	16
On Hold	3	2	4	1	3	1	1	2	3	1
Cancelled	9	7	5	7	4	1	2	0	2	3
Filled	90	79	65	58	36	46	50	72	42	55

FIGURE 14-20: Nationwide PM Transitions by Category

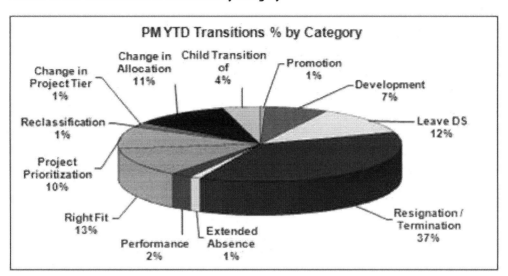

FIGURE 14-21: Nationwide Lead Time from BSA for Resources

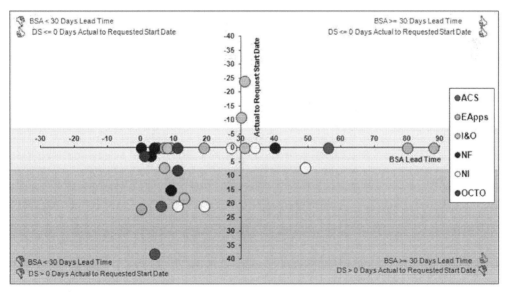

FIGURE 14-22: Nationwide Program / Project Management Career Path

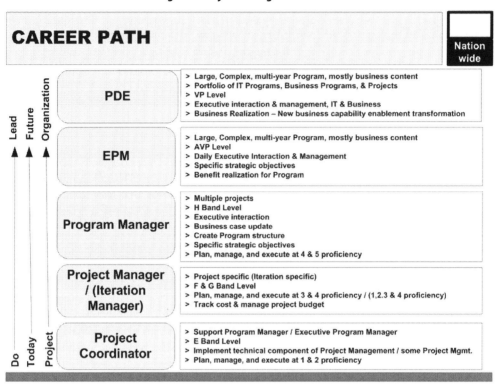

14.3.4.1 – Describe the organizational structure and process used for corporate strategic business planning.

The PMO is a partner in the strategic planning. Our Business Transformation Office (BTO) handles most of the plan work and incorporates the project selection process with the business areas that are funding or requesting the work. Prioritization occurs at the highest level of the enterprise.

Does the PMO play a role in the process? If so, describe the PMOs role and responsibilities.

PMO plays a role with providing project planning and analysis information that is leveraged in the business cases. Our Executive PMs reside in the BTO organization to allow for close alignment to our most strategic and large initiatives.

14.3.4.2 – How is the strategic plan implemented with a project forecast plan?	Clarity/Workbench is leveraged to plan out (allocate) the resources and forecast the project. Once the plans are put into the tool, an analysis is performed to determine resource constraints. Then risks are documented and plans are put into place for mitigation. The Business Solution Area Portfolio Leaders are accountable inputting all new projects initial plans into the tool to determine the ability to deliver based on resource needs. Once the project is reviewed and approved, it is then moved to a PM to kickoff. Updates to the resources and forecasts then become the responsibility of the PM.
14.3.4.3 – How is strategic planning, culture, and selection of projects integrated?	The Business Transformation Council (BTC) works closely with all key business areas to determine the correct selection of projects based on strategic intent and alignment to the enterprise vision and mission. Objectives are then aligned to support the project selection at the highest level and then appropriately applied at all levels of the organization. Alignment of project and personal performance objectives helps to drive the culture and integration of project needs.

> **14.3.5 SURVEY – PMO Business Execution:** Describe what role the PMO has in project selection, prioritization, and initiation; in portfolio, pro-gram and project execution planning; in stage-gate reviews; and in performance metrics selection and application.

14.3.5.1 – How are portfolios, programs, and projects selected and initiated?	Representatives from the Business Transformation Council (BTC) select the projects to receive funding across teams. In addition, each business unit also has some funding that they can leverage for projects that only impact one line of business.
14.3.5.2 – How are projects organized and managed as a program and/or portfolio?	Projects are organized by business case. If there are multiple business cases that support the same goals, they form a program and are organized together. Portfolios are managed by business unit and then by business solution area. For example, our Nationwide Insurance projects are organized together and our Nationwide Financial projects are organized together. Under the Nationwide Insurance portfolio, projects are organized by solution area, i.e. claims, billing, etc.

14.3.5.3 – How are projects prioritized within a program and/or portfolio?

Each business unit selects and prioritizes the projects within a portfolio. A cross selection of business line leaders are brought together to decide the priority.

14.3.5.4 – How does the enterprise define what project and program success is?

In order to receive project funding, a business case is developed with business objectives. The program/projects then further define more specific scope and deliverable items. The enterprise defines success by meeting these objectives and getting a positive Post Implementation Commitment Review (PICR) score (see above).

14.3.5.5 – Does the PMO support the management of projects that would be considered operational in nature? If so, describe the types of projects.

No, Delivery Services does not handle the small operational projects.

We allow Business Solution Areas to handle small application enhancements, rate, and regulatory type work.

> **14.3.6 SURVEY – PMO Sustainability:** Describe the overall impact of the PMO over a sustained period (e.g., customer satisfaction, productivity, reduced cycle time, growth, building or changing organizational culture, etc.). If available, please provide quantitative data to illustrate the areas in which the PMO has had the greatest business impact.

14.3.6.1 – What is included in a comprehensive project monitoring and control system and how is it implemented?

Projects are monitored via normal project status reports and are reviewed in monthly Operation Reviews with each Chief Information Officer and Business Solutions Area. Project status can also be monitored and compared to statistics pulled on cost performance index (CPI), schedule performance index (SPI), etc.

A business management department (outside of the PMO) runs reports on project status on a regular basis and provides these reports to our leaders. Information for these reports is pulled directly from the project system (Clarity / Workbench).

Selected projects are also monitored via a 7 Leading Indicators review. These reviews are conducted by PM Coaches to provide insights to leadership on the progress of the projects. The seven

areas are:
1) Stakeholders are Committed
2) Benefits are Realized
3) Work & Schedule are Predictable
4) Scope is Defined & Managed
5) Team is High Performing
6) Risks and Issues are Addressed
7) Best Practices are Leveraged and Developed

Reports are also generated on these reviews by our business management department. The status is provided via red, yellow, green indicators within the Leading Indicators report. A sample report is shown at the end of this survey area in Figure 14-23.

14.3.6.2 – How are project start-up and gate review processes structured?

We have a Begin Gate (see Classic process in Figure 14-24 shown at the end of this survey). In the Begin Gate, several questions are asked under the categories: Scope, Architecture, Quality, Project Control, Schedule, Cost, Value and General Questions.

These questions identify whether the Begin Gate criteria was met or not. If the criteria was not met, information must be provided by the team to justify moving forward and determine how risks will be handled. Delivery Executives are also provided with checklists to help them question the project team and assess whether each gate should be passed and allow the team to move to the next phase.

The Stage Gate process is defined as:
The Stage Gate process provides a specific point in time to evaluate if the project should continue based on its likelihood to deliver on the business case. Project leadership makes a go/no-go decision based on the project's achievement of the phase objectives and its readiness to begin the next phase. Additionally, the process enables project leaders to proactively identify and address common delivery issues and risks throughout the project delivery lifecycle.

Enterprise Solution Delivery Methodology Stage Gates ensure quality by providing:
- Stage Gate Report questions that enable the Delivery Executives to make a "point in time" business decision to transition to the next lifecycle phase based on project performance.

- Stage Gate Checklists for the Delivery Executives, Troika, and Test Lead to use throughout the project to identify and address delivery issues and risks.

Stage Gate Roles and Responsibilities:

IT Delivery Executive

- Is accountable for successful execution of the Stage Gate process
- Leverages Delivery Executives Checklist with Business Delivery Executive, as appropriate
- Ensures Stage Gate meeting is an effective use of the Business Delivery Executive's time (i.e., review Enterprise Solution Delivery methodology technical details with team prior to the Stage Gate meeting) and makes the Go/No Go decision with the Business Delivery Executive

Business Delivery Executive

- Is responsible to make the business' assessment of the project in the stage gate meeting and makes the Go/No Go decision with the IT Delivery Executive
- Leverages Delivery Executives Checklist with IT Delivery Executive, as appropriate

QA Lead

- Is responsible for implementing the stage gate process on the project
- Schedules and facilitates the Troika's use of the Troika Checklist throughout each phase
- Facilitates the Stage Gate meeting and its preparations
  - *Note: Many projects do not have a specific QA Lead role, and often the PM fulfills that role. This document will refer to the QA Lead role with the understanding that the role may be fulfilled by the PM. The Begin Gate and the Close Gate may not have a QA Lead role or a PM; only a Subject Matter Expert may be available, replacing the QA Lead role for those gates.*
  -

Troika

- Is responsible for preparing and participating in the Stage Gate decision making
- Collaboratively identify and address common delivery issues and risks with the QA Lead/PM through use of the Troika Checklist

Stage Gate Process:

The overall Stage Gate process is shown in Figure 14-24 at the end of this survey area. The Begin Gate occurs prior to the start of the Initiate phase. The Stage Gate process is largely the same for the Initiate, Solution Scoping, Design and Develop phase. The Implement phase supports its Close Gate a little differently in the warranty period but the basic steps are the same. Find guidance for using Stage Gates on Iterative projects in the Tailoring section.

Starting in 2012, all Stage Gate results will be stored in our Clarity Database to allow for reporting and analysis on progress and results.

14.3.6.3 – Describe the project knowledge base system and how is it developed?

Knowledge is shared on-line via shared document storage sites and blogs. In addition, we have a continuous improvement option for our methodology site, which encourages associates to "Simplify It," via improvement suggestions.

14.3.6.4 – Describe the measurement, metrics, and Key Performance Indicators (KPIs) utilized by the PMO to measure project and program success.

Key measurements leveraged by the PMO include those described above, i.e. Post Implementation Commitment Review and seven Leading Indicators. We also provide insights on project/program status and discuss all of these items at monthly operational reviews.

Metrics on resource allocations, hard booking, availability of resources, business case information, etc. are provided by other departments at Nationwide Insurance but are leveraged by our department also.

14.3.6.5 – Describe the organizational benefits and value the PMO provides to the enterprise.

The PMO provides centralized training to PMs and Requirements Analyst (RA), therefore the Business Solution Areas do not have to handle any of those responsibilities. In addition, we provide training for project roles, process, methodology, etc. We also provide ad hoc training, as needed and requested, related to any project concerns.

Our PMO sets clear role expectations and objectives. We calibrate performance across the entire PM and Requirements Analyst (RA) population, which allows for consistency in year end evaluations.

Our PMO also provides full-time PM and Requirements Analyst (RA) Coaches, who spend the majority of their time focusing on capability uplift, associate development, process improvement and associate engagement.

14.3.6.6 – Describe the economic benefits and value the PMO provides to the enterprise.

With centralization of key project resources we have removed the time necessary for Business Solution Areas to fill those positions and work with vendors on contract services. With centralization, we have also been able to build deeper relationships with a few vendors and have been able to control costs by getting a lower per hour charge by providing the vendors with volume of needs.

In addition, prior to centralization, Business Solution Areas would get funding for a year and may need several PMs and Requirements Analyst (RA). The following year they would not get the funding to sustain these positions, therefore causing morale issues and workforce planning concerns. With our centralized model, we can now move the resources to where the work is located, year after year.

The centralized model prevents the Business Solution Areas from having to use their own financial resources on growing the project delivery capabilities. We have pooled those dollars within our PMO, therefore requiring less funding for those efforts and saving the enterprise money overall.

FIGURE 14-23: Nationwide Seven Leading Indicators Color Coded Report Sample

Program Project	Stakeholders are Committed	Benefits are Realized	Work & Schedule are Predictable	Scope is Defined & Managed	Team is High Performing	Risks & Issues are Addressed	Best Practices Leveraged & Developed
Project X	Green	Yellow	Green	Red	Yellow	Green	Green

FIGURE 14-24: Nationwide IT Stage Gate Process

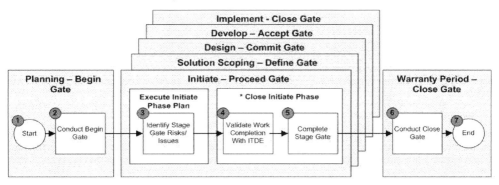

14.3.7 SURVEY – Additional Comments: Please provide any additional comments

The overall Nationwide IT core capabilities of which Delivery Services is a part is depicted below in Figure 14-25. It shows the sequential relationship from Plan to Build to Run. Delivery Services primary efforts are in the plan and build phases.

FIGURE 14-25: Nationwide IT Core Capabilities Framework

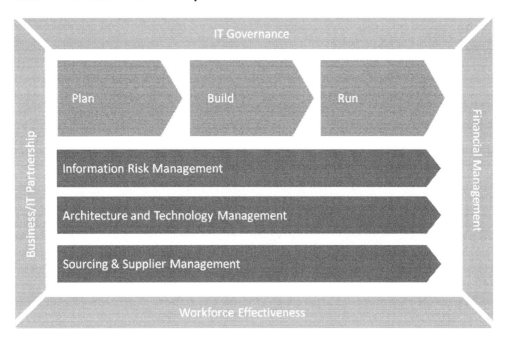

Chapter 15

Railinc PMO Case Study

Railinc is the railroad industry's most innovative and reliable resource for information technology (IT) and information services. Beginning as an information technology department within the Association of American Railroads (AAR), Railinc has evolved to meet the dynamic information needs of the railroad industry. The company was established as a wholly owned, for-profit subsidiary of the AAR in 1999.

They support business processes and provide business intelligence that help railroads and rail equipment owners increase productivity, achieve operational efficiencies and keep their assets moving. Railinc is the industry's largest and most accurate source for real-time interline rail data.

Railinc is focused on creating value for the rail system and their systems have been an integral part of the North American rail industry for almost 40 years. Railinc applications and services are embedded in critical operations and financial systems throughout the industry and support railroads, equipment owners and rail industry suppliers along every link of the supply chain.

15.1   Railinc – Enterprise and PMO Office Information

Enterprise Name:	Railinc
Country:	United States
Industry:	Transportation, Information Technology & Software
Enterprise – Annual Sales Revenue:	Small; $50 Million in US Dollars
Enterprise – Full-time Employee Equivalents:	225
World Wide Web Site:	www.railinc.com
PMO Name:	Project Management Office
Title of PMO Leader:	Director

PMO Position in Organizational Structure:	Major Projects (AAR Industry-Wide Initiatives)
PMO reports to in Organizational Structure:	Assistant Vice President, Products and Services
PMO Annual Operating Budget:	Less than $250,000 in US Dollars
PMO – Full-time Employee Equivalents:	1 (More FTE's are in reporting structure, but do not perform PMO functions)

The following are the PMO Case Study Survey question sets and the associated responses as submitted by the Railinc's Project Management Office, with minor editing for format and consistency.

15.2 Railinc PMO Background, Innovations, and Impact

In the following three parts of this case study, the Railinc's Project Management Office provides an overview of the background and structure of its PMO, various innovations and best practices by the PMO, and the potential future business impact of the PMO.

15.2.1 SURVEY – PMO Background: Describe your PMO, including background information on its scope, vision, mission, and position within the enterprise's organizational structure.

Prior to 2007, the PMO was organizationally aligned within Information Technology and reported directly to the Chief Information Officer.

The primary role was advisory at best, focused on facilitating annual project request process, status reporting, standards, and templates. As a cost center, the PMO was not viewed as an essential business function and support was tepid. The PMO changed focus beginning in the summer of 2007, when a new director was hired to implement strategic change.

The Project Management Office was re-chartered in 2007 with the following vision, mission, and objectives:

Vision:

The PMO is a support organization created for the purpose of optimizing the portfolio of projects to provide overall value and further enterprise objectives.

Mission:

To provide decision support for:

1) Project Management (to optimize project delivery process)
2) Portfolio Management (to build the right things)
3) Business Analysis (to build things right)

Objectives:

- Share project management best standards
- Create visibility into project performance
- Drive successful project delivery
- Facilitate project portfolio optimization
- Create visibility into business case realization

Since 2007, the PMO has adapted to provide value by aligning internally with the business product owners and externally with customer business executive sponsors. Organizationally, the PMO reports to the executive with responsibility for the AAR Products and Services group, from both a functional level as well as fiduciary accountability. The current scope of the PMO includes the Portfolio Management processes for customer-driven projects.

15.2.2 SURVEY – PMO Innovations and Best Practices: Address the challenges your enterprise encountered prior to implementing the new PMO practices and how you overcame those challenges. Describe clearly and concisely the practices implemented and their effect on project, program, and/or portfolio and organizational success.

The biggest challenge faced by the PMO in 2007 was one of legitimacy. The question of value was being raised by internal and external stakeholders. After a 90-day needs analysis conducted by interviewing internal stakeholders and working with senior executive management, the new approach for the PMO increased the role from advisory to strategic with emphasis on portfolio management. The executive summary (excerpted from the 2007 charter) summarizes the strategic direction and vision of the PMO, "To ensure that the right projects, and only the right projects, are correctly prioritized and holistically managed to provide overall value and further enterprise objectives."

Portfolio stakeholders and the governance model were clearly defined in the charter, which was signed by the executive management. A portfolio review committee consisting of executives and senior managers that sponsor company projects and key initiatives was initiated beginning with the 2008 budgetary (fiscal) cycle. The group convened to oversee the delivery of the portfolio of work for each fiscal year as well as approve Go/No-Go decisions for each project based on stage gate reviews and other supporting data.

Portfolio processes and the communication plan were also defined in the charter and the implementation progressed with an overview for all employees, training provided to functional groups, status meetings, status reports, and additional analyses/reporting as defined.

> **15.2.3 SURVEY – PMO Future Impact:** Briefly describe your PMO's plans for 2012 and beyond - please describe how those plans will potentially impact your enterprise and its organizational structure.

The PMO's plans for the future take into account several enterprise factors:

1) Project management methodology is aligned within product areas, implementing product strategies as defined by internal product owners and key external business sponsors (project context may be broader and more strategically positioned).

2) Current economic realities and strong leadership have surfaced significant opportunities to leverage program management capabilities with the expectation of defined business benefits (benefits realization).

15.3   Railinc PMO Model Components

In the following six parts of this case study, the Railinc's Project Management Office provides its descriptions of how they implement the six key components of the Project Business Management Organization model: Governance; Methodology; Capability; Planning; Execution; and Sustainability.

> **15.3.1 SURVEY – PMO Governance:** Describe how your PMO presents itself as an executive-level management business function, how it addresses setting policy and establishing charters, and how it provides an organizational model for the business management of portfolios, programs, and projects and the establishment of portfolio, program, and project management offices.

The Railinc PMO is aligned externally with an advisory committee comprised of our primary business customers. This committee is chartered with responsibility for the following primary roles:
- Act as ultimate sponsors for projects
- Help to prioritize Railinc's product investment
- Commit to financial and resource support for approved projects

The Railinc PMO director supports this committee by fulfilling the following duties:

- Manage project delivery
- Communicate project status
- Assess risks and escalate issues for action
- Manage the project selection process and provide supporting tools and timelines
- Publish prioritized list of approved work
- Analyze other industry product investment needs
- Support customer focused efforts with informative communications
- Provide visibility into commitment authorizations for funding and resources

15.3.1.1 – How long has the PMO been in place?	This PMO has been in place ten (10) years.
When was it started?	This PMO was started in 2001.
15.3.1.2 – What is the relationship of PMO management to the enterprise's operational management?	Correlated to operational management (direct line of business).
15.3.1.3 – How is the PMO internally structured (positions, roles etc.)?	PMO role is one of functional alliance directly with the business unit, externally focused on customer.
15.3.1.4 – How are the PMO's operations funded?	The PMO is operationally funded.
15.3.1.5 – What is the summary position description of the PMO leader?	The PMO Director sets the strategy and directs PMO activities.

The PMO Director leads the group to:

- Establish, maintain, and communicate project management methodologies, and facilitate participants through the accompanying processes
- Centrally collect and report project status
- Coach, mentor and train project managers to help them succeed with their projects
- Establish and execute a portfolio management strategy that is customer driven

- The PMO Director leads and facilitates process improvement efforts

- The PMO Director has budgetary responsibility including; planning, budgeting and allocating portfolio driven business decisions and trade-offs

15.3.1.6 – What position requirements are used as a basis for selecting the PMO leader?

The position requirements for the PMO Director are:
- Bachelor's degree in business management or related field
- A minimum of 5 to 7 years of information technology and business/marketing experience
- Significant information technology experience with a thorough understanding of Internet technologies and architectures is required
- Proven ability to work with and manage cross-functional teams
- A high degree of business acumen, sales savvy, initiative, and enthusiasm about interactive online / community-based services
- Excellent communication skills, PMI/PMP accreditation desired
- Knowledge of MS Project, MS Office Suite, Web Enabling, and other state-of-the-art technologies
- Self-motivated, team player, able to build collaborative work teams in a matrix authority environment
- Excellent interpersonal consensus building and presentation skills
- Creative decision making skills
- Previous experience managing teams
- Strong project management skills

15.3.1.7 – Is the PMO a Profit & Loss cost center or considered overhead?

The PMO is considered to be overhead.

15.3.1.8 – What current challenge is the PMO dealing with?

Maintaining customer-driven practical solutions is an on-going challenge for the PMO.

> **15.3.2 SURVEY – PMO Methodology / Standardization:** Describe what standardization your PMO has implemented across the enterprise that examines: identification and integration of processes and practices; development of standardized Project Business Management processes; and documentation of enterprise-wide portfolio, program, and project management process methodology models, including their associated policies, practices, and procedures.

The PMO links with IT to develop relevant project management lifecycle, encompasses Agile development. (See Figure 15-1: 2012 Project Management Lifecycle diagram at the end of the case study)

15.3.2.1 – Describe the standards utilized by the PMO to ensure the enterprise's project / program / portfolio management goals and objectives are achieved.	The PMO employs direct results, including customer feedback (sponsor scorecard and process survey) and budgetary allocation.
15.3.2.2 – Describe the project management process guidelines being employed by the PMO.	We use a mixture of portfolio and program management guidelines for the initiation and planning stages, and Agile development methodology for the development lifecycle.
15.3.2.3 – What systems, tools, and templates make your PMO successful?	We use SharePoint, which is extremely valuable as a business tool, including workflow elements that have been developed to support sign-off and commitment on projects that are approved.
15.3.2.4 – Describe how management at all levels is directly involved in the development of the PMO and it processes.	Senior management is directly involved with policy only. Policies that are escalated include items that are externally facing and involve the advisory committee.
	Processes are designed by the PMO Director, approved by the direct manager (Assistant Vice President of the business unit).

15.3.2.5 – Describe the implementation plan you used for establishing project / program / portfolio management standards across your enterprise.

We establish standards very lightly, enforce them using good common sense, while ensuring that the PMO provides the *right* level of rigor for the *right* process at the *right* time.

15.3.2.6 – How does the PMO use project, program, and portfolio management standards to optimize its practices?

We use published standards and guidelines sparingly, we use direct contacts and experience.

Are they based on PMI® or other industry guides and are they updated as new editions of the guides are released?

Specific answer not provided.

> **15.3.3 SURVEY – PMO Capabilities:** Describe development and assessment of the enterprise's abilities, describe any project management competency model, summarize any education and training program, describe any established career path progression plan, and outline key Enterprise Environmental Factors.

Since we are a very small organization, there is no formalized training program specifically oriented towards project management competencies. We do have a robust Agile training program and are developing product management competencies as well. In addition, we are implementing a training program focused on vertical market knowledge.

15.3.3.1 – Describe the components of your enterprise's training program.

The component within our training program include: subject matter expertise (specifically railroad), internal expertise (IT systems knowledge), Agile development methodology, product management expertise (customer focused, including business architecture development), and business analyst skills.

15.3.3.2 – Describe the value your enterprise places on education and training and its goals and objectives.	The learning and growth perspective of the company's strategy focuses on equipping our people with the competencies, attitudes, skills, and behavior to further our enterprise objectives. This includes clear roles, responsibilities and standards of excellence.

The desired outcome: increase employee engagement and drive process improvement capability through building Human Capital (competencies, attitudes, skills, behaviors); enabled by Information Capital (analytics; integrated data, tools, processes); and Organizational Capital (culture, leadership; alignment with values and principles).

15.3.3.3 – Does the enterprise have a project management career path program? If so, what are the components?	We do not have a specific career path at this time.

15.3.3.4 – Describe the measurements, metrics, and Key Performance Indicators (KPI's) utilized by the PMO to determine the organization's knowledge, skills, and level of achievement.	There are two key measurements for the PMO that directly correlate to the key areas of accountability: • Budgetary investment for future project work • Effective completion of current project work The metrics are: • Financial investment (target) • Project sponsor scorecard (results assimilated in summary format from sponsor Committee)

15.3.3.5 – Does the enterprise employ a project management competency model? If yes, please describe it. If no, why not?	No, the PMO does not specifically employ a competency model.

> **15.3.4 SURVEY – PMO Business Planning:** Discuss strategic business planning, tactical business planning, business objective (project) development and prioritization, and project identification, selection, and authorization.

Operational Excellence comprises Railinc's core strategy.

15.3.4.1 – Describe the organizational structure and process used for corporate strategic business planning.	The Operational Excellence strategy is driven across the organization in a cohesive manner by tying the annual business objectives to elements of the core strategy.
Does the PMO play a role in the process? If so, describe the PMOs role and responsibilities.	The PMO is not directly involved with this process, though the PMO Director is aligned directly with the division's objectives.
15.3.4.2 – How is the strategic plan implemented with a project forecast plan?	The project forecast is measured in terms of actual results (see above) in two ways, both financially and by customer feedback (Sponsor Scorecard survey results).
15.3.4.3 – How is strategic planning, culture, and selection of projects integrated?	Each is closely aligned with the business unit, and there is frequent communication with clear expectations with the product managers who are responsible for the products in their portfolio.

> **15.3.5 SURVEY – PMO Business Execution:** Describe what role the PMO has in project selection, prioritization, and initiation; in portfolio, program and project execution planning; in stage-gate reviews; and in performance metrics selection and application.

The PMO drives the process for project selection, prioritization and initiation in selecting new work for the future business year. The process is comprehensive (see Figure 15-2: 2012 Portfolio Selection Process diagram at the end of the case study).

15.3.5.1 – How are portfolios, programs, and projects selected and initiated?	We are the PMO for a small company, reporting directly to the Assistant Vice President who is the budgetary and resource authority over all of the work, including projects, programs and operational components.
15.3.5.2 – How are projects organized and managed as a program and/or portfolio?	Projects are organized as programs (as deemed appropriate) through direct communication with project sponsors, both external customers and internally driven through product manager strategy.
15.3.5.3 – How are projects prioritized within a program and/or portfolio?	Projects are prioritized with significant assistance from the advisory committee.
15.3.5.4 – How does the enterprise define what project and program success is?	Each project has its own measures of success that are defined by the value proposition for that initiative. That vision is further refined when planning is formalized and validated by the team, usually during the envisioning meeting (Agile process step).

These measures are documented and further validated during the development life cycle. At the conclusion of the project, participants sign off on the specific themes that comprise the value proposition and the pre-defined measures of success. |
| *15.3.5.5 – Does the PMO support the management of projects that would be considered operational in nature? If so, describe the types of projects.* | Yes, we support projects that are operational in nature. An example is a product enhancement for existing code.

Some organizations term this work "new feature" (versus maintenance or support). |

15.3.6 SURVEY – PMO Sustainability: Describe the overall impact of the PMO over a sustained period (e.g., customer satisfaction, productivity, reduced cycle time, growth, building or changing organizational culture, etc.). If available, please provide quantitative data to illustrate the areas in which the PMO has had the greatest business impact.

The largest impact that the PMO has had over a sustained period may not be directly measured at this time. Changing organizational culture is a difficult area to quantify. However, the alignment within a business unit has been instrumental in facilitating the maturity and importance of the PMO. Current initiatives include major, large programs that may ultimately drive the organization's direction for many years to come.

15.3.6.1 – What is included in a comprehensive project monitoring and control system and how is it implemented?	The project monitoring and control is under the responsibility of the individual project managers for the execution of the project product (software code) and the product manager for that line of business is accountable for the usability and "fit" for the production implementation and/or release.

The PMO governance activities include status reporting, issue/risk management, communication when sponsor decisions are required, and change management. |
| *15.3.6.2 – How are project start-up and gate review processes structured?* | Please see the Figure 15-1: 2012 Project Management Lifecycle diagram at the end of the case study. |
| *15.3.6.3 – Describe the project knowledge base system and how is it developed?* | We use a variety of tools and supporting products for knowledge dissemination and to further our product/project maturity.

Among them is the daily standup meeting, which is a core tenet of the Agile development methodology. It is an effective and quick method of relaying the most important information to the team using the least amount of time to get the day's work accomplished on the most important items, as prioritized by the team. |
| *15.3.6.4 – Describe the measurement, metrics, and Key Performance Indicators (KPIs) utilized by the PMO to measure project and program success.* | Project success is currently measured by these two criteria (at a minimum):
• Defined functionality is provided to support the business need
• Adherence to scope, quality, schedule, and budget expectations

Program success is defined as meeting expectations for industry |

return on investment, as formalized in the business case.

Measurements for benefits realization on projects will be in development during this fiscal year, with implementation for a subset of projects meeting threshold criteria to be implemented beginning 2013.

15.3.6.5 – Describe the organizational benefits and value the PMO provides to the enterprise.

Organizational benefits the PMO provides include:

- Implement selection of work annually through a cohesive process that drives business objectives
- Facilitate project portfolio optimization through a vetting and selection process with an external advisory board comprised of our major customers
- Create visibility into business case optimization through a rigorous business case development process that begins with an "opportunity definition"
- Provide comprehensive communication to external and internal stakeholders on pipeline at stage gate review checkpoints
- Monitor and control selected project work to provide visibility into issues and risk, and maintain themes or communicate changes (as dictated by business needs)
- Partner with finance, relationship directors, and other internal stakeholders to provide a holistic view for our customers

15.3.6.6 – Describe the economic benefits and value the PMO provides to the enterprise.

Benefits and value provided are:

- Annual budget realization
- Selecting the "right" work
- Elimination of redundant initiatives
- Elimination of "pet" projects
- Avoiding products that customers do not want, will not value, or do not meet business objectives
- Limits over budget projects or run away projects
- Better resource alignment and utilization through annual staffing plans that are tied to the budget

15.3.7 SURVEY – Additional Comments: **15.3.7 SURVEY – Additional Comments:** Please provide any additional comments

The Railinc Project Management Office did not provide any additional comments.

FIGURE 15-1: 2012 Railinc Project Management Lifecycle

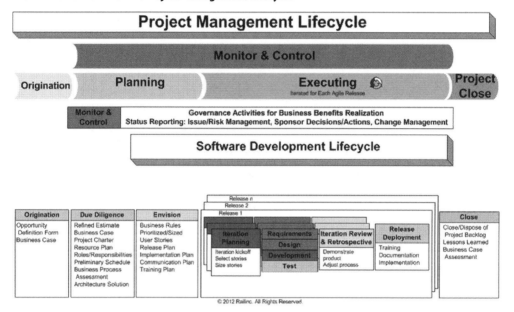

FIGURE 15-2: Railinc 2012 Portfolio Selection Process

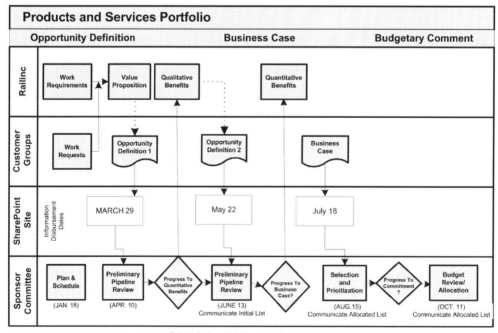

Chapter 16

Southern California Edison PMO Case Study

Southern California Edison (SCE), a subsidiary of Edison International, is an investor-owned public regulated electric utility based in Rosemead, California, providing electric service to the central, coastal and southern California regions. SCE, serves more than 14 million people in over 180 cities, in a 50,000 square-mile area. SCE's operations and work are guided by their corporate values of: Integrity • Excellence • Respect • Continuous Improvement • Teamwork.

SCE and the electric utility industry are entering an era of increasing change, driven in part by public policies, advanced technologies, and the need to replace aging infrastructure. SCE is committed to working collaboratively with all stakeholders, including customers and public officials at all levels, to implement public policies in the most cost-effective manner. SCE is committed to safely delivering reliable and affordable electricity in a responsible manner, which requires a continued focus on operational and service excellence. SCE is providing expert tips, tools, and programs to help Californians conserve energy and save money.

16.1 Southern California Edison – Enterprise and PMO Office Information

Enterprise Name:	Southern California Edison
Country:	United States
Industry:	Utility
Enterprise – Annual Sales Revenue:	Large, Over $10 billion US Dollars
Enterprise – Full-time Employee Equivalents:	Over 18,000
World Wide Web Site:	www.SCE.com
PMO Name:	Edison SmartConnect® Program Management Office

Title of PMO Leader: Senior Manager

PMO Position in Organizational Structure: Major Projects

PMO reports to in Organizational Structure: Edison SmartConnect® Program Director

PMO Annual Operating Budget: $8.2 million US Dollars (2011)

PMO – Full-time Employee Equivalents: 47

The following are the PMO Case Study Survey question sets and the associated responses as submitted by Southern California Edison, with minor editing for format and consistency.

16.2   Southern California Edison PMO Background, Innovations, and Impact

In the following three parts of this case study, the Southern California Edison's "Edison SmartConnect® Program Management Office" provides an overview of the background and structure of its PMO, various innovations and best practices by the PMO, and the potential future business impact of the PMO.

16.2.1 SURVEY – PMO Background: Describe your PMO, including background information on its scope, vision, mission, and position within the enterprise's organizational structure.

PMO Creation and Structure

In 2004, the California Public Utilities Commission (CPUC) directed Southern California Edison (SCE) and the state's other regulated utilities to explore the feasibility of upgrading electric meters for residential and small business customers to automated smart meters from which information is securely and wirelessly transmitted to the utility. SCE worked with meter manufacturers to develop an enhanced solid-state, digital electric meter aimed at lowering overall cost while providing greater customer benefits and improved grid operations. The outcome is Edison SmartConnect®, one of the industry's leading advanced metering systems and an award-winning program.

Edison SmartConnect is the company's $1.6 billion dollar advanced metering program that is replacing approximately 5 million traditional electric meters with smart meters that will help to empower customers to save electricity and money on their electric bills. Smart meter installations and back office systems implementation began in September 2009 and are expected to conclude by the end of 2012.

Edison SmartConnect smart meters are the cornerstone of SCE's upgrade to a smarter grid, which is designed to help prevent large-scale outages and to enhance system reliability and performance. By transmitting information within a secure wireless network, smart meters give customers access to information, programs and tools for greater control and management of their energy use.

The Edison SmartConnect Program transforms the way customers use energy by providing them with interval usage information so they can monitor and modify their usage. By enabling new programs and tools, such as "dynamic pricing" -- or time of day differentiated rates (i.e. rates are higher during "On-Peak" periods) – and demand response, and providing online and near real-time access energy use information, smart meters can empower customers to make informed energy usage decisions helping them save energy, money, and reduce their carbon footprint.

The project was mandated by state and federal legislation. Funding for the PMO was approved by the CPUC as part of the Edison SmartConnect business case. The Edison SmartConnect PMO, in operation from the inception of the project, was formalized in May 2006.

The success of the Edison SmartConnect Program is highly dependent on the coordinated execution of the four interrelated functional areas responsible for the overall smart metering program: the Project Management Office, Deployment, Business Design, and Information Technology (See Figure 16-1).

FIGURE 16-1: Edison SmartConnect PMO Organizational Structure & Relationships

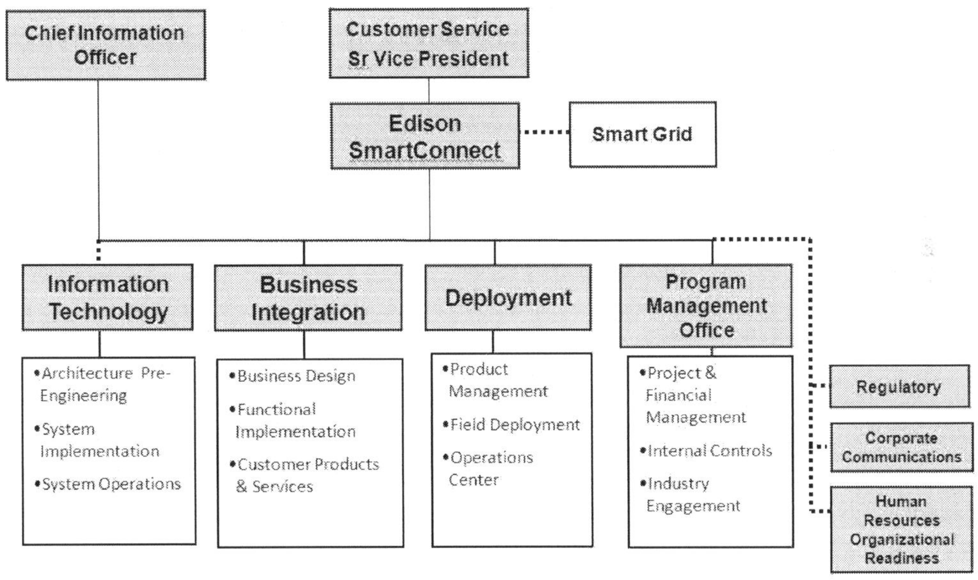

The PMO employs a highly skilled, diverse and motivated workforce, producing on-time products of the highest quality without compromising safety.

PMO Vision

The Edison SmartConnect Program Management Office will successfully develop, implement, and enforce the policies and procedures that will ensure successful scope, schedule, and budget execution of the project through program closure.

The PMO strives to be recognized as the best project management office in the electric utility and smart metering industry.

PMO Mission

The PMO's mission is to advance the Edison SmartConnect Program initiatives by employing industry best practices and providing visibility into program health, while offering independent assessments, and adding shareholder and customer value.

The PMO will provide leadership in driving Program success and achieving organizational project management maturity by offering standards, methodologies, and practices scalable to the tasks at hand.

PMO Scope

The PMO is responsible for the integration, governance, and control of Program scope, schedule, budget, earned value management, and risk management of Edison SmartConnect' smart meter deployment. The PMO also provides the overall Program governance structure and framework to ensure timely and effective decision-making, risk management, financial controls, benefits realization, and issues resolution. The PMO is accountable for effective communication among internal and external stakeholders to help them achieve an understanding of the Edison SmartConnect goals, vision, and project status.

The PMO scope is further detailed in the six functions detailed below:

Program Controls: The Program Controls group establishes and manages budgets, contract administration, schedules, risk management, change management, and audits. This group ensures organizational agreement and commitment to overall Program objectives. The group also manages and enforces standards and tools, reporting status to senior management, and represents SCE in a variety of regulatory forums.

Budgets: Costs are tracked and managed through the Systems, Applications, and Products in Data Processing (SAP) system, with reports generated periodically for review by project and program management. Financial reports are generated monthly for the twenty organizations who report into the Program. These organizations represent both project managers, whose areas are directly accountable to Program Management, and Operations and Information Technology management, who are matrixed into the Program. Following review, the appropriate project and program managers and directors provide their approvals indicating acceptance of the monthly financial results subject to any accounting adjustments required to correct for misaligned charges identified and corrected in the normal course of business and in keeping with GAAP and SCE accounting policy.

Management employs reports detailing variance to budget in weekly and monthly meetings to evaluate vendor performance and determine what if any corrective action might be needed from a financial standpoint to ensure successful completion of this phase of the Program.

Additional analysis is performed with a scenario-planning model. This model forecasts Program financial and operating performance by simulating the impact of changes in key parameters on overall Program performance. Further, all approved change requests with a financial or operational impact to the Program are recorded to the scenario-planning model, providing a detailed update to the Program baseline. Actual financial and baseline data are synchronized with Program schedules to facilitate the generation of earned value metrics.

Contracts Administration: While direct responsibility for vendor management rests with project managers who oversee each thread of work, the Program Office Contracts Department oversees the performance of each vendor selected, ensuring:

- Change orders and purchase order requests adhere to SCE policies and procedures, as well as contract and budgetary requirements as required by SCE's Supply Chain Management group;
- Invoices are correct and paid in a timely manner;
- Work executed by both parties is consistent with the terms and conditions as referenced in the contract.

In addition, the Contracts group acts as a liaison between vendors and the operations unit.

Audits: The Audits group manages a group of project managers and consultants responsible for audits and compliance for the deployment of Edison SmartConnect, including:

- Facilitating development of business process controls through participation in design workshops;
- Providing coordination between internal, external audit personnel, and Edison SmartConnect® business owners; and
- Ensuring compliance with corporate initiatives and regulatory standards, including Sarbanes-Oxley.

Program Engagement & Business Support: The Program Engagement & Business Support group manages Program outreach and representation at industry-related events and conferences, representing SCE in key forums and before industry organizations. This group also submits multiple industry award applications annually and leads internal communications, while coordinating with Corporate Communications on external communications to customers and other key stakeholders.

Organizational Readiness: The PMO is also responsible for the operational readiness of the various internal SCE departments, known as "Organization Units," through the work conducted by its Organizational Readiness team. The Organizational Readiness team works closely with operational and business area subject matter experts to assess the impacts of change associated with new technology and processes, and identify key readiness activities and risks as well as readiness mitigations needed to ensure a smooth transition at and beyond implementation.

The Organizational Readiness team leads impacted business area leads and key personnel through process walk-through events to ensure the enterprise-wide business units understand their roles and responsibilities in the Edison SmartConnect Program's multiple, large projects and releases, and is prepared to assume ownership for new business processes at implementation.

> **16.2.2 SURVEY – PMO Innovations and Best Practices:** Address the challenges your enterprise encountered prior to implementing the new PMO practices and how you overcame those challenges. Describe clearly and concisely the practices implemented and their effect on project, program, and/or portfolio and organizational success.

Introduction

The Edison SmartConnect® Program represents a leading edge approach as well as innovative technology implementation that were new to the utility industry. The over-arching challenge for the PMO was the creation of the necessary infrastructure to define and manage the ever-changing scope of the Edison SmartConnect Program. To define the scope, the PMO initiated and led 57 workshops with cross-functional groups within SCE to develop new, innovative meter functionality. For the first time in SCE's history a PMO, the Edison SmartConnect PMO, collaborated with metering and communications vendors, utility peer groups, and government agencies to develop new industry metering standards and employ best practices.

Although the Edison SmartConnect Program's dynamic environment called for project management practices that enable innovation across the Program, these practices had to be flexible to allow team members to remain productive, collaborative, and efficient in this fast-paced 5-year project. Throughout the project's life, the PMO encountered multiple challenges and identified several value-added opportunities.

The three key challenges faced by the Edison SmartConnect PMO were:
1) Formation of a Functional Project Management Organization
2) Organizational Change Management
3) Implementing the Advanced Metering Infrastructure while creating the underlying supporting technology

Challenge 1: Formation of a Functional Project Management Organization

While SCE had managed major programs in the past, Edison SmartConnect was a unique project because it required the collaboration of more than 20 organizations to develop the end product. The Edison SmartConnect Program touches multiple SCE functional areas, including Billing, Revenue Services, Transmission & Distribution,

Customer Communications, Metering Services, Information Technology, Regulatory, Corporate Communications, Local Public Affairs, Human Resources, Finance, Supply Chain, Energy Efficiency, and customer-facing programs and services. Unifying this diverse group of organizations around the single goal of executing the deployment of smart meters and their associated technologies became the PMO's single greatest challenge.

In this environment, the PMO successfully implemented and integrated core project management methodologies. Not only did the PMO demonstrate the value of key project management tools in managing the day-to-day operations, but also in anticipating future challenges and ensuring the successful completion of the Program. To facilitate the adoption of the methodology, the PMO did the following:

<u>Scheduling Reporting Tool</u>: Implemented a graphical schedule-reporting tool to produce executive-level representation of project status and earned value. These two metrics are used as a decision-making tool to determine ongoing project health.

An example of the schedule reporting tool output is shown below in Figure 16-2.

FIGURE 16-2: Edison SmartConnect Example Schedule

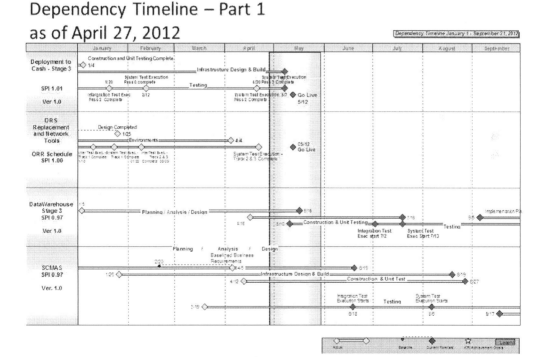

<u>Integrated Monthly Meetings</u>: Institutionalized an Integrated Monthly Meeting as a result of lessons learned from prior communications gaps in this multi-year Program. These meetings provide leadership with status of the project's financials, schedules, earned value, risks, contracts, change requests, and compliance.

Process Integration: Had PMO Project Managers serve as a single point of contact and as process integrators for all PMO policies and procedures. Integration efforts assist the program and project managers to:

- Ensure flow of communication and mitigate any technology, process or resource gaps;
- Gain trust and confidence as dedicated liaisons to all critical stakeholders to execute key initiatives by building relationships with client managers and utilizing interpersonal skills to help remove roadblocks and expedite critical activities and processes;
- Represent the PMO leadership and provide the ultimate flexibility as matrix and cross-functional team leads to provide service in all phases of the project – initiating, planning, executing, monitoring, and controlling, as well as closing; and
- Serve as internal consultants to work on continuous process improvements and service excellence for all processes in the project.

Financial Reporting Tool: Edison SmartConnect developed a sophisticated database-reporting tool to facilitate timely creation of financial reports and enhance the existing project scenario planning model. This database tool reduced reporting turnaround time by six weeks while providing staff with a comprehensive analysis engine and a ready source for accurate and multifaceted reports. The scenario-planning model aided in management decision making by producing detailed projections of the Program's costs and benefits.

Project Management Training: SCE partnered with the University of California Irvine, California Institute of Technology, and Boston University to provide ongoing project management training to PMO staff and management through various programs, such as participating in SCE's Education Reimbursement Program, which resulted in the PMO's increased adherence to the project management discipline.

Contract Management: Edison SmartConnect developed processes to vet new vendor agreements and draft contract change orders in cooperation with SCE Procurement. Employed robust processes, to validate all vendor invoices against contract terms, delivered goods, and services. Communicated status updates on change orders and new vendor agreements weekly to project managers.

Risk Mitigation: Edison SmartConnect conducted risk identification and mitigation workshops to identify potential risks, assess likelihood, and develop risk response plans, which are periodically reviewed and revised.

Challenge 2: Organizational Change Management

To ensure Edison SmartConnect® would become an operational reality, the PMO's Organizational Readiness team implemented various project management practices throughout the life of the Program to help support this challenge and in support of the multiple projects that make up the Edison SmartConnect Program. The Organizational Readiness team ensured strategic alignment with the Program's vision by working closely with impacted stakeholders, business leaders, and the Program team. Utilizing best practices, the Organizational Readiness team performed the following:

Assessed Change Impacts by conducting detailed Change Management Impact Assessment Workshops to identify how organizations within SCE would be affected and how they need to adjust their business practices.

Developed and Matured Business Transition Plans based on the results of the Change Impact Assessment Workshops. This plan identifies key Business Readiness actions necessary to ensure operational readiness for project implementations.

Supported and Assessed Business Readiness by leading Process Walk-Through events prior to project implementations, which required stakeholders to develop and execute their business processes, thereby helping key players understand new and changing workflow processes, and determined process hand-offs and coordination. This process was the result of careful planning and adherence to Change Management Best Practices. The group conducted pre-Go Live Readiness Assessments based on recognized critical success factors for technology implementations. The results were reported to senior leadership.

Participated in Post-Implementation Triage Process by assisting key stakeholders, particularly in Business Integration, to develop and implement a triage process. The team defined how the triage process would run, how issues would be identified, tracked, and escalated, as well as a process for determining the severity of issues.

The Triage Process is used to identify and resolve post-implementation issues impacting business operations. In addition, Organizational Readiness supported the identification of system stabilization metrics. These metrics provide targets that can confirm the system is performing in accordance with business requirements and expectations. When system performance stabilization metrics are met, the system can be transferred to operations for maintenance.

The PMO Organizational Readiness team's success in preparing stakeholders to transition from existing operations to new technological solutions ensured delivery of the Edison SmartConnect objectives. As an example, for the Interval Billing sub-project, which is one of the multiple projects that make up the overall Edison SmartConnect

Program, the following actions took place:

- Revenue Services Organization (RSO or customer billing) not only received and prepared to utilize the new interval billing technology Meter Data Management System (MDMS), but key personnel within RSO were able to successfully operate the MDMS, bill customers, identify and address system errors and/or billing exceptions. In addition, personnel trained in the new processes in support of Remote Service Switch (RSS) technology, allowed customers to have service activated or de-activated remotely.

- Customer Communications Organization (CCO) or phone center personnel are fully trained in the metering systems and functionalities that support customer engagement programs, such as Budget Assistant, which is SCE's web-based energy usage and cost management tool. CCO has evolved from a transactions-focused operation to a customer engagement center, addressing customer inquiries and providing information and guidance regarding energy usage and programs enabled by smart metering technology.

- SCE residential customers whose accounts have transitioned to the new interval billing system have access to sophisticated internet tools that allow them to view their hourly energy consumption data the next day. Web information has been made available to customers since 2011, which is critical to SCE's new business model.

Challenge 3: Implementing the Advanced Metering Infrastructure while Creating the Underlying Supporting Technology

The metering functionality sought by SCE did not previously exist. SCE worked collaboratively with metering manufacturers to design and build new meters with advanced functionality. SCE established key vendor partnerships and played a lead role in developing and furthering advanced metering standards.

The Program had to deliver three key meter-enabled components: energy conservation, price response, and load control. SCE pioneered the development and delivery of these key energy efficiency components.

Following a comprehensive survey of existing technologies, it became apparent that an appropriate solution did not exist. SCE developed a detailed roadmap to overcome this challenge. The roadmap included multiple threads yielding a unifying portfolio of projects that ultimately became the Edison SmartConnect Program.

The Edison SmartConnect Program is built upon innovative technology centered on wireless communication from the utility to the smart meters and back again. SCE established multiple complex back office systems capable of:

- Collecting and storing 5.5 billion energy usage data points per year for approximately 5 million accounts, and

- Hourly data collection for residential customers and 15-minute interval reads for business customers.

Edison SmartConnect meters are equipped with wireless communication components, enabling exchange between customers' smart meters and their smart appliances. Moving forward, this innovative technology will enable customers to use in-home displays to monitor their energy usage and further employ energy-saving practices.

In 2010, the Edison SmartConnect interval billing process became operational with the first deployed residential meters. Simultaneously, the Program continued to deploy the remaining meters, while building, testing, and implementing new product functionalities according to the defined roadmap that would eventually enable interval billing for all 5 million accounts by the end of 2012.

The PMO partnered with SCE's IT Department and multiple vendors to develop scenario-planning models to assess financial impacts to the various components of the roadmap.

The PMO was also integral in providing support to the other functional areas within the Edison SmartConnect Program, including Deployment, Business Design, and IT, by publishing a full deployment dashboard and schedule to support the overall management of the 5-year Edison SmartConnect Program.

> **16.2.3 SURVEY – PMO Future Impact:** Briefly describe your PMO's plans for 2012 and beyond - please describe how those plans will potentially impact your enterprise and its organizational structure.

In 2012, the PMO has been sharing best practices to strengthen project management capabilities within other SCE business areas.

The greatest impact of the Edison SmartConnect PMO is SCE's adoption of project management best practices, including:

- Change Management
- Budgets
- Contract Administration
- Schedule Management
- Communications
- Earned Value Management
- Project Closure

16.3   Southern California Edison PMO Model Components

In the following six parts of this case study, Southern California Edison's "Edison SmartConnect® Program Management Office" provides its descriptions of how they implement the six key components of the Project Business Management Organization model: Governance; Methodology; Capability; Planning; Execution; and Sustainability.

> **16.3.1 SURVEY – PMO Governance:** Describe how your PMO presents itself as an executive-level management business function, how it addresses setting policy and establishing charters, and how it provides an organizational model for the business management of portfolios, programs, and projects and the establishment of portfolio, program, and project management offices.

Executive-Level Management Business Function

The Edison SmartConnect Program Director acts as a linchpin between SCE senior management and Program leadership. The vehicle employed by the Program director to facilitate this function is the Edison SmartConnect Governance Structure. The governance structure includes senior SCE executives and leadership who are charged with overseeing Program scope, schedule, budget, and risk, while facilitating the escalation of critical Program issues to the appropriate authority. The PMO is accountable for effective communication among external and internal stakeholders to help them achieve an understanding of the Program goals and status.

FIGURE 16-3: Edison SmartConnect PMO Governance Model

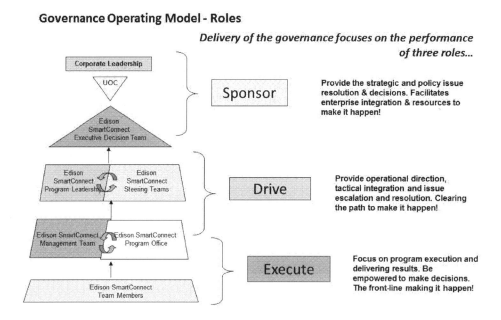

Setting Policy: The PMO leverages existing Corporate and Business Unit policies such as levels of authority, financial approvals, ethics and compliance, and safety. Beyond the existing policies, the Governance Operating Structure outlines the roles and responsibilities of the various Edison SmartConnect team members, the Program Office, and the Management team and how they each elevate necessary issues up the chain of command for resolution.

Issues generally arise as a result of brand new technology or as a result of legislative and regulatory mandates. The Edison SmartConnect Program has also created new policies due to ongoing regulatory requirements.

Establishing Charters: Charters are established by deriving business requirements and developing functional specifications to define the scope, schedule, and budget for a project. The Charter incorporates objectives, assumptions, risks, and broad design and deliverables, which are all captured in a Charter document.

To develop charters, the Business Design Team holds workshops with the subject matter experts to develop the business and technical requirements. Upon completion, the business requirements are routed to the various organizational units for review and approval.

The PMO utilizes the governance structure to obtain approval of the Charter and to establish the initial baseline for the project. Changes to the baseline are managed through the Change Control Process.

Approval of any change requests must follow the processes established in the Governance structure.

Providing an Organizational Model for the Management of Portfolios, Programs, and Projects: The PMO conducts the following three key support functions:
- Downward: Provide support to Project Managers
- Horizontal: Reporting about Program health and status to Internal and External Organizations
- Vertical: Facilitate the governance structure

16.3.1.1 – How long has the PMO been in place?	PMO has been formally in existence for six years.
When was it started?	The PMO was established in May 2006.
16.3.1.2 – What is the relationship of PMO management to the enterprise's operational management?	The relationship of the PMO Management to the enterprise's operational management is depicted in Edison SmartConnect Program's Governance Structure shown in Figure 16-3.
	The Program Office, together with the Management Team, reports up to the Edison SmartConnect Program Leadership and the Steering Teams on key decisions that need to be resolved. From there, as key decisions require, both bodies report up to the

Edison SmartConnect Executive Decision Team (EDT), made up of Company-wide cross-functional senior executives and leadership. The Program Director and the PMO Senior Manager report to the EDT on Program plans, status, and direction. This ensures the Program's alignment with all major corporate goals and initiatives.

16.3.1.3 – How is the PMO internally structured (positions, roles etc.)?

The PMO is comprised of a team of senior managers, project managers, contract management experts, project and financial analysts, and administrative support.

The PMO allows the four functional areas of the Edison SmartConnect Program – Information Technology, Business Design, Deployment, and Program Office -- to focus their attention on their Areas of Responsibility (AORs). See Figure 16-1, Edison SmartConnect® PMO Organizational Structure & Relationships shown in part 16.2.1 above.

16.3.1.4 – How are the PMO's operations funded?

The PMO's operations are funded as part of the overall $1.6 billion project.

Balancing Accounts are mechanisms for recovery of expenses not included in a utility's General Rate Case (GRC), but for which the California Public Utilities Commission (CPUC) has determined that cost recovery is appropriate.

16.3.1.5 – What is the summary position description of the PMO leader?

The PMO senior manager leads the PMO's overall planning and integration, execution of scope, schedule, and budget, as well as performance monitoring and reporting, Program compliance, industry engagement, contract administration, financial and Program controls, benefits realization, and risk management for the $1.6 billion deployment.

The PMO senior manager also ensures alignment between the corporate mission and the Program's goals.

16.3.1.6 – What position requirements are used as a basis for selecting the PMO leader?

The position requirements used as a basis for selecting the PMO leader include business leadership, personification of SCE's values, shared vision with SCE's corporate goals, and a strong project management background. The PMO leader is expected to be diligent in project planning and execution, while also having the skills of persuasion, self-management, communication, and relationship management.

16.3.1.7 – Is the PMO a Profit & Loss cost center or considered overhead?	The Edison SmartConnect PMO is treated as Overhead
16.3.1.8 – What current challenge is the PMO dealing with?	The PMO continues to deal with the growth in the number of meters capable of interval billing and the technological evolution that has been the hallmark of this Program. This includes completing the installation of the approximately 5 million meters while activating the Program's final technological solutions. The PMO is currently managing completion of the Program's business case objectives while managing attrition of key Program resources. The Program is also facing challenges associated with a regulatory mandate to allow customers to "opt-out" of replacing their mechanical meter with a smart meter. The impact of the mandate is that SCE must maintain parallel infrastructure and systems to support both advanced and legacy meters. This impacts benefits realization defined in the Edison SmartConnect business case. The PMO is also working on transitioning a Program to mainstream business-as-usual.

> **16.3.2 SURVEY – PMO Methodology / Standardization:** Describe what standardization your PMO has implemented across the enterprise that examines: identification and integration of processes and practices; development of standardized Project Business Management processes; and documentation of enterprise-wide portfolio, program, and project management process methodology models, including their associated policies, practices, and procedures.

The Edison SmartConnect Governance Model (see Figure 16-3) sets the framework of principles, policies and authorities within the Program organization. The governance set forth allows the Program to:

- Make timely decisions and define priorities;
- Assign accountability and resources;
- Establish behavior expectations and norms in accordance with SCE and Edison SmartConnect code of conduct and ethics guidelines;
- Oversee Program operations;
- Follow the Edison SmartConnect Anti-Trust Compliance Guidelines; and
- Proceed based on Regulatory Approvals, Processes and Guidelines.

The Guiding Principles are:

- Decision authority is granted to the project teams closest to the issues along with responsibility for escalating the decision when appropriate, based on the business or Program impact.

- Escalated decisions are made within the impacted business areas and not delayed by companywide consensus. Parties with opposing views are engaged in the escalation.
- The decision making process follows this escalation sequence:
  - Team Member
  - Edison SmartConnect Management Team
  - Edison SmartConnect Program Leadership/Steering Teams
  - Edison SmartConnect Executive Decision Team
  - Utility Management Committee/Utility Operations Committee
  - Corporate Leadership

16.3.2.1 – Describe the standards utilized by the PMO to ensure the enterprise's project / program / portfolio management goals and objectives are achieved.

The Edison SmartConnect business case was Southern California Edison's response to the California Public Utilities Commission (CPUC) rulemaking order to develop an Advanced Metering Infrastructure (AMI).

The PMO ensured the Program's compliance with the business case and the CPUC rulemaking order by developing a Program Charter that established the intent of the Program and created the initial Program baseline for scope, schedule, and budget to achieve the business case objectives. The Program Charter also defined an integrated management infrastructure based on a Governance Model, which established controls and levels of authority.

While the Program has some latitude in how it decides to implement the approved project authorized by the CPUC, there are a number of hard and fast guidelines based on this and prior decisions:

- The CPUC 6 - The philosophical center of the Program are the original six CPUC guidelines, which served as the governing principles behind the Program's original design and filing. The CPUC 6 stipulated the types of programs that must be enabled as part of the smart metering solution.

- The 2008 Settlement - The CPUC reviewed SCE's filing for an advanced metering system and, following testimony, negotiated a settlement with SCE. This settlement was broken down by SCE into 21 regulatory requirements and 53 business case requirements. While the Program has made a number of changes to accommodate various technological and logistical fixes, the Program's overall strategic direction is always measured against the 21 regulatory and 53 business case requirements that emerged from the original settlement.

Project Management Standards

Within the PMO, project management processes are the standard by which internal practices and controls are measured and optimized by:

- Establishing written policies governing the management of scope, time, budget, project governance, risk and procurement. These policies are reviewed and updated periodically to reflect the latest Program learnings;
- Focusing reporting to Leadership in a manner consistent with project management practices;
- Encouraging all levels of PMO staff to engage in continuing project management education; and
- Ensuring that employee evaluations are aligned with Program goals and targeted at improving project management acumen.

FIGURE 16-4: Edison SmartConnect PMO Integrated Process Control Model

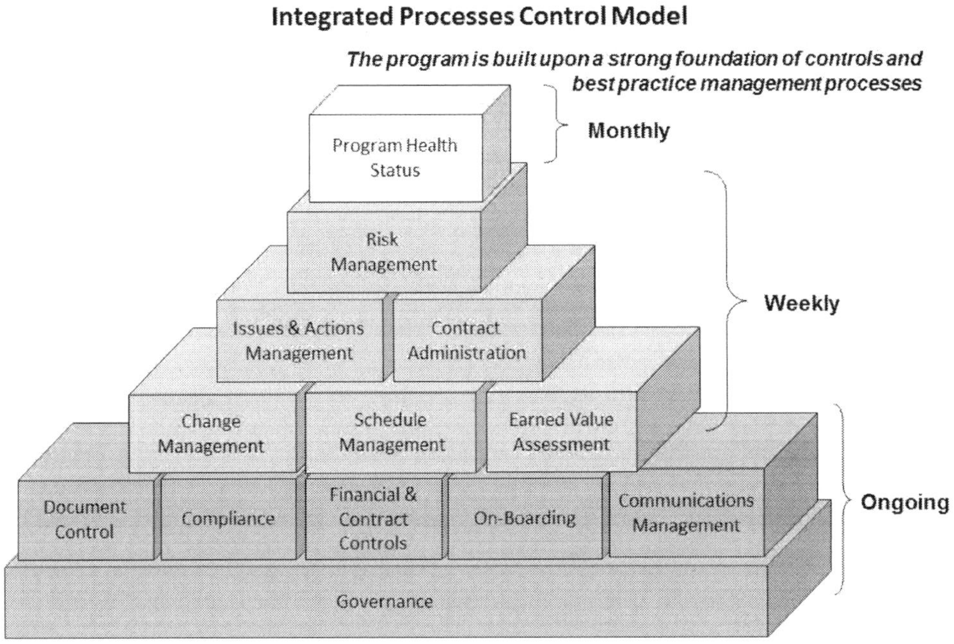

Integrated Processes Control Model

The program is built upon a strong foundation of controls and best practice management processes

16.3.2.2 – Describe the project management process guidelines being employed by the PMO.

The PMO has adapted Project Management Institute (PMI) standards to the unique requirements of SCE's regulatory environment. Within this context, Edison SmartConnect PMO uses an Integrated Process Control Model (See Figure 16-4 above). The model supports the project objectives while ensuring oversight through essential controls such as Earned Value, Change Management, Schedule Management, Risk Management, Issues and Action Items Management, and Contract Administration. The following graphic depicts the integrated model.

Infrastructure

This is the foundational base of the PMO governance structure. The blocks in Infrastructure predominantly represent the Resource, Communication, and Document Management aspects of the PMO. Resources are represented by the financial controls and "onboarding" of individuals.

Communications are represented by both internal and external communications. The documentation and compliance aspects round out the foundation of the governance structure.

Day-to-Day Operations

Resting on the foundation is the Day-to-Day operations. This level is comprised of Schedule Management with its components of Earned Value Management, Change Management, Risk Management and Contract Management. This is the heart of Edison SmartConnect operations.

Overall Program Health

Program "health" is reported via a dashboard that is delivered to the senior management and executives on a monthly basis. The reports consist of Financial, Contracts, Compliance, and Schedule information.

The Program uses a Change Control Board (CCB) to coordinate and integrate requests from key Program stakeholders, including the operations organization. The following graphic depicts the hierarchy and escalation of requests to ensure all stakeholder interests are represented (see Figure 16-5).

FIGURE 16-5: Edison SmartConnect Change Control Board

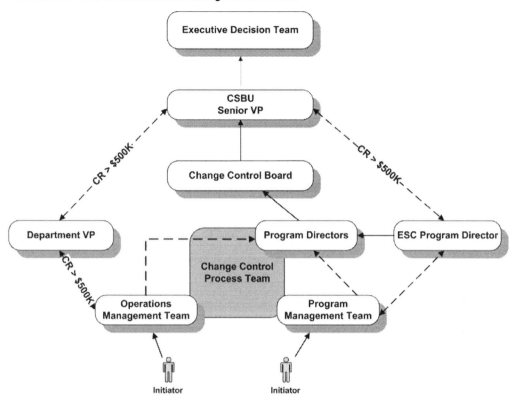

In addition to Change Management, the Program aggressively manages risks to minimize impacts and changes to the project and Program. Through continuous risk assessment, monitoring industry trends, and engaging stakeholders in risk management workshops and risk reviews, the Risk Management group ensures program success and benefits are realized.

Risk management workshops enable the program to plan for uncertainty by providing an opportunity for collaboration and integration amongst a cross section of program stakeholders to identify failure scenarios ("What If...?"), corresponding impacts, and mitigation activities.

Risks associated with the project are assessed for potential impacts and appropriate mitigation to minimize impacts to the project. If a risk is assessed as potentially impacting the project, it is escalated to the program level for further assessment and additional mitigation. If a risk is realized, the existing "Issues and Action Item" processes ensure the best resolution is derived and implemented to minimize impact. The following graphic (Figure 16-6) demonstrates the Edison SmartConnect Program risk assessment process.

FIGURE 16-6: Edison SmartConnect Risk Assessment Process

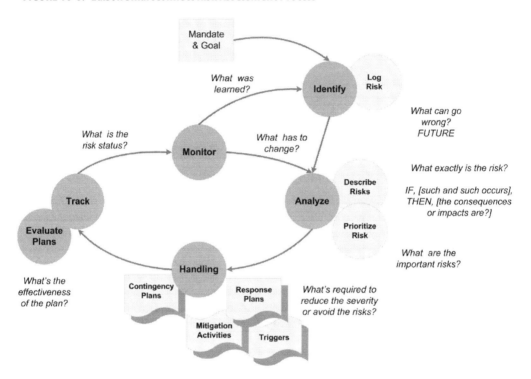

16.3.2.3 – What systems, tools, and templates make your PMO successful?

The PMO for SCE's Customer Service organization adopted Edison SmartConnect's governance model, processes, and reporting tools. Edison SmartConnect provided specific project process training, MS Project and Kidasa templates, and scheduling standards that are currently being used by the Customer Service Business Unit (CSBU) PMO.

The work that began at Edison SmartConnect is continuing beyond the life of the program. There are entities that are responsible for reporting Earned Value metrics based on the work that the Edison SmartConnect PMO started. An example of the Edison SmartConnect PMO reporting metrics using Kidasa Milestones follows in Figure 16-7.

FIGURE 16-7: Edison SmartConnect Metrics Reporting Example

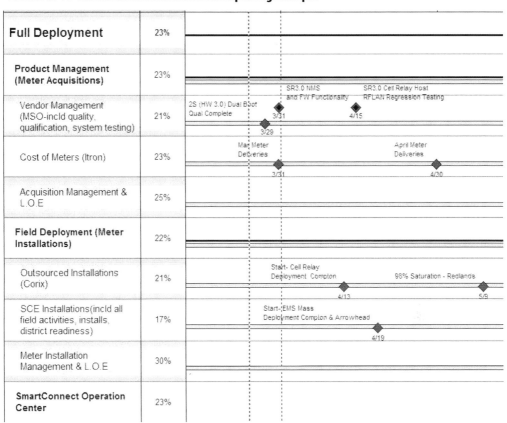

Risk Management: The PMO's risk management program and processes are on the leading edge of SCE's risk management efforts. One of the PMO's greatest value is the risk management workshop which has served as a model for SCE as a whole. The Program used risk management workshops to identify potential risks, which, if realized, could potentially halt the Program and or impact benefits. The risk management workshop process includes multiple workshops focused on potential system and/or product failures.

A cross section of department and directors and managers are represented. In 2010, the focus of the risk management workshops transitioned from "What If" to "It's Happened" with an emphasis on response and recovery. The outcome resulted in the development of response plans for the highest probable risks. One such response plan was successfully implemented in 2010, when an identified risk was realized.

The long-term corporate impact of the PMO's Risk Management processes includes adoption and use by other departments of risk management workshops and risk management training for project managers, modeled after the Edison SmartConnect PMO practices.

16.3.2.4 – Describe how management at all levels is directly involved in the development of the PMO and it processes.

Edison SmartConnect senior management was directly involved in the development of the PMO in 2006 and in its processes. Individual contributors developed the PMO processes and standards with guidance from management and through applying internal and external best practices. Once these standards were approved by management, they were reviewed and approved by senior management as well as the director of the Program.

FIGURE 16-8: Edison SmartConnect Project's Scheduling Template

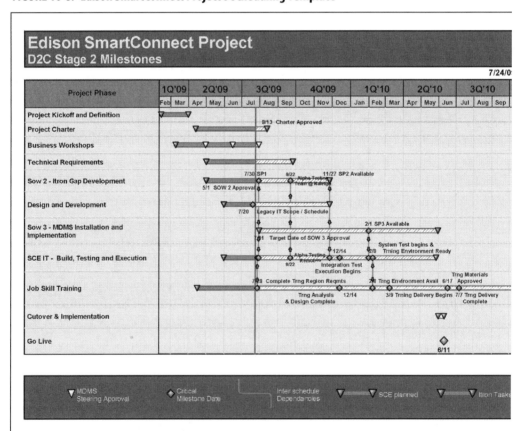

16.3.2.5 – Describe the implementation plan you used for establishing project / program / portfolio management standards across your enterprise.

The Implementation Plan used for establishing project management standards across the enterprise include:

The Project Management Office developed a Standardized Project Scheduling Template and a Scheduling Standards Document. The scheduling template was preconfigured to include data frequently used by the PMO. The scheduling template has built-in dates, as well as job titles for tasks that need to be planned and completed.

Milestones are stated at the top of the scheduling template for clear visibility of project milestone status. Also included are the project givers and receivers, which outline a statement of work of deliverables between project schedules that need to be completed by a certain timeframe.

The graphic above in Figure 16-8 is a screen capture of a project's scheduling template:

The graphic below in Figure 16-9 shows the Program Control Group's Weekly Process Update.

16.3.2.6 – How does the PMO use project, program, and portfolio management standards to optimize its practices?

Are they based on PMI or other industry guides and are they updated as new editions of the guides are released?

How the PMO uses project management standards:
Within the PMO, project management processes are the standards by which internal practices and controls are measured and optimized by:

- Having the PMO's standards for governance aligned with the Project Management Institute® (PMI) standards;
- Establishing written policies, including project charters, governing the management of scope, time, budget, project governance, risk and procurement. These policies are reviewed and updated to reflect the latest Program learnings;
- Focusing reporting to Leadership in a manner consistent with project management practices, including having a Change Request process built around a Change Control Board (CCB) that reviews project change requests on a weekly basis; employing the Scheduling Performance Index (SPI) to give each individual project's status; using the SPI and Cost Performance Index (CPI) reporting metrics during monthly updates to Executive Management;

FIGURE 16-9: Edison SmartConnect Program Control Group's Weekly Process Update

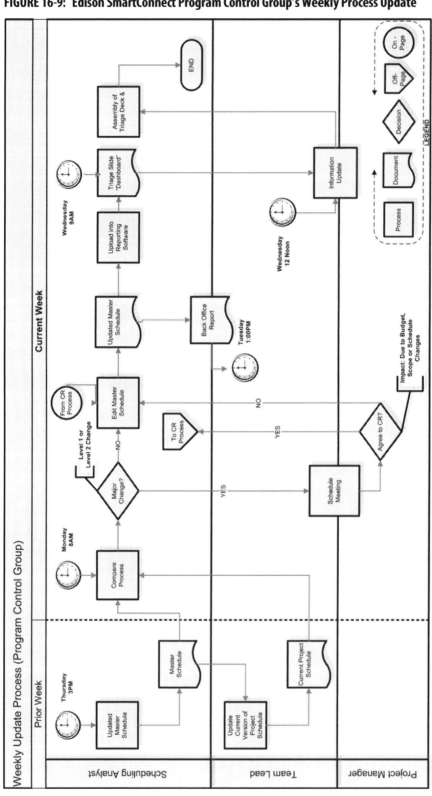

16.3.2.6 –
(Continued)

- Providing monthly financial reporting to each organization that interfaces with the Program, as well as Program leadership and executive SCE management;
- Encouraging all levels of PMO staff to engage in continuous project management education; and
- Ensuring that employee evaluations are aligned with Program goals and targeted at improving project management acumen, including having development goals reflect project management skills.

Updates to project management standards are continuously applied by the skill set of the project management team members. For example, contributors to the PMO have included various consultants including a PMI Scheduling Standards Committee Member.

16.3.3 SURVEY – PMO Capabilities: Describe development and assessment of the enterprise's abilities, describe any project management competency model, summarize any education and training program, describe any established career path progression plan, and outline key Enterprise Environmental Factors.

16.3.3.1 – Describe
the components of
your enterprise's
training program.

The components of the enterprise training program include:

- SCE's Project Management Center of Excellence Training was successfully completed by at least three members of the PMO;
- Approximately 10 PMO team members have taken the California Institute of Technology's Project Management Certification program;
- Several members of the PMO have taken the University of California Irvine Project Management course;
- Members of the PMO, as well as Management, participated in Boston University's Risk Mitigation course;
- Members of the PMO participated in Six Sigma certification courses;
- Project Management learning sessions were held for the PMO and the other functional areas;
- A mentoring program is currently being planned for certified Project Management Professionals (PMP) within

the Program to mentor others who are planning to obtain their PMP certification; and

- Several PMO members are PMP certified.

16.3.3.2 – Describe the value your enterprise places on education and training and its goals and objectives.	The enterprise places a high value on education and training. For example, the enterprise reimburses employees for Project Management certification programs, Six Sigma courses, and Master's degree programs. The enterprise's goals and objectives are to continuously improve the workforce's job skills in project management.
16.3.3.3 – Does the enterprise have a project management career path program? If so, what are the components?	Yes, Edison SmartConnect Program supports a project management career path program. For example, employees may pursue a successive Project Management track. This begins with three successive levels of Project Analyst positions followed by three successive levels of Project Manager positions.
16.3.3.4 – Describe the measurements, metrics, and Key Performance Indicators (KPI's) utilized by the PMO to determine the organization's knowledge, skills, and level of achievement.	Edison SmartConnect employees' performance evaluations contain Personal Development Goals, reflecting their varying needs of project management, time management, and other organizational skills, required to manage projects. Employee's overall goals are also mapped to program Key Performance Indicators (KPIs) and Achievement Goals.
16.3.3.5 – Does the enterprise employ a project management competency model? If yes, please describe it. If no, why not?	Yes, the PMO employs a project management competency model that is based on the enterprise-wide project management job descriptions. There are three levels of project management positions – entry level, intermediate, and senior level. These project management positions entail competency at increasing levels. The dimensional areas are: • Area of responsibility; • Decision making and impact; • Education, certification, and licensing; and • Knowledge and experience.

16.3.4 SURVEY – PMO Business Planning: Discuss strategic business planning, tactical business planning, business objective (project) development and prioritization, and project identification, selection, and authorization.

16.3.4.1 – Describe the organizational structure and process used for corporate strategic business planning.

Does the PMO play a role in the process? If so, describe the PMOs role and responsibilities.

SCE supports an annual Strategic Planning Process, which aligns corporate organizations to appropriate regulatory mandates and overall operational and financial objectives.

SCE performs an assessment of internal and external forces and key trends to develop scenarios to determine changes in environment and drive the overall strategic direction. As appropriate, each unit develops goals and objectives in support of the strategic direction.

The Edison SmartConnect PMO facilitates the strategic planning process for the Program.

The PMO partners with the Operation groups to develop and update the roadmap for the remaining Program functionalities on an annual basis. This produces a comprehensive project roadmap with scope, schedule, and budget, presented for approval to executive leadership.

16.3.4.2 – How is the strategic plan implemented with a project forecast plan?

While Program planning is conducted on a more or less continuous basis, there are key events in the course of the Program designed to highlight key strategic issues. The Program itself adheres to the original business case decision in terms of defined scope and deliverables.

Strategic decisions are made regarding how scope is facilitated. On an annual basis, Program leadership prepares a detailed plan highlighting projected spending through the end of the Program, including potential risks. The program sponsor and key stakeholders review this plan to ensure compliance with Program objectives and to validate expected deliverables against Stakeholder expectations. Specific proposals are analyzed using the Program's scenario modeling tool. This process is undertaken in addition to the risk assessment process, integrated planning meetings, annual budgeting process, and the quarterly forecasts.

Project Managers within the PMO and sponsoring organizations manage their initiatives according to the updated plans developed and approved during the planning cycle described above.

16.3.4.3 – How is strategic planning, culture, and selection of projects integrated?

The Business Design Team continuously evaluates stakeholder needs, in alignment with regulatory mandates for Advanced Metering Infrastructure. The team presents to the Executive Decision Team a preliminary Charter containing a description of the stakeholder needs for their review and approval.

16.3.5 SURVEY – PMO Business Execution: Describe what role the PMO has in project selection, prioritization, and initiation; in portfolio, program and project execution planning; in stage-gate reviews; and in performance metrics selection and application.

16.3.5.1 – How are portfolios, programs, and projects selected and initiated?

Key stakeholders (internal customers) meet with the Edison SmartConnect Management Team to discuss business needs, initiate a pre-engineering phase and full business case justification to develop a charter, discuss feasibility of the charter, and develop and execute the charter.

The team developed the portfolio of projects to present to the Executive Decision Team for their review and approval prior to proceeding with the detailed charters.

16.3.5.2 – How are projects organized and managed as a program and/or portfolio?

Projects are organized and managed as a program by strictly adhering to the following Project Management Institute Body of Knowledge® Guide process groups:
1) Project Initiation,
2) Planning Process,
3) Execution,
4) Monitoring and Controlling, and
5) Project Closure.

The portfolio of projects is strategically aligned with the original business case roadmap. The individual projects are managed through resource and cost loaded schedules ensuring integrated management within the Program.

16.3.5.3 – How are projects prioritized within a program and/or portfolio?	Edison SmartConnect projects are prioritized in logical order. The team first establishes whether a project is necessary. If a project is found to be necessary by virtue of its adherence to the regulatory mandate, it is placed in a logical sequence. Multiple projects make up the overall Program. At a high level, Edison SmartConnect projects were prioritized following this logical sequence:

1) Install meters
2) Collect billing from customers
3) Obtain interval billing from customers
4) Offer programs and services to customers, based on their energy usage

16.3.5.4 – How does the enterprise define what project and program success is?	At a high level, the enterprise defines a project's or program's success based on whether the Program has met or exceeded customers' needs.

The Program had IT testers – the Program's internal customers -- located on site to test metering and communications products to ensure the products met and exceeded customers' expectations.

The Edison SmartConnect PMO ensures that the following steps take place in defining project success:

1) Develop the business requirements
2) Design and construct the product
3) Test the product
4) Customer testing

Tight control on financials and scheduling occurs at all levels.
Project charters also define the parameters of a project and outline what project success means. The charters define initial scope and budget. Only change requests will change the schedule and/or budget for a project. If a proposed change meets or exceeds those criteria, a project is considered a success.

16.3.5.5 – Does the PMO support the management of projects that would be considered operational in nature? If so, describe the types of projects.	The Edison SmartConnect PMO supports the management of projects that are operational because the PMO continues to support the operational areas that will continue the smart metering program as it transitions from a Program to regular SCE operations, including Revenue Services, Customer Communications, Metering Services, IT Operations, and the Business Customer Division.

In fact, the Edison SmartConnect Program is impacting these organizations' metering business processes.

> **16.3.6 SURVEY – PMO Sustainability:** Describe the overall impact of the PMO over a sustained period (e.g., customer satisfaction, productivity, reduced cycle time, growth, building or changing organizational culture, etc.). If available, please provide quantitative data to illustrate the areas in which the PMO has had the greatest business impact.

PMO Impact over a Sustained Period

The overall impact of the PMO over a sustained period can be encapsulated in two words: Culture Change. The PMO has become a model for the rest of the enterprise on project and program controls, as the PMO's methodologies have been leveraged by other Organizational Units and led to the formation of a Customer Service PMO. The PMO has also been regarded as a model on financial controls and overall program deliverables, based on feedback from the California Public Utilities Commission.

The Edison SmartConnect Program's PMO best practices have been emulated in other SCE organizational units.

Additionally, the Edison SmartConnect PMO has been regarded as an industry-leading project management organization, obtaining four Project Management Institute Orange County (PMI-OC) awards in 2007, 2010, 2011, and 2012, and being named a finalist two years in a row for the PMO of the Year Award in 2010 and 2011.

16.3.6.1 – What is included in a comprehensive project monitoring and control system and how is it implemented?	Within the Program, controls are provided through standard financial and project controls practices for approved projects (as illustrated below in Figure 16-10. Proposed new initiatives are thoroughly assessed by impacted stakeholders and independently reviewed for impact by the project controls organization. Once a proposed project passes internal assessments, it is presented to the Program's Change Control Board (CCB) for approval. Projects exceeding CCB limits are reviewed by CCB and presented to the appropriate governing body for approval as specified by the Program's governance model.
16.3.6.2 – How are project start-up and gate review processes structured?	The PMO's gate review processes consist of the following elements: 1) Initiation based on business need 2) Charter approval 3) Functional specifications and business requirements are collected and approved 4) Design and code phase 5) Construction 6) Testing 7) Project implementation

FIGURE 16-10: Edison SmartConnect Program Office Controls Process

Program Office Controls

Budgeting

- Basic financial planning tools are in place:
  - Budgeting systems
  - Baseline reporting
  - Forecasting systems
- Basic accruals process has been implemented
- Cost drivers are reported along with corresponding financial data
- Analysts are embedded in key functional areas
- Financial data is reviewed with organization leads prior to meeting with organization directors and the Director of the Program
- Benefits administration is in place at CSBU Finance

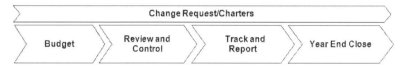

16.3.6.3 – Describe the project knowledge base system and how is it developed?

SCE Operations defines a business need for the Edison SmartConnect Program to develop.

Following this, a high level charter is produced. The Edison SmartConnect Management team seeks Executive Decision Team (EDT) approval to develop the requirements of a new charter. If approved, the team holds workshops to determine business and functional requirements in detail. Then, the Edison SmartConnect PMO develops the scope, schedule, and budget for a given project for final approval by the EDT.

The PMO uses a database as a tool to account for the different functional areas and business requirements to develop the application system and have it integrate with business operations. These business requirements are needed to build system functionality. During company-wide workshops, the databases are updated and revised.

This database information is included in the functional specifications document reviewed and approved by management.

16.3.6.4 – Describe the measurement, metrics, and Key Performance Indicators (KPIs) utilized by the PMO to measure project and program success.	The following Key Performance Indicators (KPIs) are used by the PMO to measure project/program success: • Meter deployment goal, • Tracking capital spend, and • Tracking Operations and Management. The PMO presents a monthly dashboard to the Executive Decision Team (EDT) to inform them of the Program's adherence to the above KPIs.
16.3.6.5 – Describe the organizational benefits and value the PMO provides to the enterprise.	The most prominent organizational benefit of the PMO is providing the Program with a consistent and reliable set of controls and processes for monitoring and controlling key Program functions and status. These key functions such as financial planning, contracts administration, audits, scheduling, risk management and change control have been recognized across SCE as the standard for performance and are being duplicated across the larger enterprise. An area of particular success has been the implementation of earned value for determining project status. While introduced to Edison SmartConnect as the standard metric of project performance, SCE senior leadership now requires earned value metrics for all large-scale SCE projects.
16.3.6.6 – Describe the economic benefits and value the PMO provides to the enterprise.	The economic impact of the PMO stems from two key functions. First, the PMO provides project managers with the resources and support they need to ensure their success in a dynamic environment with shifting priorities. The PMO acts as a conduit for acquiring needed financial labor and financial resources while exercising needed oversight. Second, the PMO has developed a highly effective reporting function providing Program leadership with up to date status on Program objectives and quick responses to Corporate and regulatory requests for Program information. Responsive and authoritative reporting ensures that key

management and governing bodies have the perspective necessary to make well-informed decisions on critical issues facing the Program.

16.3.7 SURVEY – Additional Comments: Please provide any additional comments

Southern California Edison's Edison SmartConnect® Program Management Office did not provide any additional comments.

Chapter 17

University of Utah Health Care PMO Case Study

University of Utah Health Care is the Intermountain West's only academic health care system, combining excellence in *patient* care, the latest in medical *research*, and *teaching* to provide leading-edge medicine in a caring and personal setting. The system provides care for the residents of Utah and five surrounding states, in a referral area encompassing more than 10 percent of the continental United States.

Whether it's for routine care or highly specialized treatment in orthopedics, stroke, ophthalmology, cancer, radiology, fertility, cardiology, genetic-related diseases, organ transplant, or many other areas of medicine, University of Utah Health Care offers the latest technology and advancements, including some services available nowhere else in the region.

University of Utah Health Care is consistently ranked among *US News & World Report's* Best Hospitals, and its academic partners at the University of Utah School of Medicine and Colleges of Nursing, Pharmacy, and Health are internationally regarded research and teaching institutions.

17.1   University of Utah Health Care – Enterprise and PMO Office Information

Enterprise Name:	University of Utah Health Care
Country:	United States of America
Industry:	Healthcare
Enterprise – Annual Sales Revenue:	Medium, $1.4 Billion US Dollars
Enterprise – Full-time Employee Equivalents:	5,000 plus
World Wide Web Site:	www.healthcare.utah.edu
PMO Name:	ITS Program Management Office

Title of PMO Leader:	Director
PMO Position in Organizational Structure:	Departmental (Information Technology Services)
PMO reports to in Organizational Structure:	Chief Information Officer
PMO Annual Operating Budget:	$730,000 US Dollars
PMO – Full-time Employee Equivalents:	Core – 4 Construction – 2 PMs and Project Support – 6

The following are the PMO Case Study Survey question sets and the associated responses as submitted by the University of Utah Health Care PMO, with minor editing for format and consistency.

17.2 University of Utah Health Care PMO Background, Innovations, and Impact

In the following three parts of this case study, the University of Utah Health Care ITS Program Management Office provides an overview of the background and structure of its PMO, various innovations and best practices by the PMO, and the potential future business impact of the PMO.

17.2.1 SURVEY – PMO Background: Describe your PMO, including background information on its scope, vision, mission, and position within the enterprise's organizational structure.

In the Beginning

Because of the large number of Information Technology projects being proposed and worked on in the organization, in October 2007, Ms. Michele Mills was asked by the Information Technology (IT) department of the University of Utah Health Care to create and manage a Program Management Office (PMO).

The purpose was to serve as a resource for Project Managers, Sponsors and others concerned about how projects were being managed. Initial objectives were to provide:

1) Project Management Best Practices
2) Project Transparency
3) Standardization
4) Outreach and mentoring services for Project Managers

We began our journey by holding an off-site retreat and invited department directors to give input on where they felt project management should go in the future. In addition, each PMO team member was asked to give a presentation on their area and provide ideas for how the PMO could optimize efforts in the future.

At that time, there was not a current Information Technology Services strategic plan, so a PMO strategic plan was created at the retreat to provide an initial Mission, Vision and Value statement, along with a multi-phased approach for implementation of the PMO. In the first 3 months, the team was able to fulfill many of the strategic plan elements that were planned at the 1-3 year milestone, including:

- Established PMO Best Practices
- Implemented Standardized Templates
- Created a Project Dashboard to fill the gap until a formal project tool was purchased
- Basic Metrics were created
- Project Management tool search began in collaboration with University of Utah campus entities

Within 6 months, the PMO began a collaborative purchase and implementation of a project and portfolio management tool. After the rollout, the team was expanded to include IT Quality Assurance/Testing programs, so was renamed the Program Management Office (PgMO).

The Program Management Office has its own budget and is currently funded through the Information Technology Services department within University of Utah Health Care.

Staff Titles

The Program Management Office has eight specific positions:
- Director, Program Management Office/ Clinical Portfolio Manager
- Team Manager/Portfolio Manager/Primary Project Tool Administrator
- Senior Project Manager [4 personnel]
- Sr. Quality Assurance and Testing/Secondary Project Tool Administrator
- Project Manager and Webmaster
- Project Manager (construction) [2 personnel]
- Project Manager [2 personnel]
- Executive Secretary
- ICD-10 Project Coordinator

Position Within Organization

The Figure 17-1 below shows the position of the Program Management Office (PgMO) within the University of Utah Health Care information technologies organizational structure.

FIGURE 17-1: University of Utah Health Care ITS Organizational Chart

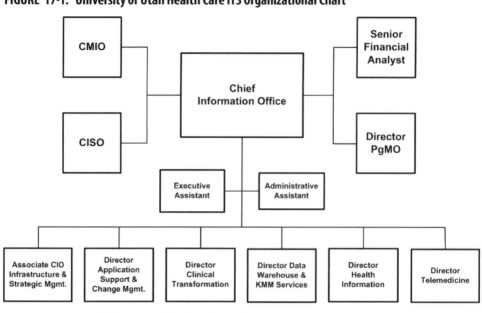

> **17.2.2 SURVEY – PMO Innovations and Best Practices:** Address the challenges your enterprise encountered prior to implementing the new PMO practices and how you overcame those challenges. Describe clearly and concisely the practices implemented and their effect on project, program, and/or portfolio and organizational success.

In 2009, the ITS Program Management Office (PgMO) implemented strategic planning using process improvement and project portfolio management tools. The focus was to reduce and prioritize project requests, based on budget and resource availability. The organization is strong and typically has funds to do what it needs to do, but with the economic problems globally, we were stretched thin. Through the leadership of our Chief Information Officer (CIO) we were able to focus PgMO time and energy on both overall strategic planning and portfolio planning. The CIO and our other senior leaders understand the importance of streamlining requests and supporting our processes. While we are still working to improve understanding among all senior leaders, they have been willing to listen to our ideas and try new ways of doing project management. Senior leadership now requires project requests to go through an IT Governance process that is standardized across all project portfolios managed by University of Utah Health Care.

The Program Management Office team members have worked very hard and accomplished a great deal over the last few years. The following activities show a small sample of the value provided to the organization and project stakeholders, since December 2009.

- University of Utah Health Care IT Governance groups established (Clinical Portfolio, Infrastructure Portfolio and Financial Portfolio)
- Initially, identified Project Managers within the department
- Created PMO Strategic Plan
- Defined Vision, Mission and Values Charter
- Developed and simplified standardized documentation, templates, job descriptions, policies, procedures and communication
- Identified minimum data sets for reporting
- Began tracking project related costs
- Converted existing projects to new methodology
- Established communication avenues with leadership team, resource managers, project managers
- Created formal project proposal process and project management process workflow
- PMO website and wiki created, enabling standardized stakeholder web access to weekly and monthly portfolio and project report
- Created "How-To" documents as a response to frequently asked questions
- Improved tracking of project work plans by implementing a Work Planning Dashboard, for Project Managers
- Achieved project management tool and time entry user adoption through one-on-one and team training of Time Entry, Project Management, and Resource Management for IT staff, management, and on-site consultants
- Process created to have consultants on-site and working within one week or less after request is received

The Project Management Office is a departmental PMO within the ITS Program Management office. PMO currently optimizes its practices through the use of standardized templates, processes, core competencies, project management computerized tool and reporting.

We were able to reduce our IT vendor market rate by an average of 25%. Saving $1,100/month per consultant using housing we secure – done through PgMO RFI process. We:

- Achieved effective cross-team collaborative work though clearly defined work products and timeline expectations. Initiated the first internal service agreement via a Scope of Work (SOW) that has been used as a model for similar work within the department. This has been a successful way to create "clear agreements."
- Developed standardized Project Test process that is used for organization wide IT QA processes and policies. Covers test scripts, test tracking, issue tracking and resolution. Teams are able to better control testing and save time through standardized scenario tracking and testing tools.
- Enhanced our Project and Portfolio Management tool with implementation of the Planview Financial Module.

As a young PMO, building project management maturity in a "Fast and Furious" way was difficult. There were many challenges, but we were able to do more than just survive. We thrived, while quietly instilling project management best practices in the organization. We have been able to deliver value to the IT department and overall organization through consistency and an expectation of excellence.

> **17.2.3 SURVEY – PMO Future Impact:** Briefly describe your PMO's plans for 2012 and beyond - please describe how those plans will potentially impact your enterprise and its organizational structure.

Historical Perspective

Project Management tools are not the answer to all your problems. We knew that creating effective processes was the first step. After standardized processes were in place we purchased a project tool and worked with the CIO, department Directors and Resource Managers to begin requiring staff to enter project time each week. After a few months of data collection, we started preparing resource utilization reports for our leaders. This allowed each team to see where they fared in comparison with their co-workers. Many teams embraced capacity planning and wanted to include more than just project work. To account for all staff time, we created what was termed "Other Planned Work" or "OPW." Time is broken up into "Portfolio Projects," "Other Planned Work," and "Operational." This provides management with a complete picture of what their staff levels are and what they should be to accomplish all their work.

By meeting with individual directors and managers, plus creating reports to help them monitor progress, we saw time entry compliance increase each month. On July 1, 2010, time entry for all project work was made mandatory by our Chief Information Officer.

Since July 2011, teams who are fully utilizing OPWs are able to more effectively plan ahead for their needs. We are anticipating by July 1, 2012, we will have the data in place to do a complete capacity planning report for our division. All the required process and system elements are in place, so now it is only a matter of maintaining time entry consistency.

Plans for 2012 and Beyond

Our next frontier will be full Capacity Planning, Forecasting (utilization and budgets), and resource based prioritization of projects. To mature our project management disciplines, we have focused time and effort to get staff consistently entering their time in the project tool – all time, not just project time. The data we have gleaned from this process has been invaluable to the teams fully utilizing it. Our goal for the upcoming year is to expand to all teams in the department, so we can get true capacity planning before the next fiscal year budgets are due.

We have already begun the process of creating a curriculum that will meet our needs for an internal certification program that would supplement outside certifications (e.g. PMP, CAPM). As part of the organization "Leader Academy", the Program Management Office is offering four (4) core competency classes – *Project Leadership, Project Communication Essentials, Negotiating for Project Success, and Basic Project Performance and Metrics.*

We plan to expand on the Project Management Track for the Leader Academy and target specific areas of need in the organization. We plan to introduce new classes every other year and provide an internal certification program to those that complete all the classes. In addition, we are now a Registered Education Provider (R.E.P.) with the Project Management Institute (PMI), so able to provide PDUs for our classes.

Prior to formal implementation of the Project Management Office, there were many ways of doing the same work in our organization. While it allowed people to do project work in their own way, it detracted from the overall success of IT projects. Project success was not consistent and was extremely subjective. Applications were randomly purchased and many stayed "on the shelf" to expire without ever being implemented.

Through the implementation of the Project Management Office and a structured project management methodology, our organization is now able to more efficiently prioritize IT projects and purchases. Resource data is being captured and is allowing for more effective capacity planning and resource requirements. Program Management Office Leader Academy classes enable us to expand our scope of influence to those outside the IT department. Our goal is to provide all staff in the hospital organization an opportunity to gain project leadership and management skills they can use in their own divisions.

Over the last few years, our Program Management Office aggressively promoted and supported project management best practices - Scope, Time, Cost, and Quality. We strategically accomplished this through user adoption, mentoring, PM core competencies, targeted Professional Development, Portfolio and Project Management methodology standardization, financial module implementation and the creation of an IT Quality Assurance framework. We can link each of the PgMO's past achievements to establishing and optimizing project management best practices.

University of Utah Health Care's Information Technology Services, Program Management Office is operational strategy in action. Our activities are consistently aligned with our organization goals of Exceptional Patient Experience, Quality, and Financial Strength (e.g. QA framework, Planview Financial Module). It is a team that has been visionary and a group of high performing, ardent "foot soldiers." Working with project teams and stakeholders to help the organization realize an effective operational strategy, we continuously demonstrate excellent process management maturity and add value.

We have accomplished much with few resources initially and with many constraints along the way. We envisioned, we thrived, and we delivered – in spite of the odds. We are slowly, but surely, building a culture of project management methodology, process planning and optimization in an environment where responding to a crisis is the "norm." Through our "PgMO Movement," we foresee a future where the delivery of project benefits and value is even more tangible. Stakeholders can look forward to continued project successes as the Program Management Office process mature and take hold throughout the organization.

Through the use of a project financial module, standardized testing process and a robust IT Strategic Plan, we are anticipating a greater return on investment in the coming years. We have a large number of mission critical major projects expected for 2011-2014. All with a great demand for project resources. We have enhanced our capacity planning abilities and knowledge, to allow for more effective resource and cost projections.

17.3   University of Utah Health Care PMO Model Components

In the following six parts of this case study, the University of Utah Health Care ITS Program Management Office provides its descriptions of how they implement the six key components of the Project Business Management Organization model: Governance; Methodology; Capability; Planning; Execution; and Sustainability.

> **17.3.1 SURVEY – PMO Governance:** Describe how your PMO presents itself as an executive-level management business function, how it addresses setting policy and establishing charters, and how it provides an organizational model for the business management of portfolios, programs, and projects and the establishment of portfolio, program, and project management offices.

The committee organizational structure for the Information Technology governance is shown below in Figure 17-2.

The following are the key features of the Program Management Office IT Governance for Portfolio & Project Management:

- Established a structure to evaluate, select, prioritize, and schedule IT projects to effectively promote the clinical and business strategy of University of Utah Health Care
- Provide coordination with other Health Science and Campus IT entities
- Developed a single, accountable organization for the delivery of IT services
- Eliminate redundancy, where feasible
- Help guide the consolidation of common IT services and solutions across campus to improve quality of service, gain efficiencies and reduce costs
  - o Defined standards and provide effective enforcement
  - o Coordinate Governance framework across all entities with defined roles and responsibilities, timely communication, and proactive, relevant reporting
- Collaboration/Service Alignment Opportunities
  - o Continuously identify, refine and confirm alignment opportunities
- Conduct detailed planning, identify organizational impact, advantages/disadvantages of alternatives and determine timing and resource needs

FIGURE 17-2-: University of Utah Health Care IT Governance Committees – Project and Portfolio Management

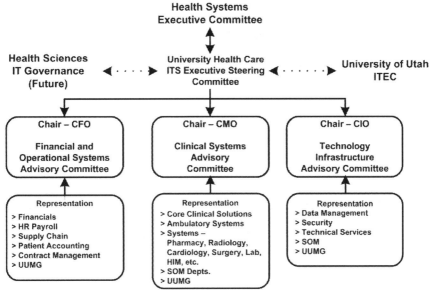

17.3.1.1 – How long has the PMO been in place? When was it started?	The PgMO evolved over time pre-2007, but was formalized as a Project Management Office in October 2007. Became a PgMO when team duties were expanded to include IT Quality Assurance.
17.3.1.2 – What is the relationship of PMO management to the enterprise's operational management?	Program Management Office reporting relationship: • PgMO to CIO • CIO to COO • COO to CEO • CEO to VP of Health Sciences • VP of Health Sciences to University President
17.3.1.3 – How is the PMO internally structured (positions, roles etc.)?	PgMO Core Positions • Director • Lead • IT Quality Assurance/Reporting This team keeps the PgMO "lights on" and provides project tool training, mentoring, support, guidance, and standard methodology.

PgMO Cloud PMs – Senior Project Managers are invited to be cloud PMs by CIO and/or Directors that provide expanded opportunities and a career path in project management.

Construction IT Project Managers – Oversee all aspects of IT requirements and implementation for hospital construction projects; work with business and application owners to ensure IT needs are met from network to desktop.

17.3.1.4 – How are the PMO's operations funded?

PMO operations are funded through University of Utah Health Care IT department - capital and operating budgets.

17.3.1.5 – What is the summary position description of the PMO leader?

The PgMO Director is responsible for overseeing the day-to-day operation of the Program Management Office and has direct responsibility for all Program Office functions, personnel and contract services associated with the Project Management, Process Redesign and ITS Quality Assurance actvities.

Works closely with internal and external departments and is accountable for:
- Actively participating in the achievement of the organization and department goals;
- Reporting directly to and supporting CIO in the execution of the Information Management Strategic Plan; and
- Developing, Implementing, and Maintaining organization wide project management, process improvement and quality assurance testing methodologies.

17.3.1.6 – What position requirements are used as a basis for selecting the PMO leader?

Qualifications/Requirements
- Bachelor's degree in business administration, healthcare administration, engineering, project management, or computer science
- Currently hold Project Management Professional (PMP) certification from the Project Management Institute (or equivalent)
- Minimum ten years professional experience in a leadership or project management capacity, preferably in an academic healthcare IT environment

- Minimum ten years of information systems experience, with at least five of the years in healthcare industry at a manager level or above
- Familiarity with Six Sigma, Lean, and Computer Simulation Software is a plus
- Demonstrates initiative, good judgment, strong service attitude and have the ability to achieve results without supervisory oversight of individual people on a project team
- Strong sense of individual accountability, team player with collaborative nature, comfortable with change and uncertainty
- Strong communication skills (written, oral, listening) with ability to present effectively to audiences of all sizes
- At minimum, a general understanding of ITIL practices and principles

Essential Functions
- Responsible for strategic planning for Program Management Office
- Direct multi-disciplinary project and portfolio staff supporting strategic plan
- Oversee all IT Governance portfolio activities
- Guide development of project charter proposals, plans and business requirements
- Assist other IT leaders in negotiating IT vendor contracts
- Provide recommendations for capacity planning through use of standard project management tools
- Ensure overall implementation of projects are in accordance with vision, strategy, and guiding principles of organization
- Oversee Program Management Office operating and capital budgets
- Hire, supervise, and evaluate Project and Portfolio Managers, and provide coaching and direction
- Lead, participate, and contribute insight on key decisions for clinical and operational business areas impacted by projects or projects impacted by business decisions
- Provide input on issues resolution and risk mitigation processes; ensure issues are resolved or escalated appropriately; identify barriers to project success and facilitate risk management planning

17.3.1.7 – Is the PMO a Profit & Loss cost center or considered overhead?	The PgMO is considered Overhead.

17.3.1.8 – What current challenge is the PMO dealing with?	Ability to provide information for true capacity planning from project data. To do this well requires the majority of staff and their leaders to consistently use project tools. Most are now using it consistently, but it must be monitored to ensure it continues. Goal is to give executive leaders quality data that is actionable for forecasting of resources and project prioritization several years in advance. We do this better than ever before, but want to raise the bar in our future capacity planning activities.

17.3.2 SURVEY – PMO Methodology / Standardization: Describe what standardization your PMO has implemented across the enterprise that examines: identification and integration of processes and practices; development of standardized Project Business Management processes; and documentation of enterprise-wide portfolio, program, and project management process methodology models, including their associated policies, practices, and procedures.

Organizational Standardization - University of Utah Health Care determined Governance types desired and implemented the model above in Figure 17-2:

- Executive Governance Committees – provide formal funding approval
- IT Governance Committees – provide funding prioritization
- Portfolio Committees – provide resource prioritization and recommendations, but is non-funding
- Portfolio Manager Group – Creation and implementation of Portfolio Management standardization and methodology

17.3.2.1 – Describe the standards utilized by the PMO to ensure the enterprise's project / program / portfolio management goals and objectives are achieved.	<ul><li>Standardized PM Core Competencies</li><li>PgMO Website, wiki, direct email address for project management and governance questions</li><li>Standard project management templates, methodology, reports, project process map and project management tool</li><li>Training is standardized and includes 1-1 targeted training, as needed</li><li>Resource utilization standards and guidance</li></ul>

17.3.2.2 – Describe the project management process guidelines being employed by the PMO.	Implemented a Project Management Process Map that incorporates PMI standard processes with "real world" activities in our organization.

The purpose is to ensure we follow all the steps and processes in a way that makes sense to everyone. This has helped our project management maturity in the organization grow, because we can always determine where someone is in the process flow.

Typically, if they are having issues we can clearly show them where they are in the process. Most of the time issues are the result of their not following the process, so we simply have them go through any missed steps that are required (e.g. Initial Project Request Submission). After having them do this a couple of times, they learn what needs to happen and future projects have fewer problems.

We utilize a standard methodology, templates, IT Governance Committees, and Funding/Non-Funding Portfolios throughout the process. The process map and all our stated tools are available to everyone internally on our PgMO website. We keep our most current copies there. |
| *17.3.2.3 – What systems, tools, and templates make your PMO successful?* | Project Management tool, One-page Process Map, website that includes project and portfolio reports - run weekly, IT Strategic Plan and tool that allows us to align projects to objectives/measurements, PgMO wiki for collaboration with team and department. |
| *17.3.2.4 – Describe how management at all levels is directly involved in the development of the PMO and it processes.* | CIO and Associate CIO were an integral part of the PgMO's success from the beginning. Both believe in project management concepts and a track record of success where implemented effectively. Both have provided consistent guidance, input and sponsorship from inception.

Chief Executive Officer and Chief Operations Officer provide an environment that allows for standardization of project management processes. |

17.3.2.5 – Describe the implementation plan you used for establishing project / program / portfolio management standards across your enterprise.

Did not have a current departmental strategic plan prior to current CIO's arrival. Employed the following:

- PMO team held a PMO retreat with four staff members;
- Invited IT Directors to attend at different times throughout the day to provide input on what they wanted to see in the future;
- Determined action items for the next 3-5 years;
- Created PMO Strategic Plan we utilized until the ITS department had one – transitioned some of our objectives and initiatives into the new one; and
- Original PMO Strategic Plan was implemented as a foundation, but can be attributed to our current success

17.3.2.6 – How does the PMO use project, program, and portfolio management standards to optimize its practices? Are they based on PMI® or other industry guides and are they updated as new editions of the guides are released?

PgMO practices and standards are based on PMI® *PMBOK Guide* and other guides - updated as new editions are released.

17.3.3 SURVEY – PMO Capabilities: Describe development and assessment of the enterprise's abilities, describe any project management competency model, summarize any education and training program, describe any established career path progression plan, and outline key Enterprise Environmental Factors.

17.3.3.1 – Describe the components of your enterprise's training program.

Basic Project Management Methodology, Leader Academy (Project Leadership, Communication Essentials, Negotiation, Basic Project Metrics and Reporting).

Soon to be introduced are Project Risk Management and Project Sponsorship Essentials.

17.3.3.2 – Describe the value your enterprise places on education and training and its goals and objectives.	As an academic medical center, University of Utah Health Care is committed to providing excellence in education and training. Many opportunities are available to students and staff. A Leader Academy was created specifically to address employee needs. The focus is on enhancing leadership skills in high performing staff. Enterprise wide goals are set each year with the current emphasis being Financial, Quality and Patient Care. There are several organizational initiatives associated with each strategic goal. This provided a framework for the ITS PgMO's alignment.
17.3.3.3 – Does the enterprise have a project management career path program? If so, what are the components?	Yes, we introduced a Cloud PM program in 2010 that provides a career path for senior level Project Managers. PMs are invited to participate by their Director and PgMO Director and work with PgMO as full team members. Receiving the benefit of mentoring, training, and team activities.
17.3.3.4 – Describe the measurements, metrics, and Key Performance Indicators (KPI's) utilized by the PMO to determine the organization's knowledge, skills, and level of achievement.	We utilize Core Competency Checklists, Personal Development Plans, and 360 evaluations.
17.3.3.5 – Does the enterprise employ a project management competency model? If yes, please describe it. If no, why not?	Yes, incorporates into Employee Evaluations that are done yearly.

> **17.3.4 SURVEY – PMO Business Planning:** Discuss strategic business planning, tactical business planning, business objective (project) development and prioritization, and project identification, selection, and authorization.

17.3.4.1 – Describe the organizational structure and process used for corporate strategic business planning.

Yearly Director retreat provides foundation for strategic planning and measurement selection in IT department leadership team. Quarterly Strategic Review meetings are held to provide alignment with the PgMO and organization IT projects.

Does the PMO play a role in the process? If so, describe the PMOs role and responsibilities.

PgMO Director participates in the yearly enterprise wide director retreat. Is also a member of the IT department leadership team and participates in quarterly strategic review meetings and all other meetings where director level leaders are invited.

17.3.4.2 – How is the strategic plan implemented with a project forecast plan?

Strategic Aligned Management (SAM) objectives align with projects in each portfolio. Our project forecast plan is based fully on the project and resource prioritization within each portfolio.

While the business side doesn't follow exactly along portfolio management alignment, over the last two years we have found less "drive by" projects than we did in the past. At minimum, we can now ask the questions "What projects should we stop or put on hold to accommodate the request?"

17.3.4.3 – How is strategic planning, culture, and selection of projects integrated?

IT Project Process Map is the central element that ties strategic planning, culture and project selection together. It is simple and easy to determine why there is an issue at any point along the way. If someone is struggling with a project anywhere in the process, we can show them where they are and where they should be in the process.

Typically, if there is an issue, it is because the project did not go through the process from the beginning. We find the requester has attempted to bypass a critical process step or did not follow it. Short cuts are quickly found, and we are able to steer the person back to the critical step they missed.

What we continuously emphasize:
- Clarify project and portfolio priorities from the beginning
- Require business justification, portfolio alignment, and approval to add to project portfolio
- Convey project priorities to each project team

- Provide clear statement of project objectives and priorities – to project teams and stakeholders
- Ensure time for planning of effective estimate
- Don't allow organization "guesses" about cost, timing and scope to dictate project planning – we provide data for better decision-making

---

17.3.5 SURVEY – PMO Business Execution: Describe what role the PMO has in project selection, prioritization, and initiation; in portfolio, program and project execution planning; in stage-gate reviews; and in performance metrics selection and application.

17.3.5.1 – How are portfolios, programs, and projects selected and initiated?

Four groups are involved:
- IT Governance Committee
- IT Executive Steering Committee
- Capital Committee
- Resource Reviews by IT Directors and Resource Managers

PgMO is involved with IT projects from project request through project closure. During capital process and project selection, IT Governance Committees follow IT Project Process Map and project request submission requirements. Requested projects must have an ROI spreadsheet that includes a portfolio scorecard. The form must be completed prior to submitters being asked to present at a capital review meeting.

Normally, two presentation meetings are held and after some discussion, each committee prioritizes project requests. The prioritized request list is sent to the organization's Capital Committee where funding is approved or projects are removed from the final list.

17.3.5.2 – How are projects organized and managed as a program and/or portfolio?

Six part process:
1) Placed in most appropriate portfolio (clinical, financial, infrastructure, security/privacy, Information Management, ICD-10).
2) IT Governance Committees fund projects, so capital project requests go there initially.
3) Once funded, they are be placed in one of the portfolios.

4) All hospital managed portfolios have standard processes, but individual chair can manage their meetings flexibly. This allows the PgMO to drive the results (e.g. prioritization of projects, resource and PM assignments), but not dictate how chairs get there.

5) Each portfolio has a PgMO Portfolio Manager assigned to it

6) PgMO Portfolio Managers meet regularly to determine and/or maintain standardization.

17.3.5.3 – How are projects prioritized within a program and/or portfolio?

Once a project or program is approved, IT Directors and Resource Managers take into account business owners and staffing requirements to determine timing of approved project implementation.

Collaboration between various entities is important, so we can get appropriate input and buy-in for timelines.

17.3.5.4 – How does the enterprise define what project and program success is?

Each portfolio has a scorecard that is included in the required Return on Investment (ROI) document. ROI also includes IT Strategic Plan Guiding Principles.

Metrics are determined at the start of a project, but additional metrics can be added throughout the project.

As the project progresses, measures are reviewed and action taken, when necessary.

17.3.5.5 – Does the PMO support the management of projects that would be considered operational in nature? If so, describe the types of projects.

Yes, but our main focus is on capital projects.

If leaders find there is a need for a project manager for an operational project, they make a request to the PgMO Director. The director reviews resource bandwidth and may provide some-one for a short-term project. Typically, the resource is not at the senior level, which gives new Project Managers an opportunity for learning.

If there is no available bandwidth, the PgMO Director will offer to have the vendor management person contact them to start the process for getting a consultant to do the work.

Types of operational projects might be to manage a maintenance roll out or coordinate an interface implementation associated with a standard upgrade. Normally, these would be handled by functional team PMs, rather than the PgMO.

17.3.6 SURVEY – PMO Sustainability: Describe the overall impact of the PMO over a sustained period (e.g., customer satisfaction, productivity, reduced cycle time, growth, building or changing organizational culture, etc.). If available, please provide quantitative data to illustrate the areas in which the PMO has had the greatest business impact.

Because of our excellent leadership at all levels of the organization, the Program Management Office has a seat at the table. We are not relegated to the back room or only as reporting and data processors.

Governance

Guidance by PgMO Portfolio Managers has streamlined the capital process. In the past, it took months to get a list of committees we could somewhat agree on. To do that, they had to meet every month throughout the year. Even then, people were not satisfied with the final request list. It wasn't based on quantifiable data, but on who had the most influence. Today, we may meet during the year for discussions about the strategic plan or other high-level purposes. Rarely, do we need to discuss the projects that were prioritized the previous year. When we do, the new request is evaluated based on the current projects in the portfolio.

Portfolio Management and Project Prioritization

Identification and prioritization of projects and initiatives has been essential in the reduction of costs. Prior to using an effective prioritization process, many software packages were purchased, put on the shelf and never used. Or an attempt to implement was made only to find out the product was not useable in our environment. Prior to the PMO and governance implementation, this occurred several times per year. Millions of dollars were wasted on systems we never implemented. With our current process, this has not occurred for any project that has gone through the IT Governance process.

Benefits Realization Tracking

We implemented our project tool financial module in fiscal year 2012, so expect benefit realization in fiscal year 2013. Tracking of estimated versus actual costs will be easier to provide. Leaders will also be able to pull their own data, if they choose to do so.

Resource allocation and coordination between projects: Requires consistent input from cross-functional teams, which we are receiving.

Executive Buy-In

Our executives have embraced project management as a means to improve competitiveness and/or for the purpose of compliance. Considering, lack of buy-in is a critical factor in the failure of PMOs, having this in our organization provides an excellent future for sustainability.

17.3.6.1 – What is included in a comprehensive project monitoring and control system and how is it implemented?

Tools include:

- Strategic Aligned Management (SAM) objective measurements
- Planview Project & Portfolio tool
- Planview Financial Module
- Project & Portfolio reports

Our organization is a two-hospital Academic Medical Center serving a regional population of approximately five million across several states.

In October of 2010, we approved the first revision of our Information Technology Strategic Plan. We had not updated the IT Strategic Plan for over ten years and in previous versions had not employed metrics.

The plan was ambitious for a health care organization with many entities already vying for our time. There were general economic and competitive pressures, federal regulatory requirements pending, and an aggressive construction program of large facility expansions underway.

While we had a rapidly maturing project management process in place, it was critical that the IT initiatives demonstrated the value delivered from investments of over $100 million. To achieve this, the IT leadership team adopted a program of Strategy Alignment Management (SAM) supported by a tightly integrated suite of software tools known as InsightVision ™.

In conjunction with project management processes and the PgMO, SAM has been fully incorporated into our strategic management process, demonstrating the value delivered from IT investments, communicating our progress against our plan, and clearly demonstrating close alignment between the IT division and the overall organization.

17.3.6.2 – How are project start-up and gate review processes structured?	Utilize formal Kick-off meetings with standard agenda.

Regular project team and project steering committee meetings held to review milestones and provide direction on moving forward (gate review).

ITS Project Process Map provides a visual source for structure.

17.3.6.3 – Describe the project knowledge base system and how is it developed?	Planview Project Management tool provides content area for storing all project related documentation.

We also use project wikis, shared folders, FAQs and web pages.

17.3.6.4 – Describe the measurement, metrics, and Key Performance Indicators (KPIs) utilized by the PMO to measure project and program success.	Determine measurements, metrics and Key Performance Indicators (KPI) at beginning of project. Utilize standard measurements, metrics and KPIs, but also project specific metrics.

Some of the current measurements we are using are:
- Percent of IT projects aligned with organization portfolio
- Amount of ITS Project Spending
- Amount of ITS Project Spending with a completed financial analysis
- Average IT Guiding Principles Alignment Rating for Approved Projects
- Average Time to Deliver Rapid-Return projects
- Number of current IT projects managed in project management tool
- Projects on-time
- Projects on-budget
- Variance of Actual versus Projected Capital Hours

17.3.6.5 – Describe the organizational benefits and value the PMO provides to the enterprise.	Better visibility, higher quality results, consistency, and agreement on prioritization process.

17.3.6.6 – Describe the economic benefits and value the PMO provides to the enterprise.	Significant reduction in software/hardware purchases that are never used. Since the implementation of the IT Governance Committees and PgMO standardization, there have not been any IT project failures. Prior to that time many projects had some element of failure

(cost overruns, late implementations, extensive scope changes) associated with them.

Evaluation of project requests and effective prioritization has prevented the purchase of systems and products that are not viable in our organization. This has been possible through the implementation of a PMO, structured requirements gathering, collaborative discussion, resource prioritization, and ROI documentation.

Because of a more robust PgMO over the last two years, along with the synergy of our Information Technology Infrastructure Library (ITIL), [which is a set of practices for IT service management that focuses on aligning IT services with the needs of business] and our Strategy Alignment Management (SAM) program implementations, the business and regulatory objectives are being met more effectively. The PgMO is now able to:

- Ensure tight alignment between Information Technology investments and initiatives with the operational strategy of the organization
- Successfully implement IT Strategic Plan objectives and initiatives
- Create transparency and visibility of the IT Strategy and objectives across the organization
- Quantify the value that IT brings to the organization
- Align daily tasks with the strategic vision
- Provide focus, challenges and engagement for workforce
- Appropriately drive change and improve agility to meet changing needs

17.3.7 SURVEY – Additional Comments: Please provide any additional comments

With the creation and implementation of the PgMO IT Project Process Map that aligns with PMI processes and the IT Strategy Aligned Management (SAM) program, we are able to provide more clarity for cross-functional groups. Project Managers at all levels, that use the process, have realized project success.

Decisive leadership from the ITS Leadership Team has provided an environment where we could hone activities to better meet the needs of the organization. With evolving support and input from executive leaders, we are confident we can expand our departmental project management influence moving forward. Meaning, the more standardized we are top-to-bottom and bottom-to-top, the more effective we will become organizationally.

We continue to validate the career path for high performing, serious minded project management professionals. Strong project managers at all levels of skill and ability are attracted to solid project management processes. We understand projects require competent project leaders and without adequate skills project performance is always at risk. Expectations are high for all project managers, and we are fully committed to continuing on a path of excellence.

In early 2012, the ITS PgMO began the first University of Utah Health Care – Information Technology Services specific Gartner PPM Maturity Assessment Survey. Participants included ITS/UIT Directors, Managers, Project Managers and various staff who participated in large project implementations over the last two years. The ITS Program Management Office is now able to report a Gartner PPM Assessment Survey score for 2012 of 3.82. This is up from our original score of 1.8 two years ago. The UUHC ITS score of 3.82 positions the PgMO to more comprehensively gain project success and maturity in the future, thus enabling our organization to become more effective, as we face continued resource challenges. While no maturity assessment is a panacea or sustained without continuous effort, it does provide an excellent way to determine what areas need specific focus.

Chapter 18

VSP Vision Care PMO Case Study

V SP was founded in September 1955 by a group of optometrists. VSP has grown into VSP Global, a complimentary group of leading companies, offering world-class products and services to eyecare professionals, employers, and more than 55 million members. These VSP Global companies provide comprehensive eyecare coverage, access to cutting-edge frame styles and brands, design of custom interiors and merchandising systems, innovative e-commerce and practice management solutions, and technologically advanced lab services.

As one of the VSP Global^{SM} companies, VSP Vision Care is the largest vision benefits company in the U.S.

18.1   VSP Vision Care – Enterprise and PMO Office Survey Information

Enterprise Name:	VSP Vision Care a VSP Global^{SM} company
Country:	United States of America
Industry:	Eyecare and Eyewear
Enterprise – Annual Sales Revenue:	Large, greater than $1 Billion US Dollars
Enterprise – Full-time Employee Equivalents:	4,860
World Wide Web Site:	www.vsp.com
PMO Name:	Enterprise Project Solutions (EPS)
Title of PMO Leader:	Vice President
PMO Position in Organizational Structure:	Enterprise-wide Division
PMO reports to in Organizational Structure:	Chief Operations Officer (COO)
PMO Annual Operating Budget:	Approximately $6 Million US Dollars
PMO – Full-time Employee Equivalents:	50

The following are the PMO Case Study Survey question sets and the associated responses as submitted by VSP Vision Care's Enterprise Project Solutions (EPS) PMO, with minor editing for format and consistency.

18.2   VSP Vision Care PMO Background, Innovations, and Impact

In the following three parts of this case study, the VSP Vision Care's Enterprise Project Solutions (EPS) PMO provides an overview of the background and structure of its PMO, various innovations and best practices by the PMO, and the potential future business impact of the PMO.

> **18.2.1 SURVEY – PMO Background:** Describe your PMO, including background information on its scope, vision, mission, and position within the enterprise's organizational structure.

Scope

In 2008, after a period of global expansion that resulted in a growing number of enterprise-wide projects, a formal Program Management Office (PMO) structure became a necessity. That is when VSP chartered the Enterprise Project Solutions Division (EPS) as a PMO.

Under the leadership of the Chief Operations Officer and the Enterprise Project Solutions Division Vice President, EPS consolidated and co-located Project Managers (PMs) and Business Analysts (BAs) from individual divisions into the PMO. EPS then developed critical staff roles and key job accountabilities, implemented robust interview processes to hire experienced project professionals, and increased its career development opportunities.

Vision and Mission

EPS focuses on three goals in support of its mission, "Bridging strategy and operational excellence through innovation, execution, and adoption." These are:

- Shaping, leading, and delivering results on enterprise projects;
- Fostering high performing employees; and
- Championing business innovations to transform the way business is done.

Position within Organizational Structure

EPS was chartered within the Vision Care line of business, yet its impact has been felt throughout the VSP Global organization as it continues to influence the practice of project management. As a change agent, the EPS PMO has been the single largest unifying force in developing an enterprise view through influencing, leading cross enterprise projects, bringing all parties to the table, and encouraging cooperation among the lines of business. The projects led by the PMO often radically change business direction, systems architecture, and the relationship between VSP and its publics, requiring true leadership to help VSP through the ensuing transition.

> **18.2.2 SURVEY – PMO Innovations and Best Practices:** Address the challenges your enterprise encountered prior to implementing the new PMO practices and how you overcame those challenges. Describe clearly and concisely the practices implemented and their effect on project, program, and/or portfolio and organizational success.

Challenges

Beginning in the 1990s, VSP became known as a vision care industry leader. As the largest not-for-profit company in the U.S., VSP sold vision benefits to both large, international clients and small-business clients. As the decade progressed and vision care benefits became a key component of employee-benefit packages, VSP experienced unprecedented growth.

To accommodate this growth, individual divisions within VSP independently employed PMs and BAs to support division-specific development and enhancement projects. This approach to project work resulted in minimal cross-divisional knowledge sharing and little coordination of project and business processes.

Effecting Change

Driven by the need to collaborate and share knowledge, a small, grassroots team of cross-divisional employees organized to address the ensuing lack of coordination among the lines of business. The team, known as the Project Professionals, was comprised of PMs, BAs, functional managers, and project sponsors.

The Project Professionals met monthly on personal time to share experiences, network, and establish a standardized project management methodology and training program. They remained active project methodology advocates for nearly eight years before becoming members of structured and strategically located project management and business analysis teams.

Implementing Practices

As EPS began maturing its skills, it also championed the development and improvement of enterprise-wide tools and processes. With much of the needed structure and methodology already in place, but inconsistently applied, the EPS PMO dedicated itself to internal process improvement and alignment. The goal was to build an enterprise point of view and increase effectiveness and business value. By creating project-tracking processes, EPS focused on establishing a baseline for project metrics and post-project assessments.

One strategy was to create participation by executives in the portfolio process by creating three unique organizational entities:

1) **Business/Technology Integration Team (Business/Technology Integration Team (BTI))** – EPS initiated the founding of the Business/Technology Integration Team, consisting of the presidents and top-level executives across the VSP lines of business. The Business/Technology Integration Team is chartered with ensuring that programs and projects align with enterprise-wide strategic initiatives and are prioritized accordingly. By involving the company's top-level executives, BTI is intended to ensure resource and budgetary support for the most critical undertakings, alignment within the enterprise, and the execution of the leadership vision.

2) **Portfolio Strategic Committee (PSC)** – The PSC is comprised of varying levels of management across the lines of business. This governance body is chartered with the approval and prioritization of enterprise projects, ensuring alignment with enterprise strategies and delivery of projects that maximize business value and return on investment. Along with the Intake Team (described below in item 3), this committee implements additional process changes and improvements designed to align the portfolio more closely with corporate strategies.

3) **Intake Team (Project Screening Board)** - Established in June 2008, the Intake Team has played a key role in driving process improvements in project portfolio management. Intake comprises experts in project execution, analysis, technology, and finance. Originally tasked with reviewing project documents prior to submission to the Portfolio Strategic Committee, the Intake Team now also ensures that projects remain in alignment with strategic enterprise initiatives. Its members also provide necessary coaching to project managers, sponsors, and projects at risk; and it researches, analyzes, and develops feasibility studies of various strategic initiatives.

> **18.2.3 SURVEY – PMO Future Impact:** Briefly describe your PMO's plans for 2012 and beyond - please describe how those plans will potentially impact your enterprise and its organizational structure.

Context

Due to competitive pressures, the "time to market" is more critical today than it was in the past. VSP can no longer afford to continue to fund and execute projects without a clear driving strategy. Therefore, as an organization VSP has made a commitment to focus its efforts on initiatives that will strategically grow its position in the marketplace.

EPS has identified an opportunity to improve the alignment of corporate strategy with project execution. The challenge is that there often is a condensed time period to vet the strategies to ensure they align with existing programs to support the enterprise mission statement and vision.

To address this challenge, EPS has improved it's project planning process by focusing on defining the program plans and divisional projects in order to align initiatives and include them as key pieces of the planning process. The VSP executive leadership team, along with PMO leadership, collaborates in an annual planning process that results in a high-level definition of new and continuing strategic initiatives that are aligned and prioritized in the enterprise portfolio.

Under the governance of EPS, coordinated portfolio planning and budget tracking processes have been developed to support a structure of responsible investment decision making. Treating projects as an investment ensures VSP is doing the right work to implement its enterprise strategy. Fiscal accountability toward project investments is a new discipline for the company, which required changes in the way annual budgets are created and monitored. The financial analyst within EPS shares responsibility with the PMO leadership team by tracking and monitoring project costs, benefits, and Return on Investment (ROI).

Future Plans

In 2012, the program management methodology will evolve through streamlined processes that eliminate redundancy and the perception of bureaucracy. Each program will have a unified program plan that has been endorsed by the program champions, program managers, and the Business/Technology Integration Team (BTI) governance team.

The new program management disciplines will increase the speed to execution through the reduction in individual project level documentation such as concepts and charters. The program plan, program roadmap, resource plan, and financial plan are dynamic tools that program managers use to manage their program in collaboration with the project managers assigned to the program.

- To aid in streamlining the execution phase of the Software Development Lifecycle, EPS is partnering with IT and operational business areas to develop standardized release management processes. The purpose is to find development, testing, and deployment efficiencies across multiple platforms for high exposure projects. The IT and EPS partnership will develop repeatable and measurable processes within the release management system, including the release plan and calendar.
  - o The outcomes will be improved productivity, decreased project resource competition, project technical architecture alignment, and preserved integrity and availability of production systems.

- EPS will also continue to emphasize the evolution and maturation of the Portfolio Analysis and Support functions to facilitate organizational decision making and readiness. The PSC reviews resource demand, risks, and changes at the portfolio level to balance the selection, sequencing, and scheduling of projects. In addition, impact assessments and timing of change to internal stakeholders, as well as external publics, are collected, maintained, and aggregated at the portfolio level.

- o EPS has formed partnerships with HR Business Partners to proactively provide portfolio data and input to strategically prepare for "change and people management" beyond the efforts at the project or program level. Likewise, partnerships are formed with stakeholders representing external publics and customers to position change and value based on a longer term, aggregated view. The PMO is currently evaluating opportunities to streamline, enhance, and automate portfolio data capture and reporting to shift more attention toward higher value analysis and expanded influence.

- As the PMO matures, so must the skill sets of the PMs and BAs. The PMO will continue to build and train the PM and BA in project management and analysis concepts, leadership, and interpersonal skill competencies and best practices. Training will range from entry-level staff development through advanced program and portfolio management.
  - o Through partnering with the award-winning VSP Human Resources Enterprise Training Team and external training partners, EPS will continue to add value to the organization by staffing increasingly complex projects and programs with highly skilled project professionals.

18.3   VSP Vision Care PMO Model Components

In the following six parts of this case study, the VSP Vision Care's Enterprise Project Solutions (EPS) PMO provides its descriptions of how they implement the six key components of the Project Business Management Organization model

> **18.3.1 SURVEY – PMO Governance:** Describe how your PMO presents itself as an executive-level management business function, how it addresses setting policy and establishing charters, and how it provides an organizational model for the business management of portfolios, programs, and projects and the establishment of portfolio, program, and project management offices.

Operating as an Executive-Level Management Business Function

The PMO governance structure was developed with the goal of building an enterprise point of view and increasing effectiveness and business value.

One strategy was to create participation by executives in the portfolio process by creating three unique organizational entities.

1) **Business/Technology Integration Team (BTI)** – EPS PMO initiated the founding of the Business/Technology Integration Team consisting of the presidents and top-level executives across the VSP lines of business. The BTI is chartered with ensuring that programs and projects align with the VSP enterprise strategic initiatives and that they are prioritized accordingly. By involving the company's top-level executives, Business/Technology Integration Team is intended to ensure resource and budgetary support for the most critical undertakings, alignment within the enterprise, and the execution of the leadership vision. The EPS PMO leads and facilitates the activities, decisions and outcomes of this group.

2) **Portfolio Strategic Committee (PSC)** – The PSC is comprised of varying levels of management across the lines of business. This governance body is chartered with the approval and prioritization of enterprise projects, ensuring alignment with enterprise strategies and delivery of projects that maximize business value and ROI. With the Intake Team, it will implement additional process changes, and improvements designed to align the portfolio more closely with corporate strategies.

3) **Intake Team (Project Screening Board)** – Established in June 2008, the Intake Team has played a key role in driving process improvements in project portfolio management. Intake comprises experts in project execution, analysis, technology, and finance. Originally tasked with reviewing project documents prior to submission to the PSC, the Intake Team now also ensures that projects remain in alignment with strategic enterprise initiatives. Its members also provide coaching to PMs, sponsors, and projects at risk; and researches, analyzes, and develops feasibility studies of various strategic initiatives.

Setting Policy and Providing an Organizational Model

As EPS organized and began maturing its team's skills, it also championed the development of enterprise-wide tools and processes. Key developments included the Project Portal, the Intake Team (Project Teaming Board) and supporting processes, operational readiness planning, and organizational impediment resolution process.

Project Portal – EPS is responsible for maintaining and enhancing an enterprise Project Portal. The Portal, organized in quick reference format, incorporates project information, project management methodology, business analysis, continuous quality improvement and various other tools.

Intake Team – The Intake Team oversees and ensures that enterprise projects remain in alignment with strategic initiatives throughout the project lifecycle.

- *Project Prioritization and Selection Criteria* – The Portfolio Strategic Committee (PSC) was in place for several years prior to the formal organization of EPS and the

Intake Team. The objective of the PSC is to approve and prioritize enterprise projects that align with enterprise strategies and that yield the greatest business value and ROI. However, before the creation of the Intake Team, prioritization was largely subjective. With the Intake Team's analysis and recommendations, the process has become more objective and results driven. Prospective projects receive scores based not only on business value and alignment with enterprise strategies, but also on growth in market share, technical infrastructure, resource availability, and relative project risk.

- *Concept* – Traditionally, the PSC approved and prioritized projects based on a project proposal. Once the PSC approved a project proposal, project initiation began with the development of a project charter and the assignment of resources.
  - o This practice resulted in a troubling trend. Too often, highly skilled teams were unable to execute quickly due to a lack of comprehensive business and systems analysis. To better utilize project resources, the Intake Team developed the project concept. The concept is a document that captures high-level ideas and resource estimates. Once the PSC approves a concept for further research, business and technical experts conduct a time-boxed analysis. The result of this analysis is a project charter appropriate for submission to the Intake Team and the PSC as a prospective enterprise project. Since implementing the concept document, average time-to-baseline has decreased significantly – from 26 weeks in 2008, to 10.3 weeks in 2009, to 6.6 weeks in 2011.

- *Project Gate Reviews* – To ensure that initiated projects remain relevant and on target to meet stated business goals, the Intake Team introduced the project gate review processes. Mandatory project gate reviews take place at predetermined project phase intervals – concept, charter, execution (project midpoint), and closing. Critical ("red") risk gate reviews are required for projects that have an at-risk status for four consecutive weeks. Project sponsors surveyed gave the gate review process an 88% satisfaction rating. Sponsors stated that they saw improvements in speed to market, increased quality control and improvements in risk mitigation to course correct at-risk projects.

- *Project Audits* – Post-project audits assist sponsors with monitoring project Return on Investment (ROI) or productivity gains over a period of time post implementation. To conduct post-project audits, the Intake Team collects baseline metrics at the project closing gate, then partners with business stakeholders to validate business value and ROI gained from the project.

- *Consultation and Coaching Services* – As the primary contact for project gate reviews, the Intake Team offers consulting and coaching services for project sponsors and PMs. Coaching for PMs, sponsors and product owners during a "red" gate review provides needed guidance that often puts a project back on track. As requested by the

PSC, the Intake Team also researches, analyzes, and develops feasibility studies of various strategic initiatives.

Operational Readiness (OR) Task Force – EPS established an OR task force in mid-2009 to ensure that divisions are prepared to manage their business at project close. The task force established new PM and BA responsibilities and developed new tools:
- Initial stakeholder assessment to identify high-level needs
- OR plan that details change management and communication efforts
- Training on the new process and updated standard documents

Organizational Impediments (OI) - VSP has experienced obstacles with certain business processes. These OIs interfered with the progress of both projects and run-the-business activities. Project teams routinely created "work-arounds" to achieve their goals and remain on schedule. To overcome and resolve these long-standing impediments, EPS now assists in identifying impediment owners and facilitates issue resolution and awareness by communicating the results of resolved OIs to all stakeholders.

18.3.1.1 – How long has the PMO been in place? When was it started?	The EPS division was chartered as a PMO in 2008, under the leadership of Chief Operations Officer and Vice President EPS.
18.3.1.2 – What is the relationship of PMO management to the enterprise's operational management?	EPS acts as the liaison to operational management to enable and support effective and efficient project execution, and to objectively align efforts for delivery of the desired business value.
18.3.1.3 – How is the PMO internally structured (positions, roles etc.)?	The PMO reports to the Chief Operations Officer.

PMO management roles and their direct reports are as follows:
<ul><li>Vice president of Enterprise Project Solutions – All EPS management</li><li>Program Portfolio Manager – Program managers</li><li>Project Portfolio Manager – Senior PMs, PMs, and PM associates</li><li>Portfolio Analysis Manager – Senior business analysts for programs, senior business analysts for projects, and business analysts</li></ul>

The EPS project manager job descriptions fall within four |

primary categories: project manager associate, project manager, senior project manager, and program manager.

- *Project Manager Associate (PMA)* – PMAs have two to four years of experience contributing to projects. They manage simple to moderate projects and frequently rely on the experience of functional managers, experienced project managers, and sponsors for guidance. Key skills include the ability to lead small teams, contribute to the development of cost-benefit analysis (CBA) and ROI forecasts, and the ability to manage project risks, issues, and changes.

- *Project Manager* – PMs have three to five years of experience leading simple to moderate projects that may cross lines of business. PMs may require moderate direction from functional managers and more experienced project managers. Key skills include the ability to build teams, manage project budgets, and have talent for recognizing risk triggers and clearly communicating risk situations to project teams, sponsors, and stakeholders.

- *Senior Project Manager* – Senior PMs have five to eight years of formal experience leading complex, highly ambiguous projects that cross the lines of business. Seniors require minimal direction from functional managers. Key skills include the ability to build teams that share an inspired vision, develop and manage project budgets, and the aptitude to facilitate the development of CBA and ROI for each project they manage.

- *Program Manager* – Program managers have seven to ten years of formal project and/or program management experience with three to five years professional experience. Key responsibilities and aptitudes include partnering with business leaders during strategic planning, developing program road maps, and establishing and managing the program governance structure, as well as effectively managing program communications.

Business Analysts (BA) are essential to successful project initiation and execution. The EPS BA team consists of three classifications of business analyst: business analyst, senior business analyst (projects), and senior business analysts (programs).

- *Business Analyst* – Business analysts have two to five years of experience in analysis and solution development and require moderate supervision to develop, research, test, and implement business process improvements, procedures, and system changes. Key skills and experience include the ability to identify, evaluate and document the business impacts and benefits of process change as well as the skill to create efficient workflows.

- *Senior Business Analyst (projects)* – these analysts have five or more years of experience analyzing business problems and providing solutions, and require minimal supervision to develop, research, test, and implement business process improvements. Additionally the senior business analyst is proficient in data and statistical analysis tools and methods.

- *Senior Business Analyst (programs)* – these analysts have seven or more years of experience in project and/or program analytics, including experience leading enterprise-wide initiatives that cross lines of business. Key skills include strategic analysis, development of feasibility studies, alternative analysis, impact analysis, financial modeling, and business process modeling as needed to further program goals.

18.3.1.4 – How are the PMO's operations funded?	The PMO's operations are funded by the standard enterprise process used for all business units.
18.3.1.5 – What is the summary position description of the PMO leader?	Vice President EPS position description:

Vice President EPS position description:
- Establish project management policies and guidelines by clarifying the role of project management in the organization
- Provide centralized services such as planning, scheduling, estimating, costing, project accounting, and risk assessment
- Review and analyze proposed projects
- Verify that projects add value to the organization and are in alignment with strategic initiatives
- Approve and prioritize projects and/or ensure consistency with corporate strategies
- Ensure the existence of a business case to justify each project or program, as well as a project charter approving each implementation

- Responsible for annual project and program budgeting, and planning
- Provide corporate-wide mentoring or training on PM-lite skills
- Mediate conflicts and provide governance across portfolio
- Ensure there is a repository of lessons learned
- Develop a customer focus
- Demonstrate that the projects and timing in the portfolio are conducted within the capacity of the organization
- Ensure responsibility is assigned within the organization for seeing that the benefits of each project are actually realized
- Conduct project portfolio modeling and analysis
- Report portfolio status and make recommendations
- Chair project portfolio governance meetings (PSC and Business/Technology Integration Team)

18.3.1.6 – What position requirements are used as a basis for selecting the PMO leader?	The PMO leader must meet the VSP requirements for the position of Vice President.
18.3.1.7 – Is the PMO a Profit & Loss cost center or considered overhead?	The EPS division is considered overhead.
18.3.1.8 – What current challenge is the PMO dealing with?	Even with the recent successes of the PMO and the excitement about its future, the PMO does face organizational challenges that continue to stretch its creativity and resourcefulness.

- EPS has identified an opportunity to improve the alignment of corporate strategy with project execution. The challenge is that there often is a condensed time period to vet the strategies to ensure they align with existing programs to support the enterprise mission statement and vision. To address this challenge, EPS has improved the planning process by focusing on defining the program plans and divisional projects in order to align initiatives and provide them as inputs into the planning process. The VSP executive leadership team, along with the PMO leadership, collaborates in an annual planning process that results in a high-level definition of new and continuing strategic initiatives that are aligned and prioritized in the enterprise portfolio.

- EPS has also developed a funding plan that would provide more structure for treating projects as portfolio investments. Currently, when projects are approved, each impacted division absorbs the salary costs and consultant fees associated with project team member hours. Project sponsors are not fiscally accountable for project budgets and resource hours. The proposal going forward is that each project will have an approved budget and executive leaders sponsoring projects will be evaluated on their ability to stay within approved project budgets.

- Planning and managing project resources also continues to be a major issue for the company and directly impacts the PMO. The program and project needs seem to be far greater than current resources support because the company is cautious about adding new resources that may not be necessary on a long-term basis.

- As VSP evolves, approved programs and projects continue to grow in complexity. In the past, a large project was about 10,000 hours. Currently, that number of hours represents a mid-size project, with large to jumbo projects equaling 20,000 hours. While the PMO attempts to keep scope tightly focused and approaches deployments iteratively when possible, it is often difficult to limit scope changes and project extensions. To assist with those "go/no–go" decisions, the PMO will continue to improve processes that will better define benefits and measure outcomes.

- Another critical challenge faced by the PMO is the need for a clearer decision-making model that can be utilized and aligned at all levels of the enterprise. With the growth and additional complexity of new lines of business and increased competition, it has become increasingly important to make well-educated, yet timely, decisions. The PMO hopes to lead the effort to promote a model that can be supported by the executives to better transition from strategic proposals to program execution without rework or delay.

> **18.3.2 SURVEY – PMO Methodology / Standardization:** Describe what standardization your PMO has implemented across the enterprise that examines: identification and integration of processes and practices; development of standardized Project Business Management processes; and documentation of enterprise-wide portfolio, program, and project management process methodology models, including their associated policies, practices, and procedures.

Identification of Need for Standard Processes

As EPS organized and began maturing its team's skills, it also championed the development of enterprise-wide tools and processes. Key developments included the Project Portal, the Intake Team (Project Screening Board) and supporting processes, operational readiness planning and an organizational impediment resolution process.

Development of Enterprise-Wide Standard Processes and Process Methodology Models

Project Portal – EPS is responsible for maintaining and enhancing an enterprise Project Portal. The Portal, organized in quick reference format, incorporates project information, project management methodology, business analysis, continuous quality improvement, and various other tools.

Intake Team – The Intake Team oversees and ensures that enterprise projects remain in alignment with strategic initiatives throughout the project lifecycle.

- *Project Prioritization and Selection Criteria* – The PSC was in place for several years prior to the formal organization of EPS and the Intake Team. The objective of the PSC is to approve and prioritize enterprise projects that align with enterprise strategies and that yield the greatest business value and return on investment. However, before the creation of the Intake Team, prioritization was largely subjective. With the Intake Team's analysis and recommendations, the process has become more objective and results driven. Prospective projects receive scores based not only on business value and alignment with enterprise strategies, but also on growth in market share, technical infrastructure, resource availability, and relative project risk.
- *Concept* – Traditionally, the PSC approved and prioritized projects based on a project proposal. Once the PSC approved a project proposal, project initiation began with the development of a project charter and the assignment of resources. This practice resulted in a troubling trend. Too often, highly skilled teams were unable to execute quickly due to a lack of comprehensive business and systems analysis. To better utilize project resources, the Intake Team developed the

project concept. The concept is a document that captures high-level ideas and resource estimates. Once the PSC approves a concept for further research, business and technical experts conduct a time-boxed analysis. The result of this analysis is a project charter appropriate for submission to the Intake Team and the PSC as a prospective enterprise project. Since implementing the concept document, average time-to-baseline has decreased significantly – from 26 weeks in 2008, to 10.3 weeks in 2009, to 6.6 weeks in 2011.

- *Project Gate Reviews* – To ensure that initiated projects remain relevant and on target to meet stated business goals, the Intake Team introduced the project gate review processes. Mandatory project gate reviews take place at predetermined project phase intervals—concept, charter, execution (project midpoint) and closing. Critical ("red") risk gate reviews are required for projects that have an at-risk status for four consecutive weeks. Project sponsors surveyed gave the gate review process an 88% satisfaction rating. Sponsors stated that they saw improvements in speed to market, increased quality control, and improvements in risk mitigation to course correct at-risk projects.

- *Project Audits* – Post-project audits assist sponsors with monitoring project ROI or productivity gains over a period of time post implementation. To conduct post-project audits, the Intake Team collects baseline metrics at the project closing gate, then partners with business stakeholders to validate business value and ROI gained from the project.

- *Consultation and Coaching Services* - As the primary contact for project gate reviews, the Intake Team offers consulting and coaching services for project sponsors and PMs. Coaching for PMs, sponsors and product owners during a "red" gate review provides needed guidance that often puts a project back on track. As requested by the PSC, the Intake Team also researches, analyzes, and develops feasibility studies of various strategic initiatives.

Operational Readiness (OR) Task Force – EPS established an OR task force in mid-2009 to ensure that divisions are prepared to manage their business at project close. The task force established new PM and BA responsibilities and developed new tools:
- Initial stakeholder assessment to identify high-level needs
- OR plan, which details change management and communication efforts
- Training on the new process and updated standard documents

Organizational Impediments (OI) – VSP has experienced obstacles with certain business processes. These OIs interfered with the progress of both projects and run-the-business activities. Project teams routinely created "work-arounds" to achieve their goals and remain on schedule. To overcome and resolve these long-standing impediments, EPS now assists in identifying impediment owners and facilitates issue resolution and awareness by communicating the results of resolved OIs to all stakeholders.

18.3.2.1 – Describe the standards utilized by the PMO to ensure the enterprise's project / program / portfolio management goals and objectives are achieved.

EPS assesses the VSP portfolio metrics quarterly.

The following factors contribute to portfolio success:

- Project pipeline – Breakdown of gate reviews conducted during the quarter, including concept, charter, execution, change, and closing
- Portfolio outcomes – Count of concepts, charters, execution gates, change requests, and closing reports approved during the quarter
- Portfolio by project type – Analysis of projects defined as nondiscretionary, enabling, growth, or transformative as a percentage of the portfolio, along with the associated cost-to-date for each project type
- Portfolio by line of business – Breakdown of project costs by line of business sponsorship
- Portfolio statistics – Total quarterly closed-project budget and schedule variance
- Portfolio baseline – Average weeks to baseline for total projects baselined during the quarter
- Satisfaction survey results – Total quarterly satisfaction survey results for sponsor to PM, project team to PM, project team to BA, and operational readiness

Project benefits – The Intake Team conducts post-project audits to assist sponsors with monitoring project ROI or productivity gains over a period of time post implementation. To conduct post-project audits, the Intake Team collects baseline metrics at the project closing gate, then partners with business stakeholders to validate business value and ROI gained from the project. Audit findings are shared with corporate executives on a quarterly basis.

18.3.2.2 – Describe the project management process guidelines being employed by the PMO.

EPS embraces the Project Management Institute's (PMI's) Project Management Body of Knowledge (PMBOK®) and the International Institute of Business Analysis' (IIBA's) Business Analysis Body of Knowledge (BABOK®) as guiding principles. This disciplined approach, coupled with staff experience, knowledge, and skill, provides the foundation for partnering with business leaders to successfully and repeatedly deliver business value.

18.3.2.3 – What systems, tools, and templates make your PMO successful?

The primary system for communicating EPS project management standards and templates is the Project Portal. This internal and proprietary portal houses the enterprise project methodology and the System Development Lifecycle with corresponding templates for use by both EPS PMs and BAs, as well as by enterprise business partners interested in managing divisional efforts. Additionally, the portal includes links to related internal information sources, such as the Agile wiki, the Enterprise Data Dictionary, the Organizational Impediments wiki, and the Tech Portal wiki.

18.3.2.4 – Describe how management at all levels is directly involved in the development of the PMO and it processes.

- *Annual Project Budgeting and Resource Planning* – Managers across the organization are directly involved in forecasting projects needed for the upcoming year in an effort to develop the annual PMO portfolio budget. The divisional project projections are foundational to developing resource plans and financial plans for the PMO.

- *Business/Technology Integration Team (BTI) quarterly program status* – Presidents and top-level executives across the VSP lines of business review programs on a quarterly basis to ensure that programs and projects align with the VSP enterprise strategic initiatives, and are prioritized accordingly. BTI quarterly status ensures resource and budgetary support for the most critical undertakings, alignment within the enterprise, and the execution of the leadership vision.

- *Financial Governance* – Management within the Finance division partners with the PMO to develop program and project CBA and to monitor Return on Investment (ROI). As additional projects or funding are required, due to changing business needs, the PMO works with sponsors to prepare business cases in order to secure additional funding from Finance's Budget Oversight Committee (BOC), led by the VSP Global Chief Financial Officer.

- *Portfolio Strategic Committee* – The PSC is comprised of varying levels of management across the lines of business. This governance body is chartered with the approval and prioritization of enterprise projects, ensuring alignment with enterprise strategies and delivery of projects that maximize business value and ROI.

- *Change Management* – The PMO partners with organizational change managers in Human Resources (HR) to develop change-management plans. The partnership between the PMO and HR has proved valuable in developing strategies to introduce successfully, process, system, and policy changes into the organization.

18.3.2.5 – Describe the implementation plan you used for establishing project / program / portfolio management standards across your enterprise.

EPS has utilized, and continues to improve, a four-step project/program/portfolio management standards implementation plan:

- *Standardization* – EPS developed a framework for consistency that included development of templates and training to ensure proper project planning, scope management, risk management, budget/cost management, and scheduling.

- *Measurement* – A series of gate-review checkpoints and supporting oversight processes were developed and deployed to provide opportunities for review of critical project/program health information. These gates include time to first baseline, review of project/program statistics at second baseline, change control, red gate reviews (when the project has been in critical status for three to four weeks), closing gate review, and post-closing audits.

- *Control* – EPS developed guidance opportunities and tools to measure overall PMO progress in managing its standards, including gate reviews and PM/program manager key job accountabilities (KJAs), as well as Project Performance feedback surveys.

- *Improvement* – PMO metrics are captured, assessed, and communicated to the PMO quarterly. Metrics are used to assist in continuous evolution and help to ensure that all established measures are realistic for the enterprise and the complexity of the portfolio of projects.

18.3.2.6 – How does the PMO use project, program, and portfolio management

PMI Standards

Consistency is a primary EPS goal. EPS utilizes PMI as its basis for establishing project/program/portfolio processes, and seeks to

standards to optimize its practices?

Are they based on PMI˚ or other industry guides and are they updated as new editions of the guides are released?

ensure and improve consistency through the use of PMO sub-teams that focus on key topics to ensure adherence to updated PMI guidelines.

Sub-teams: Aiding Continuous Enhancement

- *Estimating* – Project teams have traditionally struggled with providing realistic estimates. The Estimating Sub-team was chartered to assess the root cause of these struggles and to establish tools to assist in developing estimates. The team created and introduced several tools to the PMO, including the Project Estimating Flowchart and Charter Quick Start Guidelines to define charter development team roles and responsibilities.

- *Sponsor Training* – Creating a foundational knowledge among the enterprise project sponsors was a primary enterprise project/program maturity opportunity. The Sponsor Training Sub-team developed a series of training modules and facilitated working sessions with past, present and future project sponsors. The goal of the training was to establish common knowledge of key project topics, including vision, strategy and roadmaps, project lifecycle, role of the sponsor, and operational readiness.

- *Lessons Learned* – A Lessons Learned governance team was formed to assess all closed project lessons learned with the goal of identifying and communicating key lessons. Key lessons were defined as those lessons that are applicable to projects of multiple types, are context neutral, and represent new opportunities for PM and team education.

- *Vendor Relationship Management* – As the enterprise grows and accommodates new lines of business, consistently developing successful vendor relationships has become critical. The Vendor Management Sub-team created tools to assist project managers with initiating and developing the vendor relationship. Tools include PM On-Boarding (an expectations check list), Procurement/Vendor Engagement Matrix (vendor situations and PM role), Vendor Management Tips, and Vendor Score Card.

> **18.3.3   SURVEY – PMO Capabilities:** Describe development and assessment of the enterprise's abilities, describe any project management competency model, summarize any education and training program, describe any established career path progression plan, and outline key Enterprise Environmental Factors.

18.3.3.1 – Describe the components of your enterprise's training program.

EPS is committed to and promotes continuous learning through a variety of educational opportunities:

- *Job Skills Training* – These courses, developed by internal trainers with EPS management input, include topics such as project performance reporting, work breakdown structure development, and critical thinking.

- *External Courses and Seminars* – Management provides an annual training budget for staff to attend external courses and seminars that support their individual development plans and Project Management Professional (PMP) certification maintenance.

- *Consultants* – EPS hires top consultants from a variety of disciplines to provide coaching and/or development on specific topics. Consultant-provided education has included: ScrumMaster Certification, trained by Paul Hodgetts; Fundamentals of Six Sigma, presented by Dr. Herb Zagarow; and Enterprise Agile Adoption, presented by Scott Ambler.

- *PM and BA Forums* – Hosted monthly, forums cover a variety of career, business, and enterprise training such as COA, data management, information architecture, organizational change management, mergers and acquisitions, strategic relationships, and quality management. Forum presenters include VSP vice presidents, directors, and managers.

- *Staff-Initiated Training* – PMs and BAs share their unique aptitudes by assisting in the development and presentation of topics that will benefit their peers. The training subject matter includes topics such as "slicing the work," Scrum overview, leadership labs, and asset-based thinking.

- *Mentoring* – EPS staff partners with multiple business and IT areas to provide mentoring opportunities on project methodologies and business analysis best practices.

18.3.3.2 – Describe the value your enterprise places on education and training and its goals and objectives.	VSP is a learning organization. The enterprise values its employees and invests in their education at all levels. This investment allows the enterprise to transform itself so that it remains viable in an increasingly competitive industry. As a learning organization, VSP encourages:

- *Systems Thinking* – Tracking and communication of enterprise performance measures
- *Personal Mastery* – Individual employee learning through staff training and development
- *Enterprise Cultural Values* – Educational opportunities that promote cultural values such as trust and situational leadership
- *Shared Vision* – Encouraging a common identity to focus staff energy
- *Team Learning* – Training opportunities that allow individuals to engage in open dialogue and exercises

18.3.3.3 – Does the enterprise have a project management career path program? If so, what are the components?	Yes, PMO has two career paths team members may follow. The EPS Project Manager (PM) job descriptions fall within four primary categories: project manager associate, project manager, senior project manager, and program manager.

- *Project Manager Associate (PMA)* – PMAs have two to four years of experience contributing to projects. They manage simple to moderate projects and frequently rely on the experience of functional managers, experienced project managers, and sponsors for guidance. Key skills include the ability to lead small teams, contribute to the development of CBA and ROI forecasts, and the ability to manage project risks, issues, and changes.

- *Project Manager* – PMs have three to five years of experience leading simple to moderate projects that may cross lines of business. PMs may require moderate direction from functional managers and more experienced project managers. Key skills include the ability to build teams, manage project budgets, and have talent for recognizing risk triggers and clearly communicating risk situations to project teams, sponsors and stakeholders.

- *Senior Project Manager* – Senior PMs have five to eight years of formal experience leading complex, highly ambiguous projects that cross the lines of business. Seniors require

327

minimal direction from functional managers. Key skills include the ability to build teams that share an inspired vision, develop and manage project budgets, and the aptitude to facilitate the development of CBA and ROI for each project they manage.

- *Program Manager* – Program managers have seven to ten years of formal project and/or program management experience with three to five years professional experience. Key responsibilities and aptitudes include partnering with business leaders during strategic planning, developing program road maps, and establishing and managing the program governance structure, as well as effectively managing program communications.

Business Analysts (BA) are essential to successful project initiation and execution. The EPS BA team consists of three classifications of business analyst: business analyst, senior business analyst (projects), and senior business analyst (programs).

- *Business Analyst* – Business analysts have two to five years of experience in analysis and solution development and require moderate supervision to develop, research, test, and implement business process improvements, procedures and system changes. Key skills and experience include the ability to identify, evaluate and document the business impacts and benefits of process change as well as the skill to create efficient workflows.

- *Senior Business Analyst (projects)* – these analysts have five or more years of experience analyzing business problems and providing solutions, and require minimal supervision to develop, research, test, and implement business process improvements. Additionally the senior business analyst is proficient in data and statistical analysis tools and methods.

- *Senior Business Analyst (programs)* – these analysts have seven or more years of experience in project and/or program analytics, including experience leading enterprise-wide initiatives that cross lines of business. Key skills include strategic analysis, development of feasibility studies, alterna-tive analysis, impact analysis, financial modeling, and business process modeling as needed to further program goals.

18.3.3.4 – Describe the measurements, metrics, and Key Performance Indicators (KPI's) utilized by the PMO to determine the organization's knowledge, skills, and level of achievement.

EPS has incorporated multiple feedback loops into its portfolio management processes. These feedback loops provide information about customer satisfaction as well as individual PM competency.

The project performance feedback loops include the Project Manager, Business Analyst, sponsor and team, operational readiness, intake process, and annual enterprise-wide employee engagement surveys. This information is used to hone existing processes, develop new ones, and determine education needs.

As a result, EPS achieved the following improvements from 2009 to 2010:
- 8.6% improvement in sponsor satisfaction with PMs
- 4.7% improvement in team satisfaction with PMs
- 10.9% improvement in team satisfaction with BAs
- 6.2% improvement in sponsor satisfaction with operational readiness

18.3.3.5 – Does the enterprise employ a project management competency model? If yes, please describe it. If no, why not?

Yes, the enterprise employs a project management competency model for both its PMs and BAs.

EPS has established KJAs for its PMs. The KJAs include weighted key performance measures:
- *Leadership* – weighted at 30%, includes core competencies such as integrity and trust, customer focus, drive for results, political savvy, and robust dialogue
- *Effective Delivery of Business Value* – weighted at 30%, incorporates performance measures that addresses stakeholder engagement and readiness
- *Efficient Project Execution* – weighted at 30%, includes project execution success factors such as planning, decision-making and risk-taking
- *Project Practice Evolution and Self-Development* – weighted at 10%, encourages individual PMs to contribute to the PMO through process development and improvement, as well as individual self-development activities

EPS has established KJAs for its BAs. The KJAs include weighted key performance measures:

- *Analysts Core Competencies* – weighted at 35%, include competencies such as problem solving, tools and techniques, planning/organization, and customer focus
- *Leadership* – weighted at 30%, incorporates building effective teams, dealing with ambiguity, robust dialogue, political savvy, and drive for results
- *Soft Skills* – weighted at 25%, focus on communication and business acumen

There is also an overall expectation to actively contribute 10% of their time towards self-development and to seek and implement continuous quality improvements in all areas of the enterprise.

18.3.4 SURVEY – PMO Business Planning: Discuss strategic business planning, tactical business planning, business objective (project) development and prioritization, and project identification, selection, and authorization.

18.3.4.1 – Describe the organizational structure and process used for corporate strategic business planning.

Does the PMO play a role in the process? If so, describe the PMOs role and responsibilities.

Corporate Strategic Business Planning Process
The VSP executive leadership team, along with PMO leadership, collaborates in an annual planning process that results in a high-level definition of new and continuing strategic initiatives that are aligned and prioritized in the enterprise portfolio.

PMO Planning Role and Responsibilities
EPS has identified an opportunity to improve the alignment of corporate strategy with project execution. The challenge is there often is a condensed time period to vet the strategies to ensure they align with existing programs to support the enterprise mission statement and vision.

To address this challenge EPS has improved the planning process by focusing on defining the program plans and divisional projects in order to align initiatives and provide them as inputs into the planning process.

The VSP executive leadership team along with the PMO leadership collaborates in an annual planning process that results in a high level definition of new and continuing strategic initiatives that are aligned and prioritized in the enterprise portfolio.

Program managers, who are key members of the PMO, are aligned to strategic initiatives and partnered with the executives who will champion the efforts. These executives are responsible for developing the strategic direction and, with the program managers, the programs' roadmaps and execution plans are developed. Projects under the programs are aligned with the strategic business objectives of each program.

In addition to the involvement with strategic programs, the PMO plays a lead role in identifying annual efforts planned by individual divisions that are smaller in size, and assists with integrating the planning information into the overall process for review and prioritization.

The PMO has a key role in identifying the connections, dependencies, risks, and trade-offs that exist between programs and their projects and these other divisionally led project efforts.

Resource capacity, demand forecasting, and resource gap analysis are key responsibilities of the PMO during all enterprise planning efforts.

18.3.4.2 – How is the strategic plan implemented with a project forecast plan?

Program roadmaps are developed for the larger, strategic efforts. Program executives, program managers, senior Business Analysts, and key stakeholders work closely to define projects that will clearly support the program's vision and goals. All program executives and program managers collaborate to ensure strategic initiative alignment.

It is not uncommon for VSP programs to overlap at a high level, so it is critical to watch for interdependencies and to assess work efforts and resource usage in an integrated manner.

For projects that are not related to programs, the divisional/-business unit completes the planning, but the PMO has oversight of the definition of those project scopes and the prioritization of the work in relation to the strategic efforts that are underway. It is critical for the PMO to partner with the enterprise business leaders to ensure integration at all levels of the portfolio.

18.3.4.3 – How is strategic planning,

The Business/Technology Integration Team (BTI) oversees our cross-line of business portfolio management structure and *culture, and selection of projects integrated?* process, and the PMO has a leadership role with that group of executives.

- The PMO has made progress with recent efforts to influence changes in the decision-making approach.
- In coordination with our Enterprise Organizational Effectiveness/Change (EOEC) Management team, the PMO leaders are supporting a decision-making model that should clarify decision-making roles. Implementing such changes within the Executive levels and their direct reports will result in a more seamless and transparent communication model when moving from strategy to execution.

> **18.3.5 SURVEY – PMO Business Execution:** Describe what role the PMO has in project selection, prioritization, and initiation; in portfolio, program and project execution planning; in stage-gate reviews; and in performance metrics selection and application.

The PMO has been instrumental in the development of several project processes. It also has oversight responsibility for, and is focused on, their success.

18.3.5.1 – How are portfolios, programs, and projects selected and initiated?

Selection and Execution

1) Project selection begins with the submittal of a concept.

2) The concept is initially reviewed by the Intake Team, and then submitted to the PSC for review and approval.

3) Once a concept is approved to move to project charter, a PM, BA, and systems analyst (as appropriate) are assigned to begin charter development. The PM, Business Analyst, and Systems Analyst work together to refine the project scope, assess the Return On Investment, assess the system inventory diagram, and establish resource needs and estimate work.

4) When the charter is approved by the executive and business sponsors, it is submitted to the Intake Team for assessment and PSC readiness preparation.

5) To ensure the charter is ready for PSC prioritization, the Intake Team schedules an interview with the sponsor, PM, and BA to verify and clarify the scope, deliverables, estimates and benefits for PSC review.

6) Approved charters are prioritized and the PM and BA begin project staffing and planning.

7) The PM and BA have five weeks from the day they are assigned to kick-off the project and establish the baseline budget and schedule.

8) Second baseline is expected at project mid-point followed by the execution gate review with the PSC.

9) During execution gate, the PSC evaluates the project scope, schedule, and budget for overall health, business value, and operational readiness preparation activities.

10) Change gates are conducted at any point in the project lifecycle if there is a change to scope.

11) Additionally, red gates are conducted on projects that have been in a critical state for three to four weeks.

12) At project close, the Intake Team reviews the project closing report and the financial analyst documents the project expected benefits for audit at specified intervals.

18.3.5.2 – How are projects organized and managed as a program and/or portfolio?	Program roadmaps are developed for the larger, strategic efforts. Program managers and their champions work closely to define projects that will clearly support the program's vision and goals. They also collaborate closely with other program executives and program managers to ensure that strategic initiatives stay aligned. It is not uncommon for programs to overlap at a high level, so it is critical to watch for interdependencies and to assess work efforts and resource usage in an integrated manner.

For projects that aren't related to programs, the divisional/ business unit completes the planning, but the PMO has oversight of the definition of those project scopes and the prioritization of the work in relation to the strategic efforts that are underway. It is critical for the PMO to partner with the enterprise business leaders to ensure integration at all levels of the portfolio. |
| *18.3.5.3 – How are projects prioritized within a program and/or portfolio?* | The PSC approves and prioritizes enterprise projects that align with enterprise strategies and that yield the greatest business value and ROI. However, before the creation of the Intake Team, prioritization was largely subjective. With the Intake Team's analysis and recommendations, the process has become more |

objective and results driven. Prospective projects receive scores based not only on business value and alignment with enterprise strategies, but also on growth in market share, technical infrastructure, resource availability, and relative project risk.

18.3.5.4 – How does the enterprise define what project and program success is?

EPS assesses its portfolio metrics quarterly. The following factors contribute to portfolio success:

- *Project Pipeline* – Breakdown of gate reviews conducted during the quarter, including concept, charter, execution, change, and closing

- *Portfolio Outcomes* – Count of concepts, charters, execution gates, change requests, and closing reports approved during the quarter

- *Portfolio by Project Type* – Analysis of projects defined as nondiscretionary, enabling, growth, or transformative as a percentage of the portfolio, along with the associated cost-to-date for each project type

- *Portfolio by Line of Business* – Breakdown of project costs by line of business sponsorship

- *Portfolio Statistics* – Total quarterly closed-project budget and schedule variance

- *Portfolio Baseline* – Average weeks to baseline for total projects baselined during the quarter

- *Satisfaction Survey Results* – Total quarterly satisfaction survey results for sponsor to PM, project team to PM, project team to BA, and operational readiness

- *Project Benefits* - The Intake Team conducts post-project audits to assist sponsors with monitoring project ROI or productivity gains over a period of time post implementation. To conduct post-project audits, the Intake Team collects baseline metrics at the project closing gate, then partners with business stakeholders to validate business value and ROI gained from the project. Audit findings are shared with corporate executives on a quarterly basis.

18.3.5.5 – Does the PMO support the management of projects that would be considered operational in nature? If so, describe the types of projects.

EPS offers project management assistance and consultation, upon request, to divisions and business areas that have projects that do not meet the corporate project criteria. EPS also offers consulting services for business process reengineering efforts to operational business units across the organization, led by Six Sigma certified staff members.

> **18.3.6 SURVEY – PMO Sustainability:** Describe the overall impact of the PMO over a sustained period (e.g., customer satisfaction, productivity, reduced cycle time, growth, building or changing organizational culture, etc.). If available, please provide quantitative data to illustrate the areas in which the PMO has had the greatest business impact.

PMO Impact

- EPS has produced favorable results that have greatly benefited VSP. Through the execution of tighter schedules, EPS has managed more growth and cost reduction projects than in prior years.
  - o In 2009, EPS successfully executed and closed 20% more projects of the same size and duration, compared to 2008.
- As a result of the improvements and "best practices" that EPS has introduced, stakeholder satisfaction is at an all-time high.
  - o The satisfaction feedback scores have increased from an average score of 7.75 to 9.22 (based on scale of 1 to 10).
  - o Enterprise operational readiness scores have also increased from an average of 8.41 to 9.63.
  - o Executive Testimonials: Vice President of Product Strategy and Integration, described EPS as "focused, results-oriented and valuable assets without whom VSP couldn't accomplish its strategic objectives." Vice President of Strategic Accounts and Sales Operations, and Chief Financial Officer, refer to the EPS staff as "trusted business advisors" and "politically savvy leaders."
- Measurable results and continuous success have increased business partner confidence not only in EPS, but in project management as a discipline.
  - o Executive Testimonial: Previous Chief Information Officer, summarized the journey of project management at VSP, "When I first came here, there were project managers and business analysts but they were more hobbyists than professionals. Most of them were good, but there simply wasn't the structure in place for them to perform as well as they could. That improved over the years, but the EPS team has taken the disciplines to a much higher level of performance."

Sustainability through Continuous Improvement

EPS remains committed to the project management discipline. As part of its continuous quality improvement culture, EPS has planned the following improvements for the next 12-18 months:

- *Enhanced Business-Sponsor Education* – In partnership with HR, EPS will introduce shared accountability through management KJAs for scope, cost, schedule, and quality. Introducing sponsor metrics will assist with continued improvements in transparency, formalized change management, and in driving improvement efforts.

- *Critical Chain Analysis (Resource Management)* – EPS will identify and implement enhanced estimating and scheduling techniques, cost and change-control methods, and evaluate resource opportunity costs.

- *Business Process Maturity* – EPS continues to enhance and champion Six Sigma and Total Quality Management practices. During 2012, EPS will pilot process projects throughout the enterprise. The goal is to improve or develop predictable and effective processes with detailed measures of quality throughout VSP.

- *Enhanced Reporting* – EPS will enhance reporting tools so the right information surfaces, allowing for project course correction if needed.

- *Lessons Learned* – EPS will develop and implement a repository for actionable, project lessons learned. This will raise awareness and avoid repeating actions that slow project progress.

18.3.6.1 – What is included in a comprehensive project monitoring and control system and how is it implemented?

EPS has established a comprehensive approach to project selection and monitoring throughout the project lifecycle. The project lifecycle begins with an idea that is documented in a concept and submitted to the PSC. An approved concept will then be assigned to a PM, BA, and systems analyst for charter development. A charter, once approved and prioritized by the PSC, will be assigned to a PM and BA for resource procurement and planning. During project execution, the PM uses several key tools and processes to monitor and control the project scope, schedule, and budget:

- *Project Complexity* – This is a tool used by the PM to do an initial assessment of project scope ambiguity, project size, project technology impacts, project organizational impacts, and team/project environment factors. The tool is first completed during initiation and then revised at closing. The information helps the PM and functional manager assess the PM's ability to manage the scope, schedule, and budget based on the project's complexity.

- *Risk/Issue/Decision Log* – PMs continuously plan for, track, and monitor project risks and issues using the risk/issue log. Additionally, all key project decisions are tracked in the decision log as a tool for communication and confirmation of decisions that affect the course of the project and its deliverables.

- *Change Request Log* – The change request log serves as a comprehensive tool for the management of project schedule and budget. The tool allows for the input of approved charter, Baseline 1 and Baseline 2 approved dates, hours, and dollars. With this information accurately input, the schedule and budget variances are automatically calculated so that the PM may monitor the project health throughout the project lifecycle. Should the actual project schedule and budget begin to appear out of alignment with the calculated variances, the PM would use the tool to track and calculate approved change requests and their impacts to the overall project schedule and budget. At project close, actual schedule and budget information is input for an overall assessment of "approved" versus "actual" schedule and budget.

- *Project Execution Gate* – At project mid-point or every six months, for projects over a year in duration, the PM completes the project execution gate template. The project execution gate template allows the PM to input Baseline 1 information along with the new Baseline 2 information. Additionally, the template provides the PM with a vehicle for communicating any issues or constraints with project resources, costs, schedule, impediments, and architectural challenges. The project execution gate information is reviewed by the PSC for a mid-project health assessment.

- *Project Red Gate Review* – A PM will complete a project red gate template when project issues remain in critical (red) status for three to four consecutive weeks. The project red gate template provides the PM with a vehicle for communicating issues or constraints with project resources, costs, schedule, impediments and architectural challenges. Additionally, the red gate review allows the Intake Team to reassess project health and value to the organization for a decision on project viability and relevance given the issues.

- *Lessons Learned* – PMs facilitate retrospectives/lessons learned periodically through the project lifecycle and at project closing. The lessons learned offer the team a tool for improving their working environment and processes while serving as a tool for communicating key lessons that may transfer to other projects and teams to the PMO.

- *Project Closing Report* – At project close, the PM completes a closing report. The closing report compares the chartered scope, deliverables, goals, schedule and budget to the actuals at closing. The completed closing report is submitted to the Intake Team for the project closing gate review and the project's delivered value and benefits are traced over time after project closing.

18.3.6.2 – How are project start-up and gate review processes structured?

EPS has established a structured approach to project start-up and project gate reviews.

Project start-up begins with a concept then progresses through charter development.

Once a completed charter is approved and the resulting project planning is complete, project gate reviews are utilized to continuously monitor project health and business value.

- *Concept* – Project ideas are documented and submitted to Intake and the PSC. The PSC reviews concepts to determine whether the requested project aligns with strategic goals and adds business value. If the concept is in alignment, the PSC will approve it for charter development; a PM, BA, and systems analyst will be assigned to develop the charter. If the concept is not in alignment with VSP strategic goals, the concept will be denied.

- *Charter* – The PM, BA, and systems analyst work with the sponsor and key resources to establish project scope, deliverables, and timeline while defining benefits and Return on Investment (ROI). Once the charter is completed and approved by the sponsor, it is reviewed by the PSC and either approved as a project, returned for more information, queued as a future project, or denied.

- *Baseline 1* – Upon charter, the PM requests project resources and planning begins. Planning is complete when the team feels tasks are defined and estimated and the sponsor approves the budget/scope/schedule as Baseline 1.

- *Baseline 2* – Completed prior to the execution gate and after the second architectural review, Baseline 2 is conducted by the project team to assess the accuracy of the Baseline 1 planned work and budget given the additional knowledge gained during the course of the project. Baseline 2 is approved by the sponsor prior to execution gate.

- *Project Execution Gate* – Scheduled when a project is 50% complete or after design is completed and every 6 months for projects with durations over one year. The PSC conducts the execution gate to assess project schedule, resources, hours, deliverables, ROI, architecture and Operational Readiness plan. Upon completion of the execution gate, the PSC will determine whether the project should continue, incorporate PSC recommended changes or be discontinued.

- *Project Change Gate* – Required when a requested change to project scope, schedule, or resources exceeds the current variance. PSC assesses the change for root cause as well as for impacts to the ROI, resource allocations, and quality of deliverables, schedule, and budget. Upon change gate review, PSC will either approve the change or partial change, deny the change, or discontinue the project.

- *Project Red Gate* – Conducted by the Intake Team when a project has been in red status for three to four consecutive weeks, the goal of the red gate is to assess root cause and impacts to ROI as well as to other projects. The Intake Team will escalate to PSC if there is a recommendation to discontinue or materially change the scope of the project.

- *Project Closing Gate* – PSC assesses projects at closing to establish and track project metrics in preparation for post project benefit measurements.

- *Audit* – Intake conducts post project audit reviews to measure project benefits realized periodically as indicated by the project sponsor and PM at closing.

18.3.6.3 – Describe the project knowledge base system and how is it developed?

The knowledge based system that formed the foundation for EPS was initiated in the mid-1990s as a grassroots effort. Driven by the need to collaborate and share project management knowledge across divisions, a small team of cross-divisional employees organized to address the lack of coordination between divisional PMs. The team, known as the Project Professionals, was comprised of PMs, BAs, functional managers, and project sponsors.

The Project Professionals met monthly on personal time to share experiences, network and to establish a standardized project management methodology and training program.

The standardized project management methodology and training tools established by the Project Professionals became the foundation for the Project Portal. The Project Portal is EPS' knowledge-based system.

The Portal is based on PMI standards and provides PMs and BAs with the guidelines, tools, and examples necessary to manage project work and deliverables during all phases of the project lifecycle. Additionally, the Portal supports the System Development Lifecycle guidelines and tools for systems analysts, developers, and quality assurance testers.

18.3.6.4 – Describe the measurement, metrics, and Key Performance Indicators (KPIs) utilized by the PMO to measure project and program success.

EPS has incorporated multiple feedback loops into its portfolio management processes. These feedback loops provide information that is used by the PMO to measure both project and program success as well as to establish overall customer satisfaction. The project performance feedback loop includes the program or project sponsors, program manager, PM, BA, team, and stakeholders to assess key components of the ability of the PM, BA, and team to successfully prepare the business to receive and deliver products that meet business needs.

- PMs are assessed by their teams, sponsors and program managers on their leadership capabilities, effective delivery of business value, efficient execution and degree of team engagement.

- BAs are assessed by their PMs, teams, sponsors, and stakeholders on their:
  o Problem solving, critical thinking, and analysis;

- o   Use of tools and techniques;
- o   Planning and organization;
- o   Customer focus;
- o   Effective team building;
- o   Political savvy; and
- o   Communication skills.

- Project team members are assessed by their key stakeholders on their:
  - o   Ability to work with key business areas to identify impacts to business processes timely;
  - o   Complete transfer of knowledge from the project team to business area;
  - o   Delivery of tools necessary to support new or changed work;
  - o   Timeliness of response to questions and issues; and
  - o   Ability to collaborate.

The information provided through the project performance feedback loop has become essential to the PMO to ensure that PMs, BAs, and their teams are successfully executing projects and supporting the needs of those business areas that will incorporate project deliverables into their processes. Project performance feedback is also incorporated into PM and BA performance reviews.

18.3.6.5 – Describe the organizational benefits and value the PMO provides to the enterprise.

The PMO brings neutrality, objectivity, and leadership skills to the enterprise.

Key PMO contributions include:

- *Standardization* – Establish PM framework; consistency and standardization in process and methodology
- *Measurement* – Monitor and evaluate; establish project and program metrics
- *Control* – Performance management, resource and capacity planning, portfolio budgeting, and funding portfolio management
- *Improvement* – Capture, assess, and communicate PMO metrics quarterly
  - o   Metrics used to assist in continuous evolution and help to ensure that all established measures are realistic for the enterprise and the complexity of the portfolio of projects

341

18.3.6.6 – Describe the economic benefits and value the PMO provides to the enterprise.

The economic benefits and value of the PMO is tracked at an aggregate level through costs and benefits of the projects that are being delivered.

EPS has developed a funding model to ensure that projects and programs in the PMO are delivering business value within the stated portfolio budget. The portfolio fund is developed in the preceding year, and it is then reviewed and approved by the Budget Oversight Committee, a team consisting of the CEO, CFO, COO, and other leaders. Once approved, the costs and benefits are tracked and reported to management on a regular basis throughout the year.

Additional projects that are not a part of the approved portfolio fund are required to go through a separate approval process with the Budget Oversight Committee (BOC) to ensure business value. Each project within the portfolio requires a Cost Benefit Analysis, which is completed in coordination with a project manager and financial analyst.

Overall, this process allows the PMO to track cash flow from a project management perspective and ultimately communicate the overall ROI and payback at a portfolio, program, and project level.

18.3.7 SURVEY – Additional Comments: Please provide any additional comments

VSP Vision Care's Enterprise Project Solutions (EPS) PMO did not provide any additional comments.

Epilogue

The Future of the PMO

In the current market place, the pervasive question of "Where are PMOs going" need no longer be asked, because the research contained in this book provides the definitive answer. PMOs positioned at the executive level of an enterprise now play a key role in business planning, authorization, and execution of portfolios, programs and projects.

The research documents that PMOs who oversee the management of cross-enterprise projects do ensure projects within operational business units are managed to meet the enterprise's business needs.

A PMO, which is established and viewed as a beneficial change agent and unifying force within the enterprise, has the ability to influence outcomes, lead projects that are enterprise-wide, and encourage and drive collaborative cooperation among the various and disparate business units.

The Next Generation of the PMO

What is generically called project management has evolved substantially over time and has emerged as a true discipline and profession, which is recognized worldwide. Project management, over the last 60 years, has developed as a specific management service and created widely recognized methods for managing and delivering complex and time sensitive projects across a wide range of industries.

The profession is now reaching a point of management sophistication, however, that positions it at a crossroads at the start of the 21st century, where the practitioners need to assess the future direction of the profession.

The key question is: Should it continue to develop as a management service, or could it take a direction into the enterprise's boardroom? Currently, there is an opportunity in the maturing of the profession for this latter direction. This could be the next five to ten year direction in the evolution of project management.

The further development and maturation of the Project Business Management Organization, as defined in this book, can make that broader direction possible, and it can be the next generation of the PMO.

Sand Boxes and Rice Bowls

The world economic downturn and the massive expansion of technology have significantly increased the completion for each enterprise in the marketplace, which is forcing enterprises to be more innovative and produce more with less. Enterprises now realize that they cannot continue doing business as usual – they need to become more innovative, significantly change the way they do business, modify their cultures, and link project management activities to the business requirements of their stakeholders, clients and the marketplace. The identification, selection, and completion of projects that produce new methods, processes, technologies, and products are the life-blood of today's enterprises. Executives today are defining success as projects that deliver *Benefits* and *Value*, as defined by the enterprise. The delivery of projects *On-Time* and *On-Budget* is **expected** by executives, while the new measurement of project success is now **required** by them.

The next generation PMO discussed in this book, has the means, methods, processes, and functions that can deliver the needed innovation and cultural change. The case studies present examples of these types of PMO. However, as the PMO literature and the authors' experience and research show, PMOs, even successful ones placed at an executive level, continue to go out of existence as much today as they have in the past.

The reasons are as basic as two idiomatic business influences that are as active today as they were in the past. The first idiom, *Not in My Sandbox,* is from western culture and it means, from a business perspective, that a person or group will not be allowed to operate within another's defined sphere of business influence or organizational structure. The second idiom, *Not from My Rice Bowl,* is from eastern culture and it means, from a business perspective, that a person or group will not be allowed to take economic value (budget, funds, bonuses, etc.) from another's defined sphere of business influence or organizational structure or function.

The more recent idiomatic business organizational term of *Stove Pipe Organization* is oft used to try and represent the combination of the prior two concepts. However, it fails to convey the full meaning and extent of the organizational power and political influence that will be utilized by current executives and managers to contain, dismantle, or eliminate any new function, such as an executive level PMO, that could intrude upon the Sand Boxes and Rice Bowls of their currently established functional organizations within the enterprise.

It is the business responsibility of the enterprise's board of directors and senior executive staff to establish a functional executive level PMO as generally described in this book and shown in the case studies. It is also singularly their responsibility to ensure that such a PMO is not dismantled, disbanded, or eliminated by the business intrigue, corporate politics, and selfish interests of existing functional organizations and managers within the enterprise.

Those enterprises that can develop, organizationally integrate, and sustain an executive level PMO to manage the enterprise's new projects and cross-functional operational projects will be the business winners in tomorrow's marketplace.

Appendix

1997-2006 PMO Survey Instrument and Results

Survey Instrument 1997-2006

The following is the 1997-2006 PMO Survey instrument, which is completed online by the survey participant.

##	Question	Type of Response Requested
1	How did your PMO get started? Where did the direction to create it come from?	Enter dialog response
2	When was your PMO created and how long did the process take to complete from the concept approval process?	Enter dialog response
3	Where does the PMO fit in your organization (under what functional department or executive management level)? What is the title of the person leading the PMO organization? What executive management level does the PMO report to?	Enter dialog response
4	Is the PMO an enterprise-wide support department or is it localized to support only parts of the total organization?	Enter dialog response
5	What were (are) the biggest challenges/issues faced in the obtaining support for the PMO concept?	Enter dialog response

##	Question	Type of Response Requested
6	What were (are) some specific methods/actions taken that worked well in obtaining support for the PMO concept?	Enter dialog response
7	What were (are) some specific methods/actions taken that <u>did not</u> work well (pitfall to avoid) in obtaining support for the PMO concept?	Enter dialog response
8	What would you like to do over again (lessons learned), if you could, to get better results?	Enter dialog response
9	Was there any resistance to change in the organization? How strong was the resistance level (high, medium, low) and from what organizational level was it the strongest? What was done to reduce or overcome the resistance?	Enter dialog response
10	Was there a PMO Champion who lead or supported the approval of the PMO concept? If so, how was the Champion selected, what position in the organization structure did the Champion hold, and did the Champion add value to the process of obtaining approval? If so, how?	Enter dialog response
11	Does the PMO own, maintain, and monitor the application of documented project management processes in your organization?	Enter dialog response
12	How many concurrent projects are typically in-progress in your organization? How many total projects annually?	Enter dialog response

##	Question	Type of Response Requested
13	Please give a brief description of the types of projects that your PMO supports.	Enter dialog response
14	What do you consider, the top three project management processes requiring immediate improvements in your organization?	Enter dialog response
15	How do you rate your personal knowledge of project management processes? Check (X) the box of the letter that most closely applies	A. Little or no knowledge of the basic principles of project management B. Conversant knowledge of project management principles, but minimal first-hand experience with its application C. Formal training in applying all of the project management principles to single projects D. Extensive experience in applying project management processes across multiple projects simultaneously E. Subject matter expert experienced in developing enterprise-wide project management systems
16	How do you rate your organization's project management knowledge in general? Check (X) the box of the letter that most closely applies	Same choices as question #15.
17	Which of the following characteristics are used to select your project managers? Check (X) all the boxes that apply and comment why.	A. Technical experience B. Education level C. Previous PM experience D. PM certification
18	Does your organization have corporate project management policies, to enable the project management guidelines? Check (X) the box that most closely applies and if NO please comment why.	A. Yes B. No C. Other

##	Question	Type of Response Requested
19	How do you rate (High, Medium, Low) your organization's capabilities in the following project management processes? Check (X) all the boxes that apply and comment why. Check box in columns H = High M = Medium L = Low	A. Project Pre-Planning B. Project Scope Management C. Project Time Management D. Project Risk Management E. Project Communications Management F. Project Quality Management G. Project Resource Management H. Project Change Control Management I. Project Management Reporting J. Project Configuration Management K. Project Metrics Management
20	How do you rate your organization's management level of commitment to formal project management processes and procedures? Check (X) the box that most closely applies and comment why you believe so.	A. Non-supportive: Status-quo is fine, reluctant to accept changes in processes B. Neutral: Does not matter one way or the other, neither for or against it C. Supportive: In favor of it, but not sure how to accomplish it D. Very Supportive: Believes PM should be applied across the enterprise E. Champion: Willing to lead the effort to integrate PM across the enterprise
21	Does the organization provide formal internal/external project management training? Check (X) all the boxes that apply and comment on number of courses and frequency offered.	A. Internal Training Program B. External Training Program C. PMI Certification (PMP) D. Other
22	How do you rate your organization's commitment to formal project management training? Check (X) the box that most closely applies and comment why.	A. High B. Medium C. Low D. Other
23	Does your organization have a training budget for developing its project management expertise? Check (X) the box that most closely applies and comment why.	A. Yes B. No C. Proposed Budget D. Other

##	Question	Type of Response Requested
24	Are projects consistently staffed with skilled trained project management resources? Check (X) the box that most closely applies and comment why.	A. All of the time B. Most of the time C. Other
25	Do project management personnel have formal job descriptions, and career development plans? Check (X) the box that most closely applies and comment why.	A. Yes B. No C. Other
26	Does your organization contract project management services externally? Check (X) the box that most closely applies and comment why.	A. Yes B. No C. Other
27	How do you rate your project management (hardware/software) technology infrastructure? Check (X) the box that most closely applies and comment.	A. Adequate B. Inadequate C. Needs Development D. Other
28	How do you rate your information technology (hardware/software) infrastructure? Check (X) the box that most closely applies and comment.	A. Adequate B. Inadequate C. Needs Development D. Other
29	Are all projects audited to verify project management processes are being properly applied? Check (X) the box that most closely applies and comment why.	A. Yes B. No C. Other
30	Which of the following project management software tools are used in the PMO? Check (X) all the boxes that apply and comment how used and if multiple tools are used, why?	A. MS Project B. Open Plan C. Primavera P3 D. Artemis Views E. Other
31	Which of the following are documented as standard formats or common project	Project Summary, Scope Statement, Constraints/Limitations, Statement of

##	Question	Type of Response Requested
	management processes used on all projects? Mark (X)all items that apply and comment on level of use on all projects.	Work, Team Roles / Responsibilities PM Processes Documented, Procedures Documented, Communication Plan, OBS (Org. Breakdown Structure) RBS (Resource Breakdown Structure), CBS (Cost Breakdown Structure), WBS (Work Breakdown Structure), Project Workbook, Project Schedule Baseline Schedule, Master Schedule, Project Templates, Tracking/Counter Measures, Exception Reporting Resource Planning, Risk Assessment, Project Budget, Issues Process, Change Control Process, Metric Collection Configuration Management
32	What is the current Project Management Maturity Level of your organization? Check (X) the box that most closely applies and comment.	A. Level One: Ad-Hoc B. Level Two: Planned C. Level Three: Managed D. Level Four: Integrated, E. Level Five: Sustained
33	What roles exist within your PMO organization? Check (X) for: A = All Roles Included B = Responsibilities, Skills & Experience are Documented Please enter the number for: C= Full Time Staff D= Part Time Staff	A. Group Manager B. Project Manager C. Project Coordinator D. Planning Analyst E. Administrative Coordinator F. Schedulers G. Issues/Change Coordinator H. Risk Coordinator I. Communications Coordinator J. Project Finance Administrator K. PMIS Administrator
34	What are the low and high annual salary ranges for the following PMO positions, regardless if they are reporting to the PMO (i.e., Project Managers)? If you estimate the numbers, indicate EST. in the comments column.	Function Title: • PMO Manager • Project Manager • Project Coordinator • PMO Administrator • Planner/Scheduler • Planning Analyst

##	Question	Type of Response Requested
	Add additional functional titles and additional lines if more positions exist.	Range Information • Low • High • Bonus • Comments

Survey Results 1997-2006

The 1997-2006 survey responses are compiled into a report that is organized into five categories with a number of topics in each category that are cross referenced to the 34 questions.

1. General Information (8 topics)
2. Concept Approval (12 topics)
3. PM Knowledge (5 topics)
4. PM Capability, Commitment and Training (9 topics)
5. Staff Salaries (2 topics)

The following is a breakdown of the categories and topics that comprise the 1997-2006 PMO Survey Report:

1. **General Information**
    A. Product/Service
    B. Sales Volume
    C. Number of Employees
    D. Number of Concurrent Projects (Q#12)
    E. Number of Annual Total Projects (Q#12)
    F. Types of Projects (Q#13)
    G. PMO Staffing (Full Time / Part Time) (Q#33)
    H. Self Estimate of PM Maturity Level (Q#32)

2. **Concept Approval Issues**
    A. PMO Driving Force (Q#1)
    B. PMO Start Date (Q#2)
    C. Position In Organization (Q#3)
    D. PMO Leaders Title (Q#3)
    E. PMO Reports To (Q#3)
    F. PMO Coverage (Q#4)
    G. PMO Challenges (Q#5)
    H. Successes (Q#6)
    I. Failures (Q#7)
    J. Lessons Learned (Q#8)
    K. Resistance Level & Source (Q#9)
    L. Resistance Solutions (Q#9)

351

3. **PM Knowledge**
   A. PMO Champion (Q#10)
   B. Immediate Process Needs (Q#14)
   C. Organizational PM Knowledge (Q#16)
   D. PM Selection Criteria (Q#17)

4. **Corp. PM Policies (Q#18)PM Capability, Commitment and Training**
   A. PM Process Capability (Q#19)
   B. Commitment to PM (Q#20)
   C. PM Training Capability (Q#21)
   D. Commitment to PM Training (Q#22)
   E. PM Job Descriptions (Q#25)
   F. PM Tech. Infrastructure (Q#27)
   G. Information Tech. Infrastructure (Q#28)
   H. Process Audit (Q#29)
   I. Documented PM Processes (Q#31)

5. **Staff Salaries**
   A. Software Tools Used (Q#30)
   B. Staffing Salaries (Q334)
      1) Function Title
      2) Low Level
      3) High Level
      4) Bonus
      5) Comments

The summary report of the 1997-2006 PMO Survey results is available through the publisher's website www.PBMconcepts.com.

Glossary

ACRONYMS

BA – Business Analyst

BPM – Business Process Management

PBM – Project Business Management

PBMO – Project Business Management Organization

PgMO – Program Management Office

KPI – Key Performance indicator

EWPM – Enterprise-Wide Project Management

PBM – Project Business Management

PMCoE – Project Management Center of Excellence

PMO – Project Management Office

PO – Project Office

PSO – Project Support Office

RA – Research Analyst

DEFINITIONS

Activity: Vigorous or energetic physical or mental action. A *component* of *work* performed during the course of a *project, program, or portfolio.*

Assumptions: Factors that are considered to be true, real, or certain without proof or demonstration, when used in planning and analysis. Assumptions generally involve a degree of *risk.*

Authorization: Process of establishing, approving, funding, and communicating the *authority* to initiate *work* on a *component.*

Baseline: Approved time phased plan plus or minus approved scope, cost, schedule, risk, and technical changes. Generally refers to the current baseline, but may also refer to the original or some other baseline by applying a modifier (e.g., performance measurement baseline, technical baseline, risk baseline).

Benefit: Something that promotes or provides an advantage.

Business: A *commercial* or industrial *enterprise* and the people who constitute it. A business enterprise, usually commercial or mercantile, actively engaged in commerce as a means of livelihood. A company or other organization that buys and sells *goods*, makes *products*, or provides *services*.

Business Case: Documented feasibility study that considers economic, market, and other factors and is used to establish validity of the *benefits* and *value* of a selected *component*, which lacks sufficient definition. It is used as a basis for the *authorization* of further *project business management* activities.

Business Management: A particular kind of behavior *within* an *enterprise*. Specifically the behavior of those responsible for the decisions determining the allocation of the physical and human resources within an organization. This management function is built upon the social sciences. Management bears the same relationship to the social sciences that medicine does to such fields as chemistry, physiology, and anatomy.

Business Objective: In business and organizational *activities*, it is a clearly and broadly set target to get people together to accomplish a desired *goal* using available *resources* efficiently and effectively. Business objectives are monitored and reviewed at periodic intervals to align the business objectives with the changing market scenarios and *strategic initiatives*.

Business Plan: A high-level *document* that explains the *enterprise's* vision and mission, plus the approach that will be adopted to achieve this *mission* and *vision*, including the specific *goals* and *objectives* to be achieved during the period covered by the document.

Business Process Management (BPM): A holistic management approach focused on aligning all aspects of an organization with the wants and needs of clients. It promotes business effectiveness and efficiency while striving for innovation, flexibility, and integration with technology. BPM attempts to improve processes continuously. It can therefore be described as a process optimization process. It is argued that BPM enables organizations to be more efficient, more effective and more capable of change than a functionally focused, traditional hierarchical management approach.

Business Process Optimization: Discipline of adjusting a process so as to optimize some specified set of parameters without violating some *constraint*. The most common *goals* are minimizing cost, maximizing throughput, and/or efficiency. This is one of the major quantitative tools in industrial decision making. When optimizing a process, the goal is to maximize one or more of the process specifications while keeping all others within their constraints.

Budget: The approved cost estimate for a portfolio, program, project, any work breakdown component, or any schedule activity.

Business Unit: Any sized functional organization within the enterprise that is chartered to perform a relatively well-defined business support operation, such as accounting, a service center, product production, sales, human resources, marketing, or a project/ program / portfolio management office.

Buyer: The acquirer of products, equipment, materiel, goods, or services for an enterprise.

Capable: Having attributes, such as physical or mental power, required for performance or accomplishment. Having or showing a general efficiency and ability.

Capability: Quality or state of being *capable*, such as having a specific competency. A feature or faculty capable of development. An enterprise or resource faculty or potential for an intended use or deployment.

Commerce: Social intercourse, the interchange of ideas, opinions, or sentiments. The exchange or buying and selling of goods and services and of commodities usually on a large scale involving transportation from place to place.

Commercial: Occupied with or engaged in commerce or *work* intended for *commerce*.

Component: A constituent part, an *element*, a piece of a complex whole.

Concept: A statement of an idea.

Constraint: State, quality, sense, or reality of being restricted or driven to a given course of action or inaction. A restriction or limitation, either internal or external, that is applicable to a project, program, or portfolio, which may affect work performance and outcomes.

Construct: Something that has been systematically built or assembled from separate parts in an ordered way to create something, such as a theory, as a result of systematic thought, especially a complex theory or subjective notion.

Contract: A mutually binding agreement that obligates the seller to provide the specified *product* or *service* and obligates the *buyer* to pay to the seller a specified value.

Contract Administration: Process of: a) managing the *contract* and the relationship between the *buyer* and the *seller*; b) reviewing and documenting how a seller is performing or has performed to establish required corrective actions and provide a basis for future use of the seller; c) managing contract related changes; and d) as appropriate, managing the contractual relationship with the outside buyer.

Control: Compare actual performance with planned performance, analyze variances, assess trends to effect process improvements, evaluate possible alternatives, and recommend appropriate corrective action.

Deliverable: Any unique and verifiable *product, result*, or *capability* to perform a *service* that must be produced to complete a process, phase, project, program, or portfolio. Often used more narrowly in reference to an external deliverable, which is subject to approval by a sponsor or customer.

Discipline: A field of work requiring specific knowledge and that has a set of rules governing the conduct of *work*, e.g., engineering, consulting, programming, estimating, radiology, etc.

Document: A medium and the information recorded thereon, that generally has permanence and can be read by either a human or a machine. Examples include plans, specifications, procedures, guidelines, drawings, studies, and manuals.

Effort: Conscious exertion of power, application of hard work, and the total work done to achieve a particular end. The number of labor units required to complete an *activity* or other *component*.

Element: Denotes one of the parts of a complex whole and often connotes irreducibility.

Enterprise: A company, business, firm, partnership, corporation, or governmental agency. This includes associations, societies, for-profit entities, and not-for-profit entities.

Enterprise Environmental Factors: Any or all external environmental factors and internal organizational environmental factors that surround or influence a project's, program's, or portfolio's success. These factors are from any or all of the enterprises involved in the project, program, or portfolio and include organizational culture and structure, infrastructure, existing *resources*, commercial databases, market conditions, and software.

Enterprise Project Business Management Governance: The organizational *governance* used in performing project business management that is a blend of several governance methods, especially those of executive, operations, portfolio, program, and project management. It is employed at different decision-making levels of the enterprise and at different stages within the *project business management* methodology to support implementation of specific *business objectives* and their related business *strategic initiatives*.

Enterprise-Wide Project Management (EWPM): The application of *project business management* practices and processes on an enterprise-wide basis, using an enterprise-wide project business management office as the *business unit* to support management of the enterprise's portfolios, programs, and projects.

Estimate: A quantitative assessment of a likely amount or outcome. Usually applied to project, program, and portfolio costs, *resources*, *effort*, and durations and is usually preceded by a modifier (i.e. preliminary, conceptual, feasibility, order-of-magnitude, definitive). It usually includes some indication of accuracy.

Execute: To carry out fully. To put completely into effect. To do what is provided or required by something. To make or produce by carrying out a design. To perform indicated tasks according to plans and instructions.

Execution: The act or process of executing. Performance of work to plans.

Executive: A directing or controlling office of an organization. A person that exercises administrative or managerial control.

Goal: An objective or focused effort, an end or aim. Business goals are the things an enterprise or business unit hopes to achieve during its time in operation. It is a specific, measurable, attainable, realistic, and time-targeted objective.

Goods: Commodities, wares, merchandise.

Govern: To exercise continuous authority over a function. To control and direct the making and administration of policy in an organization. To control, direct, or strongly influence the actions or conduct of and organization or function. To exert a determining or guiding influence in or over funds.

Governance: Authoritative direction or control. The office, authority, or function of governing. The continuous exercise of authority over and the performance of functions for a business unit. The organization, machinery, or agency through which a business unit exercises authority and performs functions. The body of persons that constitutes the governing authority of a business unit or organization or enterprise.

Key Performance Indicator (KPI): A parameter or set of parameters that permits visibility into how a *business unit* meets a given criterion, how a *business objective* is being met, or a component of work is being completed.

Knowledge: Knowing something with the familiarity gained through experience, practice, education, observation, or investigation that provides an understanding of a process, practice, or technique, or how to use a tool or software.

Lessons Learned: The learning gained from the process of performing the work for the project, program, or portfolio. Lessons learned may be identified at any point and are considered a record to be included in a lessons learned knowledge base.

Manage: To handle or direct with a degree of skill.

Management: The collective body of those who manage or direct an enterprise. The act or art of managing. The conducting or supervising of something in business. The judicious use of means to accomplish an end.

Manager: A person who conducts *business* affairs; a person whose *work* or profession is *management*; a person who directs a *business unit*, including a team.

Materiel: Equipment, machinery, apparatus, and supplies used by an organization.

Method: A specific expressed way of doing a thing to be followed. A procedure or process for attaining an object or objective. A systematic procedure, technique, or mode of inquiry employed by or proper to a particular discipline or art. A systematic plan followed in presenting material for instruction. A way, technique, or process of or for doing something. A body of skills or techniques.

Methodology: An organized system of intra-related methods to be followed A body of methods, rules, and postulates employed by a discipline. A particular procedure or set of procedures. A *system* of processes, practices, techniques, procedures, and rules used by those who work in a *discipline.*

Mission: In business, a statement cogently articulating the purpose of an enterprise or business unit, giving its reason for existing. It provides the framework or context within which the enterprise's or business unit's strategies are formulated and guides decision-making.

Model: A specific version of an article or artifact, which may be a simplified version of something complex, which can be used in analyzing and solving problems or making predictions.

Monitor: Collecting performance data with respect to a plan, preparing and producing performance measurements, and reporting and disseminating performance information.

Object: Something material that may be perceived by the senses. Something mental or physical toward which thought, feeling, or action is directed.

Objective: An aim, goal, purpose, or end of action. Something toward which effort is directed. A strategic position to be attained, or a purpose to be achieved, a result to be obtained, a product to be produced, or a service to be performed by a business unit operation.

Operations: An organizational function performing the ongoing execution of *activities* that produce the same *product* or provide a repetitive *service*. Examples are: production operations, manufacturing operations, and accounting operations.

Organization: A group of persons organized for some specific purpose, to perform some type of work, within an *enterprise*. This includes business unit, functional group, department, division, or sub-agency.

Organizational Governance: Process by which an enterprise directs and controls its business, operational, tactical, and strategic activities, and by which an organization responds to the desires, expectations, and legitimate rights of its stakeholders.

Organizational Process Assets: Any or all *process* related assets, from any or all of the enterprises and organizations involved in the project, program, or portfolio that can be or are used to influence the project's, program's, or portfolio's success. Process assets include formal and informal plans, policies, procedures, guidelines, all technologies, and all systems. Organizational process assets also include all the involved organizations' learning and knowledge such as *lessons learned* and historical information.

Outcome: The tangible or intangible result of applying *capabilities, constraints,* and *effort.*

Plan: Method for achieving an end, an often customary method of doing something. A detailed formulation of a set of actions or activities. Detailed documentation for provision of some service.

Planning: Act or art of preparing plans. The establishment of goals, plans, policies, and procedures for a business unit, social or economic unit, project, program, or portfolio.

Portfolio: Management determined collection of *projects, programs,* and other *work* that are grouped together to facilitate the ability to effectively manage that collective *work* to meet the enterprise's *strategic initiatives* and *business objectives.* The projects or programs of the portfolio may, or may not, be interdependent or directly related.

Portfolio Management: Centralized management of one or more *portfolios,* which includes identifying, prioritizing, authorizing, managing, monitoring, and controlling the included *projects, programs,* and other related *work,* to achieve the enterprise's specific related *strategic initiatives* and *business objectives* and to obtain the associated benefits and value.

Practice: An established way of doing things developed through experience and knowledge. A specific type of professional or management *activity* that contributes to the execution of a *process* or *procedure* and that may employ one or more *methods, techniques* and *tools.*

Procedure: Series of steps followed in a definitive and prescribed order to accomplish something.

Process: Series of actions directed toward a specific outcome. Set of interrelated actions and activities performed to achieve a pre-specified set of outcomes, such as products, results, or services.

Product: Artifact that is produced, is quantifiable, and can be either an end item in itself or a component item within another product.

Program: Management determined set of related *projects* grouped to facilitate the ability to manage effectively, and in a coordinated way, that collective *work* to meet the enterprise's *strategic initiatives* and *business objectives* and to obtain control not necessarily available from managing those projects individually. Programs may include related *work* outside of the *scope* of the specific projects within the program.

Program Management: Centralized coordinated management of a *program,* which includes identifying, prioritizing, authorizing, managing, monitoring, and controlling the included *projects* and other related *work,* to achieve the enterprise's specific related *strategic initiatives* and *business objectives* and obtain the associated *benefits* and *value.*

Program Management Office (PMO): Centralized management of a particular program or set of programs where benefits may be realized by the sharing of management, processes, systems, resources, methodologies, tools, and techniques.

Project: Temporary endeavor, having constraints, undertaken to create a unique *product, service*, or *result*.

Project Business Management (PBM): Utilization of integrated general business management and project management knowledge, skills, tools, and techniques when applying portfolio, program, and project processes to meet or exceed stakeholder needs, and to derive benefits from and capture value through any project-related actions and activities used to accomplish the enterprise's business objectives and related strategies.

Project Business Management Maturity: Maturity of an enterprise's policies, plans, procedures, *organizational governance*, management personnel, and project business management methodology and processes that identify, plan, implement, control, accomplish, and communicate the enterprise's business *strategic initiatives* and related *business objectives* and supporting portfolios, programs, and projects.

Project Business Management Organization (PBMO): Executive level business function accountable for enterprise-wide distribution of project management best practices. The PBMO is a corporate business function with the title and responsibility similar to traditional business functions such as finance, engineering, marketing, sales, manufacturing, information technology, etc., which provide leadership and have "ownership" of their respective functional disciplines. The organizational structure within the enterprise that will institute and manage the project business management processes for portfolios, programs, and projects. To be effective in managing the initiating, authorizing, planning, controlling, and executing processes of project business management, the PBMO is located at the executive level of the enterprise.

Project Management: Application of *knowledge, skills, systems, processes, tools*, and *techniques* to project *activities* to meet the project *requirements* and obtain the related *benefits* and *value*.

Project Management Center of Excellence (PMCoE): A functional role that is an alternative title for the PBM Office [and used in Bibliography Reference 1] because the name implies its primary mission and can be applied when the function is not positioned at the corporate level but has the same responsibilities. Its primary focuses are strategic forecast planning and the establishment of corporate standards that include the effective use of a common project management methodology, processes, tools, templates, education, training, and project management competency.

Project Management Office (PMO): A business unit assigned various responsibilities related to the centralized and coordinated management of those projects under its domain.

Project Manager (PM): Individual having the responsibility and authority for managing a project.

Project Support Office (PSO): The organizational business unit within the enterprise responsible for operational master planning, which oversees the effective application of the project management standards established by the Project Business Management Office in direct support of all projects within a functional department.

Resource: Skilled human resources, materiel, equipment, services, supplies, commodities, budgets, or funds.

Result: Something that proceeds or arises as a consequence, issue, or conclusion of effort and something that is a beneficial or tangible effect of the effort. One of the outputs from performing project business management processes and activities. Results include *outcomes* and *documents*.

Risk: Uncertain event or condition that, if it occurs, has a positive or negative effect on a project's, program's, or portfolio's *objectives*.

Scope: Sum of the products, services, and results to be provided as a project, program, or portfolio.

Service: Useful work performed that does not produce a tangible product or result, such as performing any of the enterprise's work supporting production or distribution.

Sponsor: Individual person or group that provides the financial resources, in cash or in kind, for the project, program, or portfolio.

Stakeholder: Individuals, organizations, and enterprises that are actively involved in, or whose interests may be positively or negatively affected by, the authorization, execution, or completion of the project, program, or portfolio. They may also exert influence over the deliverables of the project, program, or portfolio.

Standard: Something established by authority, custom, or general consent as a model or example. Something set up, established by consensus, and approved by a recognized body that provides, for common and repeated use, rules, guidelines or characteristics for activities or their results, which is aimed at the achievement of the optimum degree of performance and *outcomes* in a given context.

Strategic: Necessary to, or important in, the initiation, conduct, or completion of a strategic plan. Of great importance within an integrated whole or to a planned effect. Designed or trained to strike a competitor at the sources of its commercial, economic, or political power.

Strategic Initiative: An endeavor intended to achieve three interrelated outcomes. Setting a boundary-spanning vision or "strategic intent." Defining an enterprise's intended achievements in terms of business *results, benefits,* and *value* interpreted from various perspectives – financial, customer, infrastructure, products, and services. Achieving specific cultural outcomes that are measurable.

Strategy: The science and art of employing the political, economic, psychological, and physical forces and other resources of an enterprise to afford maximum support to adopted policies in commerce. The science and art of command exercised to meet the competition in commerce under advantages conditions.

Sustain: To give support to, or relief to, something. To support with substance and nourish. To keep-up and prolong.

Sustainable: Capable of being sustained. Of, or relating to, or being a method of using a resource so that the resource is not depleted or permanently damaged. Of or relating to a business style involving the use of sustainable methods.

System: Integrated set of regularly interacting or interdependent *components* created to accomplish a defined *objective* or *result*. It has defined and maintainable relationships among its components, where the whole produces or operates better than the simple sum of its components. Systems may be physical *process* based or management process based, or more commonly a combination of both.

Tactic: A device for accomplishing an end. A method of employing forces in commerce.

Tactical: Adroit in employing tactics that include the planning and execution of small-scale plans, actions, or activities that serve a larger purpose, such as a strategic initiative, which then maneuvers the enterprise to accomplish a related business objective, result, or purpose.

Tactics: Science and art of disposing and maneuvering forces in business. The art or skill of employing available means to accomplish an end.

Task: A term for *work* whose meaning and placement within a structured plan for work varies by the application area, industry, and brand of management software.

Value: A fair return or equivalent in goods, services, or money for something expended or exchanged. The monetary worth of something. The relative worth, utility, or importance of something.

Vision: In business, a statement of the desired and imagined end-result, which an enterprise or business unit envisions, plans, and commits to achieve—an organizationally desirable end-point. It is roughly similar to the concepts of purpose or aim, since the anticipated result guides action towards the object, either a physical object or an abstract object or both, that has intrinsic value. It can include economic, commercial, political, environmental, social, or technological aspects. It is a clear, distinctive, and specific vision of the future desired state of the enterprise or business unit.

Work: Activity in which one exerts strength or faculties to do or perform something. Sustained physical or mental effort, exertion, or exercise of *skill* to overcome obstacles and achieve an *objective* or *result*.

Bibliography

REFERENCES

1. Bolles, D.L. (2002) *Building Project Management Centers of Excellence*. New York, NY: AMACOM.

2. Bolles, D.L. & Hubbard, D.G. (2007) *The Power of Enterprise-Wide Project Management*. New York, NY: AMACOM.

3. Aubry, M. & Hobbs, B. (2011) *Identifying the Forces Driving Frequent Change in PMOs*. Newtown Square, PA; Project Management Institute.

4. Aubry, M. & Hobbs, B. (2010) *The Project Management Office (PMO) A Quest for Understanding*. Newtown Square, PA: Project Management Institute.

5. Project Management Institute. (2008) *A Guide to the Project Management Body of Knowledge (PMBOK® Guide)* (4th ed.). Newtown Square, PA: Project Management Institute.

6. Project Management Institute. (2006a) *The Standard for Program Management* (2nd ed.). Newtown Square, PA: Project Management Institute.

7. Project Management Institute. (2006b) *The Standard for Portfolio Management* (2nd ed.). Newtown Square, PA: Project Management Institute.

8. ESI ™ International. (2012) The 2012 Global State of the PMO: On the Road to the Next Generation; An ESI ™ International Study

About the Authors

Dennis L, Bolles, PMP

Dennis Bolles is the President of DLB Associates, LLC and has more than 40 years of experience in multiple industries providing business and project management professional services. He has been a member of the Project Management Institute (PMI®) since 1985 received his Project Management Professional (PMP®) certification in 1986 (#81) and is a founder/charter member of the PMI Western Michigan Chapter serving on its Board of Directors in several positions since its 1993 inception.

He utilizes PMI Chapter and Communities of Practice (CoP) speaking engagements and Webinars to promote helping enterprises achieve their strategic initiatives and business objectives through analyzing their business process improvement needs and implementing a Project Business Management (PBM) concept and Project Business Management Organization model to manage their organizations.

Dennis is the PMI Standards Project Manager who led the project core team to a successful completion and on-time delivery of the *PMBOK® Guide* Third Edition in 2004. He has served on and contributed to multiple PMI Standards over the past 20 years.

He is a published author of many project management articles, served as Key Note speaker at PMI Congresses in St. Petersburg, Russia, Athens, Greece, and Santiago, Chile, and. is a guest speaker at PMI Chapter Dinner meetings and Professional Development Days across the USA. He is the author of *Building Project Management Centers of Excellence*, AMACOM, NY, June 2002 and co-author of *The Power of Enterprise-Wide Project Management*, AMACOM, NY, January 2007. He is the Co-Editor of *The PMOSIG Program Management Office Handbook*, JRoss, January 2011. He is the co-author of *A Compendium of PMO Case Studies: Reflecting Project Business Management Concepts*, PBMconcepts, 2012.

Visit his websites at www.dlballc.com for information about DLB Associates, LLC and at www.PBMconcepts.com for information about current and future book projects.

Darrel G. Hubbard, PE

Darrel G. Hubbard is President of D.G.Hubbard Enterprises, LLC providing executive consulting and assessment services. He has 45 years of experience in executive, consulting, line management, and technical positions; was a project manager on commercial projects; and a designated "key person" under government contracts. He holds a bachelor's degree in mathematics and physics from the University of Minnesota at Moorhead and is a registered Professional Engineer in the state of California.

He joined the Project Management Institute (PMI®) in1978 (#3662), and is a charter member of the PMI San Diego Chapter. He was the Exhibitor Chairperson for the 1993 PMI Symposium, and was deputy project manager for the ANSI Standard *PMBOK® Guide* Third Edition in 2004.

He is a published author of many articles, a presenter at several PMI Congresses and Symposiums, and guest speaker at Chapter meetings.

He is a contributing author to *The AMA Handbook of Project Management*, AMACOM, 1993 and to *The ABCs of DPC: A primer on Design-Procurement-Construction for the Project Manager*, PMI 1998. He is co-author of the books *The Power of Enterprise-Wide Project Management*, AMACOM, 2007 and *A Compendium of PMO Case Studies: Reflecting Project Business Management Concepts*, PBMconcepts, 2012.

Visit his website at www.PBMconcepts.com for information about current and future book projects.

Index

V

value *iv, v, vii, x, xvii, xix, xx, xxii, xxiii, xxv, 12, 13, 15, 16, 17, 18, 21, 26, 32, 34, 35, 37, 39, 40, 41, 42, 45, 46, 49, 50, 51, 52, 53, 57, 64, 73, 74, 76, 79, 82, 84, 90, 92, 100, 103, 104, 107, 112, 115, 119, 126, 132, 136, 144, 151, 152, 158, 159, 161, 162, 172, 174, 176, 178, 179, 180, 181, 184, 186, 188, 191, 192, 193, 195, 198, 208, 217, 223, 231, 232, 235, 236, 237, 243, 245, 247, 252, 253, 254, 255, 269, 274, 280, 286, 288, 289, 297, 302, 303, 309, 310, 312, 313, 314, 315, 317, 320, 321, 322, 323, 327, 332, 333, 334, 336, 338, 340, 341, 342, 344, 346*

vendors *71, 201, 206, 209, 215, 232, 253, 254, 259*

Vice President (VP) *v, vi, xviii, xxvi, xxvii, 31, 60, 65, 71, 81, 115, 132, 133, 136, 137, 145, 146, 197, 198, 212, 307, 308, 315, 317, 318, 335*

vision *vi, xvii, xix, xxiii, 12, 18, 21, 23, 32, 34, 46, 47, 50, 56, 57, 61, 75, 77, 90, 106, 115, 227, 236, 237, 245, 252, 257, 262, 292, 303, 307, 309, 310, 311, 313, 315, 318, 323, 324, 327, 330, 331, 333*